THE HARPER
HANDBOOK
OF COLLEGE COMPOSITION

THE HARPER HANDBOOK
OF COLLEGE COMPOSITION

Harry Shaw • Fifth Edition

Formerly Director,
Workshops in Composition,
New York University
and Lecturer in English, Columbia University

With the editorial cooperation of
Richard S. Larson, Lehman College, C.U.N.Y.
Elisabeth McPherson, Special Consultant, Community Colleges
Robert P. Parker, Rutgers University

HARPER & ROW, PUBLISHERS, New York
Cambridge, Hagerstown, Philadelphia, San Francisco,
London, Mexico City, São Paulo, Sydney

1817

Sponsoring Editor: *Phillip Leininger*
Senior Project Editor: *Rhonda Roth*
Designer: *Frances Torbert Tilley*
Production Manager: *Marion Palen*
Compositor: *Waldman Graphics, Inc.*
Printer and Binder: *The Murray Printing Company*
Art Studio: *Vantage Art Inc.*
Cover photo: *Michel Craig*

THE HARPER HANDBOOK OF COLLEGE COMPOSITION, *Fifth Edition*
Copyright © 1981 by Harry Shaw

Library of Congress Cataloging in Publication Data
Shaw, Harry
    The Harper handbook of college composition.

    First-4th ed. by G. S. Wykoff and H. Shaw.
    Includes bibliographical references and index.
    1. English language—Rhetoric.   2. English lan-
guage—Grammar—1950-   I. Wykoff, George Steward,
Harper handbook of college composition.
II. Title.
PE1408.W85 1981   808'.042   80-24323
ISBN 0-06-045976-X

Contents

Contents

Contents

Contents

Contents

Contents

Preface

When the first edition of *The Harper Handbook of College Composition* appeared nearly 30 years ago, it met with an acceptance, approval, and loyalty that have sustained it through three successive editions. The present (fifth) edition offers a major reworking of previous versions—emendation, addition, deletion, and expansion—but it remains a comprehensive and incisive reference work for the individual teacher and student, as well as a text for classroom use.

The Harper Handbook is designed to help students discover, develop, and refine the writing and speaking demands of a lifetime. Its fundamental objective is to provide training in clear, effective, and appropriate writing and rewriting. To this end, the book describes American English as it is employed by careful, accurate writers and speakers—and by others not always either careful or accurate. It states the facts about usage of the English language that educated people should know, whether or not they wish to adopt and follow them in whole or in part.

This new edition of *The Harper Handbook* offers a thorough reworking of previous editions with the aim of more clearly and effectively meeting current student needs. Among many changes effected in this fifth edition are the following:

1. The contents have been rearranged from beginning to end. Previous editions began with a treatment of the entire paper and ended with a discussion of punctuation and mechanics. The present edition starts with a thorough, functional approach to grammar and ends with the composition and the library paper. But the book is written in such a way that a user can begin with any of its seven major divisions and proceed backward or forward as needs dictate.

2. For the first time, treatments of grammar and usage have been separated. This separation has permitted a detailed exposition of fundamental grammatical principles while allowing a clear and direct examination of contemporary uses of the language.

3. The number of sections has been reduced from 100 to 80, thus producing a tighter, leaner treatment of essentials.

4. Each of the now-existing 80 sections has been almost completely rewritten, modernized, and updated.

5. Exercises throughout have been revised and hundreds of new ones have been added.

6. A conscious effort has been made to remove all traces of "sexist" language.

7. Although emphasis is steadily kept on writing, additional attention is given to the spoken word.

In short, this edition has been thoroughly revised, rearranged, and updated. It does preserve virtues that have attracted loyal users of previous editions while offering a radically new version that may continue to encourage, give insight, and inspire confidence.

Throughout, *The Harper Handbook* tries to make clear the many distinctions that exist between *grammar* and *usage*. A systematic description of words and their structures, patterns, and relationships differs markedly from a description of the ways in which people actually use language in various situations. The handbook is not rigid and inflexible in its prescriptive rules concerning usage, but neither does it adopt a laissez-faire attitude. Staying in the middle of the road can be fatal on a highway, but perhaps not on the highway to better composition.

I continue to believe that the writing needs of most students are best served by genuinely solid work, under teacher supervision, in thinking, planning, writing, and rewriting. Learning to think clearly and to write effectively and appropriately are worthwhile intellectual pursuits that are valuable not only in composition classes but in all intellectual endeavors throughout life.

Scores of dedicated teachers, loyal friends, perceptive students, and professional editors have helped me to evolve the present volume. Some of the counselors and hand-holders who have aided me during years of study and planning do not wish to be named. But I should be remiss in gratitude if I did not mention at least a few gifted individuals. Foremost among them is Professor George S. Wykoff, formerly of Purdue University and the senior author of four previous editions of *The Harper Handbook*. Professor Wykoff has now retired after nearly 50 years of teaching first-year college English; but every page of the present edition of this work bears the imprint of his personality, wise guidance, professional experience, and devoted industry. Without his warm friendship and constant support, I happily acknowledge that this edition would be far less helpful than I hope it is.

Among others who should be mentioned are Professor John A. Higgins of York College of the City University of New York, who read the entire manuscript, made numerous helpful suggestions, and has also prepared the workbook (study guide) that accompanies this edition; Professor Walter E. Meyers of North Carolina State University, who has graciously granted permission for some of his own writing to appear in this work; and Professor Richard S. Beal, who carefully read the complete manuscript and made numerous suggestions for its improvement.

Last but far from least should be mentioned the skilled, talented, and widely experienced teachers and critics whose names appear on the title page. Richard S. Larson, Elisabeth McPherson, and Robert P. Parker each read the entire manuscript with extraordinary care and made literally hundreds of suggestions for its improvement.

The faults and shortcomings of this book are my own, but I cannot also lay claim to what I hope will be judged its strengths and excellences—many of which are due entirely to the editorial cooperation of persons whose names are listed here but who are thanked less perfunctorily in the heart and mind of a grateful author.

Harry Shaw

THE HARPER
HANDBOOK
OF COLLEGE COMPOSITION

I.
Grammar

Grammar consists of a series of statements about the way a language works. English grammar is "the English way of saying things."

The word *grammar,* which comes from Greek *gramma* (meaning "letter" or "written symbol"), means the entire structure of a language. It concerns the form of words: their tenses, cases, and the order in which they are strung together in phrases, clauses, and sentences.

Contrary to what you may think, you already know a lot of grammar. Otherwise, you could not fully understand what others say and what you see on TV or read in a newspaper. You might have trouble ordering a hamburger, buying something in a store, or getting around town by bus or automobile.

None of us was born with a built-in knowledge of grammar, although we may have a sense of inborn patterns. In any case, during our infancy each of us picked up enough to communicate with others and to understand what they said. Learning to talk occupied much of our time from about age 1 to about age 4. What are parents being asked every day in questions such as, "Has the baby said her first word yet?" and "Does he chatter all the time?" The query is this: "How's the child doing at learning a language without any formal instruction from persons who are not concerned primarily with teaching it?" This learning experience was the first and most important English examination any of us ever took, and each of us passed it with a straight A.

Grammatical Devices

What you and I were doing was learning a language by examining data about words and making up rules to fit those data. Without being aware of what we were doing, we were learning about such important grammatical devices, or systems, for putting words together as *word order, inflections* (changes), and *function words.* (If these terms mean little to you, relax. Their role and meaning in the sentences you write or speak will be explained in later sections of this book. If you can't wait, look them up in Section 10.)

For example, at the age of 2 or 3 you might have said about a playmate, "Him want drink." As you grew older and gathered further language data by using your ears, you would say, "He wants a drink." Both sentences make sense, largely because they follow the first grammatical device for putting words together in a meaningful combination: *word order.* Even as an infant, you did not say "Want him drink" or "Drink want him."

1

Similarly, you changed *him* to *he* and *want* to *wants;* that is, you made *changes (inflections)* in the form of these words to indicate different grammatical relationships. Finally, you added a *function (structure) word, a.* The grammatical devices of word order, inflections, and function words—about which each of us knew a great deal long before we entered the first grade—are essential for clear writing and speaking.

At this point you may ask, "If I already know enough grammar to get along with others, why study it further?" This question is not altogether silly. It's true that knowledge of grammar in itself will not necessarily help you improve your writing. As a scientific study, grammar is unconcerned with what is "correct" and what is "incorrect." But grammar *is* concerned with the principles of a language. It is also concerned with the terms used to describe and explain those principles. An understanding of grammatical terms will help you enlarge and enrich your use of language.

Usage

Closely linked to grammatical terms and grammatical devices is the matter of *usage.* Unlike grammar, usage is directly concerned with *choices* in handling language in speech and writing. Usage involves differences between formal and informal, standard and nonstandard English. The difference between "She mailed the letter" and "The letter was mailed" is a grammatical one. Between "He done it" and "He did it," the difference is in usage. Usage is also involved in the difference between "She don't know" and "She doesn't know." Knowledge of the choices available to you in using language will help you improve your writing and speaking.

Usage is not so much a matter of grammar as it is a concern of *rhetoric,* the principles of presenting ideas, facts, and opinions so that they will produce the effect we want them to produce. We choose one expression over another not just because it seems appropriate or has some special standing but because we want to get across to our readers what we have in mind. All our choices in usage require that we consider how our readers will react, how fully and immediately they will understand what we are writing, and whether they will be satisfied or offended by the way we express ourselves.

As a college student, you are expected to use language as others with your educational advantages use it. In carrying on your affairs through language, it will be natural to take pride in being able to use words and expressions that are customary to English as it is spoken and written by other educated people. That is, your language ought always to be standard but may be informal or formal according to the situation involved.

Making Words Work For You

An important part of education is learning to make words work for you. In a writing course you have an unexcelled opportunity to refresh your knowledge of grammar and to learn new subtleties of language. But before you can profitably study *how* to use language effectively you need to learn or relearn the terms used to describe the principles of language, that is, grammar. Knowledge of any field requires knowing the vocabulary—the jargon—of that field. When a plumber asks for a Stillson wrench, you don't want to produce a pair of pliers. When someone points out to you that a sentence you have written doesn't make sense because it contains a misplaced modifier, you need to know something about the grammatical device of word order and the meaning of the term *modifier.*

The ten sections that follow provide you with the names and uses of the tools needed in learning and applying the principles, rules, and suggestions you will encounter in the remainder of this book.

If you get stuck, turn to Section 10 for explanations of terms that are clarified further in other sections of this book.

Parts of Speech

The first six sections deal with words. All words are classified according to their function in larger constructions explained in the three subsequent sections: phrases, clauses, and sentences.

This functional, or use, classification results in the *parts of speech,* which are the groups of words that work similarly in larger units. All words fall into one or more of these groups, depending on how they are used in sentences. The same word, therefore, may be two or more parts of speech, depending on its use and meaning. In fact, *functional change* or *shift* means that a word assumes a new function without a change in form, as when a noun is used as an adjective. For example, *iron* is a noun in "wears like iron," an adjective in "an iron bar," and a verb in "to iron a shirt."

The following classes of words, grouped by purpose and meaning, constitute the eight parts of speech:

Naming words:	Nouns and pronouns
Asserting words:	Verbs
Modifying words:	Adjectives and adverbs
Joining words:	Conjunctions and prepositions
Exclamatory words:	Interjections

Of these eight parts of speech, four are called *form-class* words; they correspond roughly to nouns, verbs, adjectives, and adverbs. The other four parts of speech—pronouns, prepositions, conjunctions, and interjections (in a loose, vague manner)—are called *function* or *structure* words. Form-class words provide basic meaning, and structure words provide information about the relationships among form-class words. In short, all words work together to convey sentence meaning. The way words work together in sentences is what grammar is all about.

1. Nouns

The word *noun* comes from the Latin word *nomen*, meaning "name." Therefore, the usual definition of a noun as the name of something is not really helpful because all it says is that "a name is a name." It is not inaccurate, however, to state that a noun designates a person, place, idea, quality, action, or an event or point in time.

This less–than–complete definition can be made clearer by noting the ways in which nouns may be identified, characterized, and classified. Seven characteristics of nouns, listed here in ascending order of importance, may be identified.

1a. Characteristics of nouns

1. Determiners

Nouns are usually preceded by *determiners*, or *markers: the, a, an, my, your, her, his, some, each, every, this, their,* and *that: the* desk, *a* book, *an* orange, *my* friend, *this* car.

2. Endings

Certain nouns have characteristic endings: *-al, -tion, -ness, -ment, -ure, -dom, -ism, -ance.* These endings distinguish nouns from related words of other classes: *arrive* (verb) and *arrival* (noun); *determine* (verb) and *determination* (noun); *lonely* (adjective) and *loneliness* (noun); *govern* (verb) and *government* (noun); *depart* (verb) and *departure* (noun); *wise* (adjective) and *wisdom* (noun); *real* (adjective) and *realism* (noun); *rely* (verb) and *reliance* (noun).

3. Pronunciation

Some nouns and verbs that are spelled the same way may be distinguished by accent. The first of each of these pairs of words is a noun, the second is a verb: *per'mit, permit'; rec'ord, record'; ob'ject, object'; sur'vey, survey'.*

4. Set positions

Nouns are found in set positions, such as before a verb (a *bird* sings), after a verb (wash the *floor*), or after a preposition (working for *money*). Nouns can be preceded or followed by adjectives (thirty *days*, a *house* deserted).

5. Gender

Some nouns have *gender;* that is, they are *masculine (man, boy); feminine (woman, girl);* or *neuter (chair, bicycle).* When a noun may be either masculine or feminine, it has a *common* gender (*teacher, doctor, friend*). Gender in English is a matter of sex and is reflected grammatically only in the choice of pronouns to refer to nouns.

6. Case

Nouns may have three *cases:* (a) *nominative,* (b) *objective,* and (c) *possessive* (genitive). Nouns in English have a common form for the nominative and objective cases (*Tom* loves *Sue, Sue* loves *Tom*). An apostrophe is used to indicate the possessive case: *Martha's* coat, *Robert's* moped, the *sun's* rays, our *neighbors'* yards. It is correct to say that nouns in English really have only two cases: *common* and *possessive.*

7. Number

Nouns may be singular or plural in number (referring to one or more than one). The following rules apply to the formation of plurals:

1. Most nouns form the plural by adding *s* to the singular form: *book, books; girl, girls; hammer, hammers; college, colleges.*
2. Nouns ending in *ch, sh, s, x,* and *z* add *es: church, churches; bush, bushes; glass, glasses; fox, foxes; buzz, buzzes.*

3. Nouns ending in *y* form the plural in two ways, depending on the letter that precedes the *y:* If a vowel precedes the *y* (*ay, ey, iy, oy, uy*), add *s: ray, rays; key, keys; toy, toys, guy, guys.* If a consonant precedes the *y*, change the *y* to *i* and add *es: library, libraries; study, studies; activity, activities.*

4. Nouns ending in *o* and *f* form the plural in a variety of ways; consult your dictionary, since no general rule exists to guide you.

5. A few native words exist as relics of classes of words that formed their plurals in other ways: *man, men; foot, feet; tooth, teeth; mouse, mice; child, children; ox, oxen.*

6. Foreign words that have brought their plurals with them have a number of different forms: *alumnus, alumni; phenomenon, phenomena; crisis, crises; datum, data; hypothesis, hypotheses.* Some words have both a native plural (with *s*) and a borrowed plural: *antenna, antennas, antennae; stadium, stadiums, stadia.* Consult your dictionary if you are uncertain about the plural of a borrowed word.

7. For plurals of figures, letters of the alphabet, and words referred to as words, see Sections 26 and 33.

1b. Classification of nouns★

1. Common

A *common noun* is a name given to all members of a class: *dozen, infant, farm, street, city, boy, structure.* Common nouns can be recognized as such because they do *not* begin with a capital letter (except at the beginning of a senteence or as part of a name).

2. Proper

A *proper noun* names a particular member of a class; it *does* begin with a capital letter: *Rover, Michael, Twin Cedars, Roosevelt Free-*

★This classification of nouns does not mean that a particular noun cannot belong to more than one group. For instance, the noun *herd* is common, concrete, and collective.

way, Atlanta, Bob Dylan, Eiffel Tower, Lonely Hearts Club. Proper nouns are not normally preceded by an article or any other limiting modifier such as *any* or *some.*

3. Abstract

An *abstract noun* is the name of a quality or general idea that cannot be seen or heard: *faith, happiness, courage, fear, love, intelligence.*

4. Concrete

A *concrete noun* names a material (tangible) thing that can be perceived by one or more of the senses: *fire, odor, notebook, hamburger, stone, record, cake.*

5. Collective

A *collective noun* names a group of individuals. Although it refers to more than one, it is singular in form: *pair, committee, squad, team, crowd, crew, assembly, army.*

EXERCISE 1

Pick out the 20 nouns in the following sentences. If so instructed, be prepared to give the classification of each (common, proper, abstract, concrete, or collective).

1. Loud arguments were common in that household.
2. Using a mirror, Renata painted her own portrait.
3. Roland has a well-deserved reputation for kindness.
4. A few years later, I knew how to behave better.
5. After that assembly, Suzanne was tired and bitter.
6. He thought for a moment, rubbed his forehead, and then produced a slow smile.
7. My uncle thought that Lisa would become a successful physician.
8. His was an old face, one marked by courage and showing numerous lines.

2. Pronouns

A *pronoun* is a word that can be replaced by a noun in a sentence, clause, or phrase. Like nouns, pronouns can act as the subject of verbs and the object of verbs and prepositions. Many pronouns, like nouns, have a plural form and a possessive (genitive) case.

Although most pronouns can substitute for nouns, the meaning of a pronoun may depend on that of a noun (or a group of words serving as a noun) that acts as an antecedent. The word *antecedent,* derived from Latin words meaning "coming before," refers to a word, phrase, or clause that is replaced by a pronoun later (occasionally earlier) in a sentence or in a following sentence. Note these examples:

Isadora Duncan revitalized modern dance with *her* fresh approach. [*Her,* a pronoun, refers to its antecedent, *Isadora Duncan.*]

Their match was won easily by Austin and Ashe. [*Their* refers to *Austin and Ashe.*]

Whichever she selects will be expensive. [The full meaning of *whichever* depends on that of an antecedent appearing before or after this sentence.]

2a. Kinds of pronouns

Pronouns are of eight kinds: (1) personal, (2) relative, (3) demonstrative, (4) interrogative, (5) reflexive, (6) intensive, (7) indefinite, and (8) reciprocal. Despite this relatively large number of types, pronouns are a small class of words, only about eighty in all.

1. Personal pronouns

A *personal pronoun* refers to an individual or set of individuals. Personal pronouns have several case forms, some of which include all genders and some of which have masculine, feminine, and neuter forms.

Personal pronouns also can be first, second, or third person. *First-person pronouns* indicate the speaker or writer, either singular or plural (*I, we*). *Second-person pronouns* indicate the person or persons spoken to and have identical forms for singular and plural (*you, you*).

Gender (or sex) is the same for all first- and second-person pronouns. Third-person pronouns indicate the person or persons spoken of or written about and therefore involve considerations of number and gender, as shown in the following table:

	Nominative (Subject Case)	Possessive (or Genitive)	Objective (Object Case)
Singular			
1st person	I	my, mine	me
2nd person	you	your, yours	you
Masculine	he	his	him
Feminine	she	her, hers	her
Neuter	it	its	it
Plural			
1st person	we	our, ours	us
2nd person	you	your, yours	you
3rd person (all genders)	they	their, theirs	them

2. Relative pronouns

A *relative pronoun* is usually part of a dependent clause, and its antecedent is part of a main clause. These pronouns—*who, whose, whom, which,* and *that*— have no separate forms for number, gender, or person. The distinctions among *who, whose, whom,* and *which* are determined by case; *that* lacks separate forms for case. (Remember: If any of the terms used in this and following sections are unclear to you, refer to Section 10.)

Relative Pronouns			
	Subject	Possessive	Object
Human	who	whose	whom
Nonhuman	which	whose, of which	which
Either	that	—	that

As the table shows, *who, whose,* and *whom* are used with antecedents that refer to humans; *which, whose,* and the phrase *of which* are used with antecedents that refer to nonhumans. *That* may be used with antecedents that refer to either. *That* has no possessive form.

The candidate *who* wants to get elected must campaign hard.

The old car, *which* was badly in need of repair, soon broke down.

The novel *that* I read has become a classic.

Each of these relative pronouns has an antecedent (*candidate, car, novel*), and each introduces a subordinate clause.

The relative pronoun forms—*who, whose, whom, which, that*—have no specific gender or number. Their having gender or being singular or plural depends upon their antecedent. Choice of a relative pronoun is also determined largely by its antecedent:

We are looking for a graduate *who* has studied chemistry. [Subject of clause; compare "*A graduate* has studied chemistry."]

We are looking for a graduate *whose* grades are superior. [Possessive; compare "*The graduate's* grades are superior."]

We want a graduate *whom* we can train. [Object of verb; compare "We can train *a graduate.*"]

The EPA, *which* approves fuel additives, is fostering gasohol research. [Subject of clause; compare "*The EPA* approves fuel additives."]

Gasohol, *which* the EPA is studying, is a mixture of gasoline and alcohol. [Object of verb; compare "*The EPA* is studying *gasohol.*"]

Whoever, whomever, whichever, and *whatever* are relative pronouns that do not require antecedents:

We are looking for *whoever* can do the job. [Subject of clause; compare "*Someone* can do the job."]

The company will promote *whomever* it judges most qualified. [Object of verb; compare "It judges *someone* most qualified."]

The use of a relative pronoun in its own clause determines its case: *whoever,* the subject form, is used because the relative pronoun is the subject of the dependent clause; the whole clause, not just the pronoun, is the object of the preposition *for.* In the second sentence, the entire clause is the object of *promote; whomever* is the object of *judges.*

3. Demonstrative pronouns

A *demonstrative pronoun* points out or identifies a noun or another pronoun. It changes its form only for number, not for case or gender.

The demonstrative pronouns, which can also be used as adjectives, are *this* and *that* (singular), *these* and *those* (plural), and *such*.

PRONOMINAL USES: *This* was their finest hour.
These are the times that try men's souls.
That's the bike for me.
Those are your shoes, not mine.
She claimed to be my friend, but she was not *such*.

ADJECTIVAL USES: *This* land is your land.
These sentences illustrate demonstrative adjectives.
That park was built by girls in the neighborhood.
Those pens have felt tips.
Such magazines are worth reading.

4. Interrogative pronouns

An *interrogative pronoun* introduces a question. The important interrogative pronouns are *who, whom, whose, which, what,* and occasionally *whoever, whichever,* and *whatever*.

Who is the quarterback today?
My sister asked me *who* was coming to dinner.
Whom did they expect to play in the finals?
Which of the experts did they recommend?
What can I say, dear, after I say I'm sorry?
Whose Corvette has the best chance of winning the race?
Whatever do you mean by that comment?

5. Reflexive pronouns

A *reflexive pronoun* refers to the subject of a sentence or clause. It is a compound of one of the personal pronouns plus *-self* or

11

-selves: myself, yourself, herself, himself, itself, ourselves, yourselves, themselves.

Did you hurt *yourself?*
He gave *himself* a cake for his birthday.
They appointed *themselves* to the panel.

6. Intensive pronouns

An *intensive pronoun* is used to draw attention to a noun. Intensives take the same forms as reflexives.

We must give the same privileges to the workers *themselves.*
The doctor *herself* examined the X-rays.
I *myself* will pay the bill.

7. Indefinite pronouns

An *indefinite pronoun* is less specific in reference and less exact in meaning than other pronouns. It is often difficult to pin down a precise antecedent for an indefinite pronoun. Of these pronouns, those that are used most frequently are *all, another, any, anyone, anything, everybody, everyone, everything, few, many, nobody, none, one, several, some,* and *each.* The pronoun *one,* its compound forms, and the compound forms built on the element *-body* form the possessive in the same way as nouns *(anybody's, everyone's).*

Was *anyone's* calculator left in the room?
Everyone left for the party.

Another, any, all, each, every, few, many, several, and *some* are indefinite pronouns when they function as subjects, objects, or objects of prepositions in sentences; they may also be used as adjectives.

Few could complain about the party decorations. [Pronoun]
Sylvia saw *many* at the raceway who seemed more interested in parties than in the race. [Pronoun]
Many suggestions were submitted, and we will take action on *several.* [Adjective, pronoun]
Ken has only a *few* dollars left. [Adjective]

8. Reciprocal pronouns

Reciprocal pronouns indicate an interchange of the action stated by the verb. We have only two in English, *each other* for an interaction involving two, and *one another* for an interaction involving three or more.

After the tennis match, the players shook hands with *each other*. The members of the party exploring the cave shouted to *one another*.

EXERCISE 2

Certain pronouns are italicized in the following sentences. Classify each as one of the eight kinds of pronouns.

1. That battered heap is *yours;* it's not my car.
2. *Which* of you is going to lend me the money I need?
3. *All* of the children were waiting eagerly for the clowns to appear.
4. That's the girl *who* won first honors.
5. Please stay out of this; I want to handle the matter *myself.*
6. I then learned what *it* means to be hungry.
7. As for the convicted prisoners, *theirs* is not to reason why.
8. We employees are *ourselves* at fault.
9. It should be possible for us to be kind to *one another.*
10. Ms. Sanchez, *this* is a gross mistake in arithmetic.

3. Verbs and verbals

A *verb* is a word that indicates (expresses, specifies) actions or events that take place in time. To show their number and time-related meanings, verbs are *inflected,* meaning that they undergo changes in spelling or that various endings are added.

Verbs may also be defined as members of a class of words (parts of speech) that express action or a state of being (existing) or that show a relationship between two objects or ideas. Verbs act as the main element of a *predicate* (what is said about the subject of a sentence). In short, a verb is the heart, the core, of a sentence.

Consider the ways in which verbs can be classified and characterized.

3a. Classification of verbs

Verbs can be classified as *transitive, intransitive,* and *linking.*

1. Transitive verbs

The word *transitive* means "going across." In the sentence "Juan hit the ball," *hit* shows the relationship between *Juan* and *ball.* The action is begun by *Juan* and passes to *ball.* A transitive verb takes an object—a noun, pronoun, or group of words that tells who or what receives or experiences the action of the verb. In the following sentences, each of the italicized words is a transitive verb:

Susie *gave* a brief twitch of a smile.
Raoul *has* a part-time job at a playground.
The grumpy attendant *filled* my gas tank.

2. Intransitive verbs

An *intransitive verb* does not require or take an object. That is, no action passes from subject to object.

The split end *ran* straight down the sidelines.
Moneta *jogs* around town every day.

In these sentences, both *ran* and *jogs* express action but not action that requires a noun or noun equivalent for completion.

Many verbs can be used both transitively and intransitively:

We *read* the bulletin board carefully. [Transitive]
They *read* until late at night. [Intransitive]
Deborah *won* the match easily. [Transitive]
Deborah *won* easily. [Intransitive]

3. Linking verbs

A *linking verb* shows the relationship between a subject and a noun, noun equivalent, or adjective that follows it. Its function is to unite or couple, and therefore it is also known as a *copulative* verb. Among the most often used linking (copulative) verbs are *appear, be, become, feel, look,* and *taste.* A noun that follows a linking verb is called a *predicate noun;* an adjective that follows such a verb is called a *predicate adjective*. Some verbs that are usually linking can also be used in a transitive sense:

Gerald *is* my new partner. [Linking, predicate noun]
The new auditorium *was* multilevel. [Linking, predicate adjective]
Sue *tasted* the hot coffee. [Transitive]
Sue said the hot coffee *tasted* too sweet. [Linking, predicate adjective]

For further information about linking verbs, see Section 16.

3b. Characteristics of verbs

Knowledge of certain characteristics of verbs is helpful in understanding them and their functions. A verb has eight principal characteristics:

1. Base form   5. Auxiliaries
2. Principal parts   6. Voice
3. Inflectional endings   7. Mood
4. Prefixes and suffixes   8. Tense

1. Base form

All verbs have a base, or primary, form. This base, often referred to as the *infinitive form,* is the one that appears in boldface type as the entry word in a dictionary. It is often preceded by the word *to: dance, to dance; sleep, to sleep; be, to be.*

2. Principal parts

An English verb has three *principal parts: present tense, past tense,* and *past participle.* Another verb form, sometimes referred to as a principal part, is the *present participle.*

The *present tense* of every verb in English except be is the same as the base (infinitive) form: *ride* (to ride); *start* (to start).

The *past tense* of a verb varies, depending on whether the verb is *regular* or *irregular.* Regular verbs form their past tense by adding -*ed* (or -*d* or -*t*) to the base form: *walk, walked; organize, organized;*

mean, meant. The past tense of irregular verbs differs from one word to another, but most past tense forms are familiar to native speakers of English: *say, said; go, went; throw, threw.*

The *past participle* of a regular verb is identical to its past tense: *solve* (present tense), *solved* (past tense), *solved* (past participle). The past participles of irregular verbs differ widely. They are the forms that make sense and sound right with some form of the verb *have: have gone, have written, has drawn.*

The *present participle* of a verb is formed by adding *-ing* to the base form: *rain, raining; speak, speaking.*

For further comment on the principal parts of verbs, see Section 15.

3. Inflectional endings

When a verb in the present tense follows the words *he, she,* or *it,* or a noun or noun equivalent that may be substituted for *he, she,* or *it,* the letter *s* (or *es*) is added to the base form: *he laughs, she smiles, it rains, the snow falls, the door catches.*

Also in the present tense, a verb changes its ending when its subject changes from singular (one) to plural (more than one): a bird *sings,* the birds *sing;* Maria and David *dance,* Maria *dances.*

4. Prefixes and suffixes

Certain *prefixes* and *suffixes* (beginnings and endings of words) are used with some verbs. The prefixes *be-* and *en-* for example, appear often: *become, befriend, begrudge; enable, enforce, entail, entitle.* The suffixes *-ify, -ize,* and *-ate* often indicate that a word is a verb:

testify, verify, magnify, terrify
civilize, symbolize, colonize, urbanize
locate, speculate, automate, suffocate

5. Auxiliaries

Verb markers called *auxiliaries* (helpers, aids) often signal verbs. The most common auxiliaries are *be* (and its forms *was, are, were, is*), *have, had, has, do, did, does, can, could, shall, should, would, may, will, might, must,* and *ought.*

As we *were* leaving, we *were* stopped by a guard.

Miguel *has left* the money for you.

It *should be* warmer tomorrow.

For further discussion of auxiliaries, see Section 16.

6. Voice

All transitive verbs can be active or passive in voice.

A verb is in the *active voice* when the noun or pronoun that names the performer of the action specified by the verb is the actual subject of the verb.

We *built* a shack in the country.

The engineers *have developed* new types of electric refrigerators.

The Marshall Plan *helped* to reconstruct Europe.

A verb is in the *passive voice* when its grammatical subject is not the actual performer of the activity specified by the verb. When verbs appear in the passive voice, the noun that names the actual performer of the action either appears in a prepositional phrase at the end of the sentence or is not specifically named at all. The actual performer of the action of passive verbs can often be determined by converting the verb to the active voice.

The criminal was apprehended by the police. [Passive]

The police apprehended the criminal. [Active]

The firm was run by one woman. [Passive]

One woman ran the firm. [Active]

The money was found in the subway. [Passive]

(A man) found the money in the subway. [Active]

Note: The passive voice always consists of some form of the verb *be* followed by the past participle form of the verb.

7. Mood

Mood (occasionally spelled *mode*) is a characteristic of verbs that indicates the attitude of the speaker or writer to what he or she is expressing. This attitude may be one of certainty or uncertainty, hesitancy, doubt, emphasis, wish, or command. The three kinds of mood are indicative, subjunctive, and imperative.

Indicative Mood

The *indicative mood* is used in making a statement or asking a question:

This road car is engineered for today's driving.
Does this photograph dramatize the fact that Earth is a closed life system?
Do you regret having bought that dress?
Let's leave before we are thrown out of the house.

Subjunctive Mood

The *subjunctive mood* is used to express a condition contrary to fact (something that just isn't so), uncertainty, and doubt, and in clauses following *that* which express necessity or a parliamentary motion or demand:

If I *were* you, that's what I would do. [Condition contrary to fact]
He worked as if he *were* never going to have another chance. [Uncertainty]
Dottie moved that the contractors *be* authorized to finish the job. [Parliamentary motion]
The judge insisted that she *tell* the whole story. [Necessity]

Imperative Mood

The *imperative mood* is used to express a command, a polite or strong request, or to give an order:

Watch your step!
Take the first numbered street on your right.
Please go with me to the store.
Stop whining!

For further discussion of mood, see Section 18.

8. Tense

The *tense* of a verb indicates the time of the action or the state of being expressed by the verb—past, present, or future. Tense can be thought of as *simple* (I *see*) or *progressive* (I *am seeing*). The simple tenses (past, present, and future) designate actions or states of being that have occurred or existed in the past, that are occurring or existing now, or that will occur or exist in the future. The present perfect, past perfect, and future perfect tenses indicate action in either present, past, or future time. (See Section 17.)

3c. Verbals

Verbals are verb forms that are used not as verbs but as nouns, adjectives, and adverbs. Verbals are often referred to as nonfinite verb forms because they cannot by themselves serve as the predicate of a sentence. You will encounter three kinds of verbals: (1) infinitives, (2) participles, and (3) gerunds. They differ in both form and function.

1. Infinitives

An *infinitive* is the base form of a verb. It is used either alone or accompanied by *to,* the "sign of the infinitive." When used alone, it is part of the complete predicate of the sentence and follows an auxiliary verb. When used with *to,* it serves a double function in a sentence: it may be a verb used as a noun, a verb used as an adjective, or a verb used as an adverb.

Ron LeFlore will *start* tonight in center field. [Infinitive form as a verb and part of predicate, following *will*]

You can *find* those books on the second floor. [Infinitive form as a verb and part of predicate, following *can*]

To change sparkplugs is a simple job. [Infinitive form as a noun and subject of the sentence; as a verb it has a direct object, *sparkplugs*]

The best tool *to buy* is a 19/32″ socket wrench. [Infinitive form as an adjective, modifies the noun *tool*]

Jerry wants *to see* your notes from sociology class. [Infinitive form as a noun and direct object of the verb *wants;* as a verb it has its own direct object, *your notes*]

I came *to see* how you were feeling. [Infinitive form as an adverb, modifies the verb *came;* as a verb it has its own direct object, the clause *how you were feeling*]

3c

2. Participles

A *participle* is a word that has the functions of both a verb and an adjective. It has some properties of a verb, such as voice and tense, and can take an object and be modified by an adverb. It also functions as an adjective and can modify a noun.

> *Spoken* language is in many ways easier to describe than written language. [The participle *spoken* functions as an adjective, modifying the noun *language*.]
>
> *Releasing* helium from the bag, Peggy brought the balloon to earth in France. [As an adjective, *releasing* modifies *Peggy;* as a verb, it has the direct object *helium*.]
>
> The rapidly *tiring* center moved in desperation to block the shot. [As an adjective, *tiring* modifies *center;* it is itself modified by the adverb *rapidly*.]
>
> The question *having been asked,* Marianne proceeded to answer it. [*Having been asked* tells *what* question was answered.]

3. Gerunds

A *gerund* is a word ending in *-ing* that has the functions of both a verb and a noun. Here is the chief source of confusion between participles and gerunds: although both the gerund and the present participle end in *-ing,* the gerund functions as a noun, the present participle as an adjective. As a verb, the gerund can take an object and be modified by an adverb; as a noun, it can be modified by an adjective and can be the subject or object of a verb or the object of a preposition.

> *Playing* badminton is good exercise. [The gerund *playing* is the subject of the sentence, but as a verb it takes a direct object, *badminton*.]
>
> The engineer avoided *making* changes needlessly. [As a noun, the gerund is the object of the verb *avoided;* as a verb, it has its own object, *changes,* and is modified by an adverb, *needlessly*.]
>
> Steady *running* won the race for Francie. [As a noun, the gerund is the subject of the sentence and is modified by the adjective *steady*.]
>
> Your job will be *assigning* new customers account numbers. [As a noun, the gerund is the predicate nominative; as a verb, it has both an indirect object, *new customers,* and a direct object, *account numbers*.]

EXERCISE 3

Write a complete sentence using each of the following verbs in a *transitive* sense. Use any tense form you choose.

allow	harass
congratulate	pursue
determine	rattle
expedite	slap
follow	throw

EXERCISE 4

Write sentences using each of these *linking* verbs: *appear, grow, look, smell, stand.*

EXERCISE 5

Write two complete sentences using each of the following verbs. In the first of the two sentences, make the verb *active;* in the second, *passive.* Use any tense you prefer.

capture	drive
carry	hit
deny	throw

EXERCISE 6

Make a list of verbals from the following sentences. After each verbal, write an identifying letter: P for participle, G for gerund, or I for infinitive.

1. Spoken words are naturally kept in mind with much more difficulty than those one reads, but a well-trained person can retain amazing amounts of conversation that he or she has heard.
2. The game already having been won, we decided to leave soon after the intermission.
3. Bathing, shaving, and dressing are necessary preliminaries to my eating breakfast.
4. To know more about a subject than other people know is a worthy ambition; not to make a parade of one's learning is even more worthy.
5. Jim's tackling and running are excellent, but I don't believe that he will ever learn to punt or catch passes.

6. As it flowed down the gray rock wall, the swiftly falling water seemed to have lost its liquid quality; it looked like a smooth and solidified pillar of green.
7. Having written with more than usual care, I was surprised when the teacher said that my writing was illegible.
8. The woman buying her ticket is a local merchant going to New York.
9. Dewey liked to swim and dance with me, but I always felt that he would rather read than do either.
10. A smiling face is better than a discontented one; to smile is one way to win friends.

4. Adjectives and adverbs

Just as there are two large classes of basic words, nouns and verbs, so there are two large classes of words that modify nouns and verbs—adjectives and adverbs.

The concept of modification is central to grammar, and a few examples will show why. Consider a noun like *book.* We can modify it in many ways and specify exactly what book we want to talk about: *large* book, *red* book, *old* book, *any* book, *illustrated* book. If we had to have a single noun to express the concept of each of these phrases, the size of the vocabulary would be increased enormously and would be less efficient as well. Similarly, verbs can be modified to specify exactly the nature of the action or state we want to talk about: ran *clumsily,* ran *well,* ran *swiftly,* ran *gracefully,* and so on.

Modifiers can also be combined to modify a noun or verb, thereby limiting or describing it more precisely still: *any large old red illustrated book;* ran *gracefully* and *swiftly.*

4a. Adjectives

An *adjective* modifies a noun or pronoun by describing it, limiting it, or otherwise making its meaning more nearly exact. Adjectives are of three general types: (1) *descriptive* (a *yellow* dress, a *broad* horizon, a *tired* laborer); (2) *limiting* (the *third* phrase, her *given* name, *several* weeks); and (3) *proper* (an American policy, a *Florida* orange).

Some adjectives—indeed, many—have endings that mark them as adjectives. The most important of these include

-able (-ible):	workable, serviceable, combustible, payable
-al:	partial, radial, experimental, optional, musical
-ary:	auxiliary, beneficiary, primary, arbitrary, secondary
-en:	golden, smitten, hidden, rotten, wooden
-ful:	sinful, rueful, scornful, dutiful, faithful
-ic:	artistic, pessimistic, altruistic, rustic, metric
-ish:	slavish, peevish, reddish, babyish, selfish
-ive:	restive, festive, corrosive, explosive, excessive
-less:	faultless, guileless, fearless, mindless, lawless
-ous:	marvelous, viscous, luscious, amorous, nervous
-some:	lonesome, fearsome, awesome, tiresome, handsome
-y:	sticky, risky, funny, catty, dreamy, stony

In sentences such as "The seat felt *hard*" and "The path is *treacherous*," each adjective is related to the subject, the word it modifies, by a linking verb. In these sentences, *hard* and *treacherous* are called *predicate adjectives,* or *complements.*

Also sometimes classified among adjectives are the words *a, an,* and *the.* These articles (or *determiners*) tell whether we are talking about a particular thing or not: the *indefinite articles, a* and *an,* specify that the noun they modify refers to any member of the class: *a* doctor, *an* orange. The *definite article, the,* specifies some particular member of the class: *the* doctor, *the* orange.

4b. Adverbs

An *adverb* modifies a verb, an adjective, or another adverb. Adverbs generally tell *how, when, why, how often,* or *how much.* In "The high cliff loomed *forbiddingly* above him," the adverb modifies the verb *loomed* and tells how. In "We are *nearly* ready for supper," the adverb modifies the adjective *ready.* In "Close the hatch *very* quickly," the adverb modifies the adverb *quickly.*

Adverbs have the following characteristics:

1. Adverbs are frequently, but not always, distinguished from corresponding adjectives by the suffix -ly: *true, truly; poor, poorly; sharp, sharply; quick, quickly.*

2. Certain adverbs are distinguished from corresponding nouns by the suffixes *-wise* and *-ways: sideways, lengthwise, clockwise, counterclockwise.*

3. Certain adverbs are distinguished from corresponding prepositions in not being connected to a following noun:

   ADVERB: Mr. McKay fell *down.*
   PREPOSITION: He fell *down* the staircase.

4. Like adjectives, but unlike nouns and verbs, adverbs may be preceded by *intensifiers* such as *very, somewhat, rather,* and *least:*

   It was the *least costly* furnished house.

   We must see her *right now.*

For suggestions on how to use adjectives and adverbs in sentences, see Section 19.

EXERCISE 7

Certain adjectives and adverbs are italicized in the following sentences. Determine which is which.

1. If Sallie comes, will the others be *far* behind?
2. The humidity increased *greatly,* and we realized that a storm was upon us.
3. Under the terms of the agreement, the attorney could not make *other* arrangements.
4. Christopher made his popsicle last as long as he *possibly* could.
5. *Skillfully* the policeman dispersed the *milling* crowd.
6. His manners are *disgusting,* and his personality is *barely tolerable.*
7. My friend is willing but not *able* to complete her obligations.
8. Do you know whether the Giants scored their last touchdown *after* Dimbulb left the game?
9. I know that the menu in this cafeteria has been revised *greatly* since January.
10. Is that the *same* address you had before you left for college?

5. Conjunctions

A *conjunction* is a word (sometimes several words with the force and meaning of one word) that is used to join or link or connect or relate. Conjunctions join both words and series of words. They also introduce and tie together phrases and clauses.

The principal kinds of conjunctions are (1) *coordinating,* which join words and word groups of equal grammatical rank; (2) *subordinating,* which introduce subordinate (dependent) constructions; and (3) *correlative,* which always appear in pairs.

> Renee *and* Manuel are in the library. [Coordinating]
>
> Renee went to the chemistry laboratory, *but* Manuel stayed in the library. [Coordinating]
>
> We cannot go *because* we are short of money. [Subordinating]
>
> *Either* she *or* I will perform the experiment. [Correlative]

Still another kind of joining word, called a *conjunctive adverb,* may be used to join two sentences or two main clauses and has the added effect of an adverb:

> The candidate spoke indistinctly; *besides,* she presented no real facts.

5a. Coordinating conjunctions

The principal coordinating conjunctions are

and	or	nor	neither
but	for	either	yet

Marcia *and* Jesse left the party early.
The keys must be in the car *or* in the house.
Mimi does not wish to go skating, *nor* does she wish you to.

5b. Subordinating conjunctions

The principal subordinating conjunctions are

after	before	since	until
although	how	so that	when
as	if	though	where
because	in order that	unless	while

Jason did not look in my direction *because* he was angry.
If that is your opinion, speak up.
She offered me the money *so that* I could pay the bill.
I won't leave *unless* you go with me.

5c. Correlative conjunctions

The principal correlative conjunctions are

both . . . and	so . . . as
either . . . or	whether . . . or
neither . . . nor	not only . . . but also

Both Susie *and* Mark are working on the problem.
Either the points *or* the spark plugs need changing.
Whether I vote *or* not is none of your business.

5d. Conjunctive adverbs

The most often used conjunctive adverbs are

also	however	otherwise
anyhow	in addition	still
besides	in fact	then
consequently	likewise	therefore
furthermore	nevertheless	thus

Learn to speak more slowly; *otherwise,* no one can understand you.
You seem to be certain of your facts; *however,* I do not agree.

For a more detailed discussion of conjunctions, see Section 20.

EXERCISE 8

Identify as one of the four kinds of connecting words explained in this section the italicized words in the following sentences:

1. She never writes to me; *furthermore,* she won't even answer the telephone when I call.
2. *Not only* Teresa *but also* Tasha chases woodchucks all over the field.
3. Jan will let you know *when* she thinks the tide is going out.
4. *Inasmuch as* Santa Fe and Taos are both celebrating authentic southwestern art, Carlotta plans to visit New Mexico soon.
5. The ones you mention are excellent colleges, *although* I prefer the one I am attending.

6. *Unless* you season the hamburgers properly, they won't taste good.
7. Priscilla can't decide *whether or* not to study chemistry this term.
8. We laughed *and* danced until sunrise; *therefore,* we needed sleep.
9. *Neither* time *nor* energy was wasted at that factory.
10. *After* we lit the fire, we sat back *and* waited for the steaks to cook.

6. Prepositions

A *preposition* is a word that is used to show the relationship of a noun or pronoun to some other word in the sentence.

Lydia was competent *in* mathematics. [The preposition *in* joins the noun *mathematics* to the adjective *competent.*]

I have no need *for* more *of* your excuses. [The preposition *for* joins the pronoun *more* to the noun *need;* the preposition *of* joins the pronoun *more* to the noun *excuses.*]

The following list contains all the simple prepositions that are commonly used in English:

about	beside	inside	through
above	besides	into	throughout
across	between	like	till
after	beyond	near	to
against	but	notwithstanding	toward
along	by	of	under
alongside	concerning	off	underneath
amid	despite	on	until
among	down	onto	up
around	during	outside	upon
at	except	over	with
before	excepting	per	within
behind	for	regarding	without
below	from	save	
beneath	in	since	

6a. Uses of prepositions

Members of a small class of words (parts of speech), prepositions express such relationships between words as space and time. All prepositions (1) require an object and (2) show the relationship of the object to another word.

Nouns, pronouns, gerund and prepositional phrases, and noun clauses can serve as the object of prepositions:

> The mugger ran *into* the park. [The noun *park* is the object of *into*.]
>
> I did it all *for* you. [*You,* a pronoun, is the object of *for*.]
>
> Malvina took great interest *in* running the contest. [*Running the contest,* a gerund phrase, is the object of *in*.]
>
> We came *to* within a foot of the fallen tree. [The prepositional phrase *within a foot* is the object of *to*.]
>
> You can quote *from* whatever source you select. [The noun clause *whatever source you select* is the object of *from*.]

A preposition and its object are called a *prepositional phrase*. Such phrases, which can be used as adjectives, as adverbs, and sometimes as nouns, are explained fully in Section 7.

6b. Position of prepositions

A preposition normally precedes its object, as is shown in examples given earlier. A preposition, however, may follow its object:

> *In what town* do you live? [*In* comes before *what town*.]
>
> What town do you live *in*. [*In* follows its object.]
>
> The supervisor *for whom* I am working is named Marcia Lopez.
>
> The supervisor *whom* I am working *for* is named Marcia Lopez.

6c. Simple and compound prepositions

There are two kinds of prepositions, *simple* and *compound*. Note these examples of simple prepositions:

> the knock *at* the door [knock–door]
>
> the house *by* the river [house–river]
>
> a letter *from* home [letter–home]
>
> a cat *in* the hat [cat–hat]
>
> a handful *of* dust [handful–dust]

the face *on* the floor [face–floor]

going *to* Santa Fe [going–Santa Fe]

The following phrases contain compound prepositions:

the room *across from* the library [room–library]

places *apart from* the city [places–city]

results *due to* circumstances [results–circumstances]

Many of the problems involved in correctly using prepositions concern idiomatic usage. (See Section 37e.)

EXERCISE 9

Insert prepositions in blank spaces in the following sentences. Use simple or compound prepositions, but try not to use the same preposition twice.

1. For many reasons, he was a man ——— a country.
2. ——— our late start, we had a successful trip.
3. We always walk in the forest ——— sunset.
4. The leaflets were distributed ——— the student demonstrators.
5. ——— you and me, I prefer drawing to writing.
6. The professor sought the answer ——— the pages of her notes.
7. Chichi sat ——— her favorite uncle.
8. Willie made his way ——— the wind, rain, and hail.
9. We plan to borrow the power mower ——— Dick and Karen.
10. ——— the discovery, Maria went out and celebrated.

Note: An eighth part of speech, the *interjection,* is defined and illustrated in Section 10. Interjections have no direct grammatical relationship with other words in the sentences in which they appear and accordingly provide little trouble in writing. If you are curious about this part of speech, turn to Section 10.

7. Phrases

A *phrase,* which has the functions of a part of speech, is a group of two or more related words that does *not* contain both a subject and a predicate. Five kinds of phrases may be classified as to form and use.

7a

7a. Types of phrases

1. Prepositional phrases

A *prepositional phrase* is a group of words that begins with a preposition and ends with a noun or pronoun:

on the table	of interest	in the house
for you	to them	into the wall
at the corner	beside me	by the barn

The road winds *through the mountains* and *down into a valley.*
The person standing *beside the door* seems angry.

2. Participial phrases

A *participial phrase* includes a participle together with its modifiers or objects:

Having completed the essay, he switched on the TV.
The village, *ravaged by a cyclone,* is now a ghost town.
Kenyo, *striding easily,* won the race by twenty yards.

3. Gerund phrases

A *gerund phrase* contains a gerund (verbal noun) and may also include one or more modifiers and other related words:

Lying to one's closest friend is a serious mistake.
Winning the speech contest was our first aim.
Jackie enjoyed *the screening of the prize-winning film.*

When a phrase is introduced by a preposition that is followed by a gerund, it is sometimes called a *prepositional–gerundive* phrase:

We lost the game *by failing to get back on defense quickly enough.*
After graduating from college, both Mary Jo and Steve plan to enter medical school.

4. Infinitive phrases

An *infinitive phrase* contains an infinitive:

To settle the dispute was the task of the referee, not the umpire.
Surely there must be some way *to stop this leaking faucet.*
Your next move should be *to visit the employment office.*

5. Absolute phrases

An *absolute phrase,* sometimes called a *nominative absolute,* consists of a noun followed by a participle or a participial phrase. Such a unit is a phrase because it cannot stand alone as a sentence. It is called "absolute" because it modifies no single word in the sentence of which it is a part. An absolute phrase does, however, have a thought relationship to the entire sentence or some part of it.

Night having come, the rangers ordered everyone out of the park.
She left the game early, *her foot hurting badly.*
My difficult and tiring job completed, I headed for the beach.

7b. Uses of the phrase

A phrase usually fulfills the function of a noun, adjective, or adverb. Phrases containing adjectives modifying nouns or adverbs modifying verbs are labeled "adjectival" or "adverbial," depending on their more important, or stronger, words.

1. Noun phrases

A noun phrase is used in a sentence as a subject or an object:

To play in a championship game was Joanne's greatest ambition. [Phrase as subject]
Some politicians seem to like *making a lot of money.* [Phrase as object]
He planned *keeping the moped for a thorough trial.* [Phrase as object]

2. Adjective phrases

An adjective, or adjectival, phrase is used in a sentence as a single adjective would be.

Some people *in that dormitory* are noisy and thoughtless. [The phrase tells *what* people.]
No person *filling our needs* has applied so far. [*Filling our needs* modifies *person.*]
This gift *from you* means a great deal. [*What* gift?]
Most magazines *in our dentist's office* are five years old. [The phrase modifies *magazines.*]
The very next day, many persons *striking the company* went back to work. [The phrase modifies *persons.*]

3. Adverb phrases

When a phrase is used to modify a verb, an adjective, or an adverb, it is an adverb (adverbial) phrase.

Our college choir sings *with enthusiasm*. [The phrase modifies the verb *sings*.]

The team's star player fumbled *near the goal line*. [The phrase modifies the verb *fumbled*.]

Baby sitters sometimes claim that children are unpredictable *in the extreme*. [The phrase modifies the adjective *unpredictable*.]

The crowd grew quiet *after the second explosion*. [The phrase modifies the adjective *quiet*.]

Vicki claimed she was too busy *to attend the party*. [The phrase modifies the adjective *busy*.]

Please drop the ice slowly *into the punchbowl*. [The phrase modifies the adverb *slowly*.]

A *verb phrase* consists of a group of words that have the function of a verb with its modifiers. Such phrases consist of a main verb and auxiliaries:

Soon your first year in college *will be completed*.

Verb phrases are fully explained in Section 16.

EXERCISE 10

Pick out the complete phrases in the following sentences. List the word (or words) each phrase modifies. State what kind of phrase each one is. Indicate the part of speech represented by each.

1. Seen from a distance, the night train, creeping up the mountain grade, looked like an animated glowworm.
2. In the summer, Carlos loves to read under a shady tree in the park.
3. Smith being pretty well exhausted, the coach sent in Olivetti to replace him as center.
4. To get along well with people, you must learn to share their interests.
5. A motion was made to close the nominations, no other names being proposed.
6. Having reached the age of 18, I have no desire ever to fall in love again.
7. Your teacher has no objection to your turning in well-written papers.
8. Through the night the huge four-engined jet roared on to its destination.

9. To get experience, not to make money, was her goal in seeking a summer job.
10. Having been elected president, I expressed my gratitude for the honor bestowed upon me.

8. Clauses

A *clause* is a group of words having a subject and a predicate. Some clauses are *independent* (main, principal), meaning that they can stand alone as sentences or may appear within sentences as grammatically complete statements. Other clauses are *dependent* (subordinate), meaning that they cannot stand alone and therefore depend for their meaning upon the remainders of the sentences in which they appear.

8a. Independent clauses

Independent clauses express the central act of predication in a sentence. The subject and predicate of such a clause are the sentence elements to which everything else in the sentence is related.

The couple danced around the room to increasing applause. [A sentence]

The Battlestar Galactica always escapes. [A sentence]

Although the Cylons keep trying, *the Battlestar Galactica always escapes.* [Independent clause]

Not only *will she make a contribution herself,* but *she will also ask her friends to help.* [Two independent clauses]

Come early and *stay late.* [Two independent clauses]

8b. Dependent clauses

A *dependent,* or *subordinate,* clause contains a subject and a predicate but also contains a linking word that shows its grammatical connection to the remainder of the sentence. Such a linking word (usually a subordinating conjunction or relative pronoun) shows the relationship of the dependent clause to the main clause.

The elephant, *which had a long ivory tusk,* rumbled toward the forest. [A relative clause, introduced by the subordinating relative pronoun *which,* includes the predicate *had.*]

When Terry drives, other motorists should get off the streets. [An adverbial clause, introduced by the subordinating conjunction *when,* includes the verb *drives.*]

A special kind of dependent clause is called *elliptical.* In such a clause the subject, and usually part of the predicate, may be omitted because they are understood from information provided in the main clause.

Although I was ill, I insisted on doing the shopping.
Although ill, I insisted on doing the shopping. [Elliptical clause]
While she was drying her hair, Anne looked at television.
While drying her hair, Anne looked at television. [Elliptical clause]

8c. Uses of dependent clauses

Dependent clauses can perform the functions of nouns, adjectives, and adverbs and are named according to that function.

1. Noun clauses

A noun clause acts within a sentence as a noun. In this use, a clause is usually introduced by *that, what, whatever, who, whoever, which, when, where, wherever, how,* or *why.*

What you paid was too much. [The italicized clause, introduced by the relative pronoun *what,* could be replaced by a noun, *price.*]

The manager promised *that he would run the film for us again.* [The italicized clause acts as the object of the verb *promised.*]

The doctor came to the conclusion *that his patient was out of danger.* [The italicized clause acts as an *appositive;* see Section 2 as well as the glossary in Section 10.]

The dog's owner will be *whoever finds it and feeds it.* [The italicized clause is used as a predicate complement—see Section 10.]

2. Adjective clauses

An *adjective clause* is used to modify a noun or pronoun just as an adjective would. Such a clause is usually introduced by a relative pronoun—*who, which, that, whom*—or by a subordinating conjunction—*when, where, why.*

Drivers *who live on that street* have to watch out for potholes. [The italicized clause acts as an adjective modifying *drivers*; it tells *what* drivers.]

She is the very person *whom I wanted to go with me.* [The italicized clause tells *what* person.]

Alicia is a person *I have come to know and like.* [In this italicized clause, *whom* after *person* is understood.]

You know perfectly well the reason *why I could not pay the bill.* [The italicized clause modifies the noun *reason.*]

3. Adverb (adverbial) clauses

An adverb clause, which is used to modify a verb, an adjective, or an adverb, can express several relationships:

Time: **when, before, while, since**
When you row a canoe, you must keep control of the oar. [Adverbial clause modifies *must keep*]

Place: **where, wherever**
After finding the bicycle *where I had left it,* I hurried back into the house. [Adverbial clause modifies the gerund *finding*]

Manner: **as, as if**
She kicked the can *as if it were a football.* [Adverbial clause modifies the verb *kicked*]

Condition: **if, so, unless, provided that**
Unless you pay the bill, service will be cut off. [Adverbial clause modifies the verb *will be cut off*]

Cause: **because, as, since**
The train, two hours late *because the engine had broken down,* was full of irate passengers. [Adverbial clause modifies the adjective *late*]

Purpose: **in order that, so that**
The students worked hard all day *so that the hall would be ready for the party.* [Adverbial clause modifies the verb *worked*]

Result: **that, so that, so . . . that**
We were *so* hungry *that we ate stale bread.* [Adverbial clause modifies the adjective *hungry*]

Degree or comparison: **than, as much as, as . . . as, just as**
Moneta climbed farther *than you did.* [Adverbial clause modifies the adverb *farther*]

Concession: **though, although**
Although she did not score, she made the best play of the game. [Adverbial clause modifies the verb *made*]

EXERCISE 11

Pick out every clause in each of the following sentences. Indicate its function in the sentence by one of these abbreviations: IND for independent, N for noun, ADJ for adjective, or ADV for adverb.

1. Among other kinds of people we can single out these two: those who think and those who act.
2. The people of that section have been marketing a great quantity of vegetables in the city this summer.
3. He jumped up and down; he shouted and yelled; and yet, for some strange reason, no one paid him the slightest attention.
4. I recommend a visit to Cincinnati, but when you go, remember that your impressions will be determined by where you get off the bus.
5. Whenever my high school friends assembled, we listened to the new records in anyone's collection.
6. I have often heard it said that people are funny, and I am sorry to admit that the statement is true.
7. As it was getting late, we began looking for a place where we might land and camp for the night.
8. Not all people in the library are scholars: across the table from me a boy is enjoying himself looking at the cartoons in a magazine; sitting farther away in a quiet corner are a boy and a girl reading newspapers.
9. The botanists who have been working in the experiment station are trying to develop a plant that will grow in any kind of soil.
10. The highlight of my childhood summers was a visit to my grandparents' farm; letting me do everything, it seemed, was their idea of showing me a good time.

9. Sentences

A *sentence* has traditionally been defined as "a group of words containing a subject and predicate and expressing a complete thought." This is hardly a full and accurate definition, however, for two reasons: (1) some "sentences" that are accepted as such do not contain both an expressed subject and predicate; (2) not all sentences express a complete thought because they depend for full meaning on statements that come before or after them.

A more accurate definition, although one that is not easy to grasp, is this: "A sentence is a grammatical unit of one or more words, bearing little grammatical relationship to words that precede or follow it, often preceded and followed in speech by pauses, having one of a number of characteristic patterns, and expressing an independent statement, question, command, or request."

Put simply, a written sentence is a stretch of writing that begins with a capital letter and ends with a terminal mark (see Section 21) and that an educated reader will recognize and accept as "a sentence" (see Section 41).

9a. Sentence meaning and purpose

Sentences can be classified according to the kinds of statements they make. They are *declarative, interrogative, imperative,* or *exclamatory.*

1. Declarative sentences

A *declarative sentence* states a fact or expresses an opinion:

That car has eight cylinders.
If it rains tomorrow, exercises will be brought indoors.
To lead a good life is to know true inner peace.

2. Interrogative sentences

An *interrogative sentence* asks a direct question.

Does that car have eight cylinders?
If it rains tomorrow, will the exercises be brought indoors?
Is it true that inner peace comes from leading a good life?
Has leading a good life brought her inner peace?

3. Imperative sentences

An *imperative sentence* expresses a command or request.

Fill out the application blank and mail it immediately.

Ask everyone in your class to come to the meeting tonight.
Stop quibbling: Lend me the money now!

4. Exclamatory sentences

An *exclamatory sentence* expresses strong feeling, intense emotion, or surprise.

Thank goodness, you finally got here.
Oh, if I could only take back what I said to him!
I can't believe that time has run out on us!
Let's get going!

9b. Sentence structure

Structurally, a sentence can be *simple, compound, complex,* or *compound–complex.*

1. Simple sentences

A *simple sentence* contains only one subject (simple or compound) and one predicate (simple or compound).

Workers warm up around one of the smudge pots. [Simple subject, simple predicate]
Pear and apple orchards are warmed and protected by smudge pots. [Compound subject, compound predicate]
Smudge pots and rotating wind machines protect pears and apples during cold spells. [Compound subject, compound predicate]

2. Compound sentences

A *compound sentence* contains two or more independent (main) clauses. Each of the clauses of a compound sentence is grammatically capable of standing alone as a complete sentence.

The milk was warm and sweet, but the bread was old and crusty.
Not only is she a brilliant student, but she also works as a stock analyst every afternoon.
Some of the United States Virgin Islands are large; others are just rocks jutting out of the sea.

3. Complex sentences

A *complex sentence* contains one independent (main) clause and one or more dependent (subordinate) clauses.

Our town, which has serious financial problems, will soon ask for a tax increase.

I knew quickly that I had made a mistake.

As the pain began to sharpen, I wondered whether I had encountered a lion fish.

She is an athlete who trains vigorously and who always keeps her muscles pliant and supple.

4. Compound–complex sentences

A *compound–complex sentence* contains two or more independent (main) clauses and one or more dependent (subordinate) clauses.

When the legislature passed a sales tax, many persons complained; but the governor agreed to use most of the money for better schools.

While the storm increased in force, and while thunder and lightning became more violent, Jock crawled under the bed and Stella covered her head with a pillow.

Although liability insurance is required in this state, you should be sure that your coverage is adequate and you should also be careful to check the reputation of your insurer.

9c. Sentence word order

Sentences may be classified according to the arrangement of their content. The words in a sentence may be arranged in *loose, periodic,* or *balanced* form.

1. Loose form

A *loose* sentence is so arranged that its thought may be completed, or seem to be completed, before the end. In both speech and writing, most sentences are constructed in this way.

Act quickly or you will be too late to get tickets for the game tonight. [The complete meaning of this sentence is not reached until the last word, but it makes sense if it is stopped at *quickly, late, tickets,* or *game.*]

My best friend likes to listen to tapes and to race on her motorcycle, but more than anything else she likes to ride her surfboard.

2. Periodic form

A sentence in which the words are set down in such a way that its full meaning is not complete until the end, or near the end, is called a *periodic* sentence.

If you do not intend to pay this bill, please say so.

Only if we extend our armed conflicts to other planets will the Moon become of military importance.

According to a former college president, to be at home in all lands and ages; to count Nature a familiar acquaintance and Art a familiar friend; to gain a standard for the appreciation of other men's work and the criticism of one's own; to make friends among men and women of one's own age who are to be the leaders in all walks of life; to lose one's self in generous enthusiasm and to cooperate with others for common ends; and to form character under professors who are dedicated—these are the returns of a college for the best four years of one's life.

3. Balanced form

A *balanced* sentence is so constructed that similar or opposing thoughts or statements have similar grammatical phrasing.

Wise people change their minds, fools never.

In the morning I go to classes; in the afternoon I work; at night I study.

Honesty suggests that I speak up; self-interest demands that I keep quiet.

9d. Sentence patterns

A sentence is composed of a series of words that can convey meaning only because certain of those words are structurally related. That is, the words are related in such a way that they express an act of predication (make sense). Various sentence patterns indicate the kinds of words that sentences contain. They specify the

types of words that have to be present in a sentence before it can
be called a sentence.

In English, there are seven basic sentence patterns:

Pattern 1

Subject	Predicate (Verb)
Fires	burn.
Dogs	bark.
We	talk.

Pattern 2

Subject	Predicate (Verb)	Direct Object
Jeanne	teaches	Joseph.
Musicians	play	instruments.
You	need	me.

Pattern 3

Subject	Predicate (Verb)	Indirect Object	Direct Object
Babs	gives	them	presents.
Peggy	wrote	him	notes.
The teacher	assigned	Jack	poetry.

Pattern 4

Subject	Linking Verb	Predicate Noun
Tom	is	the underdog.
Susie	was	the coffee manager.
Carol	will be	an architect.

Pattern 5

Subject	Linking Verb	Predicate Adjective
Dogs	are	loving.
Garlic	smells	strong.
It	seems	silly.

Pattern 6

Subject	Predicate (Verb)	Direct Object	Object Complement
Wanda	named	her cat	Archie.
José	called	his boss	a fool.
Joanne	considered	Will	her enemy.

Pattern 7

Subject	Predicate (Verb)	Direct Object	Adjective Complement
Ms. Lashar	painted	the barn	red.
Henry	made	his room	tidy.
Josie	thought	the situation	messy.

Expanding Sentence Patterns

Several types of modifiers may be used to expand the basic elements of any of the seven patterns illustrated. They may be definite and indefinite articles and other noun determiners or markers. (See Section 1a.)

The Girl Scouts built *a* lean-to. [Pattern 2]
My uncle lost *his* temper. [Pattern 2]

Single-word adjectives and adverbs often modify the elements of the basic patterns.

The *energetic girls soon* built a shack. [Pattern 2]
She is an *accomplished* pianist. [Pattern 4]
They elected a *capable* person judge. [Pattern 6]
He *sleeps well*. [Pattern 1]

Phrases of various kinds (see Section 7) frequently modify the basic words in patterns:

In the morning, they left *for St. Louis.* [Pattern 1]
Hoping to win the cup, Tom entered the competition. [Pattern 2]
San Francisco, *a truly beautiful city,* is a popular place *for tourists.* [Pattern 4]
He gave his parents a present *by staying out of trouble.* [Pattern 3]

Clauses of various kinds (see Section 8) frequently modify basic words in patterns.

Because he had failed twice already, David lost his incentive to try again. [Pattern 2]
Athens, *which enjoys a temperate climate,* is the capital of Greece. [Pattern 4]
She always struggled *for what she believed in.* [Pattern 1]

When infinitive and gerund phrases or noun clauses serve as either subjects or objects, they may be considered as integral parts of basic patterns. Note the following examples:

To err is human. [Pattern 5]
The team tried *to win*. [Pattern 2]
Developing new territories was the sales manager's constant aim. [Pattern 4]
They tried *growing Jerusalem artichokes*. [Pattern 2]
That he had won was clear. [Pattern 5]
He knew *what to say*. [Pattern 2]

Any essential part of a sentence pattern may be compounded through the use of a conjunction. (See Section 5.) Compound subjects, predicates, and complements are considered as single units as far as the patterns are concerned: Val *and* Ned gave them presents. [Pattern 3]

9e. Variations in sentence patterns

Knowledge of a few other variations or transformations will increase your understanding of an English sentence.

1. The passive variation

Sentences employing a verb in the passive voice are common in English; they are usually developed from pattern 2 sentences. The *passive variation* is formed by moving the direct object into the subject position and making the subject into the object of a preposition in a prepositional phrase. The verb also changes to the passive voice, which is always made up of a form of the verb *to be* followed by the past participle:

Subject	Predicate	(Prepositional Phrase)
The bridge	was struck	(by Grace).
The treasure	was hidden	(by Captain Kidd).
The soldiers	were scolded	(by the colonel).

The prepositional phrases appear in parentheses because they are optional. In some passive sentences the prepositional phrase is omitted.

Pattern 6 and 7 sentences can also be changed into the passive voice. Note the changes that occur in the following examples:

PATTERN 6: Wanda named her cat Archie.
            The cat was named Archie (by Wanda).

PATTERN 7: Ms. Lashar painted the barn red.
            The barn was painted red (by Ms. Lashar).

When a pattern 2 sentence is changed into the passive, it may be considered a pattern 1 sentence. When patterns 6 and 7 are changed, the revisions may be considered pattern 4 and 5 sentences, respectively.

2. The question variation

Sentences that ask questions are as common in English as in any other language. The *question variation* follows certain set patterns.

If in an affirmative statement a verb has one or more auxiliaries, the first auxiliary is switched so that it comes before the subject:

AFFIRMATIVE: The contest was over.
              The arrest will be made.
              The house could have been reshingled.
              The guest has gone.

QUESTIONS: Was the contest over?
             Will the arrest be made?
             Could the house have been reshingled?
             Has the guest gone?

If the affirmative statement contains no auxiliary, some form of the verb *do* is placed in front of the subject:

AFFIRMATIVE: The girl runs fast.
              Bill enjoys his enemies.
              Joe flew an airplane.
              Marcelle likes physics.

QUESTIONS: Does the girl run fast?
             Does Bill enjoy his enemies?
             Did Joe fly an airplane?
             Does Marcelle like physics?

These same rules apply when questions begin with common question words like *where, when, why,* and *how.*

3. The imperative variation

The imperative is commonly viewed as having the subject "you" either understood or implied. The following are examples of the *imperative variation* in each of the seven basic patterns:

Stop! [Pattern 1]
Begin the trial! [Pattern 2]
Give him a break. [Pattern 3]
Be a jerk. [Pattern 4]
Remain dumb. [Pattern 5]
Name the animal Bozo. [Pattern 6]
Color my face red. [Pattern 7]

EXERCISE 12

Indicate the kinds of sentences that follow, using these symbols: S for simple, CP for compound, CX for complex, or CC for compound–complex.

1. Students are not allowed to park cars in this area; if they do, they are subject to a fine.
2. Can anyone tell me what time the play begins?
3. If you want advice, your counselor is available, but be sure that your problem is really important.
4. Traffic lights and signs are intended to help, not hinder, the flow of traffic.
5. Having reached a decision, the three judges returned to the auditorium and announced it.
6. The yacht race was stopped after fifty miles, but it will be continued after the storm.
7. It is a lonely homecoming when no one is at home to greet you.
8. Our final game was the victory of the season; therefore, we will have a holiday on Monday.
9. The administration is threatening to make rules concerning proper behavior on campus.
10. Among the certain things in life, one is this: no one can foretell what the future will bring.

EXERCISE 13

Revise each of the following sentences. If it is loose in construction, make it periodic; if it is periodic, make it loose.

1. If you will lend me money for a ticket and if you will promise not to eat popcorn, I'll go.
2. Lucy Martinez was honored by a one-artist show after notable exhibitions in London and other major foreign cities.
3. Winning hands down for enthusiasm about the future of natural gas is a group of Soviet scientists.
4. I am a night person, soothed by shadows, my spirit lifted by stars in the heavens.
5. Banking the north and west sides of a large triangle are several exhibition spaces.

EXERCISE 14

Determine the sentence patterns in the following statements. Example:

Susie bought her brother a popsicle. [Answer: subject–predicate–indirect object–direct object (3)]

1. We will meet you later.
2. Locating the address seemed hopeless.
3. Many hours of work produced a beautiful display.
4. The pilot considered the day perfect for flying.
5. If we look hard enough, we might find a perfect gift.
6. Having looked all over town and having been convinced that a good used car could not be found for three hundred dollars, the boys, disillusioned but not completely hopeless, went home.
7. Loving is its own reward.
8. The cold drink tasted wonderful.
9. Several persons applied for the job without success.
10. Millard knew a good bargain when he saw one.

EXERCISE 15

Write one sentence illustrating each of the seven patterns explained in Section 9d.

EXERCISE 16

Now that you have studied Sections 1–9 and have refreshed your memory about parts of speech, phrases, clauses, and sentences, you are ready to *analyze* a sentence, that is, identify and explain every word, phrase, and clause in it. Start with the following sentence, which is complex in structure:

> The little old woman across the street is lovingly knitting a sweater for her grandson, who is a musician.

Start your analysis like this: *The* is a definite article modifying the noun *woman*. *Little* and *old* are adjectives modifying the noun *woman*. *Woman* is a noun used as part of the subject of the sentence. *The little old woman* is the subject of *is knitting*. Now keep going.

10. A glossary of grammatical terms

The following list briefly defines those elements of grammar that are most often involved in the writing of sentences. Most of the items are discussed in greater detail at appropriate places in Sections 1–9, 12–20, and throughout this book. If you do not find what you need in this glossary, consult the index.

absolute expression An absolute expression (also called nominative absolute) is one that has a thought relationship but no direct grammatical relationship with the remainder of the sentence in which it occurs. An absolute expression does not modify any individual word or word group in the sentence. An absolute expression is usually composed of a noun or pronoun and a participle:

> *The reason for our trip having been explained,* we set out with enthusiasm.

abstract noun The name of something (a general idea or quality) that cannot be touched, seen, or known directly by any other of the senses: *freedom, honor, dread, culture, sorrow*. (See Section 1b.)

accusative A case name meaning the same thing as *objective* case. (See Section 14.) The term *accusative case* is rare in English, but it is common in the study of such foreign languages as Latin and German.

active voice The form of an action-expressing verb which tells that the subject does or performs the action. (See Section 3b.)

adjective A word used to describe or limit a noun or noun equivalent. (See Sections 4 and 19.)

adjective clause A dependent, or subordinate, clause used as an adjective. (See Section 8c.)

adverb A word used to describe or limit the meaning of a verb, adjective, or other adverb, or a sentence. (See Section 4b.)

adverb clause A dependent, or subordinate, clause used as an adverb. (see Section 8c.)

agreement Correspondence, or sameness, in number, gender, and person. When a subject agrees with its verb, they are alike in having the same *person* (first, second, or third) and *number* (singular or plural). Pronouns agree not only in person and number but also in gender. (See Sections 12 and 13.)

> *Martha is* my sister.
> *Martha* and *Priscilla are* my siblings.
> A *man* hopes to retain *his* youthful appearance.
> Many *women* retain *their* youthful appearance.
> Gray is one of those *boys who are* always well behaved.

antecedent The substantive (noun or pronoun) to which a pronoun refers is its antecedent. (See Section 13.)

> The *girl* has lost *her* chance. [*Girl* is the antecedent of *her.*]
> Remember that *pronouns* agree with *their* antecedents in gender, number, and person. [*Pronouns* is the antecedent of *their.*]

antonym A word that is opposite, or nearly so, in meaning to another word. (See Section 39e.)

appositive A substantive that is added to another substantive to identify or explain it. It is said to be "in apposition."

> One important product, *rubber,* is in short supply in that country. [*Rubber* is in apposition with *product.*]
> More hardy than wheat are these grains—*rye, oats,* and *barley.* [*Rye, oats,* and *barley* are in apposition with *grains.*]

An appositive agrees with its substantive in number and case. It is set off by commas if its relationship is loose (nonrestrictive) and is used without punctuation if the relationship is close (restrictive):

> my brother Jake [Restrictive]
> Jake, my brother [Nonrestrictive]

article The articles (*a, an, the*) possess limiting or specifying functions. *A* and *an* are indefinite articles; *the* is the definite article: *a* phonograph, *an* error, *the* surgeon.

> *The* soprano has *a* lovely voice and *an* appealing manner.

aspect In grammar, aspect is usually defined as a set of ways in which a verb is inflected (changed) to indicate duration, quality, or completion of the action or state denoted. Actually, aspect is commonly conveyed by particular verbs or verb–adverb combinations, as in "Del started to run" and "Del was about to run" (both beginning action); "Del stopped running" (completed action); and "Del kept on running" (continuing action).

auxiliary A verb that is used to "help" another verb in the formation of tenses, voice, mood, and certain precise ideas. Examples are *be (am, is, are, was, were, been); have (has, had); do (does); can, could; may, might; shall, should; will, would; must; ought; let;* and *used.* (See Section 16.)

Althea *has* left town for the weekend.
We *should have been* working with the stevedores on the dock.
Will you please turn off the light?

cardinal number A number such as *two, four,* or *thirty* (2, 4, 30). (See *ordinal number.*)

case A term referring to the forms that nouns or pronouns take (nominative, possessive, objective) to indicate their relationship to other words in the sentence. (See Section 14.)

clause A group of words that contains a subject and a predicate and makes a complete statement or forms part of a sentence. (See Section 8.)

When the cheering stopped, *Effie was sad.* [Independent clause]
This is the present *that I bought.* [Dependent adjective clause]
Wherever we go, we shall have trouble. [Dependent adverb clause]
Maury insisted *that he had tried his best.* [Dependent noun clause]

collective noun The name of a group that is composed of individuals but is considered as a unit: *class, audience, jury.*

common noun A noun that names a member or members of a general or common group: *automobile, coat, quintet.*

comparison The change in form of an adjective or adverb or the addition of related words to indicate greater or smaller degrees of quantity, quality, or manner. (See Section 19.)

complement A word or expression used to complete the idea indicated or implied by a verb. A *predicate complement* (sometimes called a *subjective complement*) may be a noun, a pronoun, or an adjective that follows a linking verb and describes or identifies the subject of that verb. An *object (objective) complement* may be a noun or an adjective that follows the direct object of a verb and completes the meaning.

Ms. Black is a *lawyer* [Subjective]
George is *mournful.* [Subjective]
The club members are *youthful.* [Subjective]
They called the dog *Willie.* [Objective]
We dyed the dress *blue.* [Objective]

complex sentence A sentence that contains one independent clause and one or more dependent clauses. (See Section 9b.)

compound sentence A sentence that contains two or more independent clauses. (See Section 9b.)

compound–complex sentence A sentence that contains two or more independent clauses and one or more dependent clauses. (See Section 9b.)

You may send candy or you may send flowers, but you must certainly send something to Mother because she expects a gift.

conjugation The changes (inflections) in the form or use of a verb to show tense, mood, voice, number, and person. (See these terms in this glossary and in Sections 3, 17, and 18.)

conjunction A part of speech that serves as a linking or joining word to connect words or groups of words. (See Section 5.)

conjunctive adverb An adverb that can also be used as a conjunction coordinating two independent clauses: *also, furthermore, nevertheless, besides, however, therefore, thus, so, consequently, hence, likewise, still, then, moreover.* (See Sections 5d and 20.)

The library is open on Saturday; *therefore,* you can take the books back then.

connective Any word or phrase that links (joins) words, phrases, clauses, or sentences. The term includes conjunctions, conjunctive adverbs, and prepositions.

consonant In phonetics, a sound in which the breath is somewhat restricted or even stopped. Consonant sounds may be contrasted with *vowel* sounds, which are made with less friction and fuller resonance. The vowels in our alphabet are *a, e, i, o, u,* and sometimes *y.* All other letters are consonants.

context The parts of a piece of writing or speech that precede or follow a given word or passage with which they are directly connected. If we say that such and such a passage in a novel is obscene but that *in its context* it is significant and not shocking, we mean that what comes before or after the passage provides meaning that is important, even essential, to understanding and judgment.

coordination The giving of equal grammatical value to two or more parts of a sentence. (See Section 43.)

copula A word or set of words that acts as a connecting link. (See Section 16.)

count noun A noun that typically refers to a countable thing and that can be used with an indefinite article and in the plural: *apple, ten apples, an apple.*

declension The inflectional changes in the form or use of a noun or pronoun to indicate case, number, and person. "To decline" means to give these grammatical changes.

Case	Singular	Plural
Nominative	man, I, who	men, we, who
Possessive	man's; my, mine; whose	men's; our, ours; whose
Objective	man, me, whom	men, us, whom

degree One of the formations of adjectives and adverbs to express differences in quality, quantity, or intensity. For example, *low* and *careful* are the *positive degree; lower* and *more careful* are the *comparative degree; lowest* and *most careful* are the *superlative degree.* (See *comparison* and Section 19.)

determiner A determiner may be an article (*a, an, the*), a possessive (*my, your, its, their, hers, his*), or a demonstrative pronoun (*this, that, those*). In general, a determiner is any member of a subclass of adjectival words that limits the noun it modifies and usually is placed before descriptive adjectives. A determiner is sometimes referred to as a *marker*.

diagraming A mechanical device to aid in identifying words as parts of speech, identifying phrases and clauses, and indicating the uses or functions of these words, phrases, and clauses in a sentence. The parts of a sentence are put on lines in the positions shown in the following skeleton diagram. The three most important parts of the sentence (subject, predicate, object) are usually put on a horizontal line; any modifiers are appropriately placed on lines underneath.

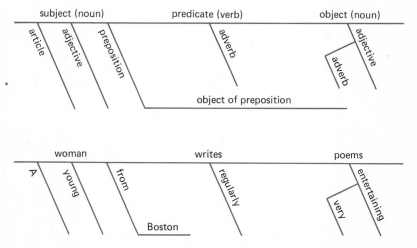

A young woman from Boston regularly writes very entertaining poems.

Another method of diagraming, which is somewhat cumbersome and little used, consists of placing each word in a sentence in a box. This plan results in a set of boxes, each enclosed in another box; the last box encloses the entire sentence.

Still another method of diagraming uses lines that branch like the limbs of trees. The first branch is from the sentence (S) to the subject (noun or noun phrase, N or NP) and the predicate (verb or verb phrase, V or VP). Further branchings reveal as many levels and varieties of structural relationships as the sentence contains.

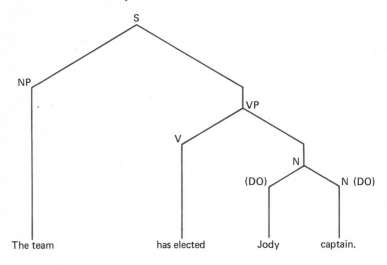

In this diagram, the sentence consists of a noun phrase (NP) and a verb phrase (VP). The latter contains both a direct object (DO) and an object complement (also DO), both referring to the same person.

direct address In this construction, also called the *vocative*, the noun or pronoun shows the person to whom speech is addressed:

> *Jimmy*, where are you?
> What did you say, *Mother?*
> After you mow the grass, *Fred*, please take out the garbage.

direct quotation A quotation that reproduces the exact words written or spoken by someone:

> "Please use your dictionary more often," the office manager said. "These letters will all need to be retyped."

(See *indirect quotation* in this glossary.)

double possessive A form using both *of* and *'s:* a book *of Marie's*. (See Section 26c.)

ellipsis (elliptical clause) The omission of a word or words that are not needed because they are understood from other words or from context. In the following examples, the words shown in brackets are often omitted in speaking and writing.

Some drove to Miami, others [drove] to Palm Beach.
While [we were] swimming, we agreed to go to a movie later.

expletive A word or phrase added either to fill out a sentence or to provide emphasis. The latter function is performed by exclamatory or profane expressions. The more frequently employed function of the expletive is complementary, however; in this sense, *surely, indeed, why,* and *yes* may be considered expletives:

This is *indeed* a happy occasion.
It and *there* are commonly used as expletives, that is, as "subject delayers."
It was Alice sitting there.
It is a truism that men love freedom.
There are 2,400 people present.

Some grammarians further classify *it*. For example, the late Paul Roberts discussed "impersonal *it*," "situation *it*," and "expletive *it*," illustrating each as follows:

IMPERSONAL: It's dark in here.
It is Saturday.
It snowed last night.
SITUATION: It was Ben who started the trouble.
It's Lois and the children.
Was it the dog?
EXPLETIVE: It is hard to believe that Winifred is 16.
It is true that we were once great friends.

finite verb A verb form or verb phrase that serves as a predicate. It has number and person and asserts that an action or state of being is taking, has taken, or will take place. A nonfinite verb form (participle, gerund, or infinitive) cannot serve as a predicate. (See Section 3c.)

functional shift The process by which a word or form comes to be used in another grammatical function (part of speech), as when a verb is used as a noun:

This is a hard *rock*. *Rock* the baby gently.

function word A preposition, conjunction, or other "structure" or "form" word used to show a grammatical relationship in a phrase, clause, or sentence. A function word is more important to structure than to meaning.

A glossary of grammatical terms

gender The gender of nouns and pronouns is determined by sex. A noun or pronoun denoting a member of the male sex is called *masculine: man, boy, lord, executor, he.* A noun or pronoun denoting a member of the female sex is called *feminine: woman, girl, lady, executrix, she.* Nouns that do not denote members of either sex are referred to as *neuter: house, book, tree, desk, lamp, courage.* Some nouns and pronouns may be either masculine or feminine and are said to have *common* gender: *child, teacher, friend, doctor, visitor, it, they.*

genitive A case name meaning the same as *possessive.* (See Section 14.)

gerund A verbal noun ending in –ing (*speaking, singing*). Because the gerund has the same form as the present participle, note the difference in their functions: the participle is a verbal *adjective;* the gerund is a verbal *noun.* A gerund can take an object and be modified by an adverb; as a noun, it can be the subject or object of a verb or the object of a preposition. (See Section 3c.)

> *Playing* squash is good exercise.
> All the skiers enjoy *eating.*
> They welcomed our *coming.*

idiom The usual forms of expression of a language; the characteristic way in which it is put together. In speaking of French idiom, for example, we refer to distinct usages such as the fact that adjectives follow nouns or that an adjective has forms for singular and plural and for masculine and feminine gender. *Idiom* also refers to expressions that are accepted but differ from usual constructions, such as *a hot cup of tea, how do you do, the law's delay,* and *jump the gun.* (See Sections 37e and 14m.)

impersonal construction A method of phrasing in which neither a personal pronoun nor personal noun is stated as the actor. The passive voice is used, or words like *it* or *there.* (See *expletive.*)

> I have four reasons for my decision. [Personal]
> There are four reasons for this decision. [Impersonal]
> We must consider three suggestions. [Personal]
> It is necessary to consider three suggestions. [Impersonal]

indefinite pronoun A pronoun such as *anybody* or *someone.* (See Section 2.)

indirect object A noun or pronoun that usually precedes the direct object of a verb, representing the person or thing with reference to which the action of the verb is performed. When an indirect object follows the direct object, a preposition (*to, for*) is used:

> Yesterday I bought *him* a soda. Yesterday I bought a soda for *him.*

indirect question Restatement by one person of a direct question asked by another:

When will you pay me? [Direct]

Joe asked when I would pay him. [Indirect]

indirect quotation Restatement by one person in his or her own words of the words written or spoken by someone else:

Eileen said, "I'll be there on Sunday." [Direct]

Eileen said that she will be here on Sunday. [Indirect]

(See *direct quotation*.)

infinitive A word that functions as both verb and noun and also may be employed as an adjectival or adverbial modifier. The infinitive is usually introduced by the sign *to: to* speak, *to* sing. (See Section 3c.) Like a *gerund*, an infinitive can take an object and be modified by an adverb; in its function as a noun, it can be the subject or object of a verb and the object of a preposition.

We should now plan *to leave*. [Infinitive as noun, object of the verb *plan*]

Will you please *return* by the next bus. [Please *to return;* infinitive as verb and part of a predicate]

The person *to see* is the manager. [Infinitive as adjective]

She is waiting *to tell* us of her recent trip. [Infinitive as adverb]

inflection (1) A change in the form of a word to show a change in use or meaning. *Comparison* is the inflection of adjectives and adverbs; *declension* is the inflection of nouns and pronouns; *conjugation* is the inflection of verbs. (2) A change in the pitch or tone of voice.

intensifier A word or element used to strengthen or enforce meaning. *Certainly, very,* and *extremely* are examples of intensifiers. So are *quite* and *rather*.

interjection The interjection (1) has no grammatical connection with the remainder of the sentence and (2) expresses emotion—surprise, dismay, disapproval, anger, fear. Grammarians distinguish two kinds of interjections. First are the forms that are used only as interjections, never occurring otherwise in speech: *oh, ouch, tsk-tsk, psst, whew, alas.* Some of these contain sounds not used otherwise in English and consequently difficult to represent in writing; *tsk-tsk,* for example, is an inadequate representation of the clucking sound made to indicate disapproval. Second are the forms that occur sometimes as interjections and sometimes as other parts of speech: *goodness, well, my.*

intonation See *pitch*.

intransitive verb See *transitive verb*.

irregular plurals See *number* and Section 1a.

irregular verb Sometimes called *strong* verbs, irregular verbs do not follow a regular pattern in forming their principal parts. Instead, these are usually formed by a change in the vowel: *see, saw, seen; choose, chose, chosen.* Your dictionary is your guide to such changes. (See Section 15.)

juncture This word has several meanings, all of which involve the act or state of "joining" or "connecting." In grammar and linguistics, juncture is a distinctive sound feature or modification of a sound feature marking the *sound* boundary of a word, clause, or sentence. Juncture indicates that words as we speak them are not usually separated (spaced out) to the extent that they are in writing. Our words tend to flow together without the pauses that in writing are shown by spaces. For example, if we speak the sentence quoted in Section 46a, "The person who can do this well deserves praise," we would need briefly to interrupt our flow of sound after either *this* or *well* in order to be understood fully. Such interruptions vary in length and are frequently combined with variations in *pitch*.

linking verb This verb is called a *joining* verb, a *copula*, or a *copulative* verb. It does not express action, only a state of being. It serves to link the subject with another noun (predicate noun), pronoun (predicate pronoun), or adjective. These words following the linking verb are called *predicate complements* or *subjective complements*. Common linking verbs are the forms of *to be, look, seem, smell, sound, appear, feel, become, grow, prove, turn, remain,* and *stand*. (See Sections 3a and 16.)

marker (See *determiner* in this glossary.)

mass noun A noun that refers to an indefinitely divisible substance or an abstract notion and cannot be used, in such a sense, with an indefinite article or in the plural: *air, happiness, water*.

modify To limit or describe or qualify a meaning, adjectives are used with nouns and pronouns and adverbs are used with verbs, adjectives, and other adverbs. (See Section 4.) The noun form is *modification*.

LIMITING: *five acres*, the *only* meal.
DESCRIPTIVE: *blue* skies, *large* houses, speak *rapidly*

mood The mood (or mode) of a verb indicates the manner in which a statement is made. Thus, if we wish merely to express a fact or ask a question of fact, we use the *indicative mood:*

The building *is* tall. [Statement]
Is the building tall? [Question]

If we wish to express a desire or a condition contrary to fact, we use the *subjunctive mood:*

Oh, how I wish I *were* in Austria! [Desire]
If I *were* rich, I should give you your wish. [Contrary to fact]

If we wish to give a command, we use the *imperative mood:*

Shut the gate, please.

(See Sections 3 and 18.)

morpheme A term used in linguistics to refer to the smallest meaningful unit in an utterance. A morpheme may be a single phoneme (such as the article *a*), a prefix or suffix (*ad-*, and *-ism*), a single syllable or several (*girl, instruct, miscellaneous*).

morphology The patterns of word formation in language, including derivation and inflection. Morphology and syntax together form a basic division of grammar.

nominal A word or word group used as a noun.

nominative absolute (See *absolute expression*.)

nonfinite verb A verb form that cannot serve as a predicate, since it shows neither person nor grammatical number. Nonfinite verb forms— the verbals—are gerunds, participles, and infinitives. (See Section 3c.)

noun See specific kinds of nouns (Section 1b).

noun clause A subordinate clause used as a noun. (See Section 8c.)

number The change in the form of a noun, pronoun, or verb to show whether one or more than one is intended. The formation of the plurals of nouns is discussed in Section 1; the few pronouns that have plural forms are listed in Section 2.

Plurals of verbs are relatively simple. Main verbs have the same form for singular and plural except in the third-person singular, present tense, which ends in *-s* (*talks, thinks*) or occasionally *-es* (*goes*). Of the verb *to be*, in the present tense, *am* (first person) and *is* (third person) are singular, *are* is second-person singular and first-, second-, and third-person plural; in the past tense, *was* is first- and third-person singular, *were* is second-person singular and first-, second-, and third person plural. Of the verb *to have*, *has* is the third-person singular, present tense form. Of the verb *to do*, *does* is the third-person singular, present tense form. Use a dictionary when in doubt concerning the singular or plural form of a noun, pronoun, or verb.

object The noun, pronoun, noun phrase, or noun clause affected by a transitive verb or a preposition.

Your coat is on the *floor*. [Object of preposition]
She struck *him* with a newspaper. [Object of verb]
I see *what you think*. [Object of verb]

A *simple object* is a substantive alone; a *complete object* is a simple object together with its modifiers; a *compound object* consists of two or more substantives.

The Cohens built the *house*. [Simple]
The Cohens built *the large yellow house on the slope*. [Complete]
The Cohens built *the house and the barn*. [Compound]

object complement A word, usually a noun or adjective, used after the direct object of certain verbs and intended to complete the meaning of a sentence:

We have chosen Margie *leader*.
Let me make this story *simple*.

ordinal number A number such as *first, third, fortieth*. (See *cardinal number*.)

paradigm An illustration of the changes (inflections) in such words as pronouns and verbs to show their forms. See the paradigm in Section 2 (personal pronouns) for an example.

participle A verb form that has the function either of a verb used as part of the predicate or of an adjective. The three forms of participles are *present, past,* and *perfect*. (See Section 3c.)

The player *swinging* the bat is Abigail.
Words *spoken* in anger are often regretted.
Having finished my essay, I turned it in.

parts of speech Words are classified according to their use in larger units of expression, that is, sentences. This functional division results in the so-called parts of speech; every word in the English language belongs to one or more of these parts of speech. There are eight such parts: *noun, pronoun, verb, adjective, adverb, conjunction, preposition, interjection.*

Many words are always used in a certain way, as a particular part of speech. But since our language is constantly changing, the functions of words sometimes reflect that change. *Chair,* for example, is usually thought of as a noun (a seat, a position), yet the poet A. E. Housman tells of carrying a victorious athlete shoulder high in a parade through his hometown:

The time you won your town the race
We *chaired* you through the marketplace.

And of course, one can *chair* committees and meetings.

Words *name, assert, modify,* and *join*. To determine what part of speech a given word is, observe how the word is used in a sentence of which it is a part.

passive voice The form of an action-expressing verb that tells that the subject does not act but is acted upon. Literally and actually, the subject is *passive*.

person A change in the form of a pronoun or verb to indicate whether the "person" used is the person speaking (*first person*), the person spoken to (*second person*), or the person or thing spoken about (*third person*): *I* read, *you* read, *he* reads, *we* read, *you* read, *they* read, *it* plays.

phoneme A *phone* is an individual speech sound; a *phoneme* is one of the set of the smallest units that distinguish one word from another in sound. In themselves, phonemes usually have no meaning. Two phonemes in English are the *b* of *boat* and the *c* of *coat*. Linguists differ in their analysis of the sounds of language but are generally agreed that some fifty phonemes exist in English.

phonetics The science of speech sounds and their production.

phrase A group of related words that does not contain a subject and a predicate and serves as a single part of speech. (See Section 7.)

pitch The combination of pitch, stress, and juncture forms what is known as *intonation,* an important item in any analysis of spoken language. Intonation means "the significant speech pattern or patterns resulting from pitch sequences and pauses (juncture)." *Pitch* refers to the degree of height or depth of a tone or of sound, depending upon the rapidity of the vibrations by which it is produced. Pitch also is a particular tonal standard with which given tones may be compared with respect to their relative level. It is closely connected with *stress;* the latter, which refers to loudness, may be *primary, secondary, tertiary,* or *weak* (neutral). One linguist (Paul Roberts) used the sentence "The White House is a white house" to indicate the different emphases given *White House* and *white house.* Pitch is usually numbered from 1 to 4 (low to high or high to low, depending on what linguist is speaking or writing). Pitch signals help in distinguishing spoken questions from statements, just as question marks and periods do in writing.

plurals (See *number* and Section 1a.)

possessive The case form of nouns and pronouns that indicates ownership: *my* hat, *your* job, the *man's* coat. This form also appears in such idiomatic expressions as *a day's work* and *an hour's time.*

predicate The verb or verb phrase in a sentence that makes a statement— an assertion, an action, a condition, a state of being—about the subject. A *simple predicate* is a verb or verb phrase alone, without an object or modifiers; a *compound predicate* consists of two or more verbs or verb phrases; a *complete predicate* consists of a verb with its object and all its modifiers.

The next player drove the ball 200 yards down the fairway. [*Drove* is the simple predicate; *drove the ball 200 yards down the fairway* is the complete predicate.]

I *wrote* the paper last night and *submitted* it this morning. [compound predicate]

predicate adjective An adjective used in the predicate after a linking verb; this adjective modifies or qualifies the subject:

Today seems *colder* than yesterday.

The players appear *ready* for the match.

predicate complement A predicate noun or pronoun, or a predicate adjective (also called a *subjective complement*).

predicate nominative A substantive (noun equivalent) following any form of the verb *to be* and referring to the subject.

A glossary of grammatical terms

predication The expression of action, a state of being, or a quality by a grammatical predicate, that is, a verb and its modifiers.

prefix (See Section 39f.)

preposition A word that is used to relate a noun or pronoun to some other word in a sentence. (See Section 6.) A preposition and its object form a *prepositional phrase*. (See Section 7.)

progressive The form of a verb used to describe action occurring but not completed: I *am reading,* you *are sleeping.*

pronoun One of a class of words used as replacements or substitutes for nouns and noun phrases. (See Section 2.)

proper noun A noun not usually preceded by an article or other limiting modifier that refers to only one person or thing or to several persons or things that constitute a class having the same name: *Jefferson, Californians.* (See Section 1b.)

reference A term used in referring to pronouns and their antecedents to indicate the relationships between them. The pronoun *refers* to the antecedent; the antecedent is indicated (or *referred to*) by the pronoun. (See Section 13.)

regular verb Also called *weak verbs,* regular verbs are the most common verbs in English. They usually form their past tense and past participle by adding *-d, -ed,* or *-t* to the present infinitive form: *move, moved, moved; walk, walked, walked; mean, meant, meant.*

relative clause (See Section 8.)

retained object An object in the passive construction is identical with the direct or indirect object in the corresponding active construction: *me* in "The picture was shown me" ("They showed me the picture").

rhetoric The art or science of literary uses of language, the body of principles and theory concerning the presentation of facts and ideas in clear, effective, and pleasing language. Rhetoric is only loosely connected with grammar and correctness and with specific details of the mechanics of writing.

Logic, grammar, and rhetoric made up the basic trivium of medieval study, but rhetoric had been important long before that time. The founder of rhetoric, Corax of Syracuse, laid down fundamental principles for public speech and debate in the fifth century B.C. more than 300 years before the Christian era. Aristotle described rhetoric as the art of giving effectiveness and persuasiveness to truth rather than to the speaker. (The word *rhetoric* comes from the Greek word *rhetor,* meaning "orator.") Aristotle believed that rhetoric depended upon, and derived from, proof and logic and that its values could be taught as systematized principles. He distinguished between the appeal of rhetoric to one's intellect and the presentation of ideas emotionally and imaginatively, which he discussed in his treatment of poetics.

Many philosophers and orators through the centuries, however, have tried to make rhetoric a mere tool of argumentation and persuasiveness. Plato condemned rhetoric because he felt that many of those who practiced it used questionable techniques; he also quoted Socrates as declaring rhetoric to be "superficial." This tendency to downgrade rhetoric persists today; when we say something is "mere rhetoric," we mean it is something empty, showy, without genuine substance. Although it is undeniable that some modern politicians and writers use tricks of presentation to conceal both lack of thought and outright dishonesty, it is equally true that *how* we say or write something is important; that legitimate and time-tested rhetorical devices can increase the value and appeal of our writing and speaking; and that although rhetoric without intellect is ineffective, so too are fact unadorned and opinion presented bare.

rhetorical question A query designed to produce an effect, not to draw an answer. It is used to introduce a topic or emphasize a point; no answer is expected:

There's no good answer to this question, is there?
How can we let these people die of neglect?

root The base of a word, a morpheme to which may be added prefixes and suffixes. (See Section 39f.) An approximate synonym for *base* and *root* in this sense is *stem;* all mean the part of a word to which suffixes and prefixes are added or in which phonetic changes are made. Thus, we say that *love* is the root (stem or base) of the word *loveliness, form* of the word *deform,* and so on.

sentence element A functional part of a sentence, such as the subject or direct object.

simple sentence A sentence containing one subject (simple or compound) and one predicate (simple or compound). (See Section 9b.)

singular (See *number.*)

stress (See *pitch.*)

strong verb (See *irregular verb.*)

structure word (See *function word.*)

subject The person or thing (noun, pronoun, noun phrase, noun clause) about which a statement or assertion is made in a sentence or clause. A *simple subject* is the noun or pronoun alone; a *compound subject* consists of two or more nouns, pronouns, noun phrases, or noun clauses; a *complete* subject is a simple subject together with its modifiers.

subordination The giving of minor emphasis to minor elements or ideas. In syntax, making one element grammatically dependent upon another. (See Sections 8c and 44.)

substantive An inclusive term for nouns, pronouns, verbal nouns (gerunds, infinitives), and phrases or clauses used like nouns. The following are examples of substantives:

> My *car* is three years old. [Noun]
> *They* will leave tomorrow; in fact, *everyone* is leaving tomorrow. [Pronouns]
> Your *playing* is admired. [Gerund]
> *To better myself* is my *purpose*. [Infinitive phrase, noun]
> *From Chicago to San Diego* is a long distance. [Noun phrase]
> *What you think* is no problem of mine. [Noun clause]
> Do *you* know *that he is a thief?* [Pronoun, noun clause]

suffix An ending that modifies the meaning of a word. (See Section 39f.)

syllable In phonetics, a segment of speech uttered with one impulse of air pressure from the lungs; in writing, a character or set of characters (letters of the alphabet) representing one sound. A syllable contains at least one vowel and may or may not have initial or final consonants. (See *syllabication* in Section 39c.)

synonym A word that has about the same meaning as another word. (See Section 39e.)

syntax The arrangement of words in a sentence to show their relationship. *Syntax* is a rather general term, but one for which our language has no adequate substitute. It is a branch of grammar.

tense The time of the action or state of being expressed by a verb: present, past, future, present perfect, past perfect, or future perfect. The first three of these six are sometimes named the *simple* or *primary tenses;* the last three are sometimes named the *secondary* or *perfect tenses*. (See Section 17.)

tone A particular style of writing and speaking: the defeatist *tone* of Toynbee's writing; the sinister *tone* of Edgar Allan Poe. The word *tone* can also be applied to certain forms of verb usage. (See Section 17c.)

transitive verb Verbs are classified as either transitive or intransitive. A *transitive verb* is regularly accompanied by a direct object that completes the meaning of the verb:

> They *refused* his resignation.

An *intransitive verb* requires no direct object:

> He *will obey*.

Whether a verb is transitive or intransitive depends upon meaning, on the idea the writer wishes to show: *will obey* in "He *will obey* our orders" is transitive.

verb See specific kinds of verbs; see also Sections 3, 15, 16, and 17.

verb phrase A verb together with an auxiliary or auxiliaries, or with its object or modifiers: *is going, was finished, shall have taken, will have been taken, studied the assignments, flows slowly, whispers nonsense to himself.* Distinguish between a *verb phrase* and a *verbal* (participle, infinitive, or gerund).

verbals Certain verb forms—participles, gerunds, and infinitives. These serve at various times as adjectives, adverbs, nouns, parts of the predicate—but *never* as a predicate alone. (See Section 3c.)

> *Skiing* is delightful. [Gerund used as a noun]
> *To succeed* is exciting. [Infinitive used as a noun]
> The *shaking* house may collapse. [Participle used as an adjective]
> Sandy was glad *to have come.* [Infinitive used as an adverb]

vocative (See *direct address.*)

voice (See *active voice, passive voice.*) The active voice normally provides greater force, strength, and life than does the passive.

vowel In phonetics, a speech sound articulated so that there is a clear channel for the voice through the middle of the mouth. In spelling, a letter representing such a sound: *a, e, i, o, u,* and sometimes *y.*

weak verb (See *regular verb.*)

word order An English sentence consists not of a string of words in free relationship to one another but of groups of words arranged in patterns. Words in an English sentence have meaning because of their position. (See Section 46.)

II.
Usage

The first ten sections of this book present a description of *grammar*. These sections, which have little to do with rules or so-called "correctness," were placed first so that you can now identify, name, and understand the tools needed to move into what is often called a standard use of language.

Grammar and usage overlap and are mutually dependent, but they do not always mean exactly the same thing. *Grammar* is concerned with the structure of a language, the way it works. It is involved with the forms that various kinds of words take, various groups of words that are meaningful in the language, and the way language shows the varied grammatical relations it can communicate: predication, modification, and the like. Grammar remains constant, or nearly so, over long periods. Usage, however, is constantly changing. One does not have a problem in usage until a choice is involved. One can split an infinitive or not split an infinitive; one can say or write "I be" or "I am." What is involved here is less grammar than usage.

What you have had stuffed into you from early school days in much the same way an animal is force-fed at a zoo is *usage* rather than grammar. You have probably been expected to learn endless lists of rules and then to write sentences applying them. Over and over you have been warned by teachers and textbooks:

1. Don't say "ain't" in the classroom.
2. Don't say "I think Mary *done* it."
3. Don't use *media* as a singular noun.
4. Don't say "between him and *I*."
   and so on through

MCMXXX. Don't split an infinitive.

Such cautions are matters of language etiquette, of conventional requirements, of a prescribed or accepted code of usage. They are not sacred, but you have heard and read them perhaps as often as they show up disguised as correction symbols on your papers.

The sections that follow are intended to alert you to those items of usage, of language etiquette, that disturb or offend careful observers, teachers, and writers. Sections 12–20 label items of divided usage and indicate what is appropriate in a given situation. They ignore some outmoded notions about usage—changes are part of the life of a language—and try to present the options, the choices, you have in writing contemporary, generally accepted English. These sections suggest that you stop worrying about rules and regulations and concentrate instead on remembering that the suitability and fitness of your language are determined by who is writing or speaking to whom about what and under what circumstances. For instance, if you wish to get someone out of your room, it might be effective and appropriate to say "Get lost," or "Beat it," or "Scram" or to use some more vigorous or even profane direction. In another situation, effective usage might suggest that you say "Please leave," or "Go away," or "Goodbye," or "Au revoir." Whatever expression you select, your choice is dependent upon usage, not grammar.

11. Levels of usage

11a. Suitable levels of usage

Attitudes about usage have become far less rigid in recent years. Almost any expression is now considered fitting if it has the wanted and intended effect upon the person reading or hearing it. Yet everyone has faced situations in which knowledge of acceptable English is either desirable or important. Such a situation confronts you now in a class in English composition.

Outside of class, you may not wish or need to use "correct" English at all times, but one of the aims of first-year English is to inform you what preferred usage directs when you are writing class papers, business letters, minutes of club meetings, and indeed all compositions intended for reading by others, with the possible exception of love letters. It helps to know what are acceptable expressions when you are talking with, or writing to, persons you wish to impress favorably. Regardless of the idioms, accents, and other language customs of your geographic or social background, the language you write and speak will often be subjected to certain standards wherever you go. It will *have* to look or sound standard because otherwise you may find yourself being snubbed socially or rejected for a job without really knowing why. Here is one of the few outright *don't's* in this book: Don't confuse a right to complain with an excuse for ignorance.

Neither in speaking nor in writing should you appear stuffy and overly precise. There is, or should be, however, a marked difference between the *what* and *how* of communicating in relaxed conversation and the *what* and *how* of writing for formal and semiformal occasions. Material in Sections 12–20 is *not* designed to put your speech and writing into a straitjacket. It *is* designed to inform you about what's what in contemporary standard English usage.

Before digging into the problems of usage discussed in Sections 12–20, it might be helpful for you to discover just how much, or how little, you really know about what is currently accepted as educated use of English. Here are a dozen remarks that the author recently overheard in a high school cafeteria, on a college campus, and on the streets of the town in which he lives. Would you make such remarks? Does each of them sound all right to you?

A Test on Usage

1. Are you going to meet Joe and myself tonight?
2. When you finished the job, who did you ask to look at what you had done?
3. The coffee shop is crowded; there's ten people waiting for seats.
4. Between you and I, the food at that pizza place is too highly seasoned.
5. If Jack don't come soon, he will miss the bus.
6. Everyone should watch out for their own personal belongings.
7. Dave asked me who he should give the money to.
8. Sue and me were not invited to the party.
9. When we arrived, the school bus had already went.
10. He hated everything and everybody which caused him to lose his afternoon job.
11. Mama be working on the night shift this week.
12. Either the operators or the foreman are to blame for what happened.

Each of these twelve statements reveals usage that is considered by some people to be inaccurate, ineffective, or an outright error. Can you identify the expressions that cause the trouble? Even if you can, many other problems in usage discussed in the next nine sections still deserve study. If most or all of the sentences seem all right to you, the sections that follow merit careful study. In them you will find answers to scores of problems in using English in addition to these suggested corrections for the sentences just listed:

1. *me,* not *myself*
2. *whom,* not *who*
3. *there are,* not *there's*
4. *me,* not *I*
5. *doesn't,* not *don't*
6. *his* (or *her*), not *their*
7. *whom,* not *who* (also a preposition at end of sentence)
8. *I,* not *me*
9. *gone,* not *went*
10. *who,* not *which*
11. *is,* not *be*
12. *is,* not *are*

11b. Varied levels of usage

Each of us employs a different level of usage, depending upon whether we are speaking or writing, our readers and audience, and upon the place and occasion involved.

We are normally more relaxed in speaking than in writing. We are directly concerned with getting across our ideas and comments to our hearers and often have little concern for so-called rules and errors. As speakers, most of us use shorter sentences than we do in writing. We depend upon our voices and gestures to help get our comments across. But these differences between speaking and writing do not mean that speaking is without standards of usage. Nor should the ease and naturalness of oral communication lull us into the belief that none of our listeners will be favorably or unfavorably impressed by what we say and how we say it.

In both speech and writing, different levels of usage exist. As a distinguished scholar, John S. Kenyon, has pointed out, what are often grouped together as different levels of language are combinations of two kinds: *cultural levels* and *functional varieties.*

Cultural levels

Among *cultural levels* may be included narrowly local dialect, illiterate speech, slovenly vocabulary and construction, exceptional pronunciation, and excessive and unskillful use of slang. On another level is the language used generally by educated people over wide areas; it is both clear and grammatically correct. These cultural levels are called nonstandard and standard language, respectively.

Functional varieties

The term *level* does not properly apply to *functional varieties:* colloquial, familiar, formal, legal, scientific. As Professor Kenyon suggests, these varieties are equally suitable for their respective functions and do not depend on the cultural status of the users.

In a general and practical sense, the most helpful distinction is between *informal* and *formal* ways of speaking and writing. Five groupings may be mentioned, but it is not easy to say precisely where one ends and another begins.

1. *Carefully Selected Written English.* Thoughtfully prepared and painstakingly edited books and magazines exhibit this level of usage. In addition, the writing of many educated men and women in all parts of the country falls into this category, which is largely (but not exclusively) the usage described in sections that follow.

2. *General Written English.* Most newspapers, radio and television scripts, business letters and reports, and several widely circulated magazines employ this second level of usage. It does not have all the polish of carefully selected written English, but it is acceptable and represents the level all students should try to attain in written work.

3. *Choice Spoken English.* This is the language heard in serious or formal addresses and talks and in the conversation of educated people who normally apply the requirements of carefully selected written English to the spoken variety. It is neither as "correct" nor as inflexible as the two earlier varieties mentioned, because oral English is nearly always freer than written English.

4. *General Spoken English.* Most well-educated people employ this level in ordinary conversation. It is somewhat more easy-going than level 3, employs more newer and shorter forms (slang, contractions), and is sometimes referred to as "colloquial."

5. *Nonstandard English.* This term is used to characterize illiterate or vulgar expressions. Such expressions, which are associated with the uneducated, also appear in the speech of many educated persons who choose to express themselves this way.

The distinctions just made can be labeled at their centers but run together at their extremes. Further, most expressions are identical on all levels. A person who says or writes "I spoke slowly" is using an expression that has no distinct level of usage. The five categories can, however, be illustrated as follows:

CAREFULLY SELECTED WRITTEN ENGLISH:	I shall not go.
GENERAL WRITTEN ENGLISH:	I will not go.
CHOICE SPOKEN ENGLISH:	I'll not go.
GENERAL SPOKEN ENGLISH:	I'm not going to go.
NONSTANDARD ENGLISH:	I ain't gonna go.

In addition to being influenced by the general distinction between formal and informal usage, language is loaded with rules about grammatical structure and word choice that are themselves modified by considerations of time, place, and situation. No standards of usage are absolute and unvarying.

The discussion that follows is presented in terms of what is generally appropriate in carefully selected and general written English. Nine major items are discussed:

agreement of subject and verb
pronouns and antecedents
case forms of pronouns
principal parts of verbs
linking and auxiliary verbs
tense
mood
adjectives and adverbs
conjunctions

In still later sections, contemporary usage concerning words, punctuation, and the construction of sentences is described fully.

12. Agreement of subject and verb

Agreement means "sameness" or "oneness" or "correspondence." When a subject and a verb agree, they have the same number and person. In standard English, singular subjects require singular verbs and plural subjects require plural verbs.

This general rule of usage (and grammar) is simple and easy to follow, but tricky situations and variations require correct answers to two questions: (1) What is the real subject of a given sentence? (2) Is that subject singular or plural?

12a. A verb agrees with its subject in number.

She asks too high a price for her used car. [*She* and *asks* are singular in number and both are in the third person.]

They ask too high a price for their used cars. [*They* and *ask* are plural in number and in the third person.]

I seek a reasonable price for this used car. [*I* and *seek* are singular and in the first person.]

This general rule covers most subject–verb agreement situations, but watch out for the following tricky constructions.

12b. A verb does not agree with words and phrases that come between subject and verb.

The *safety record* of our employees *is* among the best in the state. [*Is* is singular because the subject, *safety record,* is singular. The phrase *of our employees* has no grammatical bearing on the relationship between the real subject and its verb.]

Personnel managers from that company regularly *interview* candidates for summer work. [*Personnel managers* and *interview* are both plural.]

The little *boy,* as well as all other members of the family, *was* ill with flu. [*Boy,* the real subject, and *was* are singular.]

I, together with Rafael and Maria, *am* going to the party. [*I,* the true subject, requires the singular first-person verb *am.*]

12c. A verb agrees with its subject, not with a predicate noun.

When a form of the verb *to be (am, is, was, were, has been)* comes between two nouns or a pronoun and a noun, the noun or pronoun that comes first is the real subject.

The hardest *part* of the job *is* the bending and lifting. [The subject of the verb is *part*, not *bending and lifting*, so that a singular verb is needed.]

Bending and lifting are the hardest part of the job. [The plural subject, *bending and lifting*, requires a plural verb. *Part* is a predicate noun and does not affect the number of the verb.]

The *reason* for J. P. Getty's wealth *was* successful investments in oil.

Successful *investments* in oil *were* the reason for J. P. Getty's wealth.

12d. *There* and *here* are not subjects.

After *there* and *here*, verbs are singular or plural according to the number of the subjects that follow.

There *are parties* in the gym after every home game. [*Parties* is plural and needs a plural verb.]

There *is* a *party* in the gym after every home game. [*Party* is singular, requiring a singular verb.]

Here *are* the *books* to go back to the library. [*Books* and *are* are plural.]

Here *is* the *book* to go back to the library. [*Is* and *book* are singular.]

12e. Singular pronouns require singular verbs.

The following pronouns are singular: *another, anybody, anyone, anything, each, either, everybody, everyone, everything, many a one, neither, nobody, no one, one, somebody, someone.*

Each *has* her job to perform.

No one *was* at the store.

One of you *is* not telling the truth.

Someone in the room *was* making unnecessary noise.

None (literally *no one* and also meaning "not any") may be followed by either a singular or a plural verb. Today, it is as frequently followed by a plural verb as by one in the singular, especially when the phrase that modifies *none* contains a plural noun (*none of the persons*). The traditional rule, however, is that *none* requires a singular verb.

Agreement based on meaning and agreement based on grammatical form sometimes conflict. In the sentence, "Each of the girls in this group *is* 16 years old," *each* and *is* are in grammatical agreement. But in "*Each* of the girls in this group *are* 16 years old," *are* is plural because the meaning of "each of the girls" is construed to be "all of the girls." A somewhat similar principle may be illustrated thus: "*Everyone* in the apartment house tuned *his* TV (or *their* TVs) to that channel." Careful speakers and writers follow grammatical agreement in such sentences, but agreement based on meaning is becoming more widespread in both speech and writing.

Certain pronouns are considered singular or plural according to the number of the key word in a modifying phrase. The pronouns *some, all, half, none (no one* or *not any), what,* and *which* may be either singular or plural. Usually they are followed by an *of* phrase containing a noun that helps determine their number. Mentally remove the *of,* making the pronoun an adjective. The number of the noun it modifies will be the number of the pronoun:

Some of my *money has* been lost. [Some money has . . .]
Some of our *students have* won scholarships. [Some students have
. . .]
Half of this *building is* to be completed by summer. [Half this
building is . . .]
Half of these *buildings are* dormitories. [Half the buildings are
. . .]
Which (room) of the rooms *is* reserved for the meeting?
Which (rooms) of the rooms *are* reserved for students?

What may present problems. When used to mean *that thing which,* it takes a singular verb; when used to mean *those persons who* or *those things which,* it takes the plural:

What is to be covered on the test is a mystery to me. [*that thing
which* . . .]
What are to be covered are chapters three to seven. [*those things
which* . . .]

12f. A collective noun usually takes a singular verb.

Common collective nouns are *army, assembly, clergy, committee, company, couple, crew, crowd, family, flock, group, herd, jury, mob, orchestra, pair, personnel, squad, team, union.* These collective nouns take a singular verb and singular pronouns when the collection of individuals is thought of as a unit. However, they take a plural verb and plural pronouns when the members of the group are thought of as individuals acting separately.

The jury [a unit] *is* having trouble reaching a verdict.

The jury [members] *have* ordered their suppers and are going to eat them in the jury room.

The committee [a unit] *has* appointed a new recording secretary.

The committee [members] *have* been unwilling to charge for personal expenses.

The couple [a unit] at the head table *is* from Buffalo.

The couple [members] *were* assigned simple tasks during the celebration.

The family [members] *disagree* about my plans.

The family [a unit] *was named* Shary.

12g. Nouns that are plural in form but singular in meaning usually require a singular verb.

Grammarians and even dictionaries differ about the number of many such nouns. The following, however, are nearly always considered to be singular and take singular verbs: *athletics, economics, ethics, headquarters, mathematics, mechanics, mumps, news, physics, politics,* and *whereabouts.*

A few nouns that are plural in form but singular in meaning take a plural verb:

Len's pants *are* now ready to wear.

My scissors *were* sucked into the centrifuge.

A good rule, according to usage, is, "When in doubt, use a singular verb."

Physics, we soon learned, *is* a study of light, heat, sound, mechanics, and electricity.

Dramatic *news* of the signing of the treaty *was* broadcast at noon.

Politics is a fascinating subject for study.

12h. **Subjects that are plural in form and indicate a quantity or number require a singular verb when the subject is regarded as a unit.**

Fifteen miles *seems* too far to walk.
Three-fourths of the land *is* under water.
Three from six *leaves* three.
Sermons and Soda Water is the title of a book by John O'Hara.

12i. **Two or more subjects joined by *and* take a plural verb.**

Television and radio *have revolutionized* the entire country.
On the landing field *stand* a helicopter and an ambulance.
Valerie and Ned *are* running for the presidency of our class.

When two subjects form a single thought, have a closely related meaning, or mean one person or thing, a singular verb may be used:

Peanut butter and grape jelly *is* my favorite snack.
Her kindness and generosity *is* well known.
The secretary and treasurer of our club *is named* Peter Dennison.

12j. **Singular subjects joined by *or* or *nor, neither . . . nor*, and *either . . . or* usually take a singular verb.**

Either Mimi or Richard *was* to be blamed for the accident.
Neither the doctor nor the nurse *is* willing to take responsibility.
My sister or my brother *is* going to help you.

12k. **If the subjects differ in number or person, the verb agrees with the nearer subject.**

Neither Pat nor the other boys *know* the answer.
None of the other boys or even Pat *knows* the answer.
The people in that car or I *am* at fault.

**s/v
agr**

121

Either Sue or some of her friends *are* ready to help with this problem.

121. A relative pronoun (*who, which, that*) is singular or plural according to the word to which the pronoun refers.

The only way to tell whether a relative pronoun is singular or plural is to examine the part of the sentence that precedes it and decide to which word in the sentence the pronoun refers. This word is called the *antecedent* of the pronoun. If the antecedent is singular, the pronoun will be singular, and the verb that goes with it must be singular.

Angelina is the only one of the golfers who *has* maintained a consistently good score. [*Who* is the subject of the relative clause. It refers to *one* and is therefore singular.]

Monieka is one of the six mission stations that *are* supported by our church. [*That* is the subject of the relative clause. It refers to *stations* and is plural.]

She is the best musician who *has* ever attended our school.

She is one of the best musicians who *have* ever attended our school.

EXERCISE 1

Select the correct form of the verb from the italicized forms in the following sentences:

1. Homecoming weekend we freshmen had to sleep on the floor, for there *wasn't weren't* enough beds.
2. This dam, with the four or five other dams along the river, *form forms* part of the network of hydroelectric plants.
3. Neither one of my parents *know knows* much about mathematics.
4. The only other equipment you will need *are is* eating utensils, a flashlight, and a pocket knife.
5. My keeping of New Year's resolutions *has have* always failed in past years.
6. Liking outdoor work *is* one of the reasons that *make makes* me want to go back to the farm.
7. Whenever either of us *has have* a problem, we talk it over until we reach a solution.

8. There *are is* in my family my mother, my father, my sister, and I.
9. I am one of the millions of people who *has have* been bitten by the quiz games on TV.
10. Building model airplanes *require requires* a great deal of time and patience.
11. Each of the houses in this restored village *has have* antique furniture.
12. The location of the complimentary close and of the signature *seem seems* unusual in some business letters.
13. Neither the other students nor the instructor *was were* surprised when I came in late.
14. Charles Dickens' greatest achievement *is are* the novels that he wrote.
15. For breakfast there *was were* ham, fried potatoes, eggs, and toast.

EXERCISE 2

What is the subject of each verb in the following sentences? What is the acceptable form of each verb? (Not all of the sentences are nonstandard.)

1. Dave smilingly disgreed when someone remarked that *The Dynasts* were great literature.
2. Measles, for adults, are often a serious disease.
3. Each of the girls in the drama club is an aspiring television star.
4. Whoever finds Margaret Mead a dull and uninteresting writer are, I fear, devoid of intellectual curiosity.
5. Dolores insisted that champagnes from a domestic stock was not to be considered.
6. Everybody, students and instructors alike, are glad that school is over.
7. Your letter, together with your check, was received yesterday.
8. The tastiest part of most school lunches are the spaghetti and meatballs.
9. Except for a few scattered cousins, the seven aunts was all the family Wesley had.
10. Either you or I are going to have to push the car out of the ditch.
11. Fifteen dollars were all the Old Stone Peers could collect for playing at the dance.
12. The loss of three friends and a job were the price Carl had to pay for his curiosity.
13. Semantics is a good thing for a student to be interested in, and so is athletics.
14. The real meaning of success for many people are making more and more money.
15. For those who want to join clubs there is the ski club, the drama club, and the chorus.

13. Pronouns and antecedents

As pointed out in Section 12, *agreement* is the grammatical relationship between a subject and its verb (predicate). Agreement also concerns the patterns that govern the relationship between a pronoun and its antecedent. In addition, because a pronoun depends upon a noun or another pronoun for its meaning, it is important to place pronouns as close as possible to their antecedents and to make pronoun references exact. Section 13 deals with *agreement* and *reference*.

13a. A pronoun agrees with its antecedent in number, person, and gender.

The meaning of a pronoun is not clear unless it has the same number, person, and gender as its antecedent, the noun or noun equivalent for which it stands. Questions of person and gender cause little trouble, but number can be tricky.

> Rayon is an important synthetic material, but *it* has been replaced by nylon and Orlon in the making of some yarns. [*It* refers to the antecedent, *rayon*. Both *rayon* and *it* are singular.]
>
> Orlon and nylon are such useful materials that *they* have replaced rayon in the making of certain yarns. [*They* refers to the plural antecedent, *Orlon* and *nylon*.]
>
> Janet put on *her* goggles and stepped into the cockpit. [*Janet* and *her* are singular and feminine.]

13b. Singular pronouns refer to singular antecedents.

The words *any, anybody, anyone, each, either, everybody, man, neither, nobody, one, person, somebody,* and *woman* are singular. In standard, formal English, a pronoun referring to any one of these words should be singular (*he, her, hers, him, his, it, its, she*).

In spoken English and informal writing, this rule of usage is frequently ignored. Speakers who wish their language to sound casual and relaxed often use *their* to refer to *everybody*. And when the sense of *everybody, anyone,* and so forth is "*many*" or "*all,*" the plural personal pronoun referring to these indefinite pronouns is found in both formal and informal English: "Everybody is expected to do *their* share of the work." Such use is preferable to the somewhat awkward "Everybody is expected to do *his or her* share of the work." Notice, however, that a singular, not a plural, verb form is used.

INFORMAL: Each of the boxers was accompanied by *their* manager.

FORMAL: Each of the boxers was accompanied by *his* manager.

INFORMAL: Anyone can try *their* luck at this game.

FORMAL: Anyone can try *her* [or *his*] luck at this game.

13c. Collective nouns used as antecedents take singular or plural pronouns.

As an antecedent, a collective noun takes a singular pronoun if the group is thought of as a unit and a plural pronoun if it is considered in terms of its individual members.

The excited crowd shouted *its* cheers. [The crowd acted as a unit.]

The excited crowd shouted *their* cheers. [The crowd acted as individuals.]

The class was divided in *its* opinion of the test.

Members of the class were divided in *their* opinion of the test.

Once you have decided whether a collective noun is to be singular or plural, stick to your decision. If you use it as the subject with a singular verb, make sure that all the pronouns referring to it are singular; if you use it with a plural verb, make sure that all the pronouns are plural.

NONSTANDARD: The family *was* discussing *their* problems.

STANDARD: The family *was* discussing *its* problems.

STANDARD: The family *were* discussing *their* problems.

13d. A pronoun agrees with the nearer of two antecedents.

Two antecedents that differ in gender or number may occur in a sentence. With two antecedents and only one pronoun, the pronoun referring to the nearer antecedent should be used.

> She loves everybody and everything *that* is connected with her dance studio.
>
> She loves everything and everybody *who* is connected with her dance studio. [However, *that* would also be acceptable; see 13e]
>
> In this cool room, neither the plant nor the pansies will lose *their* freshness.

13e. *Who* refers to persons, *which* to things, and *that* to persons or things.

> The woman *who* owns this store is a good merchant.
>
> This book, *which* I borrowed from the library, contains some dirty stories.
>
> The investor *that* stayed out of the stock market was lucky.

In speech, *that* appears much more often than *which,* although either may be used if reference is not to persons. *That* is preferable to *which* when the clause being introduced is restrictive or limiting or defining. (See Section 25b.) That is, if the clause could be omitted without leaving the noun it modifies incomplete or altering the meaning of what is being said, use *which.* Otherwise, use *that.*

> The Shenandoah River, *which* flows north, passes by Harpers Ferry.
>
> The river *that* passes by Harpers Ferry is the Shenandoah.

13f. When the antecedent is a singular noun of common gender, employ a masculine pronoun unless the noun clearly refers to a woman.

> Each member of the group indicated *his* choice of a play for the production.
>
> Each member of the girls' glee club was asked to name *her* favorite song.

Some people feel that the use of the masculine pronoun unfairly excludes women. Although the standard practice just described is acceptable, sensitive writers try to avoid this construction. Some alternatives are the following:

1. Use *he or she*. (This expression tends to be awkward and should be used sparingly.)
   Each committee member did *her or his* assigned work.
2. Change the wording from the singular to the plural.
   All committee members did *their* assigned work.
3. Reword the sentence to avoid the generic pronoun.
   Each committee member performed an assigned job.

13g. A noun or an indefinite pronoun used as an antecedent takes a pronoun in the third person.

Nouns and indefinite pronouns are in the third person except when used in direct address or in apposition with a pronoun of the first or second person. A phrase such as *of us* or *of you* between the pronoun and its antecedent does not affect the person of the pronoun.

INFORMAL AND NONSTANDARD:	If a student wants to succeed, *you* must study hard.
FORMAL:	If a student wants to succeed, *he* [or *she*] must study hard.
BETTER:	A student who wants to succeed must study hard.
INFORMAL:	Neither of you has finished *your* assignment.
FORMAL:	Neither of you has finished *his* assignment.
BETTER:	Neither of you has finished *the* assignment.

13h. The antecedent of a pronoun should be actually expressed or clearly implied.

The relationship of a pronoun to its antecedent should be unmistakable. Words coming between a pronoun and its antecedent sometimes cause confusion. A relative pronoun must be in the same sentence as its antecedent, but personal and demonstrative pronouns are often placed some distance away.

Sam is the boy *who* should be elected. [*Who* is a relative pronoun.]

Sam is the boy who should be elected. For some reason, *he* is not interested in the race. [*He* is a personal pronoun.]

Implied reference occurs when the antecedent of a pronoun is not actually expressed but must be inferred from the context. One form of implied reference is the use of the pronoun *it, this, that,* or *which* to refer to an entire preceding statement rather than to some noun or pronoun in that statement. You must decide whether such words refer to an implied antecedent or whether their antecedent occurs in a preceding or even following statement. Frequent use of implied reference is found in the work of many reputable writers, and *when confusion is not possible,* the use may be effective.

Faults in the implied reference of *it, which, this, that, these, those,* and so forth may be corrected by (1) summing up the idea of the preceding statement in a noun that acts as the antecedent or (2) rephrasing the sentence so as to eliminate the pronoun or give it a clear and appropriate antecedent.

VAGUE: I worked for a department store last vacation and enjoyed *it* very much.

IMPROVED: I was employed by a department store last vacation and enjoyed the work very much.

VAGUE: You will have a lot of hiring and firing to do, and *this* requires tact.

IMPROVED: You will have a lot of hiring and firing to do, a task that requires tact.

VAGUE: Strewn over the floor were broken bottles and old rotor heads. *That* solved the mystery.

IMPROVED: Strewn over the floor were broken bottles and old rotor heads. That mess solved the mystery.

VAGUE: He was in bad shape, *which* was made obvious by his persistent coughing.

IMPROVED: He was in bad shape, a condition that was made obvious by his persistent coughing.

13i. The pronoun *you* is often used in a vague, indefinite sense.

In informal speech and writing, expressions such as "You can see how important money is" or "Dancing makes you graceful" are permissible. Formal English requires the use of *one* or *anyone* or *a person* or *people*.

Anyone can see how important money is.
Dancing makes one graceful. [You may substitute *people* for *one*.]

13j. Double or ambiguous reference for a pronoun may cause confusion.

Double reference occurs when two antecedents are possible for a single pronoun. The antecedent should be clear and definite.

Ambiguous (double) reference can be corrected by (1) repeating the antecedent, (2) using a synonym for the antecedent, or (3) changing the wording of the sentence so that the antecedent of each pronoun is unmistakable.

VAGUE: When a mother hands over the car to her daughter, *she* is not always sure it is in good condition.

IMPROVED: A mother is not always sure the car is in good condition when she hands it over to her daughter.

VAGUE: The actor told Ramon that *he* should move upstage. [Who should move: Ramon? the actor?]

IMPROVED: The actor said, "I shall move upstage." [The actor will move.]

The actor told Ramon of his intention to move upstage. [The actor will move.]

The actor advised Ramon to move upstage. [Ramon should move.]

13k. The pronoun *it* and impersonal *it* appearing in the same sentence may cause confusion.

VAGUE: We can send the refrigerator today, or we can keep *it* in the factory for a few days if *it* is necessary.

IMPROVED: We can send the refrigerator today, or if necessary we can keep *it* for a few days.

In informal English *it* sometimes refers to an idea instead of a single antecedent.

INFORMAL: He was nervous, but he tried not to show *it*.

FORMAL: He was nervous, but he tried not to show his uneasiness.

131. Indefinite use of *it* and *they*

It as a third-person singular pronoun, neuter, should usually have an appropriate antecedent. Also, when *it* is used impersonally and acceptably (*it* seems, *it* is possible, *it* is raining, etc.), do not use another *it* in the same sentence to refer to a definite antecedent. (See Section 13k.)

They, their, theirs, and *them* should have definite antecedents: plural nouns or other pronouns in the plural. Otherwise, do not use these pronouns.

VAGUE: In this article, *it* shows that war is horrible.

IMPROVED: This article shows that war is horrible.

VAGUE: *They* have good roads in Delaware.

IMPROVED: Delaware has good roads.

VAGUE: *They* say that Argentina is a wealthy nation.

IMPROVED: Economists say that Argentina is a wealthy nation.

It is sometimes used impersonally to introduce an idea.

It will be clear tomorrow.

It was Lincoln who made the "House Divided" speech.

It is necessary, it is true, it is certain, it is likely, and *it is imperative* are standard expressions.

EXERCISE 3

Detect all errors of agreement between pronouns and antecedents in the following sentences:

1. The youth hostel is an inexpensive place to stay, and any young people traveling can use them.
2. If you desire any further information or references, I shall be glad to send it.

3. The hero of the novel was moody, and it became worse in the course of the narrative.

4. My reaction to the TV mystery program is favorable, for I enjoy most of them.

5. Jake was always attentive, which earned for him his instructor's respect.

6. I feel sorry for an only child because they have no chance to share experiences with their brothers and sisters.

7. If Dominic does not understand the directions, he should ask the teacher to explain it to him.

8. It is the mosquito who causes malaria and yellow fever.

9. A friend of mine borrows money and never pays it back; this really bothers me.

10. When we were in high school, we sometimes didn't make our own decisions without first talking it over with your parents, teachers, or friends.

11. Your surroundings should be pleasant, which will make your stay more enjoyable.

12. The library stacks may be the perfect place to study for some people, but I find it too quiet.

13. Each person has their own individual way of writing a letter.

14. I do not know whether this has been the feelings of anyone before.

15. It is believed that if one carries a rabbit's foot, it will bring them good luck.

16. Where is the skilled craftsman of yesterday? Very few of them are left.

17. If students fail to take advantage of the library, he is losing a valuable helper.

18. I am sure that winter months will always be as interesting to almost everyone as it is to me.

19. St. Francis spent part of his life caring for the lepers, which were isolated from their fellow men.

20. We hear rumors about different instructors. Some are that she gives terrible exams or that her lectures are boring or that he is unfair in his grading.

EXERCISE 4

(See Directions for Exercise 3.)

1. In New York City they have regular cruises around Manhattan Island.

2. I do not mind early-morning classes except for that long walk to the classroom.

3. My mother, my sister, and myself go downtown often for our dinner.

4. We began scouting around for a haunted house, but found them rather scarce.

5. My roommate is the kind of person that you like to live with.

6. Either you or I is going to fail the test.

7. There is an advantage in living in a small town. One of these is that everyone knows everyone else.

8. If problems are taken care of immediately, you will have no future worries about it.

9. Now that I have decided to become a doctor, I believe it runs in the family.

10. As for quotation marks, I failed to use it properly to set off words from the remainder of the sentence.

11. Samuel Johnson was a lexicographer; after taking eight years to complete it, it sold out two editions within a year.

12. The published papers are written by English students, which, incidentally, are mostly freshmen.

13. John would go out of his way to help someone in distress, someone who was feeling sorry for themselves.

14. Although I am looking forward to starting classes on Monday, I keep wondering what it will be like.

15. Not every pharmacist works in a drugstore; in fact, many of them work in research or in the wholesale business.

16. Some of the college professors have received a doctor's degree in her particular field.

17. I have two brothers and two sisters which are all younger than myself.

18. If a person drives at high speed on an icy road, they may end up in a ditch.

19. Cars have safety belts, and if this is buckled, you have a good chance of surviving a crash.

20. I never thought it was possible that I could get up in front of a group and say something that made sense, but I did it. I cannot really say that I enjoyed it, but it wasn't really as bad as I thought it was going to be.

14. Case forms of pronouns

Case is a grammatical term that refers to the forms a noun or pronoun takes to indicate its relationship to other words. The three cases in English are *nominative, objective,* and *possessive.* In the statement "I want a week's vacation," *I* is in the nominative case, *week's* in the possessive, and *vacation* in the objective.

Case causes usage problems mainly with pronouns. Nouns have the same form for nominative and objective and present few difficulties in the possessive. Major concerns of usage occur with personal pronouns and with the pronoun *who,* which can be both relative and interrogative.

A good start on usage problems with pronouns is to study the table of personal pronouns in Section 2. Mastering this information about the *cases* and *persons* of personal pronouns will take care of nearly all questions about the *forms* of pronouns. Add to what you learn from the table the following: The relative and interrogative pronoun *who* is in the nominative case, both singular and plural. *Whom* is the objective form, singular and plural. *Whose* is in the possessive (genitive) case, singular and plural.

Nominative case

14a. The subject of a sentence or clause is in the nominative case.

My mother and *I* [not *me*] have gone on many fishing trips.
Who [not *whom*] is speaking, please?

14b. A predicate complement is in the nominative case.

A predicate complement is a noun (no difficulty with case), a pronoun (nominative case, essentially), or a predicate adjective (no case involved) used after a linking verb. (See Section 16.) After a linking verb, use only the nominative case of a pronoun:

That is *he* [not *him*] speaking.
It was *they* [not *them*] who smashed up the car.
It was *I* [not *me*] who was blamed for the fight.

In informal speech one often hears (and perhaps says), "It's me" or "This is me" or "That's him." Such expressions are steadily becoming more acceptable, but careful speakers and writers continue to use the nominative case in such constructions. If saying "It's I" sounds stilted to you, why not say "It's" or "This is" and follow with your name?

Objective case

14c. The object of a verb or preposition is in the objective case.

All nouns and the pronouns *it* and *you* cause no difficulty in this construction because they are the same in the nominative and objective cases. But choose carefully between *who* and *whom, I* and *me, she* and *her, he* and *him, they* and *them, we* and *us.*

Whom did the faculty blame for the trouble? [*Whom* is the object of the verb *blame.*]
The building superintendent accused *us* of being careless.
This matter concerns only *her* and *me.*
A group of *us* is going to a hamburger stand.
The band leader doesn't seem to like either *her* or *him.*
Mother met Elena, Hilda, and *me* at the bus station.
Between Abbie and *him* there is a good understanding.

14d. The indirect object of a verb is in the objective case.

An indirect object is a noun or pronoun before which *to* or *for* is either expressed or understood.

You owe *me* a better explanation than that. [You owe to me . . .]
If you do *her* this favor, she may not appreciate it. [If you do *for* her . . .]
Give *him* a call about your plans for the trip. [Give to him . . .]

14e. The subject of an infinitive is in the objective case.

Apparently she expected *me* to wait for her. [*Me* is the subject of *to wait.* The phrase *me to wait for her* is the object of *expected.*]
His desire to be completely honest made *him* say that. [*Him* is the subject of (to) *say* . . .]

The instructor let Oz and *me* leave class early. [*Oz* and *me* are subjects of (to) *leave.*]

14f. The object of an infinitive, gerund, or participle is in the objective case.

The coach said that she wanted to see *us* after the game. [*Us* is the object of the infinitive *to see.*]

Seeing *you* at this party is a pleasant surprise. [*You* is the object of the gerund *seeing.*]

Having recognized *him* at once, I crossed to the other side of the street. [*Him* is the object of the participle *having recognized.*]

14g. The object (objective) complement of the infinitive *to be* is in the objective case when the subject of the infinitive is expressed.

This rule of usage is tricky because it calls for the objective case after a linking verb. This situation occurs only when (1) the infinitive form *to be* is used and (2) the subject of the infinitive is actually expressed.

I thought you were *he* [Here the form is *were,* not the infinitive *to be.* Therefore, the objective case is not used.]

I thought you to be *him.* [*You,* the subject of *to be,* is in the objective case and is followed by a pronoun in the same case.]

Nearly everyone there took Lucinda to be *me.*

Nominative or objective case

14h. *Who* and *whoever* are used as subjects of verbs and as predicate pronouns. *Whom* and *whomever* are used as objects of verbs and prepositions.

This principle of usage causes many problems and arguments.

I demand membership for *whoever* wishes it. [*Whoever* is the subject of the verb *wishes;* the whole dependent clause is the object of the preposition *for.*]

case

14h

The question of *who* can ask for membership should not arise. [*Who* is the subject of *can ask;* the whole dependent clause is the object of the preposition *of.*]

This book tells *who* is *who* in America, and that one tells *who* was *who.* [Each *who* before *is* and *was* is the subject; each *who* after *is* and *was* is a predicate pronoun.]

This is the same man *whom* I saw at Oak Bluffs last summer. [*Whom* is the direct object of *saw.*]

Ask *whomever* you desire. [*Whomever* is the direct object of *desire;* the dependent clause is the object of *ask.*]

The letter began, "To *whom* it may concern." [*Whom* is the direct object of *concern;* the dependent clause is the object of the preposition *to.*]

My boss tells the same yarns to *whomever* he meets. [*Whomever* is the direct object of *meets;* the dependent clause is the object of the preposition *to.*]

The nominative and objective cases are frequently confused because of intervening words. The case of a pronoun depends on its use in its own clause and is not influenced by words that come between the pronoun and other words that determine its case.

He asked me *who* I thought would be chosen. [Check by omitting *I thought.*]

Who do you suppose drew up these plans? [Check by omitting *do you suppose.*]

I danced with the person *whom* no one suspected we had chosen "Beauty Queen." [Check by omitting *no one suspected.*]

Current usage studies indicate that *who* is rapidly replacing *whom* in some uses, partly because keeping them straight is difficult and partly because many people start a relative clause or an interrogative sentence with *who,* not knowing how it is going to end. Many authorities agree that in informal English *who* may replace *whom* when it stands before a verb or preposition of which it is the object, but *whom* should be used when as object it directly follows the verb or preposition.

INFORMAL: *Who* are you visiting in Buffalo?

Who are you selling your typewriter to?

The people *who* we met were on a tour similar to ours.

FORMAL: You said you were visiting *whom* in Buffalo?

To *whom* are you selling your typewriter?
The people *whom* we met were on a tour similar to ours.

14i. An appositive is in the same case as the noun or pronoun it identifies or explains.

Two people, *she* and *I*, are the only candidates with a chance to win. [Nominative]
The dean gave friendly advice to both of us, Dave and *me*. [Objective]
Last evening the club pledged two additional persons, my roommate and *me*. [Objective]

14j. An elliptical clause of comparison, preceded by *than* or *as*, takes the case called for by the expanded construction.

An *elliptical clause* is one with a word or words missing. The omitted word(s) are understood from other parts of the sentence. If the missing words are supplied, it is not difficult to choose the correct case form for the pronoun.

I am as strong as *he* (is). [Nominative]
You are much taller than *I* (am). [Nominative]
Mother does not drive a car as well as *I* (do). [Nominative]
I do not like her as much as (I like) *him*. [Objective]
This TV program amused you much more than (it amused) *me*. [Objective]
This TV program amused you much more than *I* (amused you). [Nominative]

Possessive case

In English, the principal use of the possessive case is to indicate ownership. It may also be required to indicate measurement of time or space and to show some relationship or association.

14k. A noun or pronoun linked immediately with a gerund is in the possessive case.

AWKWARD: He resents *you* being more popular than he is.

Most of the members paid their dues without *me* asking them.

The teacher praised Miguel for *him* taking careful lecture notes.

The other girls objected to *Mary* spreading such a rumor.

IMPROVED: He resents *your* being more popular than he is.

Most of the members paid their dues without *my* asking them.

The teacher praised Miguel for *his* taking careful lecture notes. [Or omit the pronoun.]

The other girls objected to *Mary's* spreading such a rumor.

When the possessive case with a gerund is awkward as, for example, when other words come between the two, recast the sentence.

AWKWARD: No rules exist against *anyone's* in this class saying what he thinks.

IMPROVED: No rules exist against any class *member's* saying what he or she thinks. [Or *against class members saying*]

Do not confuse possessive-with-gerund with noun-or-pronoun-with-participle constructions.

CLEAR: The class members heard their *teacher* asking for greater care in their written work. [Participle]

The class members responded to their *teacher's* asking for greater care in their written work. [Gerund]

14l. The possessive case of an inanimate object is usually to be avoided.

An inanimate object may be in the possessive case, but such use is sometimes awkward. Precise writers use an *of* phrase to indicate possession, although in current written English the possessive form is fairly widely used.

case

14m

AWKWARD:

The *trees'* leaves were turning green.

The *wastebasket's* contents were on fire.

We waxed and polished the *diningroom's* floor.

IMPROVED:

The leaves *of the trees* were turning green.

The contents *of the wastebasket* were on fire.

We waxed and polished the floor *of the diningroom*. [Or *the diningroom floor*]

Both awkward and incorrect is the use of a phrase containing *one of the,* then a plural possessive, and then a singular noun. Rephrasing is needed.

AWKWARD:

The waiter accidentally spilled coffee on *one of the girls' dress.*

We held our after-graduation party at *one of the boys' home.*

ACCEPTABLE:

The waiter accidentally spilled coffee on the dress of *one of the girls.* [Or *on one girl's dress*]

We held our after-graduation party at the home of *one of the boys.* [Or *at one boy's home*]

The home *of my parents* [or my *parents'* home] is on Laurel Avenue.

The report *of the committee* [or the *committee's* report] is due next week.

Note: An acceptable but usually wordy and unnecessary idiom is the *double possessive,* an *of* phrase followed by a noun in the possessive case:

A classmate of my *sister's* spent the weekend with us. [My sister's . . .]

We are reading two plays of *Shakespeare's.* [. . . two Shakespearean plays]

14m. The possessive case may be used to express extent of time or space.

Although inanimate objects are rarely put in the possessive case, English idiom prefers the possessive case for certain nouns of measure, time, and the like. It is not a question of ownership or possession; it is simply an expression of measure, extent of time, or other considerations. The usual time nouns are *second, minute, moment, hour, day, week, month, semester, year, decade, century, winter, spring, summer, autumn, today, tomorrow, yesterday.* Instead of an awkward *of* phrase, the following expressions are preferable:

a day's work	a dollar's worth
a moment's notice	a stone's throw
10 minutes' walk	at his wits' end
three years' experience	the law's delay
a summer's work	tomorrow's weather report
two semesters' study	4 inches' space
at arm's length	for charity's sake

For some of these ideas, of course, hyphenated expressions are sometimes preferable: *a 10-minute walk, a five-mile drive, a two-semester course, a 95-yard run* (vs. *a 95 yards' run*).

EXERCISE 5

Write brief sentences in which you use *he and I* or *she and I* (1) as subject of an independent clause, (2) as subject of a dependent clause, and (3) in apposition. Write brief sentences in which you use *him and me* or *her and me* (1) as direct object of a verb, (2) as indirect object of a verb, (3) as object of a preposition, and (4) in apposition.

EXERCISE 6

Rewrite errors in the use of case in the following sentences:

1. Everyone believes in some kind of superstition, even me.
2. A person such as me can study only so many hours without a break.
3. His marriage to Elizabeth Barrett was a love story that lifted both he and his wife to greater poetic activity.
4. Each night we have a contest among my friends and myself to see who can finish his assignments first.
5. Jacques grew up by showing off his knowledge even to those who knew far more than him.
6. Most sports fans belong in this category, especially us.
7. With defeat on the faces of we students, we sadly left the stadium and the Homecoming game.
8. There in my room stood a girl about the same height as me.
9. We, a few friends and me, were on our way to a picnic.

10. At the bus station, I saw another boy; I conjectured that he, like I, had been home for a short vacation.

EXERCISE 7

Detect all errors in the use of case in the following sentences:

1. Our doubts about us ever getting there began to grow.
2. The horn should also be used to warn unsuspecting pedestrians of the automobile's presence.
3. I don't mind you asking me a few questions.
4. I have had four years experience working in machine shops.
5. After 10 minutes deliberation, the judges' announced that they had reached a decision.
6. When I was very young, I recall my mother telling me about my birth.
7. Mr. Brown was a great teacher; hardly a day goes by without him being remembered.
8. I did not do as well as I expected to do in my last semester's courses.
9. If you have typhoid shots, there is less chance of you getting typhoid fever.
10. In the spring the canyon's trees again put forth their leaves.

EXERCISE 8

In the following sentences select the italicized word that precise writers would probably use:

1. I would get into an argument with *whoever whomever* said anything about my driving habits.
2. In college I hope that I meet the person *who whom* I want to marry.
3. A few other campers had arrived *who whom* also needed to purchase supplies.
4. With the assistance of these people, *who whom* Jane later discovered were her cousins, she established a school for poor children.
5. We always kept a sharp lookout for old Mr. Jones, a man *who whom* we children seemed to fear.
6. What a surprise to have a visitor *who whom* you haven't seen for eight years!
7. I believe in God: At Thanksgiving this is *who whom* I give thanks to.
8. She went to live with Michael Henchard, the man *who whom* she at the time believed was her father.
9. Every student in college will have teachers *who whom* she likes and teachers *who whom* like her.
10. I had four older brothers and sisters *who whom* I had to obey.

15. Principal parts of verbs

Verbs in every language have principal parts, sometimes three (as in German) and sometimes five (as in Spanish, Italian, and French). An English verb has three principal parts: (1) present tense (the infinitive form), (2) past tense, and (3) past participle. A good way to recall these parts is to substitute those of any verb for the following:

I *go* today.	I *eat* today.
I *went* yesterday.	I *ate* yesterday.
I *have gone* every day this week.	I *have eaten* every day this week.

In speaking and writing, try to remember that the past tense of irregular verbs is *never* used with *have, had, has, was, were,* or *got.*

15a. Regular verbs

The past tense and the past participle of most English verbs are formed by adding *-d, -ed,* or *-t* to the present. These are called *regular verbs.*

Present	Past	Past Participle
ask	asked	asked
save	saved	saved
talk	talked	talked
mean	meant	meant
spend	spent	spent

15b. Irregular verbs

Most of the verbs that cause problems in usage are *irregular.* They are called irregular because they form their principal parts in several ways. Groups of irregular verbs do fall into patterns, however. For example, one group has a vowel change in the past tense and sometimes in the past participle as well:

Present	Past	Past Participle
come	came	come
drink	drank	drunk
sing	sang	sung
cling	clung	clung
fight	fought	fought
sit	sat	sat
shoot	shot	shot
run	ran	run
find	found	found

Some verbs in this group, in addition to the vowel change, add -*n* to the past participle:

Present	Past	Past Participle
drive	drove	driven
grow	grew	grown
break	broke	broken
fly	flew	flown
freeze	froze	frozen
write	wrote	written
eat	ate	eaten
ride	rode	ridden
fall	fell	fallen

Another group changes its form completely in the past tense and past participle:

Present	Past	Past Participle
go	went	gone
bring	brought	brought
think	thought	thought
buy	bought	bought
stand	stood	stood
do	did	done
lie	lay	lain
catch	caught	caught
wind	wound	wound

A few verbs change the last consonant, but not the vowel:

Present	Past	Past Participle
build	built	built
make	made	made
have	had	had

vb form

15c

A few others have the same form for all three principal parts:

Present	Past	Past Participle
put	put	put
cut	cut	cut
burst	burst	burst
hurt	hurt	hurt
set	set	set
spread	spread	spread
cast	cast	cast

15c. The principal parts of frequently used verbs require study.

When in doubt about the past tense or past participle of a verb, consult your dictionary. If no additional forms follow the entry word, the verb is regular. If the verb is irregular, most good dictionaries will list its principal parts.

Careful study of the following list will increase your ease in using troublesome verbs. The list covers almost every verb you are likely to write or speak.

Infinitive	Past	Past Participle
arise	arose	arisen
attack	attacked	attacked
awake	awoke, awaked	awoke, awakened
be	was	been
bear	bore	borne
beat	beat	beat, beaten
become	became	become
begin	began	begun
bend	bent	bent
bet	bet	bet
bid (make an offer)	bid	bid
bid (command)	bid, bade	bid, bidden
bind	bound	bound
bite	bit	bitten
bleed	bled	bled
blow	blew	blown
break	broke	broken
breed	bred	bred
bring	brought	brought
broadcast	broadcast, broadcasted	broadcast, broadcasted

Infinitive	Past	Past Participle
build	built	built
burn	burned, burnt	burned, burnt
burst	burst	burst
buy	bought	bought
cast	cast	cast
catch	caught	caught
choose	chose	chosen
cling	clung	clung
clothe	clad, clothed	clad, clothed
come	came	come
cost	cost	cost
creep	crept	crept
crow	crew, crowed	crowed
cut	cut	cut
deal	dealt	dealt
dig	dug	dug
dive	dived, dove	dived, dove
do	did	done
draw	drew	drawn
dream	dreamed, dreamt	dreamed, dreamt
drink	drank	drunk
drive	drove	driven
dwell	dwelt, dwelled	dwelt, dwelled
eat	ate	eaten
fall	fell	fallen
feed	fed	fed
feel	felt	felt
fight	fought	fought
find	found	found
fit	fit, fitted	fit, fitted
flee	fled	fled
fling	flung	flung
fly	flew	flown
fly (baseball)	flied	flied
forbid	forbad, forbade	forbidden
forget	forgot	forgotton, forgot
forsake	forsook	forsaken
freeze	froze	frozen
get	got	got, gotten
give	gave	given
go	went	gone
grind	ground	ground
grow	grew	grown

Infinitive	Past	Past Participle
hang (execute)	hanged	hanged
hang (suspend)	hung	hung
have	had	had
hear	heard	heard
hide	hid	hidden
hit	hit	hit
hold	held	held
hurt	hurt	hurt
keep	kept	kept
kneel	knelt, kneeled	knelt, kneeled
knit	knit, knitted	knit, knitted
know	knew	known
lay	laid	laid
lead	led	led
leap	leaped, leapt	leaped, leapt
learn	learned, learnt	learned, learnt
leave	left	left
lend	lent	lent
let	let	let
lie (recline)	lay	lain
lie (tell a lie)	lied	lied
light	lighted, lit	lighted, lit
loose	loosed	loose
lose	lost	lost
make	made	made
mean	meant	meant
meet	met	met
pass	passed	passed
pay	paid	paid
prove	proved	proved, proven
put	put	put
raise	raised	raised
read	read	read
rid	rid, ridded	rid, ridded
ride	rode	ridden
ring	rang	rung
rise	rose	risen
run	ran	run
say	said	said
see	saw	seen
seek	sought	sought
sell	sold	sold
send	sent	sent

Infinitive	Past	Past Participle
set	set	set
shake	shook	shaken
shed	shed	shed
shine	shone, shined	shone, shined
shoe	shod	shod
shoot	shot	shot
show	showed	shown, showed
shrink	shrank	shrunk, shrunken
shut	shut	shut
sing	sang	sung
sink	sank	sunk
sit	sat	sat
slay	slew	slain
sleep	slept	slept
slide	slid	slid
sling	slung	slung
slink	slunk	slunk
smell	smelled, smelt	smelled, smelt
speak	spoke	spoken
speed	sped, speeded	sped, speeded
spell	spelled, spelt	spelled, spelt
spend	spent	spent
spin	spun	spun
split	split	split
spoil	spoiled, spoilt	spoiled, spoilt
spread	spread	spread
spring	sprang, sprung	sprung
stand	stood	stood
steal	stole	stolen
stick	stuck	stuck
sting	stung	stung
stink	stank, stunk	stunk
stride	strode	stridden
strike	struck	struck, stricken
string	strung	strung
strive	strove, strived	striven, strived
swear	swore	sworn
sweep	swept	swept
swell	swelled	swelled, swollen
swim	swam	swum
swing	swung	swung
take	took	taken
teach	taught	taught

Infinitive	Past	Past Participle
tear	tore	torn
tell	told	told
think	thought	thought
thrive	thrived, throve	thrived, thriven
throw	threw	thrown
thrust	thrust	thrust
tread	trod	trodden, trod
use	used	used
wake	woke, waked	woke, waked, wakened
wear	wore	worn
weave	wove	woven
wed	wedded, wed	wedded, wed
weep	wept	wept
wet	wet, wetted	wet, wetted
win	won	won
wind	wound	wound
wring	wrung	wrung
write	wrote	written

EXERCISE 9

Give the preferred forms of the verbs (verbals) that appear in parentheses in the following sentences:

1. During the evening we were many times (bite) by gnats.
2. My friend (lead) me into reading many good books.
3. For such simple questions everybody should have (know) the answers.
4. It is not easy to remember how much money one has (give) to people who have (come) to the door.
5. Don't leave your books (lie) around; they may be (steal).
6. The horse should easily have (spring) over the barrier.
7. Children like to have pictures (hang) on the walls of their rooms.
8. Her shirts had (shrink) to the point of being almost unwearable.
9. Some students never have (bear) their share of responsibility.
10. You should not have (lend) him so much money.

EXERCISE 10

Give the preferred form of the *regular* verbs (verbals) in the following sentences:

1. Salespersons are suppose to present their material in an interesting way.
2. You might say that I am prejudice, since I have lived in a city all my life.
3. I am finding it difficult to become accustom to some of the regulations.
4. I don't know what would have happen to me if I hadn't waken up.
5. My sister has help many worried people find an answer to their problems.
6. In high school we were not use to such long assignments.
7. We couldn't have ask for any worse weather than we got.
8. When I finish basic work, I plan to enroll in some advance courses.
9. I do not always use the right words where I am suppose to use them.
10. It has been prove that handicapped people work at least as well as those not handicapped.

EXERCISE 11

Give the preferred form of the *irregular* verbs in the following sentences:

1. It is hard to work when one is wore out.
2. After dinner, songs were sang for about an hour.
3. I had never gave much thought to the matter before.
4. There are five reasons why I have chose to study a foreign language.
5. In our home we have always drank tea or coffee for breakfast.
6. Whenever the pond is froze over, we go ice-skating.
7. I've never saw my father angry with any one of his children.
8. Having went through college yourself, you know what we are facing.
9. At my job I have ran up against some puzzling problems.
10. By that time certain facts had began to stand out in my mind.

16. Linking and auxiliary verbs

Some verbs express a static condition, a state of being. Still others help out another verb in forming tenses, voice, mood, and certain precise ideas. The first of these groups comprises what are known as *linking* verbs; the second, *auxiliary* verbs.

16a. Linking verbs

Nearly all "inactive" verbs are *linking verbs,* also called *copulative* or *joining verbs.* A linking verb can couple nouns or pronouns or a noun and an adjective:

This town *is* named Jocasta. [The linking verb couples two nouns.]

She *is* my best friend. [The linking verb couples a pronoun and a noun.]

That person *seems* ill. [The linking verb couples a noun and an adjective.]

The most often used linking verb is *to be.* Other common linking verbs are the following:

appear	become	feel
grow	look	prove
remain	seem	smell
sound	stand	taste

A few verbs occur in only a limited number of "linking" meanings: *slam* shut, *ring* true. The same verb can assert action and serve as a link:

The moon *looks* pale tonight. [Linking]

Grace *looks* at every page. [Action]

We *felt* happy over our success. [Linking]

The police officer *felt* her way through the tunnel. [Action]

16b. Auxiliary verbs

An *auxiliary verb* has little meaning of its own, but it affects the meaning of the verb it accompanies. In the following sentences the auxiliary verb is italicized:

I *have* left my books on the library steps.

Our work *has* come to depend more and more on computers.

As they *were* leaving, they *did* shout threats.

You *should have been* told about your mistakes.

The meanings and uses of frequently used auxiliary verbs are explained in all good dictionaries. The principal auxiliary verbs and their uses are as follows:

1. *To be.* Used in all tenses in forming the progressive tone and the passive voice.

2. *Can.* Used to express ability or power or the idea of "being able to."
   I *can* meet him soon.
   My friend *can* fix anything.

3. *Could.* Used as a kind of "past" tense of *can* to express the same ideas in a weaker manner:
   Beverly *could* not haul in the heavy anchor.
   My friend *could* fix anything if she wanted to.

4. *Dare.* Used, usually with *say,* to express probability:
   I *dare* say that's true.

5. *To do.* Used to express emphasis (emphatic tone) in the present and past tenses:
   Please *do* come to see us soon.
   She *did* send me a present this year.
   Also used to avoid repetition of a verb or full verb expression:
   Aldo slept as soundly as I *did.*
   We shall start out when you *do.*

6. *To have.* Used in present perfect, past perfect, and future perfect tenses; also in the perfect infinitive and the perfect participle: He *has* gone, *had* gone, will *have* gone, to *have* gone, *having* gone.

7. *Let.* Used to express the ideas of "allowing" or "permitting," "suggesting," or "ordering":
   Let me go now.
   Let's have a jam session.
   Let me think about that.
   Let her finish her rap.

8. *May.* Used to express permission:
   May I have your coat?
   You *may* keep the money.
   Also used to express probability or a wish:
   It *may* hurt for a while.

9. *Might.* Used as a kind of "past" tense of *may* to express the

same ideas of possibility or probability in a weaker manner:

You *might* try tutoring handicapped children.

10. *Must.* Used to express obligation or compulsion:

You *must* list your assets.

Also used to express reasonable certainty:

Jim was here promptly, so he *must* have set his alarm clock.

I hear thunder; there *must* be a storm coming.

11. *Need.* Used to express necessity or obligation:

I *need* not give her my name.

They *need* only to speak up and speak out.

Note: As an auxiliary verb, the third-person singular form is also *need:*

He *need* not take my advice.

12. *Ought.* Used to express duty or obligation; one of the few auxiliary verbs followed by the sign of the infinitive (*to*) with the main verb:

You *ought* to learn chemistry.

Everyone *ought* to know that joke.

Note: *Have* and *had* are never used before *ought* or *must.*

WRONG: I *had ought* to start working.

RIGHT: I *ought to have started* working long ago.

13. *Shall.* Sometimes used as the precise auxiliary for the first person, future and future perfect tenses:

We *shall* start the trip tomorrow.

Also occasionally used in the second and third persons to express command or determination:

You *shall* be prompt in the future.

(See Section 40.)

14. *Should.* Used as a kind of "past" tense of *shall* in the first person, but weaker in emphasis:

I *should* not scold the children.

I *should* hope for the best.

Also used frequently in a conditional meaning:

If I *should* make other plans, I shall let you know.

If Jack *should* want food, we can provide some.

Used in all three persons to express duty or propriety or necessity:

You *should* organize your work.

She *should* be proud of him.

Used in all three persons to express expectation:

We *should* be flying over Spokane now.

The letter *should* reach her on Monday.

(See Section 40.)

15. *Used.* In the past tense only, *used* expresses custom or habitual action:

I *used* to cry a lot when I was little.

16. *Will.* Used as the precise auxiliary for the second and third persons, future and future perfect tenses: You *will* go, *will* have gone; he *will* go, *will* have gone; they *will* go, *will* have gone. Also used in all three persons to express willingness or consent:

I *will* take the examination.

17. *Would.* Used as a kind of "past" tense of *will* in the second and third persons, but less strong in meaning:

You *would* scarcely care about them.

Note: If the verb in the independent clause is in the past tense, use *would* to express futurity in the dependent clause; if the verb in the independent clause is in the present tense, use *will* in the dependent clause:

Geraldo *told* me that he *would* write.

Geraldo *tells* me that he *will* write.

Frequently used in a conditional meaning, or after a conditional clause:

If you *would* agree, they *would* be reassured.

If the traffic were heavy, he *would* take another route.

If I could, I *would.*

Used to express determination:

He *would* try, no matter how difficult the assignment appeared to be.

Also used in all three persons to express repeated or habitual action:

In the winter we *would* skate every day.

And used infrequently to express wish or desire:

Would that we all had done otherwise!

EXERCISE 12

Write two sentences using each of these linking verbs. In the first sentence, the verb should be in the present tense, in the second, the past tense. Example:

Muriel *appears* happy today. Leroy *appeared* happy yesterday.

become	smell
feel	sound
grow	stand
look	taste
seem	turn

EXERCISE 13

For each italicized verb in the following sentences, indicate its auxiliary, if it has one. Explain the purpose of the auxiliary or the meaning it expresses.

1. We should have *served* the fried chicken; in fact, we might have *served* it if the cook had not *dropped* it in the sand.
2. When I *was* a boy, Mother would *assign* me new chores every other day.
3. Must we *go?* We have not *been* here long.
4. Let no one *forget* the fight; it will *do* us all harm.
5. I will never *allow* a child of mine to be without memories.
6. Have you *tried* sky diving? It might *amuse* you.
7. She ought to *saw* tree branches carefully; otherwise, she may *find* herself out on a limb.
8. Parker used to *think* he was an expert sailor; now he *is* not so sure.
9. You may *catch* the fish, but can you *cook* it?
10. Eloise should *keep* a diary; I could certainly *profit* by reading it.

17. Tense

Tense shows the time of the action or state of being expressed by a verb. The three divisions of time—past, present, and future—are shown in English by six tenses. The three *primary,* or *simple, tenses* are the present, the past, and the future. The three other tenses are the present perfect, the past perfect, and the future perfect. These last three tenses are sometimes called *compound, perfect,* or *secondary tenses.*

17a. The correct tense is needed to express a precise time.

Difficulty with tense usage arises from (1) not knowing the functions of the six tenses or (2) not thinking carefully about the time element involved. The following table shows the tenses needed to convey precise ideas.

Active Voice	
Present	I hear (am hearing)
Past	I heard (was hearing)
Future	I shall hear (shall be hearing)
Present perfect	I have heard (have been hearing)
Past perfect	I had heard (had been hearing)
Future perfect	I shall have heard (shall have been hearing)

Passive Voice	
Present	I am heard (am being heard)
Past	I was heard (was being heard)
Future	I shall be heard
Present perfect	I have been heard
Past perfect	I had been heard
Future perfect	I shall have been heard

Verbals (Nonfinite Verb Forms)	
Present infinitive	to hear (to be hearing)
Perfect infinitive	to have heard (to have been hearing)
Present participle	hearing
Past participle	heard
Perfect participle	having heard (having been hearing)
Present gerund	hearing
Perfect gerund	having heard (having been hearing)

1. Present tense

Present tense indicates that the action or condition is going on or exists now:

The Hendersons *sing* and *dance*.
Fun *is* one thing that money can't buy.
The truth *is* known.

2. Past tense

Past tense indicates that an action or condition took place or existed at some time in the past:

The Hendersons *sang* and *danced*.
Fun *was* the one thing that money couldn't buy.
The truth *was* known.

3. Future tense

Future tense indicates that an action will take place or that a condition will exist in the future:

The Hendersons *will sing* and *dance*.
Fun *will be* the one thing that money can't buy.
The truth *will be* known.

Note: The future may also be stated by the present tense accompanied by an adverb or adverbial phrase indicating time. Constructions like this are common:

I *am going* to the races *later today*.
This Friday Mona *leaves* for Tahiti.

4. Present perfect tense

Present perfect tense indicates that an action or condition was begun in the past and has just been completed or is still going on. The time is past, but it is connected with the present. The present perfect tense presupposes some relationship with the present:

We *have lived* in this apartment for several years. [and still do]
She and I *have been* friends for six months. [and still are]
The weather *has been* too cold for outdoor swimming. [and still is]

5. Past perfect tense

Past perfect tense indicates that an action or condition was completed at a time that is now past. It shows action "two steps back."

That is, the past perfect tense presupposes some relationship or connection with an action or condition expressed in the past tense:

The floor *was crowded* because a new shipment of furniture *had arrived* early that morning.
The roads *were* dangerous because ice sheets *had formed* during the night.

6. Future perfect tense

Future perfect tense indicates that an action or condition will be completed at a future time:

All of them *will have died* before then.
By the time you arrive, *I shall have gone* to bed.

Note: The three so-called secondary or compound tenses always indicate partially or totally *completed* action, whether in the present (present perfect tense), in the past (past perfect tense), or in the future (future perfect tense).

17b. Tenses should appear in proper sequence.

When only one verb is used in a sentence, it should express the precise time involved. When two or more verbs appear in a sentence, they should be consistent in tense. Remember that the tense of a verb in a subordinate clause depends on the tense of the verb in the main clause. The following general rules should be helpful:

1. The present tense is used in a dependent clause to express a general truth.

At that time, most people did not believe that the earth *is* round.

2. The present tense is used alone to express a "timeless" truth.

An ounce of prevention *is* worth a pound of cure.

3. In writing about literature it is easy to shift the tense of verbs from present to past and from past to present. Literary works may be thought of as occurring either in

the present or in the past, but one tense should be used consistently.

> In James Dickey's *Deliverance,* some businessmen from Atlanta *decide* to take a canoe trip on a wild river. They *drive* to the river, *launch* their canoe, and *begin* their journey.
>
> In James Dickey's *Deliverance,* some businessmen from Atlanta *decided* to take a canoe trip on a wild river. They *drove* to the river, *launched* their canoe, and *began* their journey.

4. Do not use the past tense if logically the present tense is called for.

> Last summer we visited a village in Ireland. The people of that community *were* hardy and resourceful.

It is possible that the community no longer exists or that its people have since become weakened, but is that what is meant?

5. Passages in some short stories and novels are written in the present tense, although the action occurred in time that is past. This use of what is called the *historical present* sometimes makes narrative more vivid, but it quickly becomes monotonous.

6. Use a present infinitive except when the infinitive represents action completed before the time of the governing verb.

> I made a note *to talk* (not *to have talked*) with you about it.
> The coach is happy *to have made* Sally a member of the team.

7. A present participle indicates action at the time expressed by the verb; a past participle indicates action before that of the verb.

> *Eating* in so many restaurants, Lena *is* introduced to some exotic foods.
> *Having been* a benched player himself, he *felt* sympathy for Hector.

8. When narration in the past tense is interrupted for reference to a preceding event, use the past perfect tense.

Last week they *fixed* the pipes, which *had been frozen* all winter. She *confided* that she *had been* in the city for over a month.

As a summary, these two formulas for the sequence of tenses may be helpful to you:

PAST ⟵――――― PRESENT ⟶ FUTURE

PAST PERFECT ⟵― PAST ⟶ FUTURE

17c. Aspect

Aspect is a category, or set of categories, in which a verb is inflected (changed) to indicate the duration, repetition, completion, or quality of the action or state of being denoted by the verb. Such forms (categories) help to express exactly what the writer wants to say: simple (*sleep*); progressive (*am sleeping*); emphatic (*did sleep*).

The *simple* category is a concise statement of a "snapshot" or instantaneous action of a verb: I *walk* (present tense); I *walked* (past tense); I *shall walk* (future tense); I *have walked* (present perfect tense); I *had walked* (past perfect tense); I *shall have walked* (future perfect tense).

The *progressive* form, which shows action in progress, consists of a form of the verb *to be* and the present participle of the main verb: I *am walking, was walking, shall be walking, have been walking, had been walking, shall have been walking.*

Applied to aspect, the word *progressive* has much the same meaning as it does when applied to tense. It indicates a category of the verb showing the relationship of the action to the passage of time in reference to duration, completion, or repetition.

The emphatic form, which indicates emphasis, consists of some part of the verb *to do* and the present infinitive of the main verb. The emphatic form is used only in present and past tenses: I *do walk,* I *did walk.*

EXERCISE 14

In the sentences that follow, change the tense of any verb that appears to be inconsistent:

1. When the teacher explained that all bodies are subject to the law of gravity, my visiting brother, a former paratrooper, yells "Amen."
2. Unfortunately, I had not had time to have played the entire concerto.
3. After we went a half-dozen miles, we ran out of gas.
4. Cynthia believes that the principal effect of *Hamlet* was catharsis.
5. When the plumbers laid the pipeline on the surface, they forgot that water became solid at below-freezing temperatures.
6. When the Dolphins lost, Francine felt that life is no longer worth living.
7. By the time the new hay crop was ready, the barns are almost empty.
8. After Cortez subdued the Aztecs, all Mexico will be quickly explored by the Spanish.
9. I ought to have paid this utilities bill before the discount period ends.
10. Some historians think that Napoleon's chief hope in conquering Italy was that he may win the admiration and love of Josephine.

EXERCISE 15

Change the inconsistent tenses of the verbs in the following sentences:

1. After my parents lived on a farm for ten years, they moved into town.
2. Having opened the manuscript, the editor lunges for her blue pencil.
3. Vivian wanted desperately to have received an A in history.
4. Harvey circled until he saw an opening; then he grabs the giraffe by the ears.
5. When I stopped at the teacher's desk as requested, she says to me, "Where's your term paper?"
6. When Marlena sees the grade on her term paper, she screamed like a wounded panther.
7. Modern historians have concluded that Troy had been besieged for commercial rather than personal reasons.
8. After he had pacified the usher, Jack leads his seven sisters down the aisle.
9. By the time we reached Washington, we were too low on money to have stayed at the Marriott Motor Hotel.
10. Last week I was just too tired to have pruned the peach trees.

18. Mood

Verbs appear in one of three moods: *indicative, imperative,* or *subjunctive.* Nearly all the verbs that you use appear in the indicative mood because this is the mood for making a statement, expressing a fact, or asking a question. The imperative mood is not often used in writing, because few of us are in the bad habit of regularly issuing orders and making demands. The subjunctive mood is the troublemaker. Its uses are explained fully in Section 3b.

18a. Learn to distinguish between the subjunctive and indicative moods.

Although you may need to use the subjunctive form of verbs only rarely, it will help to familiarize yourself with the following table, in which *be* and *come* are used as illustrations:

Present Indicative		Present Subjunctive	
I am	we are	(if) I be	(if) we be
you are	you are	(if) you be	(if) you be
he/she is	they are	(if) he/she be	(if) they be
Past Indicative		**Past Subjunctive**	
I was	we were	(if) I were	(if) we were
you were	you were	(if) you were	(if) you were
he/she was	they were	(if) he/she were	(if) they were
Present Indicative		**Present Subjunctive**	
I come	we come	(if) I come	(if) we come
you come	you come	(if) you come	(if) you come
he/she comes	they come	(if) he/she comes	(if) they come

18b. Subjunctive verb forms are rapidly dropping out of use in contemporary English.

Distinctive subjunctive forms are disappearing in favor of more commonly used indicative verb forms.

FORMER USE: If it *be* at all possible, I shall [or *will*] lend you the car.

CURRENT USE: If it *is* at all possible, I shall [or *will*] lend you the car.

Careful writers, however, continue to use the subjunctive forms of verbs when expressing ideas that are contrary to fact or involve doubt or uncertainty.

18c. Use the subjunctive forms employed in certain customary and standardized expressions.

Our language retains a number of subjunctive forms in sayings that have been handed down from times when this mood was more widely used. Write expressions like the following in their original form: Heaven *forbid,* if *need* be, she *need* not speak, Thy Kingdom *come,* Thy will *be* done, *suffice* it to say, *come* what may, far *be* it from me, *be* that as it may, God *bless* you, long *live* the King, the public *be* damned, *be* it known by these presents, the devil *take* it, so *be* it.

18d. In parallel constructions the mood of verbs should not shift.

INCONSISTENT: If I *were* in your position and *was* not prevented, I should certainly go.

If it *does* not rain and if I *be* not called out of town, I shall attend the meeting.

Last summer I *would* play tennis every morning and *swam* every afternoon.

CONSISTENT: If I *were* in your position and *were* not prevented, I should certainly go.

If it *does* not rain and if I *am* not called out of town, I shall attend the meeting.

Last summer I *would* play tennis every morning and *would* swim every afternoon.

Last summer I *played* tennis every morning and *swam* every afternoon.

EXERCISE 16

Review what is said about mood in Section 3 and in Section 18. Then select in each of the following sentences the italicized form that you believe is the preferred choice:

1. Assume, now, that she *was were* to be our official delegate.
2. If she *be is* chosen our delegate and *was were* sent to Bloomington, would we be well represented?
3. To put this campaign over, it *be is* necessary that the class president *be is* here Tuesday to make final plans.
4. My only hope is that John *receive receives* full recognition for his work.
5. Heaven *grant grants* that he *be is* not seriously injured.
6. I strongly advocate that a vote of censure *be is* ordered.
7. Even though extreme measures for our safety *are be* taken, the consequences are dubious.
8. My, how he wished he *was were* a few inches taller.
9. It is imperative that there *is be* not the slightest delay.
10. It hardly seems possible that the doctor *is would be* willing to give that anesthetic to a baby.

19. Adjectives and adverbs

Adjectives and adverbs are defined and explained in Section 4. Give some attention to that section before considering the following suggestions for using these two parts of speech.

Here are the three important statements to remember about the use of adjectives and adverbs:

1. Some adjectives and adverbs have identical forms.
2. Idiomatic usage sometimes violates the distinction between adjectives and adverbs. (See Section 37e.)
3. After a *linking* verb (see Section 16), use an adjective if reference is to the subject, an adverb if reference is to the verb.

19a. Some words may be either adjectives or adverbs.

The form of a word does not always reveal whether it is an adjective or an adverb. Some adjectives and adverbs have identical forms (e.g., *far, fast, little, less, least, much, more, most, well*). These naturally cause no trouble.

Some adverbs, however, have two forms: the first form is exactly like the adjective and the second has *ly* added: Examples are *cheap, cheaply; direct, directly; late, lately; loud, loudly; quick, quickly; slow* (hence the road signs that say *Drive slow*), *slowly.*

Most words ending in *ly* are adverbs, but some are not: words like *deadly, goodly, holy, sickly,* and *weakly* are adjectives. Also, *ly* is an adjective suffix meaning "like" in *earthly, friendly, heavenly, homely, saintly,* and *timely.*

A sprinter is a runner who runs *fast.* [Adverb]

A sprinter is a *fast* runner. [Adjective]

Grandfather was a *kindly* [adjective] person; he treated *kindly* [adverb] everyone he met.

19b. Adverbs modify verbs, adjectives, and other adverbs.

I think that all of us spend money too *rapidly.* [The adverb *rapidly* modifies the verb *spend.*]

Some people take themselves too *seriously.* [*Seriously,* an adverb, modifies the verb *take.*]

Our dog always barks *loudly* when he sees a cat. [The adverb *loudly* modifies the verb *barks.*]

The performance was *surprisingly* brief. [The adverb *surprisingly* modifies the adjective *brief.*]

She is a *really* good basketball coach. [The adverb *really* modifies the adjective *good.*]

The conductor of the tour is a *strikingly* beautiful person. [The adverb *strikingly* modifies the adjective *beautiful.*]

The lecturer spoke *very* carefully. [The adverb *very* modifies the adverb *carefully.*]

Quite lately our street has become quieter. [*Quite,* an adverb, modifies the adverb *lately.*]

It would violate standard contemporary usage to employ adjectives instead of the adverbs italicized in the preceding sentences.

19c. After such verbs as *appear, be, become, feel, look, seem, smell,* and *taste,* the modifier should be an adjective if it refers to the subject, an adverb if it describes or defines the verb.

When *be* and other linking verbs express a state of being, a following modifier refers to the subject of the sentence and should be an adjective; when the same verbs express action, then a following modifier describes or defines the verb and should be an adverb.

The boxer looked *sleepy*. [Adjective; how the boxer looked—a state]
The boxer looked *sleepily* toward his corner. [Adverb; what the boxer did—an action]
The weather turned *cold*. [Adjective; the state of the weather]
The detective turned *coldly* toward the suspect. [Adverb; how the action—*turning*—was performed]
The sunshine felt *wonderful*. [Adjective]
This pizza tastes unusually *good*. [Adjective]
He looked at his little brother *tenderly*. [Adverb]
Josephine always speaks *deliberately* when answering a question. [Adverb]

19d. Accuracy is required in the use of comparatives and superlatives.

Comparison is a change in form of an adjective or adverb to indicate greater or smaller degrees of quantity, quality, or manner. Change is indicated by the endings *-er* and *-est* or by the use of adverbial modifiers: *more, most, less, least.* The three degrees of comparison are *positive, comparative,* and *superlative.*

Positive	Comparative	Superlative
happy (adj.)	happier	happiest
soon (adv.)	sooner	soonest

In comparisons that indicate *less* of a quality, the words *less* and *least* are used with all adjectives and adverbs that can be compared.

Positive	Comparative	Superlative
ill	less ill	least ill
afraid	less afraid	least afraid
honest	less honest	least honest

This construction, however, can be avoided if it seems awkward.

FORMAL: She is less ill than she was this morning.
BETTER: She is not so ill.
She is better.

Most adjectives and adverbs of one syllable form the comparative degree by adding -er and the superlative degree by adding -est.

Positive	Comparative	Superlative
quick	quicker	quickest
tall	taller	tallest
cheap	cheaper	cheapest
tough	tougher	toughest

Although adjectives of two syllables nearly always add -er for the comparative and -est for the superlative, there are times when such adjectives have two forms for both comparative and superlative.

Positive	Comparative	Superlative
portly	more portly	most portly
	or	or
	portlier	portliest
rotten	more rotten	most rotten
	or	or
	rottener	rottenest

Adverbs that end in -ly and adjectives of more than two syllables usually form the comparative and superlative with more and most.

Positive	Comparative	Superlative
beautifully	more beautifully	most beautifully
rapidly	more rapidly	most rapidly
nearly	more nearly	most nearly
dutiful (adj.)	more dutiful	most dutiful
efficient (adj.)	more efficient	most efficient

Some adjectives and adverbs form their comparative and superlative irregularly.

Positive	Comparative	Superlative
good (adj.)	better	best
well (adv.)	better	best
bad (adj.)	worse	worst
badly (adv.)	worse	worst

19e. Avoid common pitfalls in using comparatives and superlatives.

When using the comparative and superlative degrees, keep in mind the following guidelines:

1. The comparative is used for comparing two persons or objects or actions; the superlative is used for comparing more than two.

I bought two new outfits. Which do you think is *more suitable?*
I bought three new outfits. Which do you think is *most suitable?*
Caribbean water is *greener* than Atlantic water.
Lynn's was the *most artistic* of all the flower arrangements.

In informal English the superlative is often used when only two things are compared:

This is the *best* of the two cars.

2. Avoid double comparatives and superlatives; that is, when *-er* or *-est* has been added to form the comparative or superlative, *more* or *most* before the word is not needed.

NONSTANDARD: She is *more older* than her sister.
STANDARD: She is *older* than her sister.

3. Choose the comparative form with care. Do not confuse the comparative of an adjective with that of an adverb.

NONSTANDARD: He carries trays *steadier* than Tommy does.
STANDARD: He carries trays *more steadily* than Tommy does.

4. A few adjectives are logically incapable of comparison because their meaning is absolute. Examples are *parallel*, *unique*, *square*, *round*, and *equal*. Two lines, actions, or ideas are "parallel" or they are not. They cannot be *more* parallel. However, these words have lost their superlative force and in informal English are often compared. Even good writers use adverbs like *entirely* or *quite* before them.

**ad
form**

19e

**5. Avoid including the subject in a comparison if the
subject is part of a group with which it is being compared.
Use *else* or *other* in such cases.**

> ILLOGICAL: Our boat is larger than any in the fleet.
>
> BETTER: Our boat is larger than any *other* in the fleet.
>
> ILLOGICAL: Mary is smarter than anyone in her class.
>
> BETTER: Mary is smarter than anyone *else* in her class.

EXERCISE 17

In each of the following sentences select the italicized form that is preferred:

1. Under a poor teacher the student is not able to learn very *rapid rapidly*.
2. If you treat some people *rude rudely*, they will be *rude rudely* to you too.
3. Many auto drivers wonder why other drivers do not drive *careful carefully*.
4. At the exhibitions in the past we have done very *good well* with our entries.
5. Everyone takes a written test and a driving test; the actual driving test is the *worse worst* of the two.
6. Jason's health has improved *some somewhat* since you last saw him.
7. It is *remarkable remarkably* to see operations in this factory function so *smooth smoothly*.
8. In rainy weather your brakes are not as *efficient efficiently* as on dry roads.
9. It takes more than money to make a person *real really* happy, but some money *certain certainly* helps.
10. I am glad to say that I am doing *excellent excellently* in all of my assignments.

EXERCISE 18

In the following sentences correct all errors in the use of adjectives and adverbs:

1. Other people bothered us some as we camped in the park.
2. My most favorite hobbies are dancing and bowling.
3. At times my friend feels both sadly and badly about his past record in school.
4. Papers are not graded as strict in high school as they are in college.

5. I can now see my problems clearer than I did last year at this time.
6. The harvest tells whether a farmer will be able to live comfortable or not.
7. My ankle hurt so bad the next day that I couldn't walk.
8. A student should make out a study schedule and should follow it reasonable close.
9. Once correct pronunciation is achieved, one can spell some words easier.
10. In a small college there is likely to be a more friendlier atmosphere than in a large university.
11. Here I am trying to succeed in three major fields—scholastically, athletically, and socially.
12. It soon became apparent that I was not going to do good on the test.
13. Since I am the youngest of two children, I really know what I am talking about.
14. Some activities help to draw a group of people closer together.
15. On icy roads some drivers turn corners too sharp and they apply the brakes too sudden.

20. Conjunctions

The three kinds of conjunctions, as well as conjunctive adverbs, are named, defined, and illustrated in Section 5. Consider that section before studying what follows.

Conjunctions, especially those that join clauses, should be selected carefully because they always indicate a logical relationship between ideas. Depending on your purpose, ideas may be coordinated or subordinated in several ways. Unless you know the different purposes of conjunctions and conjunctive adverbs, you may distort the meanings you wish to express. The following suggestions deal with choosing conjunctions and linking words to indicate the desired relationship of ideas.

20a. Specific purposes are served by conjunctions and conjunctive adverbs.

Your choice of a joining word can help you express one of ten different purposes. Many options are available because numerous conjunctions and conjunctive adverbs are available, some of which can express more than one purpose.

1. Addition

Linking words that suggest "along the same line" or "in the same direction of thought" include *and; both . . . and; not only . . . but also; also; besides; furthermore; in addition; indeed; likewise; moreover;* and *similarly.*

It was a gala affair *and* we all had a great time.

2. Contrast (difference)

The following linking words may be used to express a contrast or distinction between ideas: *although; but; however; instead; nevertheless; not only . . . but also; notwithstanding; still; whereas;* and *yet.*

Although it was a winter day, the sun felt warm.

3. Alternation

Certain linking words may be used to indicate a change back and forth between conditions or actions, an interchange in time, place, or thought. Such alternation may be affirmative ("She was eager to play and *moreover* she wanted to win") or negative ("She was eager to play *except that* she had a sore leg"). The following may be used to express alternation, affirmative or negative: *either . . . or; else; except that; however; instead; moreover; neither; neither . . . nor; nevertheless; nor; only; or; still; whereas;* and *whether.*

I'll give it all I have *or* I'll die trying. [Affirmative]
Juan wanted to go to the party; *nevertheless,* he had a job to finish. [Negative]

4. Reason, result, cause

Use *accordingly, as, as a result, because, consequently, for, hence, inasmuch as, in order that, since, so, so that, that, thereby, therefore, thus, whereas,* and *why.*

Fire damaged the hall, and *as a result* the party was canceled.

5. Example

Use *for example, indeed, for instance,* and *namely.*

You don't take good care of your car; *for example,* it needs an oil change.

6. Comparison

Use *in fact; moreover; so . . . as;* and *than.*

This is a pretty rose; *in fact,* it is the loveliest in the entire display.

7. Time

Use *after, as long as, as soon as, before, henceforth, meanwhile, once, since, then, until, when, whenever,* and *while.*

I will keep playing *as long as* the coach will let me.

8. Place

Use *whence, where,* and *wherever.*

Buddy wants to go *where* Althea wants to go.

9. Condition

Use *although, as if, as though, if, lest, once, provided, providing, though,* and *unless.*

Cissy will go *provided* she can borrow the price of a ticket.

10. Concession

Use *although, insofar as, notwithstanding, though, unless,* and *while.*

Although you have worked hard, the job is still unfinished.

20b. Correlative conjunctions should correlate only two ideas.

Since, by definition, correlative conjunctions are used in pairs, their clear and logical function is to relate two ideas, not more than two. Each member of the pair is followed by the same grammatical construction.

QUESTIONABLE: *Both* her good looks, charm, *and* talent appealed to the judges.

STANDARD: Her good looks, charm, and talent appealed to the judges.

Both her charm *and* talent appealed to the judges.

QUESTIONABLE: *Neither* noise, confusion, a crowded room, *nor* the scorn of his friends could keep Saul from studying.

STANDARD: *Neither* noise *nor* confusion could keep Saul from studying.

Noise, confusion, a crowded room, and the scorn of his friends could not keep Saul from studying.

QUESTIONABLE: It looks as if *either* Bud, Sharon, Mary Jane, *or* I will win the election.

STANDARD: Bud, Sharon, Mary Jane, or I will win the election.

Either Bud *or* Sharon will win the election, unless Mary Jane or I happen to win.

20c. *Like* as a conjunction

The use of *like* as a subordinate conjunction in clauses of comparison has increased greatly in recent years: "It looks *like* I might have to leave." A brand of cigarettes once proudly claimed that it "tastes good *like* a cigarette should." We do not avoid using *like* "*like* we once did." In standard English, *like* is used as a preposition with no following verb: "She acts *like* a competent attorney."

In careful usage, *as* or *as if* is considered preferable in clauses of comparison:

You should do *as* [not *like*] I tell you to.

The top of my head felt *as if* [not *like*] it had a heating pad on it.

The chief objection to *like* as a subordinating conjunction is not so much its inexactness as its overuse.

EXERCISE 19

Select conjunctions that are more suitable than those used in the following sentences:

1. My neighbor had an unpleasant disposition, yet I did not like him.
2. On the library cards are numbers, also the title and author of the book.
3. My mother's ancestry is Spanish, while my father is of Mexican descent.
4. A mirror is made by human beings, therefore cannot hold any magical powers.
5. This novel may have been good in your opinion, and it was not good in mine.
6. Being that I am only a freshman, I have not needed to choose a specific major yet.
7. My parents are the best parents in the world; I may sound prejudiced, but I hope that I do.
8. Whereas clans were prominent in Scotland in the seventeenth century, not every Scotsman belonged to a clan.
9. My coach was a benevolent sort of person, but she would always help us in any way possible.
10. Although I am next in line in our family as far as age goes, but I'd rather introduce you to my younger brother.
11. Our college has admitted a very large number of new students, and no additional instructors have been hired.
12. In college it doesn't matter to my teachers whether I study, where in high school the teachers were always after me to get my work done.
13. We drove around for a while, then returned to the motel for the night.
14. I was so sleepy when I finished studying until I just tumbled into bed.
15. I went to my room early that evening, but I had much work to do.

EXERCISE 20

In all but two of the following sentences, an inappropriate conjunction is used. Supply better ones. For the two appropriate uses write "S."

1. The huge boulder looked *like* it would topple over and crush us.
2. Beatrice could not make up her mind *if* she would wrestle the crocodile.
3. Bonnie not only found herself flat broke *but* discovered her friends had vanished completely.
4. The cannibal wanted stew, *and* there was nobody to put into the pot.

5. We had feared that you would give up, *or* you rarely ever did.

6. Family *and* friends are waiting for me in Bridgewater.

7. Fred told her *how that* his heart started pounding when the barking dog began running after him.

8. She was so wrapped up in her own problems *until* she did not want to listen to mine.

9. I heard on the radio *where* apple pie is losing its eminence as America's favorite dessert.

10. I do not care for that expensive blue shirt he chose, *and* I will pay for it anyway.

Punctuation
and Mechanics

One reason you may have trouble punctuating what you write is that the meaning, the purpose, and the importance of punctuation have never been clearly explained in terms that you could understand. Before you begin searching for guidance in Sections 21–34, give some thought to the following paragraphs.

What Punctuation Is and Does

When you talk you do not depend on words alone to tell your listener what you mean. Facial expressions and bodily gestures add much to the words themselves: you shrug a shoulder, wiggle a finger, raise an eyebrow, wink, swing your arms, clasp hands, bend forward or backward, grin or grimace, stamp your foot, nod or shake your head. The tone and stress of your voice influence the meanings of words you speak: you yell or whisper, speak calmly or angrily, lower or raise your voice at the end of a statement or a question. Meaning in talk is affected by pauses and halts that are often as significant as words themselves. Each of us has probably seen a skilled actor convey ideas and moods without using any words at all.

Similarly, when we write we cannot expect words alone to make clear to our reader what we have (or think we have) in mind. The pauses, stresses, and inflections that occur in speech must be represented in writing by various marks of punctuation if meaning is to be fully clear. The needs of the eye are different from those of the voice and ear.

Punctuation came into existence only for the purpose of making clear the meaning of written words. Every mark of punctuation is a sort of shorthand device or road sign provided to help readers along the way. Punctuation is effective if it helps the reader understand; it is harmful or ineffective if it slows or blocks the flow of thought from your mind to that of your readers.

Consider the matter this way: a question mark is related to the rising inflection in our voices when we ask a question. The mark indicates to the reader, "You have just read a group of words that should be interpreted as a question." An exclamation point conveys an idea of surprise or determination or command that would be indicated by a strongly emotional tone in speaking. A period represents the pause that occurs in speech when one idea has been stated and another is perhaps to be expressed; it signals to the reader, "What you have just read is a statement, a sentence or sentence-equivalent." A comma indicates a shorter pause than a period or question mark or exclamation point or, indeed, than several other marks of punctuation.

Conventional, acceptable punctuation is essential to clear, correct, effective writing because it actually helps express thoughts and the relationships among thoughts.

When you listen to conversation, you know who is speaking at any given moment; but when you read an account of a conversation, the dialog must be set off in paragraphs and the talk put between quotation marks if it is to be clear and meaningful. When you wish to refer in conversation to "a man's hat," you don't say "a man apostrophe s hat"; but when you write the phrase, that is precisely what you convey: *a man's hat.* We say "mans," but if we wrote the word that way we would be thought childish, ignorant, or both.

Again, the relationships among parts of a sentence are revealed by word order; words in an English sentence have meaning largely because of their position. But word order can be widely varied in both spoken and written English. *Beyond the door* and *the door beyond* may have quite different meanings. "*The door beyond* could be plainly seen, half open" is a clear and correct sentence. But what about "*Beyond the door* could be plainly seen, half open"? Note that the addition of a comma would make the meaning of the second sentence clear: "Beyond, the door could be plainly seen, half open."

In written English, various marks of punctuation suggest and indicate the grouping and relationship required to convey meaning clearly. That is, punctuation shows what to take together and what to separate in quick, silent reading; it suggests the relationships among words and groups of words and indicates something about their emphasis and importance. Punctuation is organically related to the sense of a sentence— to "sentence flow," as it has been called.

A merchant who sold only fuel oil and lumber was horrified, and his telephones were swamped with calls, because one of his advertisements mistakenly read: WE SELL FUEL, OIL, AND LUMBER. The addition of two commas changed the description of his business and cost him time, trouble, and money.

Here is another anecdote that will drive home the necessity of punctuation in writing and correct pauses and inflections in speaking so that meaning will be clear. A person walked into a friend's office and asked the friend's secretary, "Is she over eating?" "I hope not," was the prompt reply.

Now, what both the visitor and the secretary well knew was that the former meant to inquire whether the other person was away, across the street at a popular restaurant, "over there" and engaged in "eating." That is, he meant to ask, "Is she over, eating?" or "Is she over—eating?" or "Is she over? Eating?" Without a pause after *over* in speaking or without punctuation after it in writing, the secretary may be considered to have made a sensible reply to the query. Those who feel that the main purpose of punctuation is to indicate the stops, or breathing spaces, that are suitable in reading have a little truth on their side.

If you came across them in your reading, what sense would you make of these famous "trick" sentences, which are often used in stressing the importance of punctuation?

Jones where Smith had had had had had had had had had had the examiners approval.

That that is is that that is not is not is not that it it is.

These sentences can be punctuated in several ways, but here are acceptable methods illustrating that punctuation is indeed essential for clarity in writing:

Jones, where Smith had had "had," had had "had had." "Had had" had had the examiner's approval.

That that is, is. That that is not, is not. Is not that it? It is.

Accurate punctuation is organic, not merely mechanical and arbitrary. By organic is meant "belonging to, an essential part of." If you doubt that clear punctuation is an integral part of written English, ask someone to copy a page from a book or a few paragraphs from a newspaper story, omitting all marks of punctuation. Try to read what the person has written. Yes, you can probably make sense of the passage, but how much extra time and effort did you expend? Suitable punctuation is in itself a form of communication. And communication is, or should be, the primary purpose of writing.

Variations in Punctuation

Punctuation usage does vary with individual writers, but not as much as you may have thought and then only to the extent that communication from writer to reader is aided, not impeded. Possibly as much as one-fourth of punctuation is a matter of personal taste—but only to the extent that the marks used help make the words themselves fully clear. This leaves most of punctuation a fairly rigid matter of "rules." Certain basic practices and principles of punctuation remain steadfast and have done so for many decades. These principles may be called "descriptive rules," since they have been formulated from hundreds of thousands of examples as applied by reputable writers and, much more important, by professional editors and printers.

Variations in practice occur, and writers interpret the shorthand symbols of punctuation in different ways, but the areas of agreement far exceed those of disagreement. What is normally considered correct punctuation has been fixed over the years by professional workers following the advice and suggestions set forth in standard guidebooks and dictionaries. These guidebooks have slowly evolved from observed practices in carefully written English.

When a large number of examples of one use of a mark of punctuation has been gathered, a general rule is phrased thus: "Always use the . . ." When a majority of examples agree, the rule is stated as follows: "This mark is usually used . . ." When examples of the use of a mark of punctuation for a particular purpose are insufficient to make a generalization, the rule will state that "the mark is occasionally used . . ."

Certain marks are always used to accomplish a particular purpose. To fulfill other aims, other marks may be used somewhat indiscriminately and loosely. But the dominant aim of every mark of punctuation and mechanics is to aid in making writing clear. This is the only true aim of all punctuation.

Punctuation, then, is a system—call it a *method* or a *set of symbols,* if you wish—by which you try to make the meaning of what you write not only clear but unmistakable. The most important marks of punctuation are the following:

.	period	,	comma
?	question mark	;	semicolon
!	exclamation point	:	colon
—	dash	" "	double quotation marks
-	hyphen	' '	single quotation marks
'	apostrophe	( )	parentheses

Mechanics, a rather vague term, is closely related to punctuation. Mechanics applies to the conventional uses of small letters and capitals, to the writing of numbers in letters or figures, and to abbreviations, italics (underlining), accent marks, and spelling.

The Primary Purposes of Punctuation and Mechanics

In studying the sections that follow, you will apply a specific rule, principle, or convention of punctuation or mechanics to a specific sentence or part of a sentence. It may help to understand that all punctuation and some mechanical marks have one of four purposes: (1) to terminate, (2) to introduce, (3) to separate, or (4) to enclose.

To terminate

Even the most long-winded speaker eventually runs out of breath and must end a statement in order to inhale and start again. In writing, as in speech, the basic unit of thought is the sentence. Now, a sentence, whether in speech or in writing, may vary in length from one word to many hundreds, but it has to end somewhere, sometime. When you come to the end of a statement in speech, you are likely to lower (drop) your voice and pause before proceeding. In writing, the end of a statement is always correctly noted by an end stop (terminal mark of punctuation).

The period is used to end more than nine out of ten sentences. However, if your statement is in the form of a question, you use a question mark to end it. If the statement expresses surprise, strong emotion, or a command of some sort, it may properly be terminated by an exclamation point. The use of these three terminal marks has a distinct influence upon the meaning conveyed:

What do you mean? You are leaving town.

What? Do you mean you are leaving town?

What! Do you mean you are leaving town!

Other marks of punctuation are occasionally used to terminate a statement. A colon may be used to end what is actually an introductory statement when that which follows begins with a capital letter. A statement that is broken off or interrupted may be ended with a dash. Also, a statement that is left unfinished may be terminated by ellipsis periods (three or four dots).

This is what Mary Ann said to me: "Start at once and keep going."

"I hardly know what to say to express—" The speaker halted abruptly.

Perhaps I should have kept quiet. Perhaps I should have protested. Perhaps . . .

To introduce

In writing as in speech, we often lead up to a statement with a preliminary one or pave the way for a comment with words that actually serve as an introduction. Only three of the marks of punctuation are regularly used to introduce words or statements: commas, colons, and dashes. (The sentence you have just read illustrates this principle; what precedes the colon builds to what follows it.)

I need only one thing, a good moped.

Your task is simple: Get a job and hold it.

He has only one passion in life—rock music.

To separate

For writing to be clear, sometimes individual words or groups of words must be separated from others in the same sentence. To separate parts of sentences, use a comma, a semicolon, a dash, a hyphen, or an apostrophe. Remember, though, that these five marks cannot be used interchangeably for this purpose.

If you wish to go, please give me back my shirt.

This man loves his work and is happy; that one hates his and is miserable.

Money, fame, power—these were our goals.

She is now our president-elect.

This store is crowded every day from noon until 2 o'clock.

To enclose

To enclose parts of a sentence or longer units of expression, you may use commas, dashes, quotation marks, single quotation marks, parentheses, and brackets. Most enclosing marks are customarily used in pairs (two of each) except when a capital letter at the beginning of a sentence takes the place of one of them or when a terminal mark of punctuation replaces the second.

An unusual habit, *eating two breakfasts every day,* seemed to make him sluggish during morning hours.

He was not—*and everyone else knew this*—a well man.

"I am not an American," *she said fatuously;* "I am a citizen of the world."

"To say this dance is *'groovy'* is not a useful comment," remarked the young girl.

When I am ready to go (*and that will be soon*) I shall let you know.

"The supervisor on this job [*Ned Stephens*] is an excellent worker himself," remarked the superintendent.

Punctuation marks are sometimes interchangeable. Both the comma and dash, for example, can introduce, separate, and enclose material, but this ability does not mean that one is not preferable to the other in a given sentence designed to convey a particular meaning. To achieve the specific purpose of punctuation that you have in mind, select the mark that will most effectively transmit the intended meaning.

You should also note that marks of punctuation have differing degrees of strength. A period is a stronger mark than a semicolon or comma; it points out the most important division of thought, the sentence. A semicolon is weaker than a period but stronger than a comma; used within the sentence, it points out longer or more important groups than the comma usually does. The comma indicates a brief pause or less complete separation than the semicolon; it separates short groups within the sentence and suggests a comparatively close connection with what precedes and follows it.

A great deal in writing is a matter of convention and cannot be solved by resorting to common sense. Nor can all the rules and principles of punctuation be called sensible and logical. But if you are aware that something you are writing requires punctuation, apply whatever common sense is involved. Sometimes, it's considerable.

21. End stops

21a

Punctuation at the end of a sentence is called an *end stop*. Sometimes called *terminal marks,* end stops include *periods, question marks,* and *exclamation points.*

It is said that Victor Hugo, the famed nineteenth-century French writer, wrote the shortest letter on record. Wishing to know how his latest novel was selling, he sent a sheet of paper to his publisher on which appeared a single question mark. His publisher, pleased to report good news, replied with a single exclamation point. If you wish to know how you stand with an absent loved one, you might copy Hugo's letter. If you do, however, you run the risk of receiving in reply another question mark or, worse luck, a period.

The period

21a. Use a period at the end of a declarative sentence.

A declarative sentence states a fact, a condition, or a possibility and is distinguished from an interrogative sentence (which asks a question), an imperative sentence (which expresses a command or a strong request), and an exclamatory sentence (which expresses strong feeling or surprise). Sometimes, only punctuation will indicate whether a written sentence is declarative, interrogative, exclamatory, or imperative; in speech, this distinction is shown by tone of voice and inflection.

His trip began with an inspection of the missile base.
She prefers winter to summer vacations.

These are obvious statements of fact, or supposed fact, and are terminated by a period. But they might be spoken, or written, to indicate something other than a statement of fact:

His trip began with an inspection of the missile base! Did it really? What a surprise!
She prefers winter to summer vacations! Isn't this an unusual attitude? I have a different opinion.

21a

We are here concerned with punctuation, not with so-called grammar or rhetoric. But it might help to comment on the grammar of a *sentence:* by one somewhat incomplete definition, a *sentence* is a group of words containing a subject and a predicate and expressing a complete thought. Yet various kinds of statement express a complete thought without a stated or implied subject or predicate. Do they require a period or other terminal mark of punctuation? Is it incorrect so to punctuate such "sentence fragments," as they are called?

Perhaps you noticed the sentence, "What a surprise!" in the preceding examples. By definition, this is not a complete sentence: it contains no verb (predicate). But it does express a complete thought and may be ended with a terminal mark. You should be careful to write sentence fragments (or "period faults," as they are sometimes called) only for stylistic effect—and not because you don't know what a sentence is or should be. (If you are in doubt, refer to Section 41.) However, sentence fragments like the following are justifiable and effective and may be punctuated as complete statements:

"Where have you been?"
"Eating."
"Where?"
"Across the street at Dirty Joe's."
"Fricasseed hummingbird wings, no doubt!"
"At Dirty Joe's? Stale pizza—burned."

He walked as though he were in a trance. Dreaming. Dreaming? Not likely. He was more detached than that. Farther away. Lost in his own world.

21b. Use a period after an indirect question.

Words like *what, when, how,* and *why* often introduce parts of sentences that suggest a question in such an indirect way that no question mark is called for. Use a period after such sentences as these:

The supervisor asked me when I could come to work.
Please tell me what she said and how she said it.
The judge said she wanted to know why I couldn't pay the fine.

21d

21c. Use a period after a mild command or a polite request.

A direct command is usually followed by an exclamation point; a direct question is followed by a question mark. On occasion, a command or question may be so mildly imperative or interrogative that a period should be used; the purpose is to suggest, rather than to issue a command or ask a question requiring an answer.

Put first things first.
May we please have a prompt reply to this letter.
Will you kindly sign and return the enclosed form.

21d. Use a period after most abbreviations.

Mr. and Mrs. Jackson Hogan
Jeanne L. Sexton, M.D. (b. 1930, d. 1978)
Feb. 19, S.C., St., Ave., oz., bbl., Blvd., Dr., Ms.

Notes:

1. If a declarative sentence ends with an abbreviation, use only one period:
   She bought clothing, food, fuel, etc.
2. If an interrogative or exclamatory sentence ends with an abbreviation, the question mark or exclamation point follows the abbreviation period:
   Is her home in Baltimore, Md.?
   Her home is not in Baltimore, Md.! You are mistaken.

3. Inside the sentence, an abbreviation period is followed by any mark that would normally be used:
She lives in Baltimore, Md.; my home is in Severna Park.
This is the meaning of A.W.O.L.: absent without official leave.

21e. Use a period before a decimal, to separate dollars and cents, to precede cents written alone, and in metric symbols.

5.25 percent	$0.95
$15.67	3 cc. (cubic centimeters)

21f. Use three spaced periods to indicate an omission.

Such periods, called *ellipses,* indicate an omission of one or more words within a sentence or quotation. If the omission ends with a period, use four spaced periods.

"In the spring a young man's fancy . . ."
"Some books are to be tasted, others . . . swallowed, and some few . . . chewed and digested."
Susie began to recite the alphabet (*a, b, c* . . .).
The day wore on from sunrise to midmorning . . . steaming noon . . . blistering afternoon . . . cooling sunset.
Something told José to go slowly, to take his time, to think, to . . . .

21g. Avoid overusing the period.

1. Use no periods after contractions (which are shortened words but not true abbreviations): *don't, isn't, shan't, etc.*
2. Use no periods after ordinal numbers when written thus: *1st, 2nd, etc.: the 1st Battalion.*
3. Use no periods after nicknames or names that are not truly abbreviations of longer forms: *Bill, Al, Alex, Jo, Min,* etc.
4. Use no periods after familiar shorthand forms of words (which are not recommended in most writing), such as *ad, taxi, cab, auto, phone, exam, percent,* and *lab.*

5. Use no periods after certain specialized abbreviations: Station KDKA, NBC, UNESCO, WAVES, TB (for *tuberculosis*), TV (for *television*).

6. Use no periods after chemical symbols, even though they are abbreviations: O for *oxygen;* NaCl for *sodium chloride.*

7. Use no periods after Roman numerals: *Louis XIV, Chapter VII, Section XI.*

The question mark

?

21i

21h. Use a question mark at the end of every direct question.

It is usually easy to recognize a direct query, but sometimes a sentence that is declarative in form may actually be interrogative in sense. Also, remember that a question mark should never be used after an indirect question. Again, although the question mark is considered a terminal (end of sentence) mark, it may appear elsewhere in a sentence than at the end. Note the punctuation of the following:

Does he really love her?
He really does love her.
John asked, "May I go with you today?" [Direct question]
John asked whether he might go today. [Indirect question]
What is the penalty for late payment? is the question.
Who asked "When?" [Note the single question mark.]
Did you say "Get out and stay out"? [Question mark outside of quotation mark.]

21i. Use question marks to indicate a series of questions in the same sentence.

Will you go with me? or will your friend? or someone?
Who will be there? Carol? Sam? Pam? Rick?
Do you remember when you had to empty a drip pan under the icebox? When car windshields opened to let in a breeze? When men's shoestrings laced halfway up through eyes and the rest of

the way 'round the hooks? When radios came in two pieces, the speaker being separate? You could mail a letter with a two-cent stamp? Men wore garters? Grandmothers were elderly women?

Note that in the first example small letters rather than capitals follow the question marks. Actually, capital letters could be used in this situation, but they are normally employed when each of the series of questions is a sentence or nearly a sentence, as in the third illustration, or when the series consists of proper names, as in the second illustration. That is, an individual sentence normally has only one terminal mark of punctuation, and all letters preceding it are small except the first letter of the first word in the sentence and any others that are proper nouns or require capitals for some other reason.

21j. Use a question mark enclosed in parentheses to express doubt or uncertainty.

This use of the question mark is debatable and is not recommended for regular or consistent use. Usually it suggests that we have been lazy about securing exact information or are afraid to speak our minds clearly and forcefully. Sometimes, however, we have no other recourse.

This is a genuine (?) amethyst, or at least it looks like one.
Shakespeare was born on April 23 (?), 1564.

If you are not an expert and have no access to one, the question mark in the first example is justified. It is clearly indicated in the second example, since experts themselves differ about the exact date.

The exclamation point

21k. Use an exclamation point to express surprise, command, emphasis, or strong emotion.

The exclamation point has been called "the period that blew its top." This description is apt. An exclamation point is a period wearing a conical hat (on many typewriter keyboards it is made by using a period topped by an apostrophe) and resembles the period in that it is usually, but not always, a terminal mark. And it has "blown its top" in appearance and in the sense that it is a mark suggesting strong emotion, surprise, emphasis, or a direct command of some sort.

The exclamation point (or exclamation mark) should be used thoughtfully and sparingly. Overuse of this device—frequent in advertisements, informal letters, and many short stories, plays, and novels—causes it to lose much of its effectiveness. The emotion expressed should be strong, the surprise genuine, the emphasis or command really vigorous, even imperative, to warrant its use.

!

21k

A good rule to follow is this: Never use an exclamation point when another mark will serve adequately. The sentences that follow exhibit legitimate use of this mark:

So you really decided to pay the bill? What an idiot!

That was an incredibly rude remark!

The doctor said—how lucky you are!—that you will soon be all right.

Get moving at once!

"Big deal!" Miriam said scornfully.

Notes:

1. Use exclamation points rarely and only for a definite and clear reason.
2. When you do use an exclamation point, use only one.
3. An exclamation point after a long sentence looks silly. Most of us don't have sufficient breath to exclaim more than a few words at a time.

EXERCISE 1

A. Circle the periods, question marks, and exclamation points in three paragraphs in a current magazine or in a book that you are reading. Account for the use of each mark by reference to one of the principles cited in Section 21. If requested, give an oral report on your findings.

B. Use the period, exclamation point, and question mark correctly in the following sentences. If any of these marks are used incorrectly, make the necessary corrections.

1. Two planes leave this city for Rome every day, one at 9:30 AM and one at 3:00 PM

2. By now you have learned the value of a good dictionary, haven't you.

3. I thought I would not get homesick. How wrong I was.

4. Dr Smith is the best dentist in town; we and our neighbors, Mr and Mrs Thompson, have gone to him for years.

5. It is amazing how many good intentions—or should I say resolutions—I have.

6. There in the hallway was my sister, home from overseas. What a pleasant surprise.

7. They are wondering why they are not making more money, or why they did not get an advancement?

8. What is an education good for if you do not have friends.

9. Oh. Oh. Have I forgotten to turn off the stove again.

10. One may ask why something happened to Hal after a black cat crossed his path?

22. The semicolon

The *semicolon* (;) is entirely a mark of separation or division; that is, it is never used to introduce, enclose, or end a statement. It is a stronger mark than the comma, signifying a greater break or a longer pause between sentence elements. But it is weaker than the period and other terminal marks (question mark, exclamation point) and cannot be used to end a sentence. Its most common use indicates that two or more statements are not sufficiently related to require commas but are too closely related to justify being put in separate sentences.

The word *semicolon* is a misnomer. The prefix *semi-* has a meaning of "half," so that a semicolon might be thought of as "half a colon." Until about a century ago, colons and semicolons were occasionally used interchangeably, but they have distinctly different uses now. A colon is primarily a mark for introducing or summarizing; a semicolon is a mark of separation. You will have a clearer idea of the purpose of the semicolon if you think of it as a "reduced period," a "half-period," or a "semiperiod." Or you may regard this hybrid mark as a cross between a comma and a period.

The semicolon is a specialized coordinating mark of punctuation;

it is properly used only between elements of a sentence that are coordinate, that is, of equal grammatical rank. Such grammatical terminology and distinction can be troublesome; a good general rule is that in most instances (but not all) you should insert a semicolon only when use of a period could be justified, despite the fact that the semicolon is exclusively an internal (within the sentence) mark.

22a. **Use a semicolon to separate independent clauses (complete statements) that are not joined by a coordinating conjunction (*and, but, or, nor, for, yet*).**

; 22a

Complete statements are more often separated by periods than by semicolons, but the use of semicolons is justifiable and even preferable when the thought relationship of the statements is close. In both theory and practice, the following punctuation is correct:

I am certain you will like this apartment; it will suit you perfectly.

The stupid believe that to be truthful is easy; the artists, the great artists, know how difficult it is.

—WILLA CATHER

A little neglect may breed mischief: For want of a nail the shoe was lost; for want of a shoe the horse was lost; for want of a horse the rider was lost.

—BENJAMIN FRANKLIN

The first tinge of gold is in the maples; the first smell of wood smoke is in the air; the tourists are gone. The squirrels are at work; mists drop from the boughs; leaves float down.

You cannot run away from a weakness; you must some time fight it out or perish.

—ROBERT L. STEVENSON

Lord, I believe; help thou mine unbelief.

—MARK

We always like those who admire us; we do not always like those whom we admire.

—LA ROCHEFOUCAULD

We know nothing of tomorrow; our business is to be good and happy today.

—SYDNEY SMITH

The semicolon

A semicolon is needed between complete statements that are lengthy or contain internal punctuation. A period might substitute for the semicolon, but hardly a comma or a comma and a conjunction, in sentences like these:

> As long as war is regarded as wicked, it will have its fascination; when it is looked upon as vulgar, it will cease to be popular.
>
> —OSCAR WILDE

> Whatsoever thy hand findeth to do, do it with thy might; for there is no work, nor device, nor knowledge, nor wisdom in the grave, whither thou goest.
>
> —ECCLESIASTES

> It is easy in the world to live after the world's opinion; it is easy in solitude to live after your own; but the great man is he, who, in the midst of the world, keeps with perfect sweetness the independence of solitude.
>
> —EMERSON

> The days of our years are threescore years and ten; and if by reason of strength they be fourscore years, yet is their strength labor and sorrow; for it is soon cut off, and we fly away.
>
> —PSALMS

22b. Use a semicolon to separate independent clauses (complete statements) joined by a conjunctive adverb.

Conjunctive adverbs are special kinds of adverbs that can sometimes be used as conjunctions and can be moved around in sentences, whereas conjunctions have fixed positions. (See Section 5.) The most frequently used conjunctive adverbs are the following:

accordingly	henceforth	nevertheless
also	however	otherwise
anyhow	in addition	similarly
as a result	in fact	so
besides	indeed	still
consequently	instead	surely
finally	likewise	then
for example	meanwhile	therefore
furthermore	moreover	thus
hence	namely	yet

;

22b

He tried for two months to learn to use a slide rule; *then* he quit trying and admitted his failure.

The work is not simple; *however,* it is exciting and rewarding.

Jim's sister is a busy girl; *in fact,* she works harder than he does.

Keep in mind these explanatory comments:

1. Use a semicolon immediately before the conjunctive adverb when the latter comes between independent clauses. The semicolon alone separates the clauses if the conjunctive adverb is shifted in position; enclosing the adverb with commas will depend on its parenthetic strength.

22b

He tried for three months to learn to use a slide rule; he *then* quit trying and admitted his failure.

The work is not simple; it is, *however,* exciting and rewarding.

Jim's sister is a busy girl; she works harder, *in fact,* than he does.

2. When the conjunctive adverb comes between the clauses, should there be a comma after it? In the absence of an unvarying principle, use as a guide the weakness or strength of the word or phrase, parenthetically, in relation to the second clause. If it is weak, omit the comma; if it is strong, use a comma; if it is mildly strong, like *therefore,* use or omit, depending on your desire to indicate a pause. Another guide: a comma usually follows a long conjunctive adverb or phrase (*nevertheless, in fact, for example,* etc.) but rarely follows a shorter one (*thus, hence, then,* etc.).

I have trained myself to read rapidly and carefully; *thus* I save myself many hours a week.

I did not favor spending the money; *nevertheless,* I did not vote against the proposal.

This climate is subject to sudden weather changes; *consequently* (or *consequently,*) you should bring a variety of clothing.

The soldier was totally unsuited to combat duty; *therefore,* he was transferred to a base camp.

The soldier was totally unsuited to combat duty; he was *therefore* transferred to a base camp.

22c

3. Distinguish between a conjunctive adverb and a simple conjunction. A conjunctive adverb is both a conjunction and an adverb; as such, it has an adverbial function that no simple conjunction (such as *and* or *but*) possesses. Furthermore, it is used only with independent clauses, or sentences, whereas a simple conjunction may join words, phrases, dependent clauses, independent clauses, or even sentences.

4. Distinguish between a conjunctive adverb placed between independent clauses and a subordinating conjunction (*although, because, since, whereas, inasmuch as*) **introducing a dependent clause. The subordinating conjunction is preceded by a semicolon in such uses only when no coordinating conjunction joins the independent clauses.**

> I shall attend the lecture this evening, *although I can ill afford the time.* [A dependent clauses follows an independent clause.]
> I am having trouble counting money and making change; *because I was never good in arithmetic,* I think that I'll be assigned to another department. [Two independent clauses are separated, the second being introduced by a dependent clause. Two sentences might be preferable, since writing should be immediately clear to the reader.]

22c. Avoid overuse of the semicolon.

The semicolon has definite uses. Like all other marks, it should be neither incorrectly used nor overused. Especially avoid using semicolons in the following ways:

1. Do not use a semicolon to set off phrases or dependent clauses unless for the purposes indicated earlier. Ordinarily, the semicolon has the same function as a period: It indicates a complete break, the end of one thought and the beginning of another. One fairly safe guide is, "no period, no semicolon." Setting off dependent clauses or phrases with semicolons will confuse your readers.

WRONG: *Inasmuch as Joe has a fiery temper;* we have to be careful what we say to him. [Dependent clause]

WRONG: The next meeting of the club has been postponed two weeks; *because most of the members are on an inspection trip to Detroit.* [Dependent clause]

WRONG: *Being careful to observe all traffic regulations;* I am considered a good driver. [Participial phrase]

WRONG: *The excitement of our mock political campaign having died down;* we once again turned our attention to our jobs. [Absolute phrase]

To correct semicolon errors like these, use no punctuation or use a comma instead of the semicolon.

22c

2. Do not use a semicolon as a mark of introduction.

WRONG: My purpose is simple; to succeed in my job.

WRONG: (in Business Letters): Dear Sir; Dear Mr. Woods;

To correct semicolon errors like the foregoing, substitute colons or commas for the semicolons.

3. Do not use a semicolon as a summarizing mark.

Answering the phone, typing, filing; these were my duties that summer.

Use a dash or a colon instead of the semicolon shown.

EXERCISE 2

A. How are semicolons misused in these sentences?

1. We had heard that ghosts played in the cemetery nearby; and that they could be seen as cars drove along.
2. In the article, "How Ships Are Built"; I learned something about the superstitions that exist around shipyards.
3. "It won't work, I'm too old;" he said.
4. Although many people say that they do not believe Friday, the 13th, is unlucky; they are still extra cautious on that day.

5. You cannot come to class with the attitude; "Well, here I am. Teach me."

6. But whatever the case, most of her "ideas" have come true; quite a feat for a sixteenth-century author.

7. I succeeded in learning a little Portuguese; at least enough so that I could speak to the police officer.

8. This is strictly a form letter (even without salutation); although the letterhead and different-colored inks attract the reader's attention.

9. Sadness can come after a series of little disappointments; which at the time do not seem important.

10. It is a difference that is easy to see; yet hard to explain.

11. This assignment was a little odd; because I was responsible for the safety of people who were older than I.

12. It's a dreary, cold winter day; and it looks as if the racing black clouds will blanket the city with snow.

13. Finally to complete our overall picture of Mexico; we saw the churches.

14. If you like warm weather, like to travel, and have money; you would like to spend a winter in Florida.

15. An invalid's life requires not only the constant attention of the physician; but also the complete cooperation of his family.

B. The following sentences contain conjunctive adverbs or conjunctive adverb phrases. Where should semicolons (and commas) go?

1. We arrived in New York late at night thus we could not see much of the "big city."

2. A dress designer usually makes $15,000 to $20,000 a year however a famous dress designer can name his or her own price.

3. At first everyone laughed at the idea then someone said "Why not?"

4. The fog was so thick that our boat barely reached shore indeed I know of two boats that didn't.

5. The use of English refers generally to writing and speaking however my dictionary also gives information about the origin and history of words.

6. A conscience does not have a law to guide it in fact it has no guide other than one possibly developed within itself.

7. We do not plan to go on a tour therefore we can choose the places we wish to visit.

8. At home there were plenty of parties otherwise the holiday season would have been rather dull.

9. I have to choose one of four languages as a result I am seriously considering Russian, German, French, and Spanish.

10. Some people are not afraid of anything at least they do not act as if they are.

23. The colon

The *colon* (:) is a mark of expectation or addition. Its function is to signal the reader to "watch for what's coming." That is, it signals to the reader that the next group of words will fulfill what the last group promised. What comes after the colon is usually explanatory or illustrative material that has been prepared for by a word, or words, preceding the colon.

Major uses of the colon are to introduce lists, tabulations, enumerations; to introduce a word, phrase, or even a clause; to precede an example or clarification of an idea suggested before the colon; to introduce a restatement of a preceding phrase or clause; to spell out details of a generalization; and to introduce a formal quotation.

The colon is a somewhat formal mark of punctuation and is less often used than a semicolon. It does have its specific purpose, however, and should not be carelessly replaced by a dash, semicolon, or comma. Neither should it be overused, since it does mark a definite break in sentence thought.

The colon is also a mark of separation in certain instances involving several miscellaneous constructions.

23a. Use a colon to introduce a word, phrase, or clause and after an introductory statement that shows something is to follow.

Here are examples of the colon used in its primary function:

Only one course remains: to get out of here as soon as possible.

To sum up: work hard, save your money, watch your health, and trust in God.

This is my next problem: Where do I go now?

"We are never deceived: We deceive ourselves."

Two types of error occur: sampling error and non-sampling error.

Everything was in order: Chairs were arranged, windows were closed, lights were turned on.

The purpose of study is not only learning: it is also enjoyment.

Gray behaved well at the party: He spoke to all visitors, unwrapped his presents slowly, expressed his thanks, and ate his ice cream carefully.

Respect is not seized, it is earned: it is bestowed most often upon those not directly seeking it.

She thought that the main difficulty with giving back the country to the Indians was this: they would never take it and assume all the mortgages.

Jefferson concluded his First Inaugural Address as follows: "And may that Infinite Power which rules the destinies of the universe lead our councils to what is best and give them a favorable issue for your peace and prosperity."

23b. Use a colon as a separating mark in special situations.

It is not always easy to decide whether a colon introduces or separates, but in the following illustrations the colon seems to separate more than to introduce:

1. In *business letters,* the salutation is separated from the body of the letter by a colon: *Dear Sir: Dear Ms. Jammes: Gentlemen: My dear Mr. Burnside:*

2. *Titles,* and *subtitles of books* may be separated by a colon: *The English Novel: A Panorama; Education for College: Improving the High School Curriculum.*

3. *Hour and minute figures* in writing time may be separated by a colon: 10:15; 4:46 P.M. In England, a period is often substituted for the colon in such uses, a practice that is increasingly being adopted by some American publications. The colon, however, is both clear and customary.

4. *Scenes and acts of plays* may be separated by a colon: Shakespeare's *Twelfth Night,* II:v. The use of a period for the colon in this construction is increasing, but the colon seems clearer and therefore preferable.

5. *Bible chapters and verses* may be separated by a colon: Exodus 12:31. Some authorities, including the *Chicago Manual of Style* and the *Government Printing Office Style Manual,* recommend that italics not be used for names of books of the Bible, but both insist on the colon rather than the period in this construction.

6. *Volume and page references* may be separated by a colon: *The History of the English Novel,* IV:77.

7. *A publisher's name and location* may be separated by a colon: *New York: W. W. Norton & Company.*

8. *In stating proportions,* both a single colon and a double colon may be used: 2:4::4:8 (two is to four as four . . .).

23c. Place the colon properly.

A colon is placed outside quotation marks. If introductory material calling for the use of a colon ends with words in parentheses, place the colon outside the closing parenthesis. Note these examples:

> This is the first line of Jonson's "Song to Celia": "Drink to me only with thine eyes."
> For his tardiness he had an excuse (a silly one): he had failed to set his alarm clock.

23d. Avoid overuse of the colon.

The colon is a useful mark adding clarity to writing, but it should be used only to introduce and, in special situations, to separate.

1. Do not place a colon between a preposition and its object.

> I am fond of: New Orleans, Seattle, and Denver. [There is no need for the colon or, indeed, for any mark of punctuation after *of.*]

2. Do not place a colon between a verb and its object or object complement.

> He likes to see: TV plays, movies, and hockey games. [Use no mark of punctuation after *see.*]
> She enjoys such activities as: swimming, dancing, and playing soccer. [Use no mark after *as.*]

3. Do not carelessly use the colon for the dash as a summarizing mark. The colon anticipates, whereas a summarizing dash suggests that something has preceded.

Mutual funds, savings accounts, common stocks: These are popular methods of investing. [A colon can be used in this construction, but a dash is preferable.]

4. Do not use a colon after such introductory words as *namely, for instance,* **and** *for example* **unless what follows consists of a complete statement. Otherwise, use a comma, not a colon.** *As follows* **or** *the following* **normally requires the use of a colon, since the introducing words are incomplete without the illustrative or listed items that follow them.**

23d

5. A good general rule for avoiding incorrect overuse of the colon is this: Never use a colon directly after any verb or after the conjunction *that.*

<u>EXERCISE 3</u>

Some of the following sentences need colons and some already have them—used either properly or inaccurately. Check each sentence carefully and make each one correct in its use of the colon.

1. A pilot looks for two main items when checking the weather visibility and the direction and velocity of the winds.
2. Someone has said: "True achievement is measured by how much better off the world is for our having lived in it."
3. Some fields of study in civil engineering are: airport planning, architecture, bridge building, city planning, and road construction.
4. All of my jobs had one thing in common they showed me the varied reactions of many people.
5. Basically, the role Mr. Bennet assumes as both father and husband may be summed up in one word: failure.
6. Don't get me wrong I am not going to leave my future to Fate.
7. Another winter scene that I like is this a group of trees covered with snow, and a path winding down a hill.
8. Information is supplied concerning colleges such as: accreditation, control, date of founding, and location.

9. I have taught my dog a few simple tricks like: shaking hands, sitting up, rolling over, and lying down.
10. Now the thought struck me what am I doing here?
11. My dictionary has several pages of symbols on: astronomy, biology, chemistry, and mathematics.
12. At Derbytown there was everything that a person could imagine activities from horseback riding to swimming.
13. Among favorite winter sports at some colleges are: ice-skating, sledding, and tobogganing.
14. Three types of students: the mama's boys and girls, the boisterous types, and the shy, lonesome ones will be among those coming to college this September.
15. Practically all European family names were derived in one or more of the following ways (1) place of birth, (2) occupation, (3) ancestral names, or (4) a descriptive nickname.

24

24. The dash

The *dash* (—) is an emphatic mark of punctuation that is used to indicate a sudden interruption in thought, a sharp break, or a shift in thought. It has been called "the interruption, the mark of abruptness, the sob, the stammer, and the mark of ignorance." This colorful definition implies that the dash is a vigorous mark that has emotional qualities and should be used with care.

A dash is a standard mark of punctuation not represented on the usual typewriter keyboard. In typing, the dash is made by two hyphens (- -); in handwriting, it is shown by a line about as long as two hyphens. In printing, the mark is referred to as an *em dash*. Actually, printers use three dashes: an *en dash* (which in typing and handwriting is represented by a mark the length of a hyphen), the *em dash* (two hyphens), and the *2-em* (or sometimes longer) dash. The double dash, or long dash, is rarely needed in writing. The em dash (—) is what we usually have in mind when we talk about dashes in writing.

Some other mark of punctuation can usually be substituted for a dash. However, a dash lends an air of surprise or emotional tone on occasion and, if used sparingly, is a useful device for adding movement, or a sense of movement, to writing. But it is rightly called a "mark of ignorance," since some writers use it far too often.

This versatile mark of punctuation can be used to separate, terminate, interrupt, introduce, or enclose, and to indicate the omission of words, figures, or letters. You should restrict use of the dash to the purposes suggested here.

24a. Use a dash to introduce a word or group of words to which you wish to give emphasis.

What he needed most he never got—a satisfying job.
That is our most serious question—can we find a buyer for our old car?

In such constructions as these either a colon or a comma could be used; the dash adds vigor, emphasis, and a quality of emotion.

24b. Use a pair of dashes to enclose words or phrases that you wish to emphasize.

I think—no, I am positive—that you should leave at once.
If you do win the game—and try hard!—telephone me promptly.
Through clandestine channels—a small man wearing red suspenders—I discovered that the idea had originated with one of the secretaries.
Only three candidates for office—Wilson of the Order Department, Jones of Sales, and Thomas of Shipping—were present at the meeting.

A pair of commas or two parentheses could replace the dashes in each of these sentences, but they would not so sharply set off and distinguish the parenthetical material.

24c. Use a dash to indicate a sudden break or shift in thought.

When I was in high school—but I have already talked about that.
Do we—can we—dare we ask for mercy, not justice?

I started to say, "But—" "But me no *but's,*" roared the supervisor.

24d. Use a dash to separate a final statement summarizing an idea from that which precedes it.

Freedom to work as we please and where we wish, freedom to worship or not to worship, freedom to travel or stay at home—these are basic desires of most of us.

In this separating and summarizing use of the dash, no other marks of punctuation should appear with it. A colon could replace the dash but might be less effective.

24e. Use a dash (or double dash) to indicate an unfinished statement or word.

"Neither of us could spell the word *erysip—*"
When he entered, Jack began, "Mr. Pope, may I ask—"
Quickly, Mr. Pope broke in, "You may not."
Query. Did you start— *Answer.* No, Judge.

A double dash is normally used at the end of a statement, a regular em dash within the line. When a statement ends with a dash, use no other mark of punctuation.

24f. Use a dash to indicate the omission of letters and words and to connect combinations of letters and figures.

Senator S— was then charged with perjury.
We were in one h— of a predicament when that happened.
June—October (June to or through October)
She lived in that city in 1970—1972.
Ed used to fly a DC—8 on the New York—San Juan run.
The speech was carried on a CBS—NBC—ABC hookup.

24f

The dash

In typing or handwriting, a hyphen (-) might be substituted in each of these examples except the first two; in them, a long dash could also be used.

Do not use a dash in expressions like those just listed when the word *from* or *between* appears:

From June to (or through) October [Not *From June—October*]
Between 1958 and 1962 [Not *Between 1958—1962*]

A final word about the dash: use it sparingly. It is a strong and noticeable mark and should not be employed as a lazy substitute for more exact marks of punctuation or to indicate omitted ideas where you have nothing particular in mind.

24f

EXERCISE 4

A. Pick out all the dashes you can find on a page from a magazine or a book that you are reading. Account for the use (or misuse) of each.

B. Where should dashes be placed in the following sentences? Why?

1. "She stands . . . with beauty in her heart and bounty in her hands" that is how one city is described in a song about it.
2. Very soon it is a matter of only a few weeks now Monica will be a United States citizen.
3. The Plains of Abraham, the beautiful St. Lawrence River, and the Citadel these are among the places to be seen in Quebec.
4. The old gentleman had given Michael a hungry, beaten man adequate food, clothing, and shelter.
5. This area, like most, is very hilly you might even say mountainous and covered with much tall timber and brush.
6. Instead of getting up at 4 A.M. and studying as I did this morning I will sleep until the last possible moment during vacation.
7. After walking for miles at least it seemed that way to me I realized that the scenery did not look familiar.
8. My twin sister and I have always been very close a fact that has helped us many times and we give moral and physical support to each other.
9. Kings and presidents, private soldiers, and famous musicians all of these have paraded up and down Washington's Pennsylvania Avenue.
10. Although marriage plans are not in the immediate future, any person and I'm no different thinks about these plans often.
11. Finally you can be sure it took the judges quite a while my speech was declared the best given.
12. "I remember when" what a wealth of memories these words bring!

13. Just how far I shall go with the idea of building a new hi-fi set well, I'll have to wait and see.

14. This one character I can't remember his name caused all kinds of trouble to the Primrose family.

15. The numerous herds of deer, antelope, buffalo, and other wild animals what has happened to them?

25. The comma

Because the comma (,) serves so many different purposes, it is the most widely used of all punctuation marks. Its varied and distinct uses result in its being the most troublesome of those marks. In fact, comma usage varies so greatly that only a few rules can be considered unchanging. But this mark of punctuation, more than any others, can help to clarify the meaning of writing. Its overuse and misuse also obscure meaning more than the misapplication of any of the other marks.

Here are three important facts about the comma to keep in mind:

1. It is a weak mark compared to the period, semicolon, and colon.

2. It is always used *within* a sentence.

3. It has three primary purposes: (a) to *separate* sentence elements that might be misread; (b) to *enclose* or *set off* constructions within a sentence that act as interrupters; and (c) to set off certain *introductory* sentence elements.

25a. Use a comma to separate words or other sentence elements that might be misread.

The single most important use of the comma is to prevent misunderstanding. Look at this statement: "Ms. Hawley our neighbor is an attorney." Is this a comment *to* or *about* Ms. Hawley? You can make meaning clear by writing "Ms. Hawley, our neighbor is an attorney" or "Ms. Hawley, our neighbor, is an attorney."

Try reading each of these sentences, omitting each comma:

In 1978, 203 persons took this same test.

Outside, the barn needs a coat of paint; inside, the walls need plastering.

The day after, our leader was absent herself.

Soon after, Mary Lou got up and stormed out of the room.

The stock advanced five points, to twenty-one. [The comma makes it clear that the range of advance was sixteen upward, not between five and twenty-one.]

25a

1. Use a comma to separate two main clauses joined by a coordinating conjunction.

A comma between two such clauses will prevent misreading. Consider these sentences:

Last week I was sick with a cold and my sister took over.

We ate cereal and our leader ordered eggs and bacon.

I am not interested in staying for the job is dull.

Adding a comma after *cold, cereal,* and *staying* will prevent a reader from thinking that the subject of the second clause in each sentence is part of the first clause.

If the clauses are short, the comma may be left out before the conjunction. But how short is *short?* If each clause consists of only a subject and a predicate, or of only three or four words each, then the comma may be omitted:

The storm came and the river rose.

On the final day of competition, Judy did not win nor did Ben.

Even long clauses may be written without a comma between them if the subject of both clauses is the same and if the thought connection is close:

Bill looked at his new Honda quickly and then he began a close inspection of it.

2. Use a comma to separate elements in a series.

He thought only of racing strips, drag races, souped-up cars, and rally stripes.

Kristen, Allison, John, and Jamie have a wonderful mother.

This author is noted for his gloom, pessimism, and dislike of all authority.

I looked for Bertha in the library, in her dormitory room, in the cafeteria, and finally found her on the soccer field.

The revolution began as a simple, Spartan reaction to the extravagant, lascivious, pleasure-loving habits of French aristocrats.

One kind of series is represented by A, B, and C—three or more words, phrases, or clauses, with a conjunction (usually *and*) joining the last two members. Some writers omit the comma before the conjunction and use A, B and C. Present practice favors the use of a comma before the conjunction because of the greater clearness that results.

Another kind of series is represented by three or more words, phrases, or clauses without any conjunctions. Commas are used after each member except the last—unless all the clauses are independent.

This shop sells food, fishing gear, bait, soft drinks on weekends only.

Use no commas when a conjunction joins each pair of a series:

I have read nothing by Jane Austen or Poe or Faulkner or Hemingway.

All drugs must meet the same standards for safety and strength and purity.

3. Use commas to separate two or more adjectives when they equally modify the same noun.

This armless, legless, sightless wonder could actually swim.

For the costume party, Enid wore an old, faded dress and an antique, ugly, expensive hat.

When the adjectives do not modify equally—that is, when they are not coordinate—use no commas:

A large green bug settled on the dry autumn leaf.

It is not always easy to determine whether modifying adjectives are really coordinate. One test is mentally to insert the coordinate conjunction *and* between adjectives; only if it fits naturally, use a comma. In the illustrative sentence just given, you can fit *and* between *large* and *green* and between *dry* and *autumn,* but the fit does not seem natural. *Large,* for example, seems to modify *green bug.* Also, truly coordinate adjectives can be reversed: *dry autumn leaf* makes sense whereas *autumn dry leaf* does not.

4. Use a comma to separate contrasted elements in a sentence.

Such contrasted elements may be words, phrases, numbers, letters, or clauses.

Your misspelling is due to carelessness, not to ignorance.
Books should be kept on the table, not on the bed.
Lisa believes the great problem is inflation, not unemployment.
Psmith begins her name with a *p,* not with an *s.*
The harder it snowed, the faster they drove.

5. Use commas to separate absolute phrases from the remainder of the sentence.

An *absolute phrase,* a group of words that has no grammatical relationship to any word in the sentence, consists of a noun and a participial modifier, the latter sometimes being omitted but understood. (If you need further information about absolute phrases, see Section 7a.)

The task having been finished, we started on our return trip.
I went to the first desk, *my application (held) in hand,* and asked for the manager.
We needed another member for our club, *Ellen having moved to another town.*

6. Use commas to separate elements in place names, dates, and titles of people.

Harry left on May 10, 1974, to go to Akron, Ohio, for an interview.
He lives in Ogden, Utah, having been transferred there from Akron, Ohio.

Abbet, R. H., Abner, W. G., and Adams, B. R., head the list of names.

Barbara Eddy, M. D., and Robert Morgan, D. D., are the featured speakers on the program.

The son of James Adams, Sr., is listed as James Adams, Jr., in our records.

The second comma must be used when the state follows town or city and when the year follows both month and day. When only month and year are used, the use of commas around the year is optional: use two or do not use any: "Sue was born in June, 1978," or "Sue was born in June 1978."

In the dateline of a letter, punctuation is optional. It was formerly common practice to write July 7, 1977; increasingly popular is the form 7 July 1977. Both are acceptable. For clarity, always separate two numerals; where a word intervenes, the comma may be omitted if you prefer.

25b. Use commas to set off (enclose) interrupting constructions.

A word or phrase that comes between a subject and its verb is an interrupter of sentence sense. So is any element that comes between a verb and its complement or object. Some interrupters are necessary and, when used, should be set off in order not to confuse the basic pattern of the sentence.

1. Use commas to set off nonrestrictive (nonessential) phrases and clauses.

A *nonrestrictive* (nonessential) phrase or clause is *not necessary* to the meaning of the sentence. It merely adds information about a word that is already identified.

John Neiley, *who lives across the street,* is the local optician.

In this sentence the italicized clause is not needed to identify John Neiley. Since it could be omitted from the sentence, it is nonrestrictive and is set off by commas.

A *restrictive* (essential) phrase or clause, on the other hand, contains information that is *necessary* to the meaning of the sentence.

An essential element limits or restricts the meaning of the word it modifies by identifying the particular one that is meant.

The person *who lives across the street* is the local optician.

In this sentence the italicized clause is needed to identify the person. It is essential and, therefore, is not set off by commas.

Chapter 20, *which tells of the rescue,* is well written.
The chapter *that tells of the rescue* is well written.
The woman *my brother met in Santa Fe* has traveled widely.
Angela Summerfield, *whom my brother met in Santa Fe,* has traveled widely.
Tourists, *who can usually be recognized by their cameras,* seem to outnumber the native population.
Tourists *who fail to declare dutiable goods* must pay the duty plus a penalty.

Remember to use punctuation as follows:

Nonrestrictive (nonessential)—commas
Restrictive (essential)—no commas

2. Use commas to set off parenthetical words, phrases, or clauses.

A test of a *parenthetical* expression is this: It can be omitted without changing the basic meaning of the sentence. Here is another test: Frequently, though not always, its position in the sentence can be shifted without any change in meaning.

However, we do not disagree too much.
We do not, *however,* disagree too much.
We do not disagree too much, *however.*
We must, *on the other hand,* consider every aspect of the problem.
I believe, *if anyone should ask my opinion,* that action ought to be postponed.

Parenthetic elements vary in intensity, and you show their relative strength by means of punctuation (commas, parentheses). Some expressions are so weak that they require no punctuation.

3. Use commas to set off words in direct address (vocatives).

A *vocative* is a noun, pronoun, or noun phrase used in direct address. That is, a vocative indicates the person to whom something is said. A vocative may appear at various positions within a sentence.

Hey, *you,* come over here.
Ms. Brown, will you speak next?
I am proud, *Mother,* of what you have accomplished.
Will you please, *sir,* speak more distinctly?
We are assembled, *ladies and gentlemen,* to discuss an important problem.

4. Use commas to set off words in apposition.

A word in *apposition*—that is, an *appositive*—is a noun or pronoun (word or phrase) that identifies in different words a preceding noun or pronoun. Usually the appositive is explanatory and therefore nonrestrictive. But occasionally it is restrictive in meaning; then, the commas are omitted.

A friend, one *who jogs for an hour early every morning,* believes that refusal to pound one's arches indicates a yearning for the grave.
My father, a *lawyer,* has just retired from active practice.
This is Ms. Law, *our newly elected president.*
Richard *the Lion-Hearted* was a famous English king.
Carol Martin, *our supervisor,* was a considerate woman.
My task, *to write a short story,* seemed hopeless.
The river *Mississippi* is beloved of songwriters.

25c. Use a comma following certain introductory elements.

Several introductory sentence elements need to be set off from the rest of the sentence with a comma. In effect, these elements act as interrupters, delaying the main thought of the sentence. The comma serves both to separate these elements and to introduce the main idea that follows.

1. Use a comma following an introductory adverbial clause.

Before Martin started on his trip, he made a careful plan of his itinerary.
If I arrive first, I'll wait for you in the lobby.

Many introductory adverbial clauses are simply transposed elements. Inserted in their customary order, they may or may not have commas, depending on their meaning. Inserted elsewhere, they are enclosed by commas.

After you arrive on the job, various meetings will be held to help orient you.
Various meetings, after you arrive on the job, will be held to help orient you.

When the adverbial clause follows the independent clause, omit the comma if the adverbial clause is necessary to complete the meaning of the sentence.

Pedro works because he has no other way to spend his time.

Note: An introductory noun clause is not set off by a comma. Also, an adjective clause *follows* the noun or pronoun that it modifies.

That your library book was turned in late is unfortunate. [Noun clause]
The individual *whom you were talking to* is my aunt. [Adjective clause]

2. Use a comma following a series of introductory prepositional phrases or following a long prepositional phrase.

On the sidewalks, in the street, litter was everywhere.
After a long walk across the field, we were glad to rest before the fire.
In a little country store nearby, we bought some bread and cheese.

3. Use a comma following an introductory participial phrase.

Acting on the advice of Ms. Crawford, we bought some stock in the company.

Racing toward the finish line, Edith could already taste victory.

4. Use a comma to introduce a short quotation, especially in writing dialog.

Paula said, "I'll never do that again."

1. If the "he said" or its equivalent follows the quotation, it is separated from it by a comma, provided that a question mark or exclamation point is not demanded.

    "I'll never do that again," said Paula.

    "Will you ever do that again?" asked Mindy.

2. If the "he said" or its equivalent is inserted between the parts of a quotation, it is usually enclosed by commas.

    "I'll never do that again," said Paula, "unless I lose my temper."

3. When the quotation being introduced is long or formal, the colon replaces the comma. (See Section 23.)

4. Make a careful distinction between quotations that are really quotations of speaking or writing and quoted material that is the subject or object of a verb or is material identified by quotation marks such as titles, slang, and special word use. As examples of such special uses, observe the following:

    The usual remark is, "May the better team win."

    "Make haste slowly" is the motto that came to my mind.

    If the "he said" comes between parts of a quotation, it is enclosed by commas.

    "Itty-bitty" is not the exact phrase to use for "very small."

25d. Use no unnecessary commas.

Modern punctuation usage omits many commas that formerly were used. Therefore, be able to account for each comma in your writing. A comma must be *needed* for sentence construction, clar-

The comma

ity, or effectiveness. Avoid using the comma needlessly to separate closely related sentence elements. Some of the most common misuses or overuses of the comma are discussed in the following statements:

1. Do not use a comma to separate a subject from its predicate or a verb from its object or complement.

No comma is needed in any of these sentences:

We asked to hear the motion reread.
Millie found that jogging for an hour was not so hard after all.
To do satisfactory work is my aim.

2. Do not use a comma before an indirect quotation.
No comma is needed in this sentence:

The speaker asserted that she stood squarely for progress.

3. Do not use a comma indiscriminately to replace a word that has been omitted.

The word *that* in an indirect quotation, the word *that* in introducing other noun clauses as objects, and the relative pronouns *who, whom, which,* and *that* are frequently omitted in informal writing. They should not be replaced by commas. In "Janice replied, she would return next week," the comma is incorrectly used for *that.* (The comma also comes between a subject and its verb.) In "The person, I met was a friend of a friend of mine," *whom* should replace the comma, or the comma may be omitted. "She thought, that man was dead" should be written "She thought that that man was dead."

4. Do not use a comma before the first or after the last member of a series.

FAULTY: We went swimming in a cool, clear, smooth-flowing, river.
FAULTY: Avoid a mixture of, red, yellow, green, blue, and brown paints.

STANDARD: The red, white, and blue flag waved in the wind.

Omit the last comma in the first sentence and the first comma in the second.

5. Do not use a comma between two independent clauses where a stronger mark of punctuation (semicolon, period) is needed.

Confusion is always caused by this misuse, sometimes called the *comma fault* or *comma splice*. (See Section 42a.) Use a period or semicolon in place of the comma in a statement like this one:

My mother told me to be home early, I told her I couldn't.

25d

6. Do not use a comma, or pair of commas, with words in apposition that are actually restrictive.

The following italicized words really limit, identify, or define; they should not be enclosed with commas:

Goya's painting *The Shooting* is one of his greatest.
My cousin *Dorothy* is a lovely person.
Zeno *of Elea* was a follower of Parmenides.

7. Do not use a comma in any situation unless it adds clarity and understanding.

Comma usage is slowly growing more open. In the following sentences every comma can be justified, but each could be omitted since clarity is not affected in the slightest degree:

After the movie, Joe and I went home, by taxicab, because we wanted, at all costs, to avoid subway crowds.
Naturally, the last thing you should do, before leaving work, is punch the time clock.

Of all marks of punctuation, commas are the most frequently used and the most important for clarity. Use them when necessary to make your meaning clear. Avoid using them when they slow down thought, interrupt, or make your writing look as though you had used a comma shaker.

The comma

A. Choose a paragraph from a book that you are reading or from a current magazine. Underline or circle every comma. Give a reason for each comma or pair of commas according to the principles stated in Section 25. Do not be surprised if a few of the commas are unconventionally used, unnecessary, or incorrectly placed.

B. In the following sentences commas are omitted. Where should they be inserted?

1. Should you take the wrong road you may never find the right road again.
2. You may choose easy courses and get high grades or you may choose difficult courses and really learn something.
3. When one gets there she has the feeling of having conquered the mountains for she can see for miles around.
4. Through a careful examination of ourselves our ability and the requirements for safe driving everyone can live in a safer world.
5. We have not made our decision yet nor can I tell you how soon we shall.
6. If everybody would ask what he or she has to be thankful for I know many of us would be surprised.
7. Once the plane takes off the flight attendant is always there to help you.
8. By working hard for three months I received my first increase in pay.
9. Florida is visited all the year round but the busy season starts in December and lasts through March.
10. After wandering through the woods all afternoon I found enough mushrooms for our supper.
11. To demonstrate what I mean by a mean trick I'll relate an experience that happened to me.
12. The atmosphere of Holland Michigan is of the old world and all the charm of old Holland can be found there.
13. As reckless drivers we are always one jump ahead of the safety experts for we can think of other ways to kill ourselves.
14. A person who is susceptible to colds should avoid exposure to cold wet or snowy weather.
15. Many times when the snow falls and the wind blows the road to our house is drifted with the snow.
16. Little siblings come in assorted sizes shapes and dispositions.
17. In the play the king had a long curly black beard.
18. You have been in college three months now haven't you?
19. The longer I watched the ice show the more I thought I would like to be a great skater too.
20. I unloaded my clothes and my friends left immediately for home.

25d

EXERCISE 6

Directions given under Exercise 5B.

1. The time being 8 P.M. the curtain rose and the play began.
2. It takes only twenty minutes to drive to the store that is under normal conditions.
3. Freshmen who put activities above studies will very likely never become sophomores.
4. Off Marseilles France lies the island bastion Chateau d'If part of the setting of Dumas' *The Count of Monte Cristo*.
5. *Caroline* which is French and *Carolina* which is Italian are both diminutives of the medieval Latin name *Carola*.
6. My parents and I or I should say my mother decided that we would drive to Mammoth Cave Kentucky.
7. The bird dog namely the pointer is the aristocrat of hunting dogs.
8. This is how according to tradition the idea of the Christmas tree and Yule log originated.
9. At any time of the year spring summer fall or winter there is a tinge of beauty in the woods.
10. The old expression "Practice makes perfect" applies to the idea of writing effectively.

25d

EXERCISE 7

Some of the commas in the following sentences are not needed. Which ones are they?

1. It is plain to see, that in our family it is an advantage to have at least two cars.
2. In the United States the most notable days in May are Mother's Day, and Memorial Day.
3. I believe, this work demands too much of my time.
4. No doubt the pleasant weather, that usually accompanies July, is considered in vacation plans.
5. You expressed a desire to know, what type of reports we expect to write in the future.
6. Clear communication, is very important everywhere you go.
7. The last and most important part of registration is, payment of fees.
8. In our state there is a place called, "New Salem State Park."
9. Some of the students of today, have poor habits.
10. Often a question will arise in the form, "Why are superstitions used?"

26. The apostrophe

The *apostrophe* ('), which is both a mark of punctuation and a spelling symbol, has three uses: (1) to indicate the omission of a letter or letters from words or of a figure or figures from numerals; (2) to form the possessive (genitive) case of nouns and of certain pronouns; and (3) to indicate the plurals of letters, numerals, symbols, and certain abbreviations. The apostrophe is an overused mark of punctuation and mechanics, but you must know how to employ it correctly for each of the purposes indicated here if your writing is to be clear to readers.

26a. Use an apostrophe where a letter or letters have been omitted.

aren't (are not)	mustn't (must not)
can't (can not)	o'clock (of the clock)
couldn't (could not)	shan't (shall not)
doesn't (does not)	wasn't (was not)
hasn't (has not)	won't (will not)

1. Use an apostrophe to indicate pronunciation, usually in dialectal speech.

"I say it's 'bout time you start tryin' hard and quit foolin' around."
The late Will Rogers is quoted as having said, "A lot of people who don't say *ain't,* ain't eatin'."

2. Use an apostrophe with certain abbreviated expressions such as "coined" verbs and participles.

the TV'd baseball game
he O.K.'d the order.

3. Carefully distinguish between an expression with omitted letters (a contraction requiring the use of an apostrophe)

and an abbreviation (a shortened form usually followed by a period). Don't use both an apostrophe and a period.

natl., nat'l   Dan, Dan'l
sec., sec'y   Fred, Fred'ric

4. An apostrophe is usually omitted in shortened forms of certain words, although it is not incorrect—just precise—to use one:

phone (for telephone)   plane (for airplane, aeroplane)
possum (for opossum)   copter (for helicopter)
memo (for memorandum)   gym (for gymnasium)
cello (for violoncello)   chutist (for parachutist)

26c

26b. Place an apostrophe where a figure or figures have been omitted.

class of '78 (1978)   the '50's (the nineteen—or other—fifties)
spirit of '76 (1776)   gold rush of '49 (1849)

26c. Use an apostrophe to form the possessives of nouns, some pronouns, and certain phrases.

The use of an apostrophe to form the possessive case of words varies in the following ways:

1. Use an apostrophe and *s* to form the possessive of a noun, either singular or plural, that does not end in *s*.

man, man's   women, women's
men, men's   child, child's
woman, woman's   children, children's

2. Use an apostrophe alone to form the possessive of a plural noun that ends in *s*.

doctors, doctors'   girls, girls'
lions, lions'   the Smiths, the Smiths'
countries, countries'   queens, queens'

3. Use an apostrophe alone or an apostrophe with *s* to form the possessive of singular nouns that end in *s*.

One-syllable proper names that end in *s* or an *s* sound add an apostrophe and *s*: *Keats's poems, Jones's books, Marx's theories.*

In words of more than one syllable that end in *s* or an *s* sound, add an apostrophe only: *Themistocles' strategy, Aristophanes' plays, Berlioz' compositions.*

Some common nouns that do not end in *s* but have an *s* sound at the end add only an apostrophe: for *conscience' sake.*

26c

4. In compound nouns add an apostrophe and *s* to the element that is nearest to the word possessed: *the daughter-in-law's children, the daughters-in-law's children; Representative Smith of Colorado's vote.*

5. Use an apostrophe with the last element of a series to indicate joint possession: *Wolcott and Brown's store, a soldiers and sailors' home.*

6. Use an apostrophe with each element in a series to indicate *alternative* or *individual* possession: *Wilson's or Eisenhower's or Carter's administration; Authors' and Printers' Dictionary; Bob's and Jim's plans; bachelor's and master's degrees; soldiers' and sailors' uniforms.*

7. Use an apostrophe and *s* to form the possessive of indefinite pronouns.

anybody's	other's
everybody's	somebody's
no one's	someone's

Do not use an apostrophe to form the possessive of personal and relative pronouns; *ours,* not *our's; yours,* not *your's; hers,* not *her's; whose,* not *who's* (unless you mean *who is); its,* not *it's* (unless you mean *it is* or *it has*).

8. With geographic terms and names of firms, organizations, and institutions, follow the form settled

upon by usage or tradition: *Harpers Ferry, Hudson Bay, Hudson's Bay Company, St. Mary's Seminary, Citizens Union, Rutgers University, Columbia University Teachers College.*

9. Certain idiomatic expressions require the use of an apostrophe even though actual possession is not clearly indicated: *a day's wait; an hour's delay; a stone's throw; twenty cents' worth; at my wits' end.* **(See Section 14m.)**

10. Certain double possessives require both an apostrophe and *of: a book of my friend's; a brother of Jane's; a nephew of my cousins's.* **(See Section 14l.)**

11. A noun or *indefinite* **pronoun followed by a gerund (verbal noun) should have an apostrophe.**

> We objected to the *manager's* leaving early.
> *Anyone's* failing of this examination will be remarkable.

26d. Use an apostrophe and *s* **to form the plural of letters, figures, symbols, and words referred to as words.**

1. Use an apostrophe and *s* **to indicate the plurals of letters of the alphabet.**

> Mind your *p*'s and *q*'s.
> Dot your *i*'s and *j*'s.
> Your *i*'s look like *e*'s.

2. Use an apostrophe and *s* **to indicate the plurals of figures.**

> We have no more size *8*'s.
> He suffered every year during the *1970's.*
> They came by *2*'s and *3*'s.

3. Use an apostrophe and _s_ to indicate the plurals of symbols and of some abbreviations.

the three R's
indent all ¶'s three spaces
how many C.O.D's did they receive?

4. Do not use the apostrophe in forming the plural of nouns unless actual possession is shown.

"The Smiths have arrived," but "the Smiths' house was for sale."

26d

5. Use an apostrophe to indicate the plurals of words that are referred to as words.

Your remarks contained entirely too many _but's._

As with several of the other marks of punctuation, so with the apostrophe: There is a growing tendency to dispense with it. But also as with other marks of punctuation, the test for its use is clarity: Does it help make meaning clear? Without an apostrophe, _she's_ (_she is_) becomes _shes; he'll_ (_he will_) becomes _hell; she'll_ (_she will_) becomes _shell; three a's_ becomes _three as; three as's_ becomes _three ass._

EXERCISE 8

A. Circle all the apostrophes on a page of printed material and give the reason for each.

B. Where are apostrophes needed in the following sentences? Why?

1. You will find the visitors apartments in the east wing of the building.
2. Its a pleasant feeling to know that someone thinks youre brilliant.
3. After I receive my bachelors degree, I hope to continue on and obtain a masters degree.
4. By 12 oclock midnight I have all my next days planning done.
5. Stores in large cities feature by mail a personal shoppers service.
6. To me theres nothing in nature as beautiful as new-fallen snow.
7. Our various families reunion last August was a great success.
8. Recently I finished reading Nathaniel Hawthornes _The Scarlet Letter._
9. Now lets look at some possible solutions to some of todays problems.
10. Alaska has always been built up in peoples minds as a state where everythings big.

EXERCISE 9

Apostrophes are misused in the following sentences. Make all necessary corrections.

1. Many people are building new home's and spending money on luxury's like television.
2. The Norman Conquest, by reason of it's being French, brought the French language to England.
3. Every year thousands' of people swim in this lake.
4. If our neighbor is not working at his place, he is loafing at our's.
5. My teacher did'nt want anyone in her class who would'nt work.
6. Walking in wet weather make's ones' feet cold and damp.
7. Various European country's scenery is simply breathtaking.
8. The mens' and womens' residence halls even have a childrens' playroom for visiting parents and friends.
9. Many of our postage stamps have prominent peoples' pictures printed on them.
10. This magazine-index volume includes the five year's materials from 1970 to 1975.

27. Quotation marks

Quotation marks, both double ("...") and single ('...'), are marks of enclosure for words, phrases, clauses, sentences, and even paragraphs and groups of paragraphs. By definition, *quotation* means repeating (or copying) what someone has said or written; *quotation marks* are a device used principally to indicate the beginning and end of material so quoted. These marks, often called *quotes,* consist of two (or one) inverted commas at the beginning (*open quote*) and two (*or one*) apostrophes for closing a quotation (*close quote*). On a standard typewriter keyboard, single and double quotation marks are the same at the beginning and the end of the quoted material.

In some books and magazines and in most newspapers, either no quotation marks at all or single quotation marks are printed where, according to convention, double ones would be used. For example, the *New York Times* invariably uses single quotes in all headlines and subheads in which quotations are involved. A few book publishers, presumably as a typographic experiment or in an attempt to be "different," often use single quotes where American convention calls for two. Also, those of you who are accustomed to reading material printed in Great Britain are familiar with the use of single and double quotes in a way that is exactly the reverse of American usage.

You are advised to employ these marks in accordance with conventions set forth in this section unless there is a sound reason to proceed otherwise.

27a. Use quotation marks to enclose every quotation and each part of an interrupted quotation.

A direct quotation consists of the exact words of the person being quoted, that is, the original writer or speaker. You must be careful to enclose in quotes, precisely as written or spoken (even if it contains obvious errors) the material copied. In most general writing, such quotations consist of words that were really used; in fiction, they consist of imagined words in dialog or monolog. Indirect quotations, in which the sense but not the exact phrasing is quoted, should not be enclosed in quotes.

> "What will my starting salary be?" I asked the manager.
> "Well," he replied, "I'm not sure." Then, pausing, he inquired, "What do you think is fair?"
> The professor looked up the quotation he had had in mind all during the argument with his teen-age son. He found it in Plato's *Laws:* "You are young, my son, and, as the years go by, time will change and even reverse many of your present opinions. Refrain therefore awhile from setting yourself up as a judge of the highest matters." He smiled ruefully and recalled that Plato had also written, "Of all the animals, the boy is the most unmanageable."

Note that in the first brief passage just presented, direct quotations are interrupted by other words and quotation marks are used to enclose each part of the broken-into quotation. The most common of such interrupters are word groups like "he said," "said he," "she replied," and "I answered." Such an interrupter is preceded by a comma, unless a question mark or exclamation point is required. It is followed by a comma or an even stronger mark of punctuation, such as a period or semicolon, if the grammatical elements involved require it. Selection of the correct mark of punctuation will be aided by this test: What mark of punctuation would be used if the interrupter ("she said," etc.) were omitted? Use that mark after the inserted part indicating the speaker.

Sandy is a good friend, but I have not seen her for a year. "Sandy is a good friend," she said, "but I have not seen her for a year."

There is no opening here; however, we will keep your application on file. "There is no opening here," the personnel manager said; "however, we will keep your application on file."

He bought the car at Fairport. It was on sale. "I bought the car at Fairport," Walter said. "It was on sale."

On occasion, you may be writing your own account of someone's comment but desire to give his or her exact words now and then. Be careful to enclose in quotes only the actual words used, not your restatement of remarks made:

The farm agent sternly declared that "it makes no sense at all" for Congress to support aid for farmers with oratory but "willfully and maliciously" to oppose all bills designed to support farm prices.

Criminals of today, the bondsman declared, don't have the "solid respectability" of those of forty or fifty years ago.

"

27b

27b. If a quotation extends for more than one paragraph, use quotation marks at the beginning of each paragraph but at the end of only the last.

"To measure and mark time has always been a concern of people. Early systems for noting the passage of time were based on the sun, stars, and moon.

"Egyptian priests established a year of 365 days as early as 4200 B.C. and based their calculations on the passage of the seasons, the sun's shadow, and the behavior of stars.

"Under Julius Caesar, astronomers prepared the Julian calendar in which twelve months were given arbitrary lengths and every fourth year was made a leap year."

Quotation marks setting off extended quotations (more than

three lines) may be omitted if you make the lines of the quotation shorter than full measure. If you indent each line of the quotation a half-inch or so, so that it is clearly distinguished from the remainder of the text, the marks may be dropped. This device is commonly employed by book and magazine publishers and may be adapted for your own use. In double-spaced typewritten copy, quoted material that is set off is usually single spaced *unless the manuscript is being prepared for publication.*

27c. In dialog use a separate paragraph for each change of speaker.

In the conversation of two or more persons it is conventional to use a separate paragraph for the remarks of each speaker. If this is done—and exceptions occur even in careful writing—quotation marks are needed at the beginning and end of each separate comment. Here is a sample of short speeches of dialog, separately paragraphed and separately enclosed in quotes:

> Larry was dressing for tennis when Bill walked into the room. "What's up?" Bill asked. He walked over to the sofa in the corner and sat down leisurely.
> "Game with Winnie at noon," Larry replied. "But I was up so late last night that I think I'll be awful."
> "Well, who was your date?"
> "Winnie," replied Larry sheepishly. Bill grinned, picked up a copy of *Esquire,* and began looking for cartoons.

27d. Use quotation marks to enclose words and phrases that are used in a special sense.

If a word or expression is appropriate, no matter what its level of usage, no quotation marks should enclose it as a form of apology. This suggestion applies to slangy or colloquial expressions, even profanity. If the expression is not appropriate, find a substitute that is.

Occasionally, however, you may wish to shift to an expression with a specific, limited usage or level of usage in order to convey a thought realistically and emphatically. Such expressions may be illiteracies, technical words, or common words with a specialized or technical meaning; they are enclosed by double quotation marks.

> Most of the executives are estimable men, but the president is a "stuffed shirt."
>
> He referred to it as a "gentlemen's agreement," but to me it was sheer "bunk."
>
> This issue of stock was so heavily "watered" that it caused an investigation by the New York Stock Exchange.
>
> If we judge that we "have it taped," we are not likely to be curious about the ways in which other races of man have answered questions that are also our questions.
>
> The person who has "had it" so far as all religion is concerned looks with impatience on the role that religion has played in humanity's progress toward self-mastery.

Quotation marks are conspicuous and sharply focus attention on the words or expressions they enclose. Therefore, do not overuse them for the purpose just mentioned or as an excuse for inexact choice of words. Also, words that are labeled "colloquial" in your dictionary are in reputable informal use and should not be enclosed unless they represent a *marked* and *purposeful* shift from the level of writing you are employing.

27e. Use quotation marks to enclose chapter headings and the titles of articles, short stories, and short poems.

When both a chapter heading and the title of a book are cited, or when both the name of an article and that of the magazine in which it appears are given, you will need to use italics and quotation marks. The general rule is to use quotation marks with chapter headings, with the titles of articles, short stories, and short poems, and with art objects and the like. Use italics (underlining) with all other names and titles, as indicated in Section 30.

Book publishers tend to use more italics (underlining) than either magazines or newspapers. The appearance of italics in most newspapers is so rare as to be almost nonexistent, but this is no criterion for the use of italics in your own writing, which is not dependent on the kinds of type available in the printing plant of a newspaper. Note the preferred use of italics and quotation marks in the following examples:

> He found the quotation from Longfellow's "The Children's Hour" in Bartlett's *Familiar Quotations.*
>
> The article was from *National Review* and was entitled "Freedom and Virtue."
>
> Grant Wood's famed painting, "American Gothic," was recently reproduced in *American Heritage.*
>
> His most famous short story is "The Devil and Daniel Webster." It first appeared in the *Saturday Evening Post* and was later published in a book entitled *Thirteen O'Clock.*

"

27f

Some titles, it should be noted, require neither quotation marks nor italics. It is not necessary to quote or underline the names of books of the Bible or even the words Bible, Old Testament, and New Testament. Such famed titles as the Gettysburg Address and the Declaration of Independence require neither quotation marks nor italics, although of course it is not an error so to distinguish them.

A more difficult problem is whether to include such words as *the, a,* and *an* in a quoted or italicized title or name. If they are included, they may begin with a capital letter and be underlined or included within quote marks. Include or exclude *the, a,* and *an* in accordance with the practice of the newspaper or magazine being cited. You may conventionally write *Atlantic Monthly,* the *Atlantic Monthly,* or *The Atlantic Monthly.*

27f. Use quotation marks to enclose expressions that need special attention.

In order to make your meaning clear, you will occasionally need to refer specifically to a word or phrase by underlining it or placing it in quotation marks. Italics (underlining) may be preferred for this purpose, but quotation marks are permissible. Note these examples:

> Ivan said "not yet," but I thought he said "nyet."
>
> The phrase "freedom of worship" [or *freedom of worship*] has had many interpretations.

The word "ineluctable" [or *ineluctable*] is a learned word meaning "inevitable" [or *inevitable*].

Once again, do not overuse quotation marks to attract attention
to a word or phrase. It is unnecessary, although not incorrect, to
use quotation marks when mentioning terms whose meaning is
clear:

He gave a peculiar definition of the word God.
His concept of good is about the same as mine of evil.

**27g. Use single quotation marks to enclose a
quotation within a quotation.**

The standard rule in American practice is to use single quotation
marks to enclose a quotation within a quotation. (British practice
is usually the reverse.) On the exceedingly rare occasions when it
is necessary to punctuate a quotation within a quotation within a
quotation, the correct order is double marks, single marks, double
marks. If more sets of marks than this are needed, you had better
recast your sentence so as not to lose your readers entirely.

The supervisor said, "When you say, 'I'll be there on time,' I
expect you to mean what you say."
The supervisor went on, "Then this worker asked, 'What did
the boss mean when he said, "Joe, be there on time"?' "

**27h. Place quotation marks correctly with reference
to other punctuation.**

1. The comma and period *always come inside* quotation marks.
   This principle applies even when only the last word before
   the comma or the period is enclosed (but does not apply to
   letters or figures).
2. A question mark, exclamation point, or dash comes *outside*
   the quotation marks unless it is part of the quotation. The
   question mark comes *inside* the quotation marks when both
   the nonquoted and quoted elements are questions.
3. The semicolon and colon come *outside* the quotation marks.

If these statements seem confusing, perhaps the following illustrations will clarify them:

"Please lend me the money now," she said. "I won't need it tomorrow."

The prize pumpkin was rated "excellent," but one judge felt it was only "good."

She went to Gate "Y", but her ticket indicated that the proper entrance was "G".

Did Jim say, "I have enough money"?

Jim asked, "Have I enough money?"

"Have I enough money?" Jim asked.

What is meant by "an eye for an eye"?

The performance was an utter "flop"!

"My performance was a 'flop'!" she exclaimed.

"Well, I'll be—" she said and then blushed.

He arose confidently, said "My friends—" and then fell to the floor in a dead faint.

Did Jim ask, "Have I enough money?"

Read Thoreau's "Brute Neighbors"; as a nature lover, you will enjoy it.

EXERCISE 10

A. Study several pages of a short story or novel that contain dialog. Examine the use of quotation marks and their position with respect to other marks of punctuation. Discuss any uses that are not in accordance with principles given in Section 27.

B. To illustrate the use of quotation marks, write a short paper entitled "A Dialog Between _____ and _____."

C. In the following sentences make quotation marks, capitals, and commas conform to commonly accepted principles:

1. After I had completed my driver's training, Father said, "that I could apply for a beginner's license".

2. The old saying, 'The more the merrier—' well, it isn't necessarily true.

3. The area might be called "a sportsman's paradise, for the woods are teeming with game.

4. At the end of the last class before vacation, our instructor said she would like to say one more thing: Have a merry Christmas.

5. Here are words of wisdom for the ambitious, hardworking young person, "There is always tomorrow."

6. My dictionary defines *preface* as "something written as introductory or preliminary material to a book.

7. Our community recently honored my mother by naming her "the typical American housewife;" naturally her family is very proud of her.

8. What makes the automobile so deadly is the 'nut' behind the wheel.

9. "Well, son, the justice drawled, $18.75."

10. It would be so easy to sleep through those early 8 o'clock classes is a favorite thought of most students.

11. You have asked me, "Why read"?

12. Can this really be happening to me? I said to myself.

13. The home of 650 happy people and a few soreheads—this is the sign that travelers see as they enter my town.

14. I have read Keats' The Eve of St. Agnes and I think I have never read a more beautiful poem.

15. After you leave college and obtain a job the adviser told us you will find that coming in late and not appearing once or twice a week will have serious consequences.

28a

28. The hyphen

The *hyphen* (-) is a mark of punctuation, but it is most frequently used to indicate that two or more words or two or more parts of one word belong together. That is, the hyphen is used in spelling compound words and in dividing words at the ends of lines.

28a. Use your dictionary to determine whether a word combination is written as a compound with a hyphen, as one word written solid, or as two separate words.

No rules about compounding are inflexible. Our language is constantly changing; word forms undergo frequent modification. But the general principle of word joining is dictated by usage. When two or more words first become associated, through usage, with a single meaning, they are usually written as two words. As time goes on and the new compound grows to be more of a unit in thought, it is likely to be written with a hyphen—a mark that in one sense separates the parts but in a more specific way joins them. Eventually, the separate parts lose their hyphen (or hyphens) and become one word, written solid.

This principle may be seen in a word like *railroad*. It was formerly written as two words, *rail road;* then it was written with a hyphen, *rail-road.* The same principle may be illustrated by *base ball, base-ball, baseball; basket ball, basket-ball, basketball; step son, step-son, stepson; super market, super-market, supermarket.* The third word in each of these series is now the universally accepted form.

28a

But you cannot always count on this principle; some common expressions that have been in use for a long time have never progressed beyond the first stage. You may occasionally see the compound word *highschool*, but nearly all copy experts and most publications still employ the separate form: *high school.* And you are not likely to see such common expressions as these written in any other form than as two separate words: *station wagon, Boy Scout, Girl Scout, White House, sports car, summer vacation, stock market, post card, real estate, blood pressure.* Other combinations remain in the second stage (spelled with a hyphen), despite their having been used so often that they might well have reached the third stage (written solid): *son-in-law, post-mortem, clear-cut, hard-featured, heart-free.*

Still another problem with compounds should be mentioned: Their form (two words, hyphenated, solid) may depend on meaning. That is, a word group may have one meaning, and even one pronunciation, when written one way and quite a different meaning and pronunciation in another form. Note the difference in meaning in these sentences:

Driving down the *middle of the road* is not recommended.
This candidate for office follows a *middle-of-the-road* course.
The advertisement was for a *light housekeeper*, not a *lighthouse keeper.*
Lee was a *go-between* in the office quarrel.
In order to count, the ball must *go between* the goal posts.
The little boy played with a *black ball.*
Joe wishes to *blackball* this applicant.
This woman is a *well-known* member of her community.
This woman is *well, known* never to have been ill in her life.
Jim was a *battle-scarred* veteran of World War II.
The *battle scarred* Jim's body and soul.

Now you can see, if you did not already know, how confusing and involved the writing of compounds can be. (It is small wonder that the latest edition of the *Government Printing Office Style Manual* devotes fifty-eight closely printed pages to compound words.) When in doubt, *use your dictionary*.

28b. Use a hyphen to join the parts of certain groups of compound words.

In spite of the exceptions and variations involved, certain general statements about compound words can be made. Most of them involve exceptions, but they provide a few guidelines.★ It may also help to remember that the present-day tendency is to avoid using hyphens whenever possible.

1. A hyphen is used between two or more words modifying a substantive (noun, pronoun, etc.) and used as an adjective.

able-bodied	narrow-minded
above-mentionnd	never-to-be-forgotten
absent-minded	nineteenth-century
Anglo-Saxon	old-fashioned
bad-tempered	olive-skinned
bell-shaped	open-minded
best-known	pink-blossomed
city-wide	quick-witted
far-fetched	razor-keen
fast-moving	sad-looking
first-rate	six-room
good-natured	slow-witted
light-haired	twelve-foot
long-needed	velvet-draped

Note, however, that such compounds are not always hyphenated. They usually are when they precede the word they modify, but they may be written as two separate words when they follow a substantive:

Beulah touched the red-hot coil.

The coil was soon red hot.

★Not all of the exceptions within the groups mentioned are noted—in the interest of not compounding confusion as well as words.

Furthermore, adverb and verb compounds (especially with present participles) are often written as separate words preceding a noun: the *ever quickening* pace. But if the meaning is doubtful without the hyphen, by all means use it.

2. Hyphens are used in compound nouns.

Compound nouns consist of from two to as many as four parts. Nearly every part of speech can become a component of a compound noun. For example, *by-product* is a compound noun consisting of a preposition and a noun; *jack-of-all-trades* consists of a noun, preposition, adjective, and noun. Here are some examples of familiar compound nouns that require a hyphen (or hyphens):

brother-in-law	leveling-off
court-martial	looker-on
fellow-citizen	a five-year-old
forget-me-not	secretary-treasurer
go-between	take-off
great-uncle	trade-off

3. Hyphens are used in combining forms attached to a capitalized word.

Prefixes and suffixes attached to common words usually become a part of the word, written solid. Dictionaries have long lists of such combined forms; see, for example, the entries under *non, over, un,* and *under* in your dictionary: *nonessential, overtake, unarmed, understate.*

However, you should use a hyphen to join a prefix or other combining form to a *capitalized* word:

anti-British	pseudo-Protestantism
pan-German	trans-Andean
post-Civil War	ultra-Spanish
pro-Arab	un-American

4. A hyphen is used after a single capital letter joined to a noun or participle.

Our language contains many coined words of this kind, all of which should be hyphenated:

A-flat	T-square
H-bomb	U-turn
I-beam	V-neck
S-curve	X-ray

5. A hyphen is used between elements of an improvised compound.

blue-pencil (as a verb)	make-believe
know-how	never-say-die
a let-George-do-it response	a high-wide-and-handsome attitude
verbal give-and-take	long-to-be-remembered
hard-and-fast rule	stick-in-the-mud

Any ordinary good-gracious-what-next novelist would be content to spin out this plot to book length.

The promoter of securities gave me a now-you-see-it-now-you-don't impression.

Note, however, that many writers who improvise compounds do not use hyphens. James Joyce, for instance, was famous for running words together to achieve new stylistic effects. In *Ulysses* appear such compounds as *biscuitmush, lifebrightening, teadust,* and *wavenoise.* Granted that such words might be more readily understandable if they were hyphenated or written separately, they do add flavor and vigor to writing. And James Jones, in a novel entitled *The Thin Red Line,* coined adjectives like *handleopened, longpicklenosed,* and *wavywhitehaired.* To refer to an individual as "longpicklenosed" is more picturesque and economical than to mention a person "who has a long nose shaped like a pickle." In general, however, new coinages are clearer if they are written with a hyphen so that familiar elements can register with your reader.

6. Hyphens are used in some, but not all, compounds with *father, mother, sister,* or the like as the first element.

brother-workers	mother-of-pearl
father-in-law	parent-teacher
fellow-citizens	sister-nations

Note, however, that many compounds beginning with these words are not hyphenated: *father love, mother church, sister ship,* and so forth.

7. Hyphens are used between the parts of compound numerals from twenty-one to ninety-nine if they are written out.

twenty-one   forty-three
twenty-first   ninety-two

8. Hyphens are used in certain fractions.

Hyphenate fractions if they are written out, but omit the hyphen if one already appears in either the numerator or the denominator.

two-thirds   twenty one-thousandsths
four-fifths   twenty-three thirtieths
ten-thousandths   twenty-four thirty-eighths

9. A hyphen is used between a number and its unit of measurement.

a 4-yard gain   a 10-day vacation
a 35-hour week   an 8-foot board

10. A hyphen is usually, but not always, used when _ex_ or _self_ is the first element.

ex-serviceman   self-control
ex-vice-president self-respect

Note, however, that other words fitting into this classification are not hyphenated: _selfsame, excommunicate._*

11. A hyphen is used in order to avoid doubling a vowel or tripling a consonant.

anti-imperialistic   shell-like
semi-independent   will-less

12. Hyphens are used to prevent mispronunciation.

recover as distinguished from _re-cover_
recreation as distinguished from _re-creation_
retreat as distinguished from _re-treat_

---

*Dictionaries often differ among themselves about compound words. Never mind: Choose a good dictionary and follow it consistently.

28b

13. A hyphen is used as a suspensive hyphen in pairs.

When the first or second part of a compound word is used only once, a suspensive (carrying-over) hyphen is occasionally used:

This was a group of 6- and 7-year-olds.
He bought some 6-, 8-, and 10-penny nails.

28c. Use a hyphen to indicate the division of a word broken at the end of a line.

28c

Whether you are writing in longhand or on the typewriter, you often come toward the right-hand side of your sheet of paper with enough space left to begin a word but not complete it. The result is that large numbers of "rules" for the division of words have been devised. In fact, the situation is so common and the problem so vexing that the United States Printing Office has issued a supplement to its *Style Manual* devoted solely to word division. The supplement runs to 128 pages and consists of basic rules for word division and the actual breaking up of more than 12,500 words.

When using a division hyphen at the end of a line, keep the following rules in mind:

1. Divide according to pronunciation.

Words are normally (but not always) pronounced according to their syllabication.

knowl-edge, not *know-ledge*
ste-nog-ra-pher, not *sten-og-ra-pher*
sten-o-graph-ic, not *ste-nog-ra-phic*
grum-ble, not *grumb-le*

2. Place the hyphen at the end of the first line, never at the beginning of the second:

The botanist used only two specimens in his demonstration.

3. Never divide a monosyllable.

Some rather long words have only one syllable and cannot be divided. Write such words as *breath, ground, laughed,* and *through* in their entirety on the first line; if this is not possible, carry the whole word over to the next line. Also, such parts of words as -*geous* (advantageous) and -*tious* (contentious) cannot be divided, although they can be separated, *as wholes,* from the root word: *advanta-geous.*

4. Do not divide a one-letter syllable from the remainder of the word.

A word like *about* does have two syllables, *a* and *bout,* but it should not be broken up. Do not divide such words as *able, among, enough, item, many, unit, very.*

5. Do not divide on a syllable with a silent vowel.

The ending -*ed* is not fully pronounced in many words and should not be separated from the word of which it is a part. Avoid breaking up such words as *asked, attacked, climbed, massed, yelled.*

6. Do not divide a word with only four letters.

A word with only four letters can usually be crowded into the first line if necessary. If space does not permit, carry over to the second line in their entirety such words as *also, into, only, open, real, veto.*

7. Divide two consonants standing between vowels when pronunciation warrants such division.

This principle is illustrated by words like *alter-native, exis-ten-tialism, struc-ture, strin-gent.*

8. Present participles may be divided before their -*ing* ending: *ask-ing, carry-ing, giv-ing, sing-ing, tak-ing, walk-ing.*

However, note that when the ending-consonant sounds of the main word occur in a syllable with a silent vowel, such consonant sounds become part of the added -*ing; buck-ling, chuck-ling, han-dling, muf-fling, twink-ling.* Also note that when the -*ing* ending results in doubling a consonant, separation should occur between the consonants: *sin-ning,* not *sinn-ing.*

9. Most prefixes and suffixes may be divided from main words.

Such affixes should not be separated if they consist of only one letter, but others can be set apart: *ante-cedent, convert-ible, pre-pare, argu-able.*

10. Do not divide sums of money, initials in a name, proper nouns, and units of time.

Write in their entirety on the first or second line items like these and all others that might be misinterpreted or misread. For example, if you refer to $3,654,987.00, write the entire unit on one line. If a person's initials are J. L., put them together, not on separate lines.

11. Divide compound words between their main parts.

Avoid dividing *understanding,* for example, into *un-der-stand-ing.* It is preferable for each main part to stand by itself: *under-standing.*

12. Let pronunciation be your guide when three consonants come together.

Such a combination of letters is fairly common in English. Note the division of the following words: *punc-ture, chil-dren, watch-ing, hail-stone, self-made.*

Enough. If these comments don't answer your questions, consult your dictionary. This is preferable to trusting pronunciation alone or memorizing the principles just cited.

28d. Use a hyphen (or hyphens) to indicate the structure (spelling) of a word.

Notice that r-o-u-g-h and c-o-u-g-h are pronounced differently. The prefix of this word should be p-r-o, not p-e-r.

28e. Use a hyphen (or hyphens) to suggest a hesitant manner of expression.

W-e-ll, I think I can go; y-y-es, I'm sure I can.
Our family likes p-p-potatoes but not t-t-tomatoes.

28f. Use a hyphen to represent dialectal pronunciation.

The horse came a-tearin' into the stable.
We just sat there, a-drinkin' and a-gassin'.

28g. Use a hyphen with certain street addresses and telephone numbers.

We live at 109-76 189th Street.
Our number used to be Riverside 3-1165, but now it is 743-1165.

28g

EXERCISE 11

A. Circle the hyphens on one page of a book that you are reading, another textbook, or a magazine. Give the reason for each.

B. Copy the following words in a list, and make a list of the same words without the hyphens. What is the difference in meaning when the same word is hyphenated or written solid? *re-treat, re-creation, re-view, re-claim, re-dress, re-lay, re-search, re-turn, re-cover, re-act, re-collect, re-pose, re-tire, re-count, re-sign, re-prove, re-sound, re-solve, re-sort, re-cite.*

C. Indicate where hyphens should be inserted in the following sentences:

1. Most business letters are written on 8½ by 11 inch stationery.
2. On some of our trips we make use of the state owned and government owned parks.
3. My registration here was a true once in a lifetime experience.
4. On the basketball floor Tim, with his 6 foot, 8 inch frame, was able easily to reach over his smaller opponents' heads.
5. After an hour or so of study, one should take a five or ten minute break.
6. Thirty five to forty five dollars a week is good income for a 12 year old boy.
7. I have learned that a tailor made suit may be cheaper to buy than a ready to wear type.
8. I went into the kitchen where, huddled over in one corner, was a little black faced, long legged, brown eyed boxer puppy.
9. If I were a student again, I would try to make a better than average grade on every test, quiz, or recitation.
10. Easter has long been celebrated as a coming of spring festival.
11. On county roads one should drive at a 40 mile per hour speed.

12. The community sponsored activities in my home town are of high quality.
13. Too many of us take what I call an on the spur of the moment action.
14. These model airplane kits have step by step instructions for putting the planes together.
15. "Amidst the general hum of mirth and conversation that ensued, there was a little man with a puffy say nothing to me or I'll contradict you sort of countenance . . ." (Charles Dickens, *The Pickwick Papers.*)

29. Parentheses and brackets

( ) / [ ]

29

Parentheses ( ) are principally used in pairs to enclose explanatory matter in a sentence. Such material is not intended to be a part of the main statement and often has no direct grammatical relationship to the sentence in which it appears. Marks of *parenthesis* (or *parentheses* or *parens* as they are usually called) signal to the reader what speakers mean when they say "By the way," or "Incidentally," or "Here's something to consider, but it's only a side remark."

You may set off incidental (parenthetical) material by commas, dashes, or marks of parenthesis. Each of these marks is acceptable for this purpose; your choice will usually depend on the closeness of relationship between the inserted material and the remainder of the sentence. Commas are ordinarily used to enclose parenthetical material that is closely related in thought and structure to the sentence in which it occurs; dashes enclose parenthetical material that forcefully and abruptly breaks into the sentence; parentheses are used to enclose material more remote in structure or thought that runs to some length and may itself contain internal punctuation, such as commas. The following sentences illustrate this general tendency, although the marks conceivably could be used interchangeably:

Denmark, which is where he was born, was his favorite European country.
Denmark—he lived there until he was 7—was his favorite European country.
Denmark (he was a native of that country and lived there until he was 7) was his favorite European country.

Parentheses are conspicuous marks of punctuation; therefore, do

( ) / [ ]

29b

not overuse them. Also, if your writing contains many parenthetical statements that require punctuation, look to your sentence structure; it is likely that you are not writing in a clear, straightforward style. Parentheses are actually interrupters and tend to slow communication from writer to reader. Most sentences can be rephrased to avoid using parenthetical statements. For example, the first sentence of the three just presented may be recast into one that contains no parenthetical material: "Because he was born there, Denmark was his favorite country."

A *bracket* [ ] is one of two marks (brackets are always used in pairs) primarily for the purpose of enclosing material that is not part of a quoted passage. Brackets are editorial marks used to enclose *comments, corrections,* or *additions* to quoted material.

Brackets occur in professional and academic writing but have limited use elsewhere. The bracket does not appear on most typewriter keyboards and must be inserted by hand or, if desired, made on the typewriter by using a bar (virgule) and two underscores. Brackets should never be confused with marks of parenthesis. Parentheses are used to enclose your own parenthetical material; brackets are used to set off matter inserted by you into someone else's writing.

29a. Use parentheses to enclose material that is only remotely or indirectly connected with its context.

These proposals (I am fairly certain they are sensible) should be carefully studied.

If you see any fresh peaches at the store (they must be in season now), please bring me some.

If anyone has not bought a ticket yet (sales began a week ago), a few seats are left.

29b. Use parentheses to enclose numerals or letters indicating divisions.

She was studying horticulture for three reasons: (1) she likes outdoor life; (2) she has had some experience at a nursery; (3) she enjoys watching plants grow.

The committee decided to (a) appoint a new president; (b) dismiss the treasurer; (c) set a date for the next meeting; (d) adjourn.

29c. Use parentheses to enclose sums of money only when explicit accuracy is essential.

Sums of money repeated for accuracy occur often in legal papers and business writing. Ordinarily, either words or numerals will be sufficient in sentences like the following:

Our grocery bill was eighty-six dollars ($86.00).
The going price is sixty cents (60¢) a pound.

( ) / [ ]

29f

29d. Use brackets to enclose a comment that is inserted into a quoted passage.

The teacher then said, "Class is dismissed. [Cheers.] But your papers are due at the next meeting."
The talk show host then said, "I am pleased to present [obviously he was not at all pleased] our singing star."

29e. Use brackets to add to a quoted passage.

"She was fined ten pounds [$22] for the violation."
The advertisement read: "These gloves [designed by Pucci] are now on sale."

29f. Use brackets to insert a correction into quoted material.

"His heritage was Norwegian [actually, Danish], a fact of which he was proud."
"Lincoln was born on February 12, 1806 [1809]."
"I was born in Conneticut [Connecticut] in 1962," the speaker remarked.

Note: Use the word *sic* (Latin for "thus") in brackets to indicate an error that you do not choose to correct:

"I am to [*sic*] weak to get up."

197

29g. Brackets have two miscellaneous uses.

1. In some plays, stage directions may be enclosed in brackets: [Macbeth leaves].

2. Brackets may enclose parenthetical remarks that are already within parentheses.

"This incident (it is related in Chapter 10 of the biography [1976 edition]) is not believable."

EXERCISE 12

Insert parentheses or brackets where they belong in these sentences:

1. With the arrival of the relatives one never knows how many confusion reigns.

2. Sometime in April, 1564 the exact day is not known William Shakespeare was born in Stratford-on-Avon, England.

3. There are two major divisions of Christmas presents: a those of a monetary value, and b those which money cannot buy.

4. Several essays by Thoreau you do remember him? have been widely quoted.

5. My grandfather Jones Crankie as my sister and I always called him when we were children is a well-known dentist.

6. The first three years of my life 1962–1964 were spent in Germany my father was stationed there.

7. My first orchid, even though my friend did not have to pay for it his parents owned the greenhouse, had great meaning for me.

8. The magazine article began: "People these days are to sic busy to care about anyone but themselves."

9. "*Plain Sense* was published early in the nineteenth century 1826 by a New York printer."

10. Air pollution see Chapter 10 was eagerly discussed.

30. Italics

In longhand and typewritten copy, certain words and groups of words should be underlined to correspond to the conventions of using italic type. These conventions, however, have never been standardized, and the use of italic type varies widely from one publication to another.

To a printer, italic type means letters with a slope to the right that look quite unlike the so-called roman type that is ordinarily used. To a reader, italic type indicates that some word or group of words has been singled out for emphasis or some other distinction. To a writer, the use of italics (underlining) is a troublesome problem in the mechanics of writing about which few authoritative statements may be made.

One flat statement can be made: the use of italics has greatly decreased in recent years. Few newspapers now use italic type except for directions to readers, such as "continued" lines, or unless it is specified in display advertising. Magazines, even carefully edited ones, currently use italic type in fewer and fewer instances in which formerly it was regularly employed.

Another statement can also be made with some accuracy: quotation marks (see Section 27) may be used to identify or emphasize words or groups of words just as italic type can. In fact, publications of varied sorts regularly use quotation marks for such purposes—although many words that, by convention, would be distinguished in some way often appear in roman type without either italics or quotation marks.

As a careful writer, use italics (underlining) in the specific situations cited here and quotation marks in other constructions.

30a. The following groups and classes of words should be italicized (underlined).

1. Titles of books and magazines

The Thorn Birds
The Godfather
Saturday Review
The Atlantic Monthly

In such titles, the first and last words and all other important words are capitalized. If *the* is the first word in the actual title of either a book or a magazine, it may be retained (although it is often dropped), in which case it should begin with a capital: *The Atlantic Monthly,* or the *Atlantic Monthly,* or *Atlantic Monthly.* (See Section 27e.)

2. Titles of plays, operas, long poems, and motion pictures

Strange Interlude [Play]
The Barber of Seville [Opera]
The Illiad [Long poem]
The Goodbye Girl [Motion picture]

3. Names of ships, trains, and aircraft

the *Titanic* [Steamship]
the *City of Denver* [Train]
the *Spirit of St. Louis* [Aircraft]

4. Names of newspapers

The New York Times
The San Francisco Chronicle
yesterday's *Dallas Herald*

Usage here can, and does, vary. Some authorities suggest that the article *the* be dropped when such names are cited. Others recommend that only the actual name of the newspaper be underlined (italicized) and not the place of its publication: Chicago *Tribune.* Newspapers themselves, as well as many other publications, rarely italicize such names at all. Formal writing requires that *at least* the name of a newspaper be underlined. (See Section 27e.)

5. Names of legal cases

John Doe v. *Mary Doe* or John Doe *v.* Mary Doe

The citation of legal cases is not likely to concern you often, but the use of italics in such instances is standard. However, convention requires that the *v.* (for Latin *versus,* "against") appear in roman type if italics are used elsewhere in the citation, and in italics if roman is used for the actual names involved.

6. Scientific names

Ursus arctos (European brown bear)
Felis catus (an ordinary cat)

Convention decrees that the Latin (scientific) names of genera and species appear in italics. The names of groups higher than genera are usually printed in roman type, but they may appear in italics if you wish to show off your learning or your careful use of a dictionary.

7. Foreign words and phrases

There is a *je ne sais quoi* quality about this object. [French for "I don't know what"]

Honi soit qui mal y pense. [French for "shamed be he who thinks evil of it" or "evil to him who evil thinks"]

Cura facit canos. [Latin for "care brings gray hairs"]

Note that thousands of words and phrases have been so thoroughly absorbed into the English language that they need no longer be italicized. Such words as these can safely be written without italics:

ad infinitum	ex officio
alias	gratis
billet doux	hors d'oeuvres
bona fide	matinee
carte blanche	mores
delicatessen	prima facie
en route	sauerkraut
et cetera	vice versa

When you are uncertain whether a word is still considered foreign enough to be underlined, consult a dictionary. All good dictionaries use some device for indicating the domestic-foreign status of words.

8. Items for specific reference

Italics (underlining) may be used to refer to a word, letter, number, or phrase that is spoken of as such:

I misspelled *deification* on the test.

There's a difference between *horde* and *hoard*.

Your *l*'s look exactly like *t*'s. [Only the letter should be italicized, not the apostrophe or the *s*.]

Is this a *6* or a *9*?

9. Items for emphasis

On occasion—and it should be a rare occasion—you can add emphasis by underlining. When you do single out a word or phrase for emphasis, use only one line, not the two or three that sometimes appear in the informal notes of immature writers.

You should <u>always</u> sign your name to a letter.
<u>Never</u> show your bankroll in a public place.
Whatever you think, <u>whatever</u> you even <u>suspect</u>, keep quiet.
The late Will Rogers was never more humorous than when he said: "Don't gamble. Take all your savings, buy some good stock, and hold it until it goes up. Then sell it. <u>If it doesn't go up, don't buy it.</u>"

A final word about italics: Underlined words, like italic type, are conspicuous. Be sparing in your use of them; never underline without a specific and clear purpose in mind.

EXERCISE 13

Copy the following sentences, underlining the words that should be italicized:

1. Many travelers regret the passing of great transatlantic liners like the Queen Mary and the Queen Elizabeth.
2. Looking up the name Jane, we find it equivalent to Joan, and Joan is equivalent to Joanna, which is the feminine of John.
3. The British differ in their spelling of some words: They use more -our and -re endings instead of -or and -er.
4. I like to reread famous works such as Mark Twain's Huckleberry Finn and William Shakespeare's Julius Caesar.
5. When the reader specifically is meant, the pronouns you, your, and yours are recommended.
6. The Chicago Tribune is a leading newspaper in the Midwest; The New York Times and The Christian Science Monitor are leaders in the East.
7. Our music director adds spice by the way she pronounces words, such as da-reem' for dream and ka-rye' for cry.
8. Monitor comes from the Latin word monere, which means to warn; the word monitor has been used (capitalized thus, Monitor) as the name of a ship.
9. Everyone who likes to travel should read magazines like Travel, Holiday, and The National Geographic.
10. Some people say au revoir and some say auf Weidersehen; I'll stick with the plain, old-fashioned American good-by.

31. Capitals

It is impossible to state all the rules for using capital letters. The appearance of capitals is widespread; usage is not fixed and unchanging; exceptions occur for almost every "standard" rule of capitalization.

Despite the confusion that exists about capital letters, the basic principles involved are somewhat clearer than they have been in the past. In general, current tendency is toward a "down" style. (Capitals are sometimes called *upper-case* letters, since they come from the upper case of a font of hand-set type. Small letters are correspondingly sometimes called *lower-case* letters.) Books, magazines, and especially newspapers are employing fewer capitals than they formerly did.

cap

31a

The best general rule to follow is this: use capitals only for a specific purpose and in accordance with a clearly recognized principle. Unnecessary capital letters clutter up a page as much as do large numbers of dashes, exclamation points, or other obtrusive marks.

31a. Capitalize the first word of every sentence, including every quoted sentence and line of poetry.

1. Capitalize the first word of every sentence.

This is one rule that all of us know. But even this hard-and-fast practice is not always followed. It applies in nearly all instances, but just to show you how involved and perplexing much of punctuation and mechanics is, suppose you were to write the following:

Letters in the English language may be classified as vowels and consonants. *A, e, i, o,* and *u* are the principal vowels.

You do not mean that *a* is a principal vowel only when it is capitalized; the sentence really could logically begin with a lower-case (small) letter, couldn't it?

Or how about this?

The tree was not healthy (beetles are the natural enemy of leaves) and had to be cut down.

A sentence enclosed in parentheses inside another sentence *may* begin with a capital letter, but it often doesn't.

Even so, remember the basic rule. But also remember that very little about punctuation can be taken for granted; few of its "rules" admit *no* exception.

2. Capitalize the first word of a direct quotation and of a quoted sentence.

Our director said, "You have done a good job."

"I never met a man I didn't like" is a saying attributed to Will Rogers.

"Yes," Donna replied. "You have my permission to leave now and my request never to return."

Aldous Huxley once wrote: "That all men are created equal is a proposition to which, at ordinary times, no sane human being has ever given assent."

When only *part* of a direct quotation is included within a sentence, it is usually not begun with a capital letter:

The accident victim said that he felt "badly shaken," but he refused hospitalization.

3. The first word following a colon, question mark, or exclamation point is usually capitalized if it is a proper name or begins a complete sentence.

In suggesting that no one is indispensable, Stevenson wrote: "Atlas was just a gentleman with a protracted nightmare."

A wise man knows this: Advice when it is most needed is often least heeded.

The first word following a colon, question mark, or exclamation point is usually not capitalized if it introduces a supplementary remark that is closely related to what preceded the mark.

Wars are never accidental: they are planned.

Who is coming? Are you? your father? your mother?

4. In quoting (or writing) poetry, capitalize the first word of each line.

"And we are here as on a darkling plain,
Swept with confused alarms of struggle and flight

Where ignorant armies clash by night."
—MATTHEW ARNOLD

Some modern poetry is written without capital letters at the beginnings of lines. Always use the capitalization employed in the poem you are quoting.

5. The first word following a resolving or enacting clause is capitalized. The first word following *Whereas* in contracts, resolutions, and the like is usually not capitalized.

> *Resolved,* That the Congress do now . . .
> *Be it ordered,* That . . .
> *Whereas* the following parties . . .

6. Capitalize the first word and each noun in the salutation of a letter, but only the first words in the complimentary close.

> My dear Sir: Very truly yours,
> Dear Mr. and Mrs. Brown: Yours sincerely,

31b. Capitalize proper nouns and words derived from them.

Although they are not used as much today as they were in the past, capital letters are required for many classes and groups of words. The following list indicates some of the most common types of capitalized words:

1. Names of people and titles used for specific persons

> Abraham Lincoln, Eleanor Roosevelt, the Senator, the Secretary, the President, The Whitney family, Mother, Grandfather, the Major.

2. Names of countries, states, regions, localities, other geographic areas, and the like

> Canada, France, Arizona, the Orient, the Torrid Zone, the Midwest, the Blue Ridge Mountains, the Solid South, the Painted Desert, the Kanawha River, Lake Erie, the Commonwealth of

cap

31b

Virginia, the Swiss Confederation, the Gulf of Mexico, Des Moines.

3. Names of streets

Seventh Avenue, Bronson Road, Cherry Lane, Ninety-sixth Street.

4. Names of the Deity and personal pronouns referring to Him

Jesus Christ, the Almighty, God, Heavenly Father, Jehovah, Him, Thy, His, the Creator, the Holy Ghost, Allah, the Supreme Being.

5. Names for the Bible and other sacred writings

Book of Psalms, Bible, Gospels, the Scriptures, the Koran, Genesis, the Talmud, the Apocrypha, the Upanishads.

6. Names of religions and religious groups

Roman Catholicism, Episcopalian, Moslem, Protestantism, Unitarian, Hinduism, Islam.

7. Names of the days and the months (but not the seasons)

Sunday, Monday, etc.; January, February, etc.; winter, spring, summer, fall, autumn.

8. Names of schools, universities, and colleges

Salem High School, Cornell University, Virginia Military Institute, Williams College.

9. Names of historical events, eras, and holidays

Civil War, Cenozoic era, Stone Age, Renaissance, Veterans Day, Yom Kippur, Memorial Day, Christmas, the Middle Ages, Louisiana Purchase, the Treaty of Versailles.

10. Names of ethnic groups, organizations, and members of each

Eskimo, Aryan, University Club, American League, New York Mets, a Boy Scout, Celtic, Anglo-Saxon, Malayan, Caucasian.

11. Vivid personifications

Destiny, the Angel of Death, the New Frontier, the Nutmeg State, Star of Fortune.

12. Trade names

Pepsi Cola, Dr. Pepper, Cheerios, Mr. Clean, Frigidaire, Palmolive, Ry-Krisp, Kleenex.

13. Scientific names

The names of a scientific class, order, genus, or family is usually capitalized: *Carnivora, Crustacea, Felidae, Arthropoda.*

14. Ordinal numbers

An ordinal number (*first, second, third*) is capitalized when used with the name of a person or period. Such a number is spelled out if it precedes the name. Roman numerals may follow the name of the person or era:

The Thirty-ninth Congress, George VI, the Second Utah Regiment, Pope John XXIII.

15. Many abbreviations and several miscellaneous one-letter symbols are capitalized

Ms. Smolen, James C. Wing, D.D.S., the Hon. Alfred Auray, F. (Fahrenheit), C. (centigrade and Celsius), N. (North), C (one hundred).

16. Interjections

Exclamations of surprise and anger often appear at the beginnings of sentences and are capitalized for this reason only. But the interjection *O* is always capitalized:

Please come early and, oh, be sure to bring your guitar.

"Sail on, O Ship of State."

17. Words in foreign languages according to the rules of the language

The use of capital letters is made more chaotic by the fact that several foreign languages employ capitals quite differently from English usage. Perhaps you know, for example, that *all* nouns and words used as nouns are capitalized in German. But did you know that the adjectives derived from proper nouns (as *American* is derived from *America*) are not capitalized in French, Italian, Spanish, Portuguese, Danish, Norwegian, and Swedish? We would write *French literature*; and the French write *littérature française*.

If you know a foreign language well enough to write it, you probably know most of its rules for capitalization. If you are reading a foreign language, do not think that its capitalization is necessarily incorrect merely because it does not follow English practices.

1. In Greek and Latin poetry only the first word of a paragraph (stanza) is capitalized, not each line of verse.

2. In German family names *van* and *von* are usually, but not always, capitalized. Follow the preference shown in personal signatures.

3. Latin follows English practice in capitalizing proper nouns and proper adjectives; the Dutch capitalize all nouns (as the Germans do) and all proper adjectives (as the Germans do not, except for those derived from persons' names).

4. For our particle *the,* French uses *le* and *la* (masculine and feminine); for *of the,* the French use *de la, du* (*de* + *le*), *des* (*de* + *les*). These particles are capitalized when they are not preceded by a Christian name or title, and are written in small letters when they are preceded by such a name or title. Italians use *di* and *da* and the Dutch *ter* as the French use *de* and *du*:

   *Guy de Maupassant; De Maupassant; La Salle; Du Barry;
   Leonardo da Vinci; Hans ter Zeeland.*

18. Governmental terms

the House of Representatives, the Senate, the Department of Labor, the British Embassy, the United Nations, the Bureau of the Census, the Iowa State Highway Commission.

19. Titles of books, plays, musical compositions, magazines

Vanity Fair, Romeo and Juliet, The Blue Danube Waltz, U.S. News & World Report.

Prepositions, conjunctions, and articles are not capitalized except at the beginning or end of titles or unless they consist of five or more letters.

EXERCISE 14

cap

31b

A. Circle all the capitals on a page of a textbook or magazine. Give the reason for each capital.

B. Copy the following sentences, correcting the misuse or nonuse of capitals according to principles stated in Section 31:

1. Our english teacher often told us, "you can't judge a book by its cover."

2. Numerous examples can be cited from the bible and other Books about god and the greatness of his works.

3. The names of some of our States and many of our Cities have an indian origin.

4. I am registered as a Freshman in the college of home economics here at lakeside university.

5. She blurted out, "how about thursday or friday?" to which he replied, "fine!"

6. My freshman courses consist of plant science 140, english composition 101, chemistry 111 and 112, zoology 161, and speech 114.

7. The mississippi river is the most famous river in American history; the kankakee river is not so well known.

8. The climate is mild in rome, italy; the coldest months are december, january, and february.

9. In little things Happiness is sometimes found, like an a on an english paper.

10. Every summer aunt laura and aunt ida come to visit us.

11. My main interests deal with the subjects of Chemistry, Guns, Airplanes, Rockets, and the Planet Earth.

12. Some english teachers hunt for Topic Sentences and Transitional Sentences the way a hunter hunts for game.

13. To reach chatsworth you must take u.s. highway 52 to junction 24, and then turn left on state route 24.

14. During his term of service my Father was sent to live in several places in the east and in the south.

15. The poet shelley ends his famous poem, "ode to the west wind," with these words: "o Wind, if winter comes, can spring be far behind?"

32. Abbreviations

Abbreviations, shortened forms of words and phrases, save time and space. In addition, proper use of abbreviations avoids the needless spelling out of often-repeated phrases and words, a practice that annoys some readers. Coming across spelled-out items such as "Mister Jones" and "Mistress Adams" would be distracting and bothersome to most readers.

Actually, more and more abbreviations are being used as the tempo of living increases. Here, for example, are abbreviated forms of professions, industries, or types of business as they appear on one page of a city telephone directory. All save space, and all appear without periods: *catrg, consltnt, dmnds, engrvr, frght forwdrs, furn, ins, jwlrs, ofc, pblctn, plmbg & heatg, pub accnt, restrnt, rl est, stk brkr.* Are all of these readily understandable? In writing, especially if space is not at a premium, it would be preferable to spell out *catering, consultant, diamonds, engraver, freight forwarders, furniture, insurance, jewelers, office, publication, plumbing and heating, public accountant, restaurant, real estate,* and *stock broker.*

As a general rule, spell out all words and phrases that would be puzzling if abbreviated and abbreviate correctly all terms that are frequently encountered and are readily understood in shortened form.

32a. In carefully prepared, formal writing use few abbreviations.

A limited number of abbreviations are acceptable in *all* writing. Among them are the following: *Mr., Mrs., Ms., Dr., Ph.D., ibid., Col.* (Colonel), *col.* (column), A.D., B.C., A.M., P.M.

32b. Use only acceptable abbreviations in writing of all kinds.

Abbreviations should meet two criteria: (1) They must be appropriate to the context in which they appear. (2) They must be standard forms listed by reputable dictionaries. The second requirement rules out such abbreviations as *n.g.* (no good) and *g.f.*

(girl friend). The first suggests that some standard abbreviations are inappropriate in carefully prepared writing: *Xmas, advt. no., Nov., St.* (meaning "street").

The abbreviations listed in Section 32a are acceptable and customary in all writing, no matter how formal and precise. Literally thousands of other abbreviations are standard and appear frequently in ordinary prose. Here is a summary of often-used standard abbreviations:

1. *Names of days:* Sun., Mon., Tues., Wed., Thurs., Fri., Sat. (to be used only as dates and not recommended in formal writing).

2. *Names of months:* Jan., Feb., Aug., Sept., Oct., Nov., Dec. (The months of March, April, May, June, and July are not properly abbreviated. Again, the shortened forms are not recommended in formal writing.)

3. *Names of states:* Ill., Ind., N.C., Del., Mass. (These abbreviations are used chiefly in addresses and are not recommended for use in formal papers.) The U.S. Postal Department uses a different list of preferred state abbreviations, each consisting of two capital letters: IL, IN, NY, FL, DE, MA.

4. *Names of organizations:* D.A.R.; N.O.W.; A.F.L.; G.O.P.; B.P.O.E. (Preferably, spell out such terms the first time they are used.)

5. *Names of government agencies:* CIA, FBI, SEC, TVA, FDIC.

6. *Titles:* Rev., Atty., Sec., Treas.

7. *Measurements:* in., bu., ft., lb., m, l, mg, yd.

8. *Bibliographical terms:* vol., pp., op. cit., loc. cit.

9. *Money:* c; ct. (cent); dol. (dollar); U.S. $ (used in foreign trade).

If you need to use abbreviations often, consult your dictionary. All good dictionaries provide either separate lists of abbreviations, with definitions, or individual entries in alphabetical order, or both.

32c. Use a period after most, but not all, abbreviations.

Most of the abbreviations just listed, as well as many others, are followed by periods. Exceptions to this rule are numerous, however. Many agencies are abbreviated without periods (*UNICEF, FSLIC, NASA*). Metric measurements, when abbreviated, are not followed by periods (e.g., *km* for *kilometer*). Certain shortened forms, none of which is appropriate in formal writing, do not require periods: *phone, lab, ad, exam.* Nicknames appear without periods (*Jan, Al, Ben, Ned, Sal, Ted, Bill, Fran*). Contractions like *can't, aren't, doesn't,* and *wasn't* are written without periods.

num

33

EXERCISE 15

Change the use of abbreviations in the following sentences to conform to the directions given in Section 32. Assume that the sentences are part of a formally written paper.

1. I have 8 o'clock classes every Mon., Wed., and Fri. A.M.
2. The prep schools in England are often called pub. schools.
3. Our home ec courses are not as easy as some non-ec students think.
4. My brother Thomas is 21 yrs. old, is 6′2″ tall, and weighs approximately 180#; by comparison, my brother John is only 5 ft. 5 in. tall and weighs 112 lbs.
5. At Morgan Park Mil. Acad. I had an excellent teacher who was a capt. in the U.S.M. Corps; he has since become a lt.-col.
6. When I finish my college chem and lab courses, I would like to go on to grad. school.
7. Berta has recently been awarded a scholarship to Col. Univ. in N.Y.C., N.Y.
8. The parade down Penn. Ave. was something to behold; I should like to be in Wash., D.C., and see another.
9. The assignments in our English comp. book deal with all phases of comp. and with some suggestions for lit. reading.
10. The three lines of the letter heading were: 222 Indep. Blvd., Phila., Pa., Feb. 15, '79.

33. Numbers

Writing words for numerals or using numbers for words is a matter of convention and custom. A few general principles about this vexing problem of mechanics can be stated; but variations do occur, and the stylebooks of reputable newspapers, magazines, and book publishers differ widely.

Since exact and unchanging rules for representing numerals cannot be cited, it is preferable to adopt a general system and use it consistently. In arriving at a formula that will cover most of your uses of numerals, remember these generally accepted principles:

1. Never begin a sentence with an actual numeral.
2. Use words for numbers between one and ten. (This spelling-out-below-ten rule does not apply to numbers illustrated in Section 33b.)
3. Use figures for numbers above ten.
4. When a number can be expressed in no more than two words, write it in words.
5. When a number can be expressed in no fewer than three words, use figures.
6. Arabic numerals are generally preferable to Roman numerals.

num

33a

Memorizing these six principles will save you trouble. Yet not even these rules are observed by all publications. For example, many reputable newspapers use figures for nearly all numbers, regardless of size. Also, you must use some common sense in applying the rule about not beginning a sentence with a numeral. This is an undesirable sentence:

Two thousand two hundred dollars and fifty cents was his bank balance.

Recast the sentence to make it clearer and still avoid beginning with a numeral:

His bank balance was $2,200.50.

Again, these six principles admit certain exceptions, to be explained shortly. But mastering these "rules" will clear up most of your problems about numbers; applying them consistently will help make your writing clear.

33a. Use words to represent numbers in special situations.

1. A number at the beginning of a sentence

Five hundred employees are covered by group insurance.
Thirty of these couples are from another town.

2. Indefinite expressions and round numbers

The mid-twenties must have been a frantic era.
This hall will seat three hundred persons.

3. Fractions standing alone or followed by the expressions *of a* and *of an*

This cardboard is one-eighth inch thick.
His home is one-fourth of a mile from the store.

4. Numbers used with dignified and important subjects

Utah is not one of the Thirteen Original Colonies.
He died while he was a member of the Seventy-eighth Congress.

5. Numbers preceding a compound modifier containing a figure

The platform was supported by eight 6-foot poles.
Now we need six ¼-inch strips of canvas.

33b. Figures are sometimes used to represent numbers in special instances.

1. Units of measurement

Such units include age, degrees of temperature and angular distance, size, weight, and the like. These units are always expressed in figures regardless of the appearance of other numerical expressions within a sentence.

Tom's employer is 42 years old, but he himself is 64.
He lived for 54 years, 11 months, and 6 days.
The latitude is 49° 26′ 12″ N.
The thermometer registered 12° this morning.
A high temperature of 16 degrees was reported.
The rows were planted 3 feet apart.
All his stationery measures 8½ by 11 inches.

Heather poured 2 gallons into a 5-gallon can.
This huge book weighs 3 pounds and 12 ounces.
A "10-foot pole" is a "3.302-meter pole."

2. Dates, including the day or the day and the year

Please report for work in July.
My birth date is August 19, 1949.
He was in the armed services from July 15 to November 30, 1953, when he was discharged.
The proper date line for a letter is May 10, 1978.
The proper date line for a letter is 10 May 1978 [no comma].

3. Time

12 M. (noon).   3:46 P.M.   half past 7

11 o'clock [Not 11 o'clock A.M. or 11:00 in the morning]
He was in a coma for 4 hours, 14 minutes, and 30 seconds.

4. House, room, telephone, and postal zone numbers

She lives at 472 Old Mill Road, Lipton, Connecticut 06438.
His room number is 906; his telephone number is 304-6795, but it formerly was Clearwater 9-1848.

5. Highway and other comparable numbers

We took U.S. Highway 95 to New Haven.
On this set we cannot get Channel 6.
Train #176 is due to come in on Track 7.
Flight 126 will depart from Gate 4.

6. Percentages and other mathematical expressions

The interest rate is 6%.
He bought two 6½ percent bonds.
The ratio of 2 to 8 is the same as the ratio of 8 to 32.
The specific gravity is 0.9567.
Multiply by 3 to find the correct number.

num

33c

7. Money

$0.50   50 cents $5.50   10 cents each (apiece) $4 per
100 pounds $7 a pound   £2 5s. 4d.

8. Unit modifiers.

7-hour day   5-day week   8-inch plank   10-million-dollar
loan   5-foot-wide entrance

9. Chapter, page, and footnote numbers

Chapter 16   See page 14   pages 306–63
See Footnote 4 on page 65 for an explanation.

33c. Use ordinal numbers correctly.

The numbers discussed so far in this section are *cardinal numbers,*
those that we use in counting: *one, two, three,* or 1, 2, 3. *Ordinal
numbers* indicate rank or order: *first, second, third* or 1st, 2nd, 3rd.
On occasion you may need to express figures and alphabetical
letters in combination. Such combinations are correctly used in
tables, in numbering paragraphs, in indicating a numbered street
(from 10th on), and sometimes in dates (but not when the year
follows immediately).

The conventions that apply in this combination are numerous
and involved, but the following illustrations show current form in
several common expressions:

Your June 15th letter [or *your letter of June 15*] was welcome.
Your June 15, 1980, letter was welcome.
686 North Second Street   105 Fifth Avenue
The corner of 4th Road and Sixth Avenue
36th parallel   fifth precinct   7th Air Force

When two or more ordinal numbers appear in a sentence and
one of them is *10th* or more, use figures for each number:

He campaigned in the 1st, 4th, and 12th wards.

33d. Use Roman numerals correctly.

The figures with which we are most familiar come from the Arabs and hence are called Arabic numerals: 1, 2, 3, etc. But Roman letters were used exclusively until the tenth century and still have certain conventional uses today. For example, the cornerstones of most buildings and the plaques on most public monuments carry dates in Roman numerals. Such numerals also are used to number the preliminary pages of a book, to indicate the acts and scenes of a play, to refer to different individuals with the same name, and in other somewhat stylized situations.

num

33d

> Falstaff first appears in Act I, Scene ii, of *Henry IV*.
>
> Louis was the name of eighteen Kings of France ranging from Louis I to Louis XVIII.
>
> Jack had the same name as his father and grandfather and thus signed his name John William Smith, III.
>
> That article appears in Volume XIII of my encyclopedia.
>
> The date is faded somewhat, but you can make it out—MCMXII.

Roman numerals are rarely preferable to Arabic numbers, but you should know how they are formed in order to use them correctly when an infrequent need arises and also to understand what you read on cornerstones, tombstones, and monuments of various kinds. A repeated letter repeats a value; a letter before one of greater value subtracts from it; a letter following one of greater value adds to it; a line over the letter means "multiplied by 1,000." The eight basic symbols upon which the system is built are I, V, X, L, C, M, $\overline{V}$, and $\overline{M}$. The following table of Roman numerals is placed here for reference; don't waste time memorizing it.

I	1	XV	15
II	2	XIX	19
III	3	XX	20
IV	4	XXV	25
V	5	XXIX	29
VI	6	XXX	30
VII	7	XXXV	35
VIII	8	XXXIX	39
IX	9	XL	40
X	10	XLV	45

XLIX	49	CL	150
L	50	CC	200
LV	55	CCC	300
LIX	59	CD	400
LX	60	D	500
LXV	65	DC	600
LXIX	69	DCC	700
LXX	70	DCCC	800
LXXV	75	CM	900
LXXIX	79	M	1,000
LXXX	80	MD	1,500
LXXXV	85	MM	2,000
LXXXIX	89	MMM	3,000
XC	90	MMMM or M$\overline{\text{V}}$	4,000
XCV	95	$\overline{\text{V}}$	5,000
XCIX	99	$\overline{\text{M}}$	1,000,000
C	100		

EXERCISE 16

Change any unconventional uses of figures and spelled-out numbers in the following sentences:

1. The greatest attraction of Niagara Falls is the one-hundred-and-sixty-five-foot drop where two hundred thousand cubic feet of water fall every second.
2. 750 dollars a month is not unusual as a starting salary.
3. In England there are one hundred and twenty-six churches dedicated to St. George.
4. I am taking French one hundred and one and mathematics one hundred and sixty-one; I am a 1st-semester freshman.
5. My brother stands five feet four inches tall and weighs one hundred and thirty-nine pounds.
6. Will you please come to dinner at our hall at six forty-five P.M. on Wednesday, March twenty-third?
7. To be admitted you must be in the upper 3rd and preferably the upper 4th of your graduating class.
8. I was born on April twelfth in Portland, Missouri, in the year nineteen hundred and sixty-one; we now live at twelve hundred and one Seventy-ninth Street, and my telephone number is three-seven-two-one-one-six-five.
9. My home town can be reached by U.S. Highway Fifty-two or State Roads Twenty-five, Twenty-six, and Forty-three.
10. I went to the Bursar's Office on the 1st floor of the Administration Building and paid the fee of ninety-two dollars and fifty cents.

34. Miscellaneous marks

Several marks used in writing and printing are concerned as much with pronunciation and spelling as with punctuation. Some of them are important, and you should know their purposes and functions.

34a. Accent marks should be used where they are required.

When foreign words come into English, they usually do so with their original pronunciation and spelling, although most of them gradually become absorbed into English and tend to lose some of their "foreign" characteristics. Some words, however, are more slowly Anglicized (made English) and continue to cause problems in spelling and pronunciation for English-speaking people.

One aspect of this problem is the use of accent marks with certain words borrowed from other languages. The principal accent marks are, in alphabetical order, *acute, cedilla, circumflex, dieresis, grave, tilde,* and *umlaut.* If they originally had them, recently borrowed words tend to drop them as the words themselves become more widely used in English. In general, accent marks are retained in borrowed words only when they are needed to indicate pronunciation—and not always then.

1. Acute accent

In strictly formal writing, each of these words and expressions would carry an *acute accent:*

attaché	décolletage	idée fixe
blasé	décor	maté (beverage)
cliché	éclair	matériel
communiqué	éclat	passé
coup d'état	élan	précis
coupé	émigré	protégé (protégée)
curé	exposé	résumé
début (débutante)	fiancé (fiancée)	touché

219

2. Cedilla

A *cedilla* is a hooklike mark placed under the letter *c* in some borrowed words to show that it is sounded like a voiceless *s* and not like a *k*, the more usual pronunciation. In English it is used mainly with words of French origin and has more to do with spelling and pronunciation than with mechanics and punctuation. Use a cedilla under *c* in words like these if you are writing careful and formal English:

aperçu	garçon
façade	Provençal
Français	soupçon

3. Circumflex accent

A *circumflex accent* is used over a vowel in some languages, notably French, to indicate a particular quality or tone in pronunciation. The following are uncommon in English but, on occasion, admit no adequate substitutes:

bête noire	raison d'être
coup de grâce	table d'hôte
papier-mâché	tête-à-tête

4. Dieresis

Dieresis, also spelled *diaeresis,* is a mark that consists of two dots. It is used to indicate the separation of two consecutive vowels into different syllables. It is less used than formerly, having been largely replaced by the hyphen or dropped entirely. For example, the dieresis was formerly used almost universally to show that the first two syllables of *cooperate* and *zoology* are pronounced separately: *coöperate, zoölogy.* The word *re + examine* is now spelled either *reexamine* or *re-examine* but no longer with a dieresis. However, you may wish to use the mark with such words as *Chloë* and *naïve* to prevent mispronunciation.

5. Grave accent

A *grave accent* is used in French and in a few words that have been Anglicized from French to indicate the quality of the open *e*, as in the word for "dear" (*chère*). A grave accent is also occasionally used by writers, chiefly poets, to indicate that full pronunciation is to be given to an ending or syllable that is normally elided (run together) in speech: *lovèd* is pronounced "love-ed." The grave accent is increasingly being dropped from the following words and expressions, but still appears in formal usage:

à la carte   mise en scène
à la mode   pièce de résistance
crème (crème de la crème)   pied-à-terre

6. Tilde

A *tilde* is a mark placed over a letter, such as the *n* in Spanish and words that have been Anglicized from Spanish, to indicate the nasal sound represented in English by *ny*. The mark, like others discussed in this section, is being used less and less: for example, the word still spelled in Spanish as *cañon* is now almost always spelled *canyon* in English. However, precise writers continue to use the tilde in such words as *doña, mañana, piña, señor, vicuña,* and *São Paulo.*

7. Umlaut

An *umlaut* is a mark consisting of two dots (ü) that is used to indicate a vowel affected by partial assimilation to a succeeding sound. It is characteristic of Teutonic (German) languages and is sometimes used by especially careful writers. At present it is most often used in writing proper names: *Dürer, Die Walküre, Tannhaüser, Büchner, Brüning.* The name of the former Nazi leader, *Göring,* is spelled *Goering* in this country because of the rarity of umlaut usage here and also as an indication of the correct pronunciation of *o.*

Any good dictionary will indicate which of these seven accent marks is needed for any given word. But don't confuse any of these accent marks with marks used by a dictionary to divide syllables or to indicate where stress falls in pronunciation.

34b. Use asterisks sparingly.

An *asterisk* (★), a star-shaped mark now rarely used in writing, is a reference mark or a mark used to indicate that something has been omitted. It is a conspicuous mark and is used sparingly even in footnotes and in reference books and technical writing.

As a reference mark placed after a word or statement to be commented upon, the asterisk has been largely replaced by the use of a superior number (an Arabic number written slightly above the line). The employment of asterisks to indicate the omission of words from a sentence or entire sentences from a paragraph or a longer piece of writing has been almost universally abandoned in favor of ellipsis. (See Section 21.) Formerly, asterisks were also employed to suggest the passage of time in a story, much as fades and dissolves are used in television and motion pictures today. Even for this purpose they have been largely replaced by ellipsis periods or by blank space.

misc
mrks

34c

34c. The bar (also called *virgule*) has specialized uses.

A *bar* (/) is a short oblique stroke (diagonal) used in printing and in some writing. Dictionaries usually refer to this slanting mark as a *virgule,* a word that closely resembles the Latin word *virgula* ("little rod"), from which it is taken.

Primarily a mark of separation or division, the bar has miscellaneous uses in modern English. It appears in such expressions as *and/or,* primarily a business and legal term used when three alternatives are present: *boys and/or girls* may mean "boys" or "girls" or "boys and girls." Some especially careful writers object to the term *and/or,* but it is widely used and is undeniably a helpful time-saver.

A bar (virgule) is also used in quoting two or more lines of poetry in a prose passage when the lines are run together; use a bar to show the end of one line and the beginning of another. For example, these two lines from Pope's "An Essay on Man,"

> *And spite of Pride, in erring Reason's spite,*
> *One truth is clear, Whatever is, is right.*

might be written in a prose sentence:

> One of Pope's most quotable sayings, "And spite of Pride, in erring Reason's spite,/One truth is clear, Whatever is, is right" appears in his famous poem, "An Essay on Man."

The bar is also sometimes used to stand for the word *as;* an order for 500 copies of an item might read "520/500," which means that 520 copies would be shipped with only 500 being billed, the remainder being sent free to allow for damage in transit, promotional efforts, and so forth.

Occasionally the bar (virgule) is used to represent a month–day–year combination in informal letters or memoranda: November 11, 1918, may be represented 11/11/18. Also, the expression "in care of " is written informally as *c/o.* This device is sometimes used in writing fractions or in typewriting fractions that are not on standard keyboards: 7/8; 9/10.

34d. Use a brace to connect or group certain items.

A *brace* {or} is a mark used to connect two or more lines of writing and to group items in formulas, mathematical and chemical equations, and tables of statistics. Like all other marks of punctuation and mechanics, it is used solely for clarity: to make understandable to the reader the relationship between one line or group of lines consisting of words, symbols, or figures and another line or group of lines:

Conn.		Calif.	
Mass.		Wash.	Pacific Coast
R.I.	New England	Ore.	States
Maine	States		
N.H.			
Vt.			

		daily
Intervals		weekly
of Payment		monthly
		annually

34e. Use a caret to indicate an addition to writing.

A *caret* (∧) is an inverted *v*-shaped mark used to show that something between lines or in the margin should be added at the point indicated. The word *caret* has been taken over from Latin, where it means "there is lacking" or "there is wanting."

The caret is a useful device for making insertions, but do not overuse it. It is preferable for an entire page to be handwritten again or retyped to avoid numerous unsightly additions. Here is an example of how a caret may be used:

the autumn of

The first clubhouse, at 9 Brevoort Place, was leased in ∧ 1865.

34f. Use ditto marks only in special types of writing.

Ditto marks (") are a time- and effort-saving mechanical device that is frequently employed in tables of names, in bills, accounts, and similar types of writing where much repetition occurs. The word *ditto* comes from the Latin word for "saying," *dictum,* and actually means "the aforesaid," "the same as before." Ditto marks are conventionally used in preparing lists and tabulations but are rare in ordinary writing unless it is highly informal.

On the typewriter, dittos are made by using quotation marks.

Stir in one-half pound of melted butter.
Then add　　 "　　　 "　 " salted nuts.

35. Spelling

Correct spelling is essential for intelligent communication. It is taken for granted and expected at all times. Yet many people realize that their writing sometimes contains spelling errors, and are plagued by doubts and fears. Distraction, confusion, and misunderstanding result from errors in spelling.

Perhaps you are one of those people who feel disturbed by their spelling errors and have enough spelling conscience to do something about it. Or perhaps are among those who doubt their ability to master this difficult subject. You may have tried many times and failed. If so, is there any hope for you?

The answer is that *if you really have a desire to learn to spell perfectly you can, provided:*

1. You can pronounce such words as *accept* and *except* so that they will not sound exactly alike.

2. You can look at such words as *sad* and *sand* and in a single

glance, without moving your eyes, detect the difference between them.

3. You can sign your name without looking at the paper on which you are writing and without even consciously thinking about what you are doing.

4. You can tell your friend Jill from your friend Sue at a glance.

5. You can learn a simple rhyme, such as "Old King Cole was a merry old soul . . ."

6. You can remember that a compl*i*ment is "what *I* like to get."

7. You can equip yourself with a reliable desk dictionary.

8. You can learn to proofread your writing syllable by syllable.

If you can honestly meet these eight conditions, you can learn to spell *without ever making a mistake;* if you can meet only some of them, you can still double or quadruple your spelling efficiency.

The first and most important step in correct spelling is to form the *desire* to learn, really to want to become a competent speller; the second is to devote the necessary *time* to learning; the third is to use all available *means* to learn. (If you are chronically and consistently a poor speller, your instructor may recommend a special book that deals solely with spelling problems and provides spelling exercises.)

In addition to desire, time, and means, it should be easy to improve if you habitually do these seven things:

1. Pronounce words correctly.

2. Mentally *see* words as well as hear them.

3. Use a dictionary to fix words in your memory.

4. Use memory devices (mnemonics) to help remember troublesome words.

5. Learn a few spelling rules.

6. Write words carefully in order to avoid errors caused not by ignorance but by carelessness.

7. *List* and *study* the words you misspell most frequently.

35a. Proper pronunciation is an aid to correct spelling.

Mispronouncing words causes more trouble than any difference between the spelling and the sound of a correctly pronounced word. It is probably improper pronunciation that would make you write *calvary* when you mean *cavalry*. *Affect* and *effect* look somewhat alike, but they have different pronunciations as well as different meanings. A *dairy* is one thing: a *diary* is another. There is some reason why, from the sound of the word, you might spell *crowd* as "*croud*" or *benign* as "*benine*," but there may be no reason except poor pronunciation for spelling *shudder* as "*shutter*," *propose* as "*porpose*," or *marrying* as "*marring*."

Spelling consciousness, an awareness of words, depends in part on correct pronunciation. Properly pronouncing the following pairs of words will help some people spell them correctly; mispronouncing them will cause spelling trouble for almost anyone:

carton, cartoon	elicit, illicit	plaintiff, plaintive
celery, salary	finally, finely	sink, zinc
color, collar	minister, minster	specie, species
concur, conquer	picture, pitcher	tenet, tenant

Keep in mind these suggestions:

1. Do not add vowels in pronouncing and spelling the following:

athletics (not "athaletics")	grievous (not "grievious")
disastrous (not "disasterous")	laundry (not "laundery")
explanation (not "explaination")	Spanish (not "Spainish")

2. Do not drop vowels from the following:

accidentally	criticism	miniature
auxiliary	laboratory	proficient
brilliant	literature	temperament

3. Do not omit consonants in pronouncing and spelling the following:

acquaintance	environment	lightning
acquire	government	probably
candidate	library	surprised

4. Do not drop syllables in words like the following:

convenience	sophomore	tentative
interesting	temperature	wonderful

5. Watch out in spelling words with silent letters.

align	hymn	prompt
condemn	knee	psychology
dumb	knot	thumb
fourth	knuckle	wrap

6. Look carefully at the prefixes of words like the following:

antebellum	perfect
antemeridian	perhaps
anteroom	perjury
antiaircraft	predict
antifreeze	prescribe
antiseptic	prenatal

7. Be careful in spelling words with lightly stressed sounds.

actor	hypocrisy	privilege
calendar	loafer	separate
discipline	murmur	vulgar

8. Form the habit of pronouncing and spelling troublesome words syllable by syllable, writing them, and then pronouncing them aloud so as to relate sound to spelling.

35b. Words should be seen as well as heard.

The ability to visualize words, to see them in the mind's eye, is the hallmark of a good speller. When a word is mentioned, proficient spellers can "see" the word in full detail, every letter standing out, as though it were written down before them. Here is a method of learning to see words mentally:

1. With your eyes on the word being studied, pronounce it carefully. If you don't know the accepted pronunciation, consult a dictionary.
2. Study each individual letter in the word; if the word has more than one syllable, separate the syllables and focus on each one in turn.

3. *Close your eyes* and pronounce and spell the word either letter by letter or syllable by syllable, depending on its length.
4. Look at the word again to make certain that you have recalled it correctly.
5. Practice this alternate fixing of the image and recall of it until you are certain that you can instantly "see" the word under any circumstances and at any time.

Such a procedure is especially valuable when you are dealing with tricky words that add or drop letters for no apparent reason, contain silent letters, or transpose or change letters without logical cause: *explain,* but *explanation; curious,* but *curiosity; proceed,* but *procedure; maintain,* but *maintenance; pronounce,* but *pronunciation; fire,* but *fiery.*

The most frequent error in visualizing words is mistaking one word for another to which it bears some resemblance: *accept* and *except; adapt* and *adopt; affect* and *effect; all together* and *altogether; born* and *borne; breath* and *breathe; council* and *counsel; formally* and *formerly; its* and *it's; loose* and *lose; pail* and *pale; statue, stature,* and *statute; urban* and *urbane.*

35c. A dictionary is an important aid in correct spelling.

When you are suspicious of the spelling of any word you should check it immediately in your dictionary. "Doubt + dictionary = good spelling" is a reliable formula. However, it is a counsel of perfection, one that few of us are likely always to follow. Furthermore, our sense of doubt may be so great that we spend half our writing time flipping dictionary pages rather than communicating, and thus grow bored and frustrated.

Also, you may have tried to look up a word in the dictionary and been unable to find it. If your visual image of a word is weak, you can frustrate yourself even more: Look for *agast* and you may give up before discovering that the word is *aghast.* You won't find *pharmacy* and *photograph* among words beginning with *f.* A story is told of a man who was away on a trip and telephoned his assistant to send his gun to him at a hunting resort. The assistant asked his boss to spell out what he wanted. "Gun," he shouted.

"G as in *Jerusalem, u* as in *Europe, n* as in *pneumonia.*" Whether or not he received his *jep* is unknown; maybe he got a dictionary instead.

Information from a dictionary about the origin (etymology) of words is an aid in spelling. If, for instance, you know that the French word for sleep is *dormir* (from the Latin *dormitorium*), you will not spell *dormitory* with an *a* instead of an *i*. Similarly, a study of prefixes and suffixes will help you spell correctly by grouping hundreds of words in ways that emphasize their resemblance.

sp

35d

35d. Memory devices help in remembering some troublesome words.

One kind of memory device has the imposing name of *mnemonics*. The word is pronounced "ne-MON-iks" and comes from a Greek word meaning "to remember." A *mnemonic* is a special aid to memory, a memory "trick" based on what psychologists refer to as "association of ideas," that is, remembering something by associating it with something else. You have been using mnemonics for most of your life.

A mnemonic will be most helpful when you base it on some happening or some person in your life. That is, you must invent, or use, only mnemonics that associate ideas in a personal way.

Here are a few examples of mnemonics. They may not help you because they have no personal association, but they will provide ideas for the manufacture of your own.

all right: Two words. Associate with *all correct* or *all wrong.*
argument: I lost an *e* in that *argument.*
business: Business is no *sin.*
conscience: Con + science.
corps: Don't kill a live body with an *e* (*corpse*).
dessert: Strawberry sundae (double *s*).
piece: Have a *piece* of *pie.*
potatoes: Potatoes have *eyes* and *toes.*
privilege: Some special privileges are *vile.*
together: To + get + her.
vaccine: Vaccine is measured in cubic centimeters (*cc*'s).
villain: The *villain* likes his *villa* in that country.

sp

35e

35e. Some spelling rules are helpful.

If you study a number of words that have similar characteristics, you can make some generalizations about their spelling. In fact, observers have been doing just this for more than a century, with the result that some fifty spelling rules have been formulated.

Generalizations about the groupings of letters that form classes of words do help some people spell more correctly. The five basic rules given here are of particular value in spelling correctly certain classes of words.

1. Words containing *ei* or *ie*

About 1000 fairly common words contain *ei* or *ie*. It helps to know that *ie* occurs in about twice as many words as *ei*, but the problem is not thereby fully solved. The basic rule may be stated in this well-known verse:

> *Write* i *before* e
> *Except after* c
> *Or when sounded like* a,
> *As in* neighbor *and* weigh.

This rule, or principle, applies only when the pronunciation of *ie* or *ei* is a long *e* (as in *he*) or the sound of the *a* in *pale*.

There is another way to summarize the rule and its reverse: When the sound is long *e* (as in *piece*), put *i* before *e* except after *c*. When the sound is not long *e* (as it is not in *weigh*), put *e* before *i*.

Still another way to state the principle is thus: When the *e* sound is long, *e* comes first after *c*, but *i* comes first after all other consonants: *ceiling, conceit, conceive, deceit, perceive, receipt, receive, achieve, aggrieve, cashier, chandelier, handkerchief, hygiene, reprieve, retrieve*.

This much of the rule is fairly simple. The last two lines of the verse refer to words in which *ei* sounds like *a*. Fortunately, only a few everyday words, such as the following, are in this group: *chow mein, eight, feint, freight, heinous, neighbor, reign, rein, veil, vein, weight*.

A few words are exceptions to this basic *ei–ie* rule or are not fully covered by the verse. The best advice is to learn the following words by some method other than trying to apply the rule, which doesn't work: *either, Fahrenheit, fiery, financier, height, leisure, neither, protein, seize, sleight, stein, weird.*

2. Final *e*

Hundreds of everyday words end in *e,* and thousands more consist of such words plus suffixes: *care, careful, careless; hope, hopeful, hopeless.* In our pronunciation nearly all *e*'s at the ends of words are silent: *advice, give, live.* Actually, the usual function of a final silent *e* is to make the syllable long: *rate,* but *rat; mete,* but *met; bite,* but *bit; note,* but *not.*

Final silent *e* is usually dropped before a suffix beginning with a vowel but is usually retained before a suffix beginning with a consonant.

advise, advising	ice, icy
amuse, amusing, amusement	judge, judging
argue, arguing	like, likable
arrive, arrival	love, lovable
awe, awesome	move, movable
believe, believable	owe, owing
bite, biting	purchase, purchasing
care, careful, careless	safe, safety
come, coming	use, usable, useless
desire, desirable	value, valuable
dine, dining	whole, wholesome
excite, exciting	zone, zoning

This basic rule is clear enough, but it does not cover all words ending in silent *e.* Here are additions and exceptions to the general principle:

1. Silent *e* is retained when *ing* is added to certain words, largely to prevent them from being confused with other words.

    dye, dyeing, to contrast with *die, dying*

    singe, singeing, to contrast with *sing, singing*

    tinge, tingeing, to contrast with *ting, tinging.*

2. Silent *e* is retained in still other words before a suffix beginning with a vowel. Sometimes this is done for the sake of pronunciation, sometimes for no logical reason at all: *acre, acreage; cage, cagey; courage, courageous; here, herein; mile, mileage; service, serviceable; shoe, shoeing.*

3. Final *y*

Words that end in a *y* preceded by a consonant usually change *y* to *i* before any suffix except one beginning with *i: angry, angrily; beauty, beautiful; busy, business; carry, carries, carrying; dignify, dignified, dignifying; happy, happier, happiness; lucky, luckier, luckily; marry, married, marriage; pity, pitiful, pitying; study, studied, studious.*

Words that end in a *y* preceded by a vowel do not change *y* to *i* before suffixes or other endings: *annoy, annoyed, annoyance; betray, betrayal, betraying; buy, buyer, buying; employ, employer; stay, stayed, staying.*

Here are some everyday words that follow neither part of the "final *y*" principle: *baby, babyhood; busy, busyness; day, daily; lay, laid; shy, shyly, shyness.*

4. Doubling a final consonant

Most words of one syllable and words of more than one syllable that are accented on the last syllable, when ending in a single consonant (except *x*) preceded by a single vowel, double the consonant before adding an ending beginning with a vowel. This is a complicated rule but a helpful one, as may be seen from the following examples: *run, running; begin, beginning; plan, planning; forget, forgettable; prefer, preferred.* Several important exceptions should be noted, however: *transfer, transferable; gas, gases.* Note, also, that the rule applies only to words that are accented on the last syllable: *refer, referred,* but *reference; prefer, preferred,* but *preference.*

5. The "one-plus-one" rule

When a prefix ends in the same letter with which the main part of the word begins, be sure that both letters are included. When the main part of a word ends in the same consonant with which a suffix begins, be sure that both consonants are included. When two words are combined, of which the first ends with the same letter as that with which the second begins, be sure that both letters are included. Here are some examples: *accidentally, bathhouse, bookkeeping, cleanness, coolly, cruelly, dissatisfied, irresponsible, misspelling, overrated, really, roommate, suddenness, unnecessary, withholding.*

The only important exception to this rule is *eighteen,* which, of course, is not spelled "eightteen." Also, keep in mind that three of the same consonant are never written solidly together: *cross-stitch*, not "crossstitch"; *still life* or *still-life,* not "stilllife."

If you find such spelling rules helpful, you may wish to investigate others. For instance, consult your instructor or a book devoted entirely to correct spelling for rules dealing with words beginning or ending as follows:

-able, -ible	-ar, -er, -or	de-, dis-, dys-
-ally, -ly	-ary, -ery	-efy, -ify
-ance, -ence	-cede, -ceed, -sede	-ise -ize, -yze

Here is a sampling of words with these endings and beginnings:

available	concede
responsible	proceed
finally	supersede
completely	describe
allowance	dissimilar
reference	dysentery
cellar	stupefy
announcer	magnify
author	disguise
dictionary	apologize
distillery	paralyze

35f. Carelessness is a primary cause of misspelling.

When you are writing, you concentrate on what you are trying to say and not on grammar, usage, punctuation, and spelling. This concentration is both proper and understandable. But in your absorption you are likely to make errors of various sorts, including some in spelling, that result from haste or carelessness, not ignorance.

Since many English words really are difficult to spell, we should be careful with those that we actually know; yet it is the simple, easy words nearly everyone *can* spell that cause over half the errors made. The following list contains several words or phrases that are repeatedly misspelled. They are so easy that you are likely to look at them scornfully and say, "I would never misspell any of them." Yet you probably do misspell some of these words on occasion, or other words just as simple.

a lot, not alot	crowd, not croud
all right, not alright	doesn't, not does'nt

forty, not fourty
high school, not highschool
irrelevant, not irrevelant
ninety, not ninty
perform, not preform
research, not reaserch

religion, not regilion
surprise, not supprise
thoroughly, not throughly
used to, not use to
whether, not wheather
wouldn't, not would'nt

sp
35g

35g. List and study the words you misspell most frequently.

Learning to spell is an individual, personal matter. One attack on correct spelling will work for one person but not for another. Perhaps it would be more precise to say that although certain words cause trouble for a majority of people, any list of commonly misspelled words will contain some that give you no difficulty and omit others that do. The best list of words for you to study is the one you prepare yourself to meet your own needs and shortcomings.

According to one estimate, only a basic 1000 words appear in 90 percent of all writing. Several of these words appear in the following list of frequently misspelled words. You might start your list of "personal demons" with words in this group that are troublesome for you.

1. abbreviation	16. admittance	31. apparatus
2. absence	17. advantageous	32. apparently
3. academic	18. advertisement	33. appearance
4. accept	19. advisable	34. argument
5. accidentally	20. alleged	35. article
6. accommodation	21. allotted	36. astronautical
7. accompanying	22. always (all ways)	37. athletics
8. accumulation	23. among	38. attendance
9. accustomed	24. analysis	39. audience
10. achievement	25. anniversary	40. auxiliary
11. acknowledge	26. announcement	41. awkward
12. acquaintance	27. answer	42. bachelor
13. across	28. anxiety	43. balance
14. adequate	29. apartment	44. basically
15. adjustment	30. apology	45. becoming

46. beginning	86. dealt	126. excitement
47. believing	87. deficient	127. exercise
48. beneficial	88. definitely	128. exhausted
49. boundary	89. democracy	129. existence
50. brilliant	90. description	130. experience
51. business	91. desirability	131. explanation
52. calendar	92. despair	132. extraordinary
53. candidate	93. desperate	133. facilities
54. career	94. determination	134. familiar
55. category	95. dictionary	135. fascinating
56. certain	96. difference	136. February
57. challenge	97. difficulty	137. fictitious
58. changeable	98. diminish	138. fiery
59. characteristic	99. disappear	139. financially
60. chosen	100. disappoint	140. flammable
61. column	101. disastrous	141. foreign
62. commercial	102. disease	142. forty
63. committee	103. dissatisfied	143. friendliness
64. communication	104. distribution	144. fundamental
65. comparatively	105. divine	145. government
66. comparison	106. division	146. gradually
67. competition	107. dormitories	147. grammar
68. conceivable	108. economical	148. guidance
69. conference	109. efficient	149. handicapped
70. confidence	110. eighteen	150. handsome
71. conscientious	111. elaborate	151. height
72. consequently	112. eligible	152. hindrance
73. consistent	113. eliminate	153. holiday
74. contemporary	114. embarrass	154. honorable
75. continually	115. encouragement	155. hospitality
76. contribution	116. enthusiasm	156. humiliate
77. controlling	117. entrance	157. humorous
78. convenience	118. environment	158. hundred
79. correspondence	119. equally	159. hungry
80. counsellor	120. equipped	160. hurriedly
81. countries	121. erroneous	161. hypocrisy
82. courageous	122. especially	162. illiterate
83. courteous	123. exaggeration	163. imaginary
84. criticism	124. excellent	164. immediately
85. curiosity	125. except	165. incidentally

sp

35g

166. independence
167. indispensable
168. infinite
169. influential
170. inimitable

171. initiative
172. innocent
173. insistence
174. integration
175. intellectual

176. intelligence
177. interesting
178. interpretation
179. interruption
180. interview

181. intolerance
182. introduction
183. invitation
184. irrelevant
185. irresistible

186. jeopardize
187. kindliness
188. knowledge
189. laboratory
190. laboriously

191. language
192. legibility
193. legitimate
194. leisurely
195. liable

196. libraries
197. likelihood
198. literature
199. livelihood
200. loneliness

201. maintenance
202. manageable
203. manipulate
204. manufacturing
205. marriageable

206. mathematics
207. measurable
208. mechanical
209. merchandise
210. millionaire

211. miniature
212. miscellaneous
213. mischievous
214. misspelled
215. momentarily

216. monotonous
217. mysterious
218. nationalities
219. naturally
220. necessary

221. negative
222. negligent
223. neighborhood
224. neither
225. niece

226. nineteen
227. ninety
228. ninth
229. nonsense
230. noticeable

231. numerous
232. obedience
233. obstacle
234. occasionally
235. occupying

236. occurrence
237. of (off)
238. omission
239. operation
240. opinion

241. opponent
242. opportunities
243. opposition
244. optimistic
245. ordinarily

246. original
247. outrageous
248. pamphlet
249. panicky
250. parallel

251. particularly
252. peaceable
253. peculiarities
254. penniless
255. perceive

256. performance
257. perhaps
258. permanent
259. permissible
260. perpetuate

261. perseverance
262. persistent
263. personnel
264. persuade
265. physician

266. planning
267. pleasant
268. plenteous
269. politician
270. portrayed

271. possession
272. possibility
273. potential
274. practically
275. preceding

276. predicate
277. predictable
278. predominant
279. preference
280. preferred

281. prejudice
282. preliminary
283. preparation
284. presumptuous
285. privilege

286. probably
287. procedure
288. process
289. professional
290. prominent

291. promotion
292. pronunciation
293. propaganda
294. quantity
295. questionable

296. questionnaire
297. realize
298. reasonable
299. receive
300. recognition

301. recollection
302. recommendation
303. recurrence
304. reference
305. referred

306. regrettable
307. relative
308. relieve
309. religious
310. remembrance

311. removable
312. repetition
313. representative
314. reputation
315. research

316. resolution
317. resistance
318. resources
319. respectfully
320. responsibility

321. ridiculous
322. righteous
323. roommate
324. sacrilegious
325. safety

326. satirical
327. satisfactorily
328. scarcity
329. schedule
330. scholarship

331. secondary
332. secretary
333. seize
334. selection
335. semester

336. separate
337. serviceable
338. severely
339. shining
340. significance

341. similar
342. sincerely
343. singular
344. sixtieth
345. solution

346. sophomore
347. specialization
348. specifically
349. specimen
350. speech

351. sponsor
352. stratosphere
353. strength
354. substantiate
355. substitute

356. subtle
357. sufficient
358. superfluous
359. supersede
360. surprise

361. suspicious
362. technical
363. technique
364. television
365. temperature

366. temporarily
367. than (then)
368. there (their, they're)
369. thorough
370. to, too, two

371. tradition
372. transferred
373. transportation
374. truly
375. Tuesday

376. twelfth
377. unanimous
378. uncontrollable
379. undoubtedly
380. unforgettable

381. unfortunate
382. until
383. unusually
384. usefulness
385. valuable

386. versatile
387. visible
388. volume
389. voluntary
390. wealthiest

391. Wednesday
392. weird
393. welcome
394. welfare
395. where (were)

396. whether
397. wholly
398. woman (women)
399. writing
400. written

sp

35g

EXERCISE 17

Some of the following groups contain one misspelled word. Find the errors.

1. anxiety	penniless	referrence	interesting
2. literature	perdictable	persuade	reasonable
3. miniature	divine	apology	scarcity
4. enviroment	privilege	humorous	gradually
5. unnecessary	dormitories	noticeable	temperture
6. exercise	unforgetable	balance	definitely
7. contrabution	attendance	procedure	secretary
8. comparison	friendliness	auxiliary	selection
9. probably	livelihood	permanent	similiar
10. occurrence	interview	incidentaly	severely
11. roommate	research	misspelled	immaginary
12. changable	committee	truly	excitement
13. sophomore	professional	government	regrettable
14. perceive	sincerly	modifies	speech
15. argument	mathematics	oppinion	suspicious
16. studying	especially	guidance	writting
17. safety	operation	admitance	allotted
18. disatisfied	planning	occasionally	shining
19. preliminary	lonelyness	category	invitation
20. embarrass	exhausted	possession	preference
21. courageous	preferred	temporarily	necessary
22. boundary	quantity	accompaning	candidate
23. promotion	preceeding	prominent	transferred
24. outrageous	laboratory	practically	undoubtedly
25. familiar	sponsor	kindliness	fascinating

EXERCISE 18

Some of the following groups contain a misspelled word. Find the errors.

1. absence	division	imaginary	familar
2. chosen	labratory	experience	difficulty
3. shinning	accompanying	nonsense	omission
4. similar	preferrence	manufacturing	hindrance
5. hundred	foreign	argument	millionaire
6. unecessary	official	admittance	recurrence
7. eighteen	apartment	difference	occasionaly
8. ninety	confidence	negative	business
9. holiday	predictable	writing	opperation

10. studing	knowledge	temperature	relative
11. loneliness	enthusiasm	modifys	necessary
12. dictionary	regretable	across	contribution
13. monotonous	believing	continually	opponent
14. truely	naturally	preceding	language
15. reference	couragous	honorable	environment
16. incidentally	libraries	occurence	religious
17. numerous	arrival	immediately	livelyhood
18. equally	unforgettable	proceedure	almost
19. goverment	description	relieve	removable
20. original	definately	dissatisfied	righteous
21. among	sincerely	noticable	influential
22. opinion	performance	convenience	excellent
23. neither	countries	outrageous	reasearch
24. innocent	occupying	mispelled	changeable
25. grammar	perhaps	respectfully	courteous

EXERCISE 19

In the following paragraphs 50 words are incorrectly spelled. List these words on a separate sheet of paper by giving correct spellings of the misspelled words. If a word is spelled incorrectly more than once, *list it only once.*

1. After I had been admitted to Atwood University and had completed my registeration, I was very much surprised to recieve a letter from my grandfather. Now, Grandfather was never very much of a man for writting letters, but approximatly every week or so his communications continued to arrive. I am sure that at times it was not convient for him to write (he as much as said so frequently), but he had the urge, so he said, to tell me of his own experiences at Atwood.

2. Grandfather early wrote about my making friends. He had made the aquaintance, he said, of many people during his first weeks at Atwood, from whom he chose a few intimates. These people he had met in the classroom, at some of the fraternities, in the Union, in resturants, and on the atheletic field. He treated every one in a courtious manner and never cracked jokes at their expense; so doing, he had learned, was a sure way to forfiet their respect.

3. One of Grandfather's closest associates was Bill Jones, whom he had met at one of the dormatories. Bill was a very tempermental person, but he had a genius for getting along with people, and Grandfather benefited greatly from his comradship. About the middle of the first semester they became roomates.

4. From Bill Jones Grandfather learned much about the art of studying. Up to the time of their rooming togeather, Grandfather was much

dissatisfied with his scholastic record, and even though he tried to learn to study, he sometimes was so poorly prepared, usually in mathmatics and English, that he was almost too embarassed to go to class. Bill made a begining of his work on Grandfather's scholarship by giving him simple explainations of his more difficult assignments, but he was more interested in teaching the methods and dicipline of study. Once Grandfather had mastered these, the maintainance of better marks became an easy task.

5. One of Bill's secrets was concentration; if you divide your attention, you get nowhere. Another was not postponing getting to work. Grandfather admitted, for example, that the night before one test, he spent the evening playing pool at the Union. He had alloted two hours for his review, but the evening just seemed to dissappear, and when Grandfather got to his room, he was too tired to worry about his lack of knowlege, and went immediatly to bed. He was not much mistified when he failed the test, and he even thought of quiting school. But about that time he met Bill and aquired valuble study habits. No longer was he an irresponsable student, handicaped by a lack of study method. Study was now his first neccessary task. When the next test came, he was so good that he could spot an independant clause a paragraph away; and by the time of the punctuation test, he had mastered the comma, had good control of the semicoln, and was even using recklessly but correctly quite a number of appostrophes.

6. In high school Grandfather had been a notorously poor speller. The adolescent love notes that Grandfather wrote to the girl accross the aisle contained so many wrongly spelled words that the young lady broke off the correspondance. Love couldn't erradicate Grandfather's spelling disease, and after this disasterous adventure he swore that he would overcome his trouble; but he didn't. It was method, not love, that Grandfather needed, and Bill Jones supplied the answer. Grandfather still spelled a word wrong occassionally, but he became so persistent in his study of the words spelled by rule, the tricky words, and the words spelled according to sylable that when he took the spelling test for the first time, he had only one mispelled word.

7. I could go on and on telling of the refferences to college life made in Grandfather's letters, and of the many occurences of which he wrote. But I don't want to be accused of wordyness, and, anyway, I've given you a general idea of the content of these letters.

8. Long before the end of the year I became conscious of the fact that Grandfather was trying to decieve me a polite way; he was really giving me advice by means of his letters, but whenever I accused him of this fact, he swore to his innocense and vowed that his only object was to entertain me and, perhaps, keep me from becoming homesick. I never did quite beleive him.

IV.
The Word

Skillful writers leave little to chance. Just as their tones and sentence structures are chosen to be effective for their subjects and appropriate for their audiences, so do they select suitable words to achieve their purposes.

Think how the wording of a single sentence might vary depending on whether it was addressed to close friends, your parents, teachers, a prospective employer, a church or town official, a judge, and so on. Think how it might vary with the age of the listener—a younger brother or sister, perhaps, as opposed to an aged aunt or uncle. The use of words is not a matter of choosing absolutely "good" words and avoiding absolutely "bad" ones but of selecting those that will help achieve the effect you want.

Diction refers to the choice of a word or words for the expression of ideas. Defined in this way, diction applies to both writing and speaking, although the sections here deal only with writing. The following sections will help make your writing more effective.

Because there are many words to choose from, because many ideas require expression in different shades of meaning and emphasis, and because outright errors in usage should be avoided, diction is troublesome for all writers and speakers. Just as a reputable builder carefully selects materials for the construction of a house, so must writers use care in choosing the words they use. Effective communication, the primary aim of writing and speaking, is impossible without effective choice and use of words.

Diction, like sentences, should be *correct, clear,* and *effective,* but no standards can be absolute. Our language is constantly changing. Also, diction, like fashions in dress and food, is influenced by changes in taste. Again, what is acceptable in daily speech and conversation may not be suitable in formal writing. The use of this or that word cannot be justified by saying that it is often heard or seen in print. Advertisements, newspapers, magazines, and even some "good" books exhibit faulty diction, or at least diction that is not acceptable in formal writing.

As you study the following sections, keep your dictionary constantly at hand. You may disagree with some of the statements made in Sections 36–40, but it is sensible to be guided—at least at first—by the work of authors and speakers whose skill in communicating commands respect.

SUMMARY OF COMMON PROBLEMS IN DICTION

In choosing and using words, remember that

1. words should be in *current* use (Section 36).
2. words should be in *national* use (Section 36).

3. words should be in *reputable* use (Section 37).

4. words should be *exact* and *emphatic* (Section 38).

Keep in mind two primary recommendations about diction:

1. *Be specific.* Much of what we write and speak is indefinite, not clearly expressed, of uncertain meaning. Even when we have a fairly good idea of what we wish to say, we don't search hard enough for those exact, specific, and concrete words that would get across what we have in mind. *Be definite. Don't be vague.*

2. *Be concise.* Most statements of any kind are wordy. All of us, in both speech and writing, tend to repeat ideas in identical or similar words—and then write or say the same things once again. Neither speech nor writing should be abrupt or cryptic, but both should be economical. *Make it snappy!*

word use

36a

36. Current and national use

In writing, it helps to remember that words mean what your readers think they mean, not necessarily what you think they do. The first method of insuring clear communication is to use words that are in *current* and *national* use.

36a. Current use

Words should be understandable to readers and listeners of the present time. Words do go out of style and out of use. (You must have struggled with the meanings of words and expressions used by Shakespeare and other earlier writers.) Except for somewhat doubtful purposes of humor, avoid using antiquated expressions.

1. Obsolete words

An *obsolete* word is one that has passed completely out of use. An *obsolescent* word is one that is in the process of becoming obsolete. One dictionary, however, may label a given word "obsolete"; another may label the same word "obsolescent"; still another, "archaic." Your dictionary may include *infortune* for *misfortune, yestreen* for *last evening, garb* for *personal bearing, prevent* for *precede, eftsoon* for *soon afterward*, *belike* for *perhaps*, *twifallow* for *plow again*, *anon* for *coming*.

2. Archaic words

An *archaic* word is an old-fashioned word, one that has passed from everyday use but may still appear in Biblical expressions, proverbs, and legal language. Effective, up-to-date general writing will not include terms such as *enow* for *enough*, *methinks* for *it seems to me*, *lief* for *willing*, *wot* for *know*, *glister* for *glisten*, *whilom* for *formerly*, *pease* for *pea*, *oft* or *ofttimes* for *often*, *marry* as an expression of surprise or astonishment, *bedight* for *array*, *cote* for *pass by*, *presents* for *this document*, and *beget* for *procreate*.

3. Poetic words

Words that have been (and are still occasionally) used in poetry rather than prose are known somewhat loosely as *poetic diction*. Poetic words, sometimes so labeled in dictionaries, are usually archaic words found in poetry composed in (or intended to create the aura of) a remote past. Examples are the use of the endings *-st*, *-est*, *-th*, and *-eth* on present tense verbs: *dost, couldst, wouldst, leadeth, doth*. Other examples are contractions such as *'tis* and *'twas*. Usually considered "poetic" are words like *glebe, ope, orb, 'neath, eye of night, acold, thee, thine, thou, ye*, and *fain*.

4. Neologisms

A *neologism* is a newly coined word or phrase or an established term employed in a new sense. Not all neologisms are contrived and artificial, but many are and consequently have short lives. Numerous well-known columnists, broadcasters, sports commentators, and advertising copywriters repeatedly concoct neologisms. Some of their coinages are colorful, attention getting, and picturesque, and presumably will prove permanently valuable. If they do not fill a real need, they will quietly disappear from the language.

Words are coined in various ways:

1. As needed words in the fields of science, technology, and business, to describe new inventions, discoveries, applications, and occupations: *astronautics, astrogate, automation, H-bomb, cyclotron, computerize, realtor, beautician*.

2. By adaptation of common words—often by analogy, for example, by adding *-ize* to nouns to form verbs or adding a suffix like *-wise* to form adverbs: *vacationize, signaturize, bookwise, city-wise, taxwise.* Most "-ize" and "-wise" coinages are rarely suitable in formal writing.

3. Through the combination of two or more common words. Those are the so-called portmanteau words: *brunch* (*br*eakfast and l*unch*); *cheeseburger* (*cheese* and ham*burger*); *chortle* (*ch*uckle and sn*ort*); *motel* (*mo*tor and ho*tel*); *smog* (*sm*oke and f*og*); *transistor* (*trans*fer and re*sistor*); *cinemaddict* (*cinema* and *addict*); *stagflation* (*stag*nation and in*flation*).

4. By using the initial letters or syllables of common words: *loran* (*lo*ng *ra*nge *n*avigation); *radar* (*ra*dio *d*etecting *a*nd *r*anging). Such a word is an *acronym.*

5. As virtually or completely new information: *gobbledygook; blurb; jeep; bazooka.*

6. As registered trade names or trademarks (even though in dictionaries they are the property of their owners) and their derivatives: *Kodak, kleenex, Dacron, simonize, technicolor, Caterpillar* (tractor).

Depending on the dictionary you own, newly coined words that appear may have no label or be labeled "informal" or "colloquial" or "slang," with perhaps a brief history of their origin or originator. If you use neologisms, be sure they are appropriate to both content and reader, that is, easily understood by the people you are addressing.

These lines from the English poet Alexander Pope are sound advice:

In words, as fashions, the same rule will hold,
Alike fantastic if too new or old:
Be not the first by whom the new are tried,
Nor yet the last to lay the old aside.

36b. National use

Television, radio, the telephone, films, and easy transportation have helped to make American English *national.* That is, writers or speakers can assume they will be understood by American read-

word
use

36b

ers or listeners if they use words and phrases common to all parts of the country. Words should be in *national* use.

Applying this principle suggests that the writer should be aware of other limitations of diction besides geographic regions. The comments that follow deal with the subdivisions in vocabulary that can prevent or hinder a reader's understanding.

1. Americanisms and Briticisms

Broadly defined, an English *nationalism* is a word or phrase common in or limited to the English used by a particular one of the English-speaking nations. *Americanism* and *Briticism* refer to words or word meanings that are common, respectively, in the United States and the British Isles. Dictionaries label many such expressions "U.S.," "Chiefly U.S.," "British," "Scottish," or the like, not to guide us in our writing—except when we write to someone in a non-American country—but to help us understand them when we come across them in the writings of anyone writing in English anywhere in the world. For example, here are different terms associated with cars and motoring in the United States and Great Britain:

word
use

36b

American Usage	British Usage
battery	accumulator
gasoline	petrol
paved road	metalled road
hood (of a car)	bonnet
trunk (of a car)	boot
fender	wing

2. Localisms

A *localism* is a word or phrase used and understood primarily in a particular section or region. Along with certain grammatical constructions and characteristic pronunciations, localisms identify a speaker's *regional dialect*.

Various areas of the United States have localisms that add flavor to speech but may not be immediately intelligible in other areas. For residents of one of these areas, such expressions seem quite clear since they themselves have known and used them from childhood. Dictionaries label or define many words according to the geographic area where they are common. Here are some examples:

Northern (most of New England, parts of northern New Jersey and northern Pennsylvania):

pail: (Midland and Southern *bucket*)
swill: (Midland and Southern *slop*)
brook: "small stream"
down-easter: "native of New England, especially Maine"
choose: "wish"
selectman: "town official"

Midland (the rest of New Jersey and Pennsylvania; northern Delaware, Maryland, and Virginia west of the Appalachians; West Virginia, Kentucky, Tennessee, and westward):

**word
use**

36b

blinds: "window shades"
skillet: "frying pan"
green beans: "string beans"

Southern (part of Virginia; North Carolina, South Carolina, and Georgia west to the mountains):

chitlins: "chitterlings"
harp, mouth harp: "harmonica"
snap beans: "string beans"
butternuts: "brown overalls"
corn pone: "corn bread"
chunk: "throw"
tote: "carry"
poke: "sack"

Southwestern:

mesa: "flat-topped rocky hill"
mustang: "half-wild horse"
mesquite: "spiny tree or shrub"
maverick: "unbranded animal"
longhorn: "breed of cattle"

Western:

grubstake: "supplies or funds"
coulee: "narrow valley"
rustler: "cattle thief"
potluck: "food available without special preparation"
dogie, dogy: "motherless calf"

Should localisms be used? If a particular localism is in general use on all levels in your home region, then it is widely enough understood to be acceptable, although it will mark your writing as stemming from that region. If you have any doubt about whether the word or phrase will be understood, choose a substitute that is in more general use.

3. Shoptalk

The specialized or technical vocabulary and idioms of people in the same work or the same way of life are known as *shoptalk,* the language people use in discussing their particular field of activity. *To talk shop* is the verb form of this expression.

For your writing to be in national use, avoid introducing words and expressions peculiar to, or understood only by, members of a particular trade, profession, science, industry, or art. Legal shoptalk, medical jargon, and sports talk, for example, have special meanings for those in these fields and occupations. So do more than 40 other classifications of words that have special labels in your dictionary: astronomy, entomology, psychology—all the way from aeronautics to zoology.

In the last generation alone, many new words and meanings have come from fields like chemistry, electronics, nuclear physics, automation, and other sciences, arts, and recreations.

When technical words are widely used or have extended meanings, their subject labels may be dropped. Some examples (made popular by special fields) are *broadcast* (from radio), *telescope* (from astronomy), *weld* (from engineering), *diagnose* (from medicine), *daub* (from painting), and *mold* (from sculpture).

A specialist writing for or speaking to other specialists uses numerous technical terms. In that circumstance, shoptalk is appropriate. But it is another matter for nonspecialists. Few of us could understand a technical article in *Electronics* magazine. More of us could understand its treatment in *Scientific American.* All of us might understand it if it were adapted for a general-circulation magazine.

Use common sense in dealing with shoptalk. Consider the "average" educated reader and find terms that require no special or technical knowledge unless they are indispensable to what you want to say and unless you carefully define them when you use them.

word use

36b

4. Foreign words and phrases

For most Americans, a foreign word or phrase is one that comes from a non-English language. Tens of thousands of foreign words have come into our language from Greek, Latin, and French, and thousands more have come from other languages. Depending on your dictionary, you will find from 40 to 150 foreign-language abbreviations used for word origins and meanings.

Two things happen to these foreign words and phrases: (1) If they have been widely used or used over a long period, or both, they are Anglicized and become part of our everyday language, to be recorded in dictionaries like any common word. (2) If the conditions of (1) have not been met, the word or phrase remains foreign; as such, it is indicated in dictionaries as foreign, partly as a guide for writers to use italics if they use the word or phrase. (See Section 30.) Anglicized examples include *a priori, à la mode, blitz, chef, habitué,* and *smorgasbord.* Non-Anglicized examples include *Anno Domini, fait accompli, cause célèbre, ex libris, mañana,* and *Weltschmerz.*

If the word or phrase has been Anglicized or if no good English equivalent exists, use it. But why *merci beaucoup* for "thank you" or *Auf Wiedersehen* for "good-by"? Even *a* or *an* serves better than *per:* $5 *an* hour.

word
use

36b

EXERCISE 1

From an anthology of prose and poetry, compile three lists of five words each, one of obsolete, one of archaic, and one of poetic words. Check your lists against your dictionary. How many are not listed? How often did your judgment agree with that of the compilers of the dictionary?

EXERCISE 2

From an electronics or astronautics magazine or a periodical like *Scientific American* or *Popular Mechanics,* compile a list of ten words that you think may be neologisms. Compare the list with entries in your dictionary. Write a brief report on your findings.

EXERCISE 3

From time to time, study consecutive or random pages in your dictionary. Compile a list of five to ten words that are labeled "Regional

American Words," "British" or "Chiefly British," or "Scottish" or "Chiefly Scottish." Using an appropriate title, write a paper of about 500 words based on the list.

EXERCISE 4

Make a list of five or more localisms heard in your neighborhood or vicinity. Write a short paper on them to be read in class.

EXERCISE 5

From a textbook in one of the sciences, make a list of twenty technical words and investigate their meanings. Write a paper of about 500 words on "The Technical Vocabulary of——."

37. Reputable use

The choice and use of words in today's writing is more relaxed, freer from rules, and closer to the way we actually speak than ever before. This freedom of choice, however, does not mean that "anything goes" and that no standards of diction exist. In all careful writing, one should try to use words and expressions that are standard and reputable: considered to be in good and acceptable usage.

Many reputable words and expressions, however, are neither exact nor effective. This section contains suggestions for using words that (1) call things by their names; (2) are as concrete and specific as meaning allows; and (3) are direct, economical, and idiomatically sound.

37a. Exact diction

Any of several words may be available to convey a general meaning, but often a particular word or phrase will express your meaning more precisely than any other. It is your task and opportunity to find this word or phrase. In this search, a thesaurus is an excellent reference book. Frequently, too, your choice is from several words with nearly identical meanings, and a study of the synonyms for an expression listed in a dictionary or thesaurus will help you choose a more precise term. For example, before allowing a word like *happy* to stand in one of your papers, find out whether one of the following adjectives will communicate your meaning more precisely: *blithe, cheerful, gay, sportive, jocular, jolly, jovial, joyful, joyous, merry.*

For another example, consider the overworked word *pretty.* We speak and write of a pretty day, a pretty girl, a pretty flower, and so on. The word *pretty* is entirely reputable and carries a general meaning that cannot be called misleading or incorrect. Perhaps it would be more exact and accurate to write that a certain person is *attractive* or *charming* or *personable* or *winsome* or *exquisite* or *fair* or *comely* or *sensuous* or *engaging.* These words are not synonyms for *pretty,* but one of them may more exactly convey the impression you want to give.

But do not let the use of synonyms lead you into error: two words may be synonymous in one meaning but not in another. *Steal* and *pilfer* share a meaning—"to take without permission"— but *steal* can also mean "to move so slowly as to be unnoticeable." We can write "The shadows were *stealing* across the yard," but not "The shadows were *pilfering* across the yard."

Exactness and precision in diction require you to think clearly and carefully. Effective diction is achieved when the reader understands as nearly as possible what the writer intended to communicate.

37b. Specific diction

A *general* word names a broad concept: class names of nouns (*animal, clothing, devices, land, street*); conventional verbs with many meanings (*go, move, say*); and broad adjectives and adverbs (*good, bad, gladly, fast*). Especially colorless diction results from overuse of the forms of *to be* (*am, is, are, was, were*).

A *specific* word names a more limited concept (*collie, leotard, flashlight, pasture, boulevard*). As a verb, a specific word will have a more particular meaning and a more limited use (*totter, amble, saunter, drawl, shout*). A specific word is a vivid, hence a *clear* word; an active, hence a *lively* word; and a fresh, hence an *interesting* word.

Some general words are so vague that they only approximate an idea. With the aid of a thesaurus or dictionary, you can find specific words for any of the following general words and phrases:

aspect	field	manner	quality
case	fine	matter	question
character	great	nature	situation
condition	instance	nice	state
cute	interesting	personality	style
degree	item	persuasion	thing
element	job	phase	type
factor	lot	point	vital
feature	lovely	problem	way

GENERAL: a *fine* day
a *great* game
the first *thing*

SPECIFIC: a *memorable* day
a *record-setting* game
the first *argument* (*question, principle, problem,* etc.)

dict

37c

37c. Concrete diction

An *abstract* word gives no clear picture; it is a mental construct like *beauty, culture, efficiency,* or *wealth.* A *concrete* word expresses something that can be perceived by the senses: *lilacs, crimson, drumbeats, jogging, lemony, jagged.* "He *closed* the door" pictures movement; "He *slammed* the door" gives both picture and sound. *Weep* suggests sight and feeling; *sob* adds hearing and movement.

Specific and concrete nouns, colorful and dynamic adjectives and adverbs, verbs that tell of action or relate to the senses, specific and concrete phrases—all help make writing more direct, forceful, and effective.

Ordinarily, and within the bounds of common sense, choose the concrete, specific word over the general, abstract one. This sentence uses reputable words and is clear in meaning:

If you have committed a crime, escape to the woods with ammunition and clothing. People there will give you food and you need worry about nothing.

Notice the greater effectiveness of these sentences from Merimée's short story, "Mateo Falcone":

If you have killed a man, go into the *maquis* of Porto-Vecchio with a good gun and powder and shot. You will live there quite safely, but don't forget to bring along a brown cloak and hood for your blanket and mattress. The shepherds will give you milk, cheese, and chestnuts, and you need not trouble your head about the law or the dead man's relatives, except when you are compelled to go down into the town to renew your ammunition.

37d. Colloquialisms

A *colloquialism* is a conversational word or phrase that is permissible in, and often indispensable to, an easy style of speaking and writing. A colloquialism is not substandard or illiterate; it is an expression that is more often used in speech than in writing and more appropriate in informal than in highly formal speech and writing. The origin of the word is the Latin *colloquium,* for "conversation." Our word *colloquy* means "speaking together"; the word *loquacious* means "given to talking, fond of talking."

Colloquialisms are thoroughly reputable and can be used in all writing that is not painstakingly precise, learned, or stilted. If the tone of some paper that you are writing is formal, you should employ only a few colloquialisms and only those that do not alter the mood and intent of your work. But do not avoid colloquialisms entirely, because if you do your writing may sound affected and artificial. A good rule is to use colloquialisms thoughtfully and carefully and not to rely on them as a substitute for more exact and appropriate expressions.

Dictionary words and phrases are marked as colloquial ("Colloq.") when the editors judge them to be more common in speech than in writing or more suitable in informal than in formal discourse. In some dictionaries the label used is "Informal." A large number of words and phrases are so labeled. The term applies to many expressions because informal English has a wide range and because editors differ in the way they interpret their findings. Certain contractions, such as *don't, shouldn't,* and *won't,* are considered "acceptable" colloquialisms; other expressions, however, such as *brass tacks, jinx, enthuse, flop,* and *ad,* should be avoided. No objective rule or test will tell you when to use a colloquialism and when not to. In general, use a colloquialism when your writing would otherwise seem stiff, artificial, and labored.

The following are examples of colloquialisms (as in dictionaries

dict

37d

and linguistic studies, no attempt is made to indicate their comparative rank or acceptability: *angel* (financial backer), *brass* (impudence), *freeze* (stand motionless), *phone, gumption, cute, hasn't got any, show up, try and, take a try at, flabbergast, fizzle, flop, root for, make out, fill the bill.*

You might use any or all of these colloquialisms if you are reporting the conversation of a person who would characteristically use them in speech. You might use several in writing in which the tone is light or humorous or breezy. But whenever you use colloquialisms, be certain that they are in keeping with the purpose and tone of your writing.

37e. Idiomatic English

English idiom or *idiomatic English* concerns words used in combination with others. Of Greek origin, the word *idiom* meant "a private citizen, something belonging to a private citizen, personal," and, by extension, something individual and peculiar. An idiomatic expression may violate grammar or logic or both and still be acceptable because the phrase is familiar, deep-rooted, widely used, and easily understandable—for the native born. "How do you do?" is, for example, an accepted idiom, although an exact answer would be absurd.

A few generalized statements may be made about the many idiomatic expressions in our language. One is that several words, when combined, may lose their literal meaning and express something that is only remotely suggested by any one word: *birds of a feather, blacklist, lay up, toe the line, bed of roses, dark horse, heavy hand, open house, read between the lines, no ax to grind, hard row to hoe.*

A second statement about idioms is that parts of the human body have suggested many of them: *burn one's fingers, all thumbs, fly in the face of, stand on one's own feet, keep body and soul together, keep one's eyes open, step on someone's toes, rub elbows with, get one's back up, keep one's chin up.*

A third generalization is that hundreds of idiomatic phrases contain adverbs or prepositions with other parts of speech. Here are some examples: *walk off, walk over, walk-up; run down, run in, run off, run out; get nowhere, get through, get off.*

agree
$\begin{cases} \textit{to} \text{ a proposal} \\ \textit{on} \text{ a plan} \\ \textit{with} \text{ a person} \end{cases}$

contend
$\begin{cases} \textit{for} \text{ a principle} \\ \textit{with} \text{ a person} \\ \textit{against} \text{ an obstacle} \end{cases}$

differ
$\begin{cases} \textit{with} \text{ a person} \\ \textit{from} \text{ something else} \\ \textit{about} \text{ or } \textit{over} \text{ a question} \end{cases}$

impatient
$\begin{cases} \textit{for} \text{ something desired} \\ \textit{with} \text{ someone else} \\ \textit{of} \text{ restraint} \\ \textit{at} \text{ someone's conduct} \end{cases}$

rewarded
$\begin{cases} \textit{for} \text{ something done} \\ \textit{with} \text{ a gift} \\ \textit{by} \text{ a person} \end{cases}$

wait
$\begin{cases} \textit{at} \text{ a place} \\ \textit{for} \text{ a person} \\ \textit{on} \text{ a customer} \end{cases}$

Usage should conform to idiomatic word combinations that are reputable and, therefore, generally acceptable. Remember, however, that many acceptable idioms are also trite. (See Section 38h.) A good dictionary contains explanations of idiomatic usage following key words that need such explanation. It is important to consult your dictionary when using certain words such as *prepositions* with nouns, adjectives, or verbs. The following are examples of idiomatic and unidiomatic expressions containing troublesome prepositions:

Idiomatic	*Unidiomatic*
accord with	accord to
according to	according with
acquaint with	acquaint to
adverse to	adverse against
aim to prove	aim at proving
among themselves	among one another
angry with (a person)	angry at (a person)
as regards	as regards to
authority on	authority about
blame me for it	blame it on me
cannot help talking	cannot help but talk
comply with	comply to
conform to, with	conform in

correspond to (a thing)	correspond with (a thing)
desirous of	desirous to
graduated from (high school)	graduated (high school)
identical with	identical to
in accordance with	in accordance to
in search of	in search for
prefer (one) to (another)	prefer (one) over (another)
prior to	prior than
responsible for (to)	responsible on
superior to	superior than
treat of (a subject)	treat on (a subject)
unequal to	unequal for

It should be pointed out that many educated users of the language do not always follow accepted idiomatic usage. In everyday conversation, such a speaker is as likely to say "blame it on me" as "blame me for it" and "angry at" a person as "angry with." But in careful, formal writing the distinctions just listed should be followed.

Collecting idioms can be fun. For instance, what can you make of these idioms?

> *make* a date; *make* as if; *make* believe; *make* a fool of; *make* heavy weather of; *make* good; *make* off; *make* ready; *make* up; *make* a meal of; *make* it; *make* over; *make* mincemeat of; *make* do; *make* merry; *make* a fuss; *make* a mess; *make* trouble; *make* a pass

Or these?

> break one's *heart;* have one's *heart* in the right place; wear one's *heart* on one's sleeve; change of *heart;* after one's own *heart; heart* and soul; set one's *heart* on; eat one's *heart* out; take to *heart;* cold hands, warm *heart;* one's head rules one's *heart;* sick at *heart*

37f. Figurative language

Many words have an exact meaning (*denotation*) and a suggested or implied meaning (*connotation*).

The exact, literal meaning of a word is referred to as its *denotation,* its dictionary definition. It is thus different from an associated meaning, or *connotation,* that the word might have for an individual (or group) because of personal experience.

Assume that you see a small four-footed animal on the street and refer to it as a *dog*. If your purpose in using the word is to refer to the animal in exact terminology, you have succeeded in applying a denotative term that is plain, straightforward, and objective. But suppose that one grandparent of the dog was a fox terrier, another a bulldog, the third an Irish terrier, and the fourth a collie. You can denotatively express these facts by referring to the animal you see as a *dog of mixed breed*. Here you have continued to use objective phrasing. But if your purpose is to speak exactly and objectively, it would be unwise to call the dog a *mongrel*. True, this term means the same as a *dog of mixed breed,* but it is likely to arouse mingled feelings of approval or disapproval toward that dog.

Nearly all words mean more than they seem to mean. They have associated meanings, a surrounding fringe of suggestive, or connotative, values. For example, a dictionary definition of the word *gold* is "a precious yellow metal, highly malleable and ductile, and free from liability to rust." But with gold have long been associated riches, power, happiness, evil, and unhappiness. Around the core of meaning that the dictionary definition gives are associations, suggestions, and implications. These connotations are not always present, but you should be aware of this suggestive power of words.

A writer's obligation is to convey sensible comments clearly. But good writers search for words that suggest more than they say, that stimulate the reader's imagination. These words, having connotative values, suggest associated meanings: *baby sister,* not *girl; enigma,* not *problem; home,* not *house; mother,* not *woman.* By exact, or denotative, definition, a horse is "a large, solid-hoofed, herbivorous mammal," but to anyone who has ever owned, loved, and cared for a horse the word suggests many associated meanings. New Orleans is "an industrial and trade center," but its name suggests such images as Crescent City, Old French Quarter, Mardi Gras, Sugar Bowl, Superdome, and Dixieland jazz.

A *figure of speech* is one method of using words out of their literal, or ordinary, sense in order to suggest a picture or image. "He is a saint" and "sleeping like a baby" are illustrations of, respectively, the two most common figures of speech: metaphor and simile.

A *metaphor* is a term applied to something to which it is not literally applicable. That is, a metaphor is a figure of speech in which a term is transferred from the object it ordinarily designates to an object that it may designate only by comparison or analogy,

dict

37f

as in the phrases "evening of life" (later years, old age) and "A mighty fortress is our God" (strength, power).

A *simile* expresses the resemblance of one thing to another, but it does so by using the words *like, as,* or *as if.* "She is *like* a cool breeze," "heart *as* cold *as* an iceberg." Figurative language, which is often vivid and imaginative, can add color and clarity to writing.

Found occasionally in prose are the following figures of speech, which, like parts of speech, appear in both writing and speaking. In addition to metaphor and simile, these include:

1. *Synecdoche:* A figure of association. Use of a part (or an individual) for the whole class or group, or the reverse.

    PART FOR WHOLE: We have fifty *head* of cattle on our farm.

    WHOLE FOR PART: Central defeated Stratfield in the homecoming game.

    The two schools did not play, but their football teams did.

2. *Metonymy:* A figure of association somewhat like synecdoche. Use of the name of one thing for that of another suggested by it, as in "the bottle" for "strong drink":

    We all agree that the tailor *sews a fine seam.*

    i.e., does good tailoring.

3. *Personification:* Giving nonhuman objects the characteristics of a human being:

    The waves *murmured,* and the moon *wept* silver tears.

4. *Hyperbole:* Exaggeration, or a statement exaggerated imaginatively, for effect; not to be taken literally. Some similes and metaphors express hyperbole:

    The young student, *innocent as a newborn babe,* eagerly accepted the bet.

    The sweet music *rose and touched the farthest star.*

dict

37f

Because figurative language is colorful and imaginative, it adds vigor and effectiveness to writing. But do not think of figurative language as a mere ornament of style; do not use it frequently; do not shift abruptly from figurative to literal language; and bear in mind that a direct simple statement is often preferable to a series of figures and always preferable when the figures are artificial, trite, or overly elaborate. Many worn-out similes are trite phrases: *happy as a lark, cool as a cucumber, busy as a bee, mad as a hornet, quick as a wink, smooth as silk, right as rain, quiet as a mouse, hot as blazes, like a chicken with its head cut off.*

Mixed figures are those in which the images suggested by the words and phrases are unrelated. Similes or metaphors are especially likely to become mixed; they seem to describe an event or process that cannot happen or exist. Here are some examples of mixed and inappropriate figures:

After football season many a football player who was a tidal wave on the football field has to put his nose to the grindstone and study.

Three of us were the kingpins on the roost in our high school.

At any party there is always a rotten apple that throws a monkey wrench in our food and drink.

I hope to get to be a wheel here, but I don't expect to do much trotting around when I get out.

When I graduate, I hope to become a well-oiled cog in the bee-hive of industry.

dict

37f

EXERCISE 6

Substitute more effective words for those that you consider ineffective in the following sentences:

1. It seems funny how Nature provides us with so much beauty.
2. A Thanksgiving dinner without a turkey is dreadful.
3. The weather in Arizona and California is simply terrific.
4. Our building is one of the prettiest in the state.
5. Most of the brands of portable typewriters on the market are fine.
6. I am anticipating my four years of college to be very interesting.
7. Our college now has one of the nicest gyms among colleges of our size.
8. I had a feeling that my freshman year was going to be just awful.
9. Trying, not winning, is the most important factor in the game of life.
10. Sir Walter Scott has a perfectly lovely view toward knights and ladies.

EXERCISE 7

In the following sentences, the writers obviously did not say what they intended to say. What did they mean? Explain the problem in each sentence.

1. Amparo never struck me as a close friend.

2. I then stopped in across the street to learn how old Mrs. Jones is.

3. There in the street I found my eyes resting on top of the Empire State Building.

4. The dinner is to honor residents and interns who are leaving the hospital and their wives. [News item]

5. Juan and his brother would take stomachaches from the green apples.

6. We are having my aunt and uncle for Christmas dinner, and I am sure we will enjoy them.

7. I think I shall never forget a talk by the Coke machine, before I left high school.

8. We next visited a furniture factory, where hundreds of antiques are manufactured every day.

9. With nothing to do on New Year's Eve, and feeling degraded, I went to a party given by my neighbors.

EXERCISE 8

List several words that have the same general meaning as the italicized word but are more exact and emphatic: (1) a *tall* building; (2) your *nice* child; (3) a *talkative* man; (4) a *kind* person; (5) a *loud* noise; (6) he *worked* hard; (7) she *walked* in; (8) a *leading* merchant; (9) I was *surprised;* (10) a *pleasant* room; (11) a *dislike* of war; (12) a *good* mind; (13) he *got* on the carrousel; (14) he *ran* quickly; (15) a *small* animal; (16) the doorbell *sounded;* (17) a miserable *house;* (18) Dr. Jones is a *specialist;* (19) a *delightful* book; (20) an interesting *trip*.

EXERCISE 9

Make the following sentences idiomatically acceptable by listing the prepositions that would properly fill in the blanks:

1. Jane is too careless _____ her appearance.

2. Mario is now reconciled _____ living on a small salary.

3. Please don't meddle _____ affairs not your own.

4. That species is peculiar _____ this vicinity.

5. You will find Claire _____ home this afternoon.

6. Some people cannot bear to part _____ a prized possession.

7. What do you infer _____ that proposal?

8. Your mother is apprehensive _____ your safety.

9. Are you really independent _____ your father?

10. This letter means that he will accede _____ your request.

11. Some students are unconcerned _____ the consequences they will face.

12. In my opinion the study rooms are the most important asset _____ the library.

13. Our citizens are conscious _____ the fact that we have a great need for more industries.

14. The only difference _____ them and other students is that they took all the easy courses they could.

15. For many years Bernardo has had the reputation _____ being a very successful businessman.

EXERCISE 10

Each sentence or group of sentences in the following contains a figure of speech from a published writer. Number each item and give the name of the figure of speech contained in it.

1. Her black hair surrounded her brow like a forest.

    THOMAS HARDY

2. She was a phantom of delight
    When first she gleamed upon my sight;
    A lovely apparition, sent
    To be a moment's ornament.

    WILLIAM WORDSWORTH

3. Can Honour's voice provoke the silent dust,/ Or Flattery soothe the dull cold ear of Death?

    THOMAS GRAY

4. At critical times in our history, the White House in Washington has announced special TV talks to the nation.

    NEWS ITEM

5. There is the New York of the commuter—the city that is devoured by locusts each day and spat out each night.

    E. B. WHITE

6. Bliss was it in that dawn to be alive,/ But to be young was very heaven!

    WILLIAM WORDSWORTH

7. He can talk French as fast as a maid can eat blackberries.

    THOMAS HARDY

8. Above me are the Alps, the palaces of Nature, whose vast walls have pinnacled in clouds their snowy scalps.

    BYRON

9. The commuter is the queerest bird of all. The suburb he inhabits has no essential vitality of its own and is a mere roost where he comes at day's end to go to sleep.

    E. B. WHITE

dict

37f

10. You shall not press down upon the brow of labor this crown of thorns; you shall not crucify mankind upon a cross of gold.

WILLIAM JENNINGS BRYAN

EXERCISE 11

Point out any inconsistent figurative language in the following and rewrite the sentences containing it.

1. The laborer has both his calloused hands resting firmly on terra firma.
2. "We have straddled the fence with both ears to the ground at the same time too long," said the speaker.
3. By learning to fly and by becoming a doctor, I can kill two birds with one stone.
4. Make hay while the sun shines, or you may find yourself out on a limb with your nose to the grindstone.
5. Don't be surprised, if you encounter difficulties on the highways and byways of life, to find many others in the same boat.

dict

38a

38. Inexact and ineffective diction

Section 37 offers numerous suggestions for using reputable words as effectively as you can. In Section 38 you are cautioned about flaws that will lessen whatever effectiveness you may have otherwise achieved. Regard the comments that follow not as a series of *don'ts* but as a list of weaknesses in diction that are always—or nearly always—to be avoided.

38a. Illiteracies

Illiteracies are nonstandard words and phrases not normally accepted in either informal or standard usage. Also called *barbarisms* and *vulgarisms,* illiteracies are characteristic of uneducated speech; they should be avoided in writing unless put into the mouths of people being characterized as uneducated. Illiteracies are not necessarily coarse and are frequently colorful, but they should not be used without a specific purpose.

263

Dictionary editors apply different restrictive labels to "illiterate" or "vulgar" English; what may be marked *illiterate* in one dictionary may be termed *dialect* or *nonstandard* in another. And because most dictionaries record primarily "standard" usage, many illiteracies are not listed at all.

The following words and phrases are examples of illiteracies: *acrossed* and *acrost, ain't, anywheres, as how, being as, being as how, borned, brung, to burgle, concertize, couldn't of, disremember, drownded, drug* (past tense of *drag*), *et* (past tense of *eat*), *fellers, hisself, I been* or *I done, irregardless, mistakened, nohow, nowheres, ourn, them's* (for *those are*), *them there, this here, youse.*

38b. Improprieties

One class of improprieties includes words that are acceptable as one part of speech but are nonstandard as another; they may be nouns improperly substituted for verbs, verbs for nouns, adjectives for nouns, adjectives for adverbs, adverbs for adjectives, prepositions for conjunctions. Another class includes misuses of principal parts of verbs.

A word that is identified as more than one part of speech may be so used without question, but do not remove a word from one part of speech and place it in another until standard usage has sanctioned this new function. The following are examples of grammatical improprieties:

NOUNS USED AS VERBS:	*grassing* a lawn, *suppering,* to *author, ambitioned, passengered*
VERBS USED AS NOUNS:	a *sell, advise*
ADJECTIVES USED AS ADVERBS:	dances *good, awful* short
VERB FORMS:	*come* for *came, don't* for *doesn't, says* for *said, done* for *did, hadn't ought, set* for *sit, of* for *have*
OTHER COMBINATIONS:	*them kind; being that, being as* or *being as how* for *because* or *since; except as* for *unless*

For guidance consult your dictionary, which labels every word according to the part (or parts) of speech that it is. Note also the usage label—colloquial, dialect, slang, and so forth—since the same word may be acceptable as one part of speech but not as another.

Another class of improprieties includes words that are similar or vaguely similar to other words and are used inaccurately in their place. Such words include homonyms and homographs.

Homonyms are two words that have the same or almost the same pronunciation but are different in meaning, in origin, and frequently in spelling, for example, *real* and *reel; made* and *maid; hour, our,* and *are; accept, except; stationary, stationery.*

Words that are near-homonyms may also cause confusion: *farther* for *further, father* for *farther, genial* for *general, morass* for *morose, loose* for *lose, imminent* for *eminent.*

A person of such distinction is certainly one to *immolate.*
The tennis player *lopped* the ball to the back of the court.
To be an engineer one has to be able to use a *slight* rule.
All of us took too much for *granite.*
When I slipped and fell I was *humidified.*

dict

38c

Such confusion may result from hearing words inexactly rather than seeing them in print and relating their meaning to their appearance as well as their sound.

Homographs are two or more words that have the same spelling but are different in meaning, origin, and perhaps pronunciation. Examples include *slaver* (a dealer in slaves) and *slaver* (drool or drivel); *arms* (parts of the body) and *arms* (weapons); *bat* (club, cudgel) and *bat* (flying mammal).

38c. Exaggeration

To *exaggerate* is to misrepresent by overstatement: "I thought I'd die of embarrassment"; "That outfit is older than Noah"; "That is a horrible [or *ghastly* or *frightful*] tie you are wearing"; "I was scared to death."

Occasionally, exaggeration can be used to good effect, but it is *never* exact and is not intended to be taken literally. It is more often misleading and ludicrous than appropriate and picturesque. Be cautious when using such words as *gigantic, tremendous, wonderful, phenomenal, staggering, thrilling, terrible, gorgeous, horrible, marvelous,* and *overwhelming.* (See *hyperbole* in Section 37f.)

38d. Affectation

Affectation is artificial behavior intended to impress others, a mannerism or way of talking, acting, or writing that involves show or pretense. In language, it becomes apparent when a writer uses words that are not customary or appropriate to the person using them. Deliberately trying to be different or learned or impressive often results in misinterpretation, confusion, and annoyance for the reader. Pretense is an even greater sin against effective English than "bad grammar."

For example, compare these two sentences:

AFFECTED DICTION: After liquidating her indebtedness she was still in possession of sufficient resources to establish a small commercial enterprise.

EFFECTIVE DICTION: After paying her debts, she still had enough money to set up a small business.

For another example, a recent magazine contained this paragraph:

> The opportunity for options in life distinguishes the rich from the poor. Perhaps through better motivation, the upper levels of the poor could be tempted into the option track. It is important to motivate such people close to the breakthrough level in income because they are closest to getting a foot on the option ladder.

What this writer probably meant was, "The more money you have, the more choices you have." He or she fell into the error of affectation.

38e. Euphemisms

One form of affectation is the use of *euphemisms*. A euphemism is a softened, bland, inoffensive expression used instead of one that may suggest something unpleasant. In effective writing it's a good idea to call things by their names. In avoiding such nonreputable expressions as *croak, turn up one's toes to the daisies, kick the bucket,* and *take the last count,* you may be tempted to write *pass away* or *depart this life* rather than the short, direct word *die.* Other examples of euphemisms that should usually be avoided are *perspire* for *sweat, prevaricate* for *lie, expectorate* for *spit, mortician* for *undertaker, separate from school* for *expel, intoxicated* for *drunk, abdomen* for *stomach, obsequies* for *funeral,* and *love child* for *illegitimate.*

Here are a few euphemisms recently noted in magazines and newspapers:

preowned car (secondhand car)
senior citizens (old people)
experienced tires (retreads)
mortical surgeon (undertaker)
sanitary engineer (garbage collector)
comfort station (public toilet)

problem skin (acne)
custodial engineer (janitor)
motion discomfort (nausea)
food preparation center (kitchen)
extrapolation (educated guess)
creative conflict (civil rights demonstration)

38f. Jargon and gobbledygook

Jargon has two basic meanings: (1) the language of a particular trade, profession, or group, such as legal jargon or medical jargon; (2) unintelligible or meaningless talk. The first of these meanings is discussed in Sections 36b and 38g under the headings of technical words (shoptalk) and slang. In its second sense, jargon involves the use of vague terms, "big" words, and indirect, roundabout ways of expressing ideas.

In an attempt to make writing "fine," the users of jargon will write "The answer is in the negative" rather than "No." For them, "bad weather" is "unfavorable climatic conditions." Jargoneers also employ what has been called "the trick of elegant variation." They may call a spade the first time but will then refer to "an agricultural implement."

Gobbledygook is a special kind of ineffective writing. The term was coined by a former congressman, grown weary of involved government reports, who possibly had in mind the throaty sounds uttered by a male turkey.

The term *gobbledygook* is often applied to governmental and bureaucratic announcements that have been described as "masterpieces of complexity." For example, in a pronouncement from a Washington bureau "the chance of war" was referred to, in gobbledygook, as "in the regrettable eventuality of a failure of the deterrence policy."

Another example is the plumber who wrote to inform an agency of the U.S. government that he had found hydrochloric acid good for cleaning out pipes. Some bureaucrat responded with this gobbledygook: "The efficiency of hydrochloric acid is indisputable, but the corrosive residue is incompatible with metallic permanence." The plumber responded that he was glad the agency agreed. After several more gobbledygookish letters, an official finally wrote what should have been written originally: "Don't use hydrochloric acid. It eats the hell out of pipes."

Realizing how absurd gobbledygook is may ensure your never using it. Who, for instance, would prefer "Too great a number of culinary assistants may impair the flavor of the consommé" to "Too many cooks spoil the broth"?

38g. Slang

Slang is the nonstandard vocabulary of a given culture or subculture. It consists of coinages and figures of speech that are often characterized by raciness and spontaneity. Slang may also be defined as language peculiar to a particular group, language by which members of the group recognize and relate to other members of the group. The groups may be based on age—much slang begins with high school or college students—but it may come from any segment of the population: musicians, sports figures, lawyers, doctors, engineers, and even ministers and priests. Most slang terms eventually pass into the obscurity of dictionaries of obsolete slang, but some endure in wider and more general use.

Slang expressions may take one of several forms:

1. *Neologisms* (newly coined words) that remain slang, although not all neologisms are slang. A newly coined word for a new thing, such as *countdown,* will probably enter the language as a standard word; on the other hand, a newly coined word for something that already exists and has a name, such as *upper* (amphetamine), will probably be labeled as slang.

2. Words that are formed from others by abbreviating them: *legit, simp, psych out* or *psych up, snafu, mod.*

3. Words in general use that are given extended meanings: *bird* (which has been a slang term for "girl" for centuries), *creep, off the wall, grass, pot, pits, jerk, guts, grease, pad.*

4. Phrases that are made up of one or more newly coined words or one or more general ones: *blow your top, go into orbit, freak out, pork barrel, shoot the bull, conk out, cool it, bum steer, ripped off.*

Slang has no place in formal writing and only a limited place in informal writing. Why? First, many slang words and expressions last for a brief time and then pass out of use. If they are used, they violate the principle of national use. (See Section 36.) Second, using slang expressions prevents searching for the exact words needed to express your meaning. Calling someone a "creep" hardly conveys an exact and full impression. Third, most slang does not serve the primary aim of writing: conveying a clear and exact message from writer to reader. Finally, slang is not suitable in most formal or careful informal writing because it is not in keeping with the context. Words should be appropriate to the audience, the occasion, and the subject.

There are, however, some arguments in favor of slang in certain situations. It does express feeling. It also makes for effective shortcuts in expression and often prevents artificiality in writing. Furthermore, when used in recording dialog it can convey the actual flavor of speech.

dict

38h

38h. Triteness

The term *trite* applies to words and expressions that are worn out from overuse. A trite expression is sometimes called *hackneyed language* or a *cliché.* The origins of the words *triteness, hackneyed,* and *cliché* are revealing: the first comes from the Latin word *tritus,* which means "to rub, to wear out"; *hackneyed* is derived from the idea of a horse or carriage let out for hire, devoted to common use, and thus worn out in service; *cliché* comes from the French word meaning "to stereotype."

Thus, trite language resembles slang in that both are rubber stamps, "stereotyped plates" of thought and expression.

Clichés may be tags from common speech, overworked quotations, or outworn phrases from newspapers. They save writers the task of stating exactly what they mean, but their use results in writing that is stale and ineffective. Such words and phrases may seem humorous; they are, indeed, often used for humor or irony.

Used seriously, they suggest that the speaker or writer is naive or lazy.

Because trite words and expressions are familiar, they are likely to occur to us more readily than others that are more effective. Look suspiciously at each word or phrase that leaps to mind until you can be certain the expression is exact and unhackneyed. Hundreds and hundreds of examples could be cited, but here are some colorful expressions that are now ineffective because of overuse:

brave as a lion	gentle as a lamb	pure as new-fallen snow
brown as a berry	green as grass	sadder but wiser
cold as ice	like a blundering idiot	strong as an ox
fight like a tiger	like a duck out of water	trees like sentinels
free as the air	like a newborn babe	wild as a March hare

Here are some more trite words and phrases:

a must, all in all, along this (that) line, and things like that, any manner or means, aroused our curiosity, as a matter of fact

battle of life, beating around the bush, believe me, bigger and better things, bitter end, bright and early, brings to mind, butterflies in my stomach, by leaps and bounds

center of attraction, chills (shivers) up and down my spine, come into the picture, come to life, conspicuous by its absence

dear old [high school, college, alma mater], depths of despair, doomed to disappointment, dull thud

each and every, every walk of life

fair land of ours, few and far between, fill the shoes of, first and foremost, fond memories, force of circumstances

get our (their) wires crossed, give it a try, give out (up), goes without saying, grand and glorious, great [guy, job, thrill, etc.], green with envy

hang one on, honest to goodness

in dire straits, in glowing terms, in the best of health, in the long run, in this day and age, interesting (surprising) to note, intestinal fortitude, irony of fate

last but not least, last straw, leaves little to be desired, live it up, mad dash for, make the world a better place, more than pleased, Mother Nature

necessary evil, never a dull moment, nick of time, no fooling, no thinking person, none the worse for wear, needs no introduction

out of this world

proud possessor, psychological moment

raining cats and dogs, real thrill

sad to relate, safe to say, sigh of relief, sight to behold

take a back seat, the time of my life, thing of the past, tired but happy

wee small hours, wide open spaces, words fail to express, wunderbar, without further ado

38i. Wordiness

To be really effective, diction must be economical. Writing should be neither clipped nor sketchy, but using more words than are needed weakens the force and appeal of all writing and most speech.

Conciseness alone does not guarantee good writing, but it is impossible to write forcefully if you use three or four words where one would serve adequately. (The Golden Rule contains only 11 words. The Ten Commandments are expressed in 75 words. Lincoln's Gettysburg Address contains only 267 words.) The moral of "few words for many" is in the following: To the question of whether rules should be observed, an administrator wrote, "The implementation of sanctions will inevitably eventuate in subsequent repercussions." What he meant, and should have written, was "Yes."

Here are examples of some wordy expressions and their concise counterparts:

I would appreciate it if	please
in the month of June	in June
it has come to our attention that	(begin with the word following *that*)
it is interesting to note that	(begin with the word following *that*)
in the event that	if
at the present time	now
on condition that	if
in regard to	about
inasmuch as	since
are of the opinion	believe
in accordance with	by
before long	soon

When meaning is expressed or implied in a particular word or

dict

38i

phrase, repeating the idea by additional words is useless. One word of two or three expresses the idea, and the others add nothing. Common examples are using *again* with many verbs beginning with re-; using *more* or *most* with absolute-meaning adjectives; and using *more* or *most* with adjectives and adverbs that already end in *-er, -est.* The following are examples of such repetitious expressions:

repeat again	recur again
more better	necessary need
long length	first beginnings
endorse on the back	each and every one
completely unanimous	cooperate together
rise up	fellow classmates
most perpendicular	more perfect
more paramount	resume again
loquacious talker	meet up with
audible to the ear	consensus of opinion
more older	many in number
most unkindest	visible to the eye
descend down	final end
individual person	revert back
join together	reduce down
complete monopoly	cover over
this afternoon at 3 P.M.	back up
most unique	talented genius

Wordiness takes many forms. *Affectation* (Section 38d), *euphemisms* (Section 38e), *jargon* and *gobbledygook* (Section 38f), and *trite expressions* (Section 38h) are frequently wordy. Once again, use all the words you need to express your ideas fully and clearly, but try—and try hard—to eliminate the deadwood.

EXERCISE 12

Write a short paper summarizing what your dictionary tells you about these words applied to language: *barbarism, illiteracy, impropriety, solecism, vulgarism.* Use dictionary examples of each.

EXERCISE 13

In your dictionary, find answers to the following questions. If the answer is yes, explain.

Can the following words be used as indicated?

1. *corp* as the singular of *corps*
2. *conjugate* as an adjective
3. *pshaw* as a verb; as an interjection
4. *rose* as a verb
5. *holp, holpen* as past tense and past participle
6. *contrariwise* as an adjective
7. *quarry* as a verb
8. *throw* as a noun
9. *cool* as a noun
10. *complected* as a variant of *complexioned*
11. *stratums* as a plural
12. *ditto* as a verb
13. *quail* as a verb
14. *wrought* as a past participle of *work*
15. *hardy* as a noun
16. *sure* as an adverb
17. *equal* as a noun
18. *appropriate* as an adverb

dict

38i

EXERCISE 14

Following are three statements, as reported by the Associated Press, concerning a promotion refusal. Which is the least effective and which the most effective? Why?

1. Verbal contact with Mr. Blank regarding the attached notification of promotion has elicited the attached representations intimating that he prefers to decline the assignment.
2. I have spoken to Mr. Blank about this promotion; he does not wish to accept the post offered.
3. Blank doesn't want the job.

EXERCISE 15

What are the meanings of the following words and expressions?

burg, mum, numbskull, primp, uppish, fizzle, type, catch (*n.*), rambunctious, middy, highfalutin, lab, bossy, grapevine, fluke, preachify, sleuth, buddy, buck fever, pass the buck, pitch in, freeze out, war horse, small potatoes, yes man, yours truly, square shooter, blue streak, rubber stamp, Dutch treat, salt away, close call, play up to, walking papers, make time, sweet tooth, fill the bill, cut a figure

EXERCISE 16

What are the meanings of the following slang words and phrases? (Any difficulty you have with this question should tell you something about the short life of some slang.)

1. sound off
2. on the make
3. shyster
4. cahoot
5. get one's goat
6. stool pigeon
7. sad sack
8. hooey
9. nix
10. tizzy
11. kibosh
12. pork barrel
13. high-hat
14. long green
15. goo
16. on the loose
17. jittery
18. stuffed shirt
19. mooch
20. a yard

dict

38i

EXERCISE 17

The following letter of 78 words can be written in clear, simple language in about 30 words. See how close to that number you can come in your revision.

Dear Sir:
    We are in receipt of your favor of the tenth instant in re order for five television sets and wish to advise that according to our records your order was shipped on Oct. 19. Inasmuch as the order was carefully checked on this end, we would ask you to wait for three days. If the material has not been received in that time, we would ask that you use the card attached hereto and give us due notice.

EXERCISE 18

Substitute more effective expressions for those that you consider trite in the following sentences:

1. After all, one does not have to stay out to the wee small hours of the morning simply because it is New Year's Eve.
2. When I applied for my first job, I must admit that I had butterflies in my stomach.
3. The movie ended with the hero driving down the highway, like a ribbon winding over the hills, and into the reddening glow of the setting sun.

4. Her marks have improved by leaps and bounds. The main underlying reason for it is that she has worked like a dog.

5. At a ripe old age she died, having lived out her life in the wide open spaces.

EXERCISE 19

Shorten each of the following sentences as much as you can without losing meaning:

1. There were only about one-third of our group who made it back.
2. There should be greater emphasis placed on our tutoring program.
3. Saturdays are the only days I am able to have the car.
4. When I ask for a raise in my allowance, my parents' answer is usually in the negative.
5. In the event that I make the honor roll, I plan to have a party.
6. Some people are resentful with regard to the way the dues have been raised.
7. The story was basically dreary, and it was plain to see that the author had tried to enliven it.
8. I had hoped to become a good student in the field of mathematics.
9. It was at midnight that I awoke to a most astounding sight.
10. It was after the 1975 drought that my father dug himself another well.

dict

38i

EXERCISE 20

See directions for Exercise 19.

1. In case I am offered the opportunity, I may fly to Chicago.
2. We heard that stores would remain open a longer length of time during the Christmas season.
3. I have always shied away from the field of mechanical engineering.
4. About 20 miles north of Sommerville is a camp called Whistlewood; this is my summer camp.
5. It has been called to my attention by the secretary that a board of directors meeting has been scheduled for June 8.
6. I do not feel the necessity for a conference at the present time.
7. Upon arriving at the Bar-X Ranch, we were assigned horses for the pack trip into the hills.
8. There is still a great deal to be explained in the area of flying saucers.
9. I would like to take this opportunity to introduce myself.
10. I endorsed on the back a check for $10 that my aunt had sent me for expenses.

The dictionary and vocabulary building

To write and speak competently, everyone needs as a guide a reliable dictionary. No speaker or writer of English knows all the words that are available. Every user of English needs help with the meaning, spelling, pronunciation, and use of certain words.

If you have not done so yet, make the acquaintance of your dictionary *now*. Better still, make it your constant companion. Best of all, make it your friend.

39a. Choose a reliable dictionary.

Appealing to "*the* dictionary" as an authority is as illogical as saying, "Don't buy me a book; I already have one" or, "It must be so; I saw it in print." Dictionaries may be good, mediocre, or bad. Some, like pocket dictionaries, are so small that they are not fully reliable. The following dictionaries are recommended:

The American College Dictionary (ACD) (New York: Random House)
The American Heritage Dictionary of the English Language (AHD) (New York: American Heritage; Boston: Houghton Mifflin)
Funk & Wagnalls Standard College Dictionary (SCD) (New York: Funk & Wagnalls)
The Random House Dictionary of the English Language, College Edition (RHD) (New York: Random House)
Thorndike-Barnhart Comprehensive Dictionary (CD) (Glenview, Ill.: Scott, Foresman)
Webster's New World Dictionary of the American Language (NWD) (Cleveland: William Collins and World Publishing Company)
Webster's New Collegiate Dictionary (NCD) (Springfield, Mass.: Merriam)

Any of these dictionaries represents an excellent investment in a practical, constantly useful, and reliable aid in speaking and writing.

Larger dictionaries are also available. Each of them contains at least three times as much information as those just listed. Entries are more numerous, frequently are more detailed, and often provide finer shades of meaning. Such dictionaries are called "unabridged" versions. However, unabridged dictionaries are more expensive than those suggested, more awkward to handle, and difficult to carry around. Such sizable and valuable dictionaries are often placed in classrooms, in libraries, and in teachers' offices and staff rooms. The best known of the unabridged dictionaries are the following:

Funk & Wagnalls New Standard Dictionary of the English Language (New York: Funk & Wagnalls)

New English (Oxford) Dictionary (New York: Oxford University Press: *The Shorter Oxford Dictionary* appears in both one- and two-volume editions; the larger work is in twelve volumes and a supplement)

The Random House Dictionary of the English Language (New York: Random House)

Webster's Third New International Dictionary (Springfield, Mass.: Merriam)

39b. Learn how to use and interpret a dictionary.

Many persons consult a dictionary to find the spelling or meaning or pronunciation of a word. However, to use it for only these purposes is to ignore other useful information.

Dictionaries differ in their presentation of material. If you have never done so before, examine your dictionary carefully and critically. Read its table of contents. Examine the material given on the inside of front and back covers. Read, or at least skim, some of the prefatory pages as well as any supplementary material at the back.

After you have done this, you should read the articles headed "General Introduction," "Guide to the Use of This Dictionary," "Guide to Pronunciation," "Etymology Key," "Explanatory Notes," and "Symbols and Abbreviations Used." Your dictionary may not have sections entitled precisely thus, but it will contain equivalent material. You cannot use your dictionary with full effectiveness until you are acquainted with its plan and method of presentation.

Although dictionaries differ in their methods of listing entries and citing information, all reliable dictionaries have a common purpose: They report on the way language is currently used and, occasionally, on how it has been used in the past.

Lexicographers (the people who make dictionaries) do not themselves decide what words mean or even how they should be spelled or pronounced. A good dictionary is a product of careful study and research, a report on what is known as *standard English,* that is, the English of most educated speakers and users of the language.

A dictionary is not an "authority" in any exact meaning of the word. It does not dictate or prescribe except in the sense that it records and interprets the status of English words and phrases. It indicates what is general practice in the language; only in this way can it be said to constitute authority. When you have a specific problem about usage, apply in your own writing and speaking the information recorded in your dictionary. But do not think of it as a final arbiter of what is right and what is wrong.

39c. Master the information given for word entries.

Time spent in learning words thoroughly will save time, errors, and annoyance later.

For any word listed in an adequate dictionary, each of the first five of the following items is given. For many words, some of the last five kinds of information are provided:

1. spelling
2. syllabication
3. pronunciation
4. part(s) of speech
5. meaning(s)

6. level(s) of usage
7. derivation (origin)
8. synonyms
9. antonyms
10. other information

abridge \ə-'brij= *vt* **abridged; abridg·ing** [ME *abregen,* fr. MF *abregier,* fr. LL *abbreviare,* fr. **L** *ad–* + *brevis* short—more at BRIEF] **1 a** *archaic:* DEPRIVE **b :** to reduce in scope : DIMINISH ⟨attempts to ~ the right of free speech **2 :** to shorten in duration or extent ⟨modern transportation that ~s distance⟩ **3 :** to shorten by omission of words without sacrifice of sense:CONDENSE *syn* see SHORTEN *ant* expand, extend—**abridg·er** *n*

abridg·ment *or* **abridge·ment** \ə-'brij-ment*n* **1 :** the action of abridging : the state of being abridged **2 :** a shortened form of a work retaining the general sense and unity of the original *syn·* ABRIDGMENT, ABSTRACT, SYNOPSIS, CONSPECTUS, EPITOME. *shared meaning element* : a shorter version of a larger work or treatment *ant* expansion★

1. Spelling

The basic, or "entry," word is given in black (boldface) type. Associated with the main entry may be other words in black type

---

★By permission. From *Webster's New Collegiate Dictionary,* © 1980 by G. & C. Merriam Company, Publishers of the Merriam-Webster Dictionaries.

indicating run-on entries. (Endings such as *-er* and *-like* may be added—*begin, beginner; clerk, clerklike*—and alternative entries of variant forms—*Bern, Berne; diagram, -gramed, -graming* or *-grammed, -gramming*.) Note especially the following:

1. The plurals of nouns are given if a noun forms its plural other than by adding *s* or *es.*
2. The comparative and superlative degrees of adjectives and adverbs are given if a spelling change is made in the addition of *er, est.*
3. The past tense, past participle, and present participle of verbs are given in some dictionaries when these forms differ from the present tense form or if the spelling changes in the addition of an ending.
4. Many compound words spelled with a hyphen, as one word, or as two words are so indicated.

When a word has two or more spellings, the more common spelling is usually given first. Sometimes the variant spelling is also listed separately.

The spelling of proper names (people, places, etc.) is given either in the regular place in the alphabetical listing or in a special section or sections at the back of the dictionary, depending on the dictionary.

2. Syllabication

Learn to distinguish between the light mark, or dot (·), which is used to separate syllables (ri · dic · u · lous), and the hyphen (-), which is used to show that the word is a compound (*hardhitting*). All reliable dictionaries use the dot system of indicating syllabication. Some substitute an accent mark after the stressed syllable.

Knowledge of syllabication is important in two ways. First, it helps in the pronunciation of words, which in turn helps in correct spelling. Second, it shows where to divide words between syllables if division is necessary at the end of a line. (see Section 28c.)

3. Pronunciation

Pronunciation is based on *accent* or emphasized syllables and on the *sound* given to letters or letter combinations.

Both accent marks and syllabication dots are included in the entry word by some dictionaries. Other dictionaries carry only the syllabication dots in the entry word and include the accent marks in the "pronunciation" word.

Learn to distinguish the accent marks. Primary, or heavy, stress is shown by a heavy mark (′) and secondary, or less heavy, stress by a light (′) or double (″) mark: com′ pass′, com′ pass″; dif′ fer′, dif′ fer″; spell′ ing′, spell′ ing″; pro′ nounce′, pro″ nounce′. Secondary stress may also be shown by a mark below the line.

In pronunciation, with 26 letters of the alphabet, some 45 to 65 sounds, and 250 common spellings of sounds, you need all the help your dictionary can give. Note the respelling-as-pronounced form after the main entry. Refer as needed to the main pronunciation key and to its more frequently used items (usually inside the cover or at the bottom of each right-hand page). Your dictionary may have a separate key for foreign sounds.

Generally, when two or more pronunciations of a word are included, the one that is more commonly used is given first. A variant pronunciation may occasionally be labeled "British" or "Chiefly British" (*Brit.* or *Chiefly Brit.*) to show that this pronunciation is the common one in Great Britain.

4. Part(s) of speech

Since all English words are parts of speech, the part of speech of every entry is generally given. If the word is used as more than one part of speech, such information is provided and the particular meaning or meanings for each one explained. Also shown are the singular or plural forms of many nouns, the comparative and superlative degrees of many adjectives and adverbs, and the correct use of verbs as transitive, intransitive, or both.

Study the following excerpt:

sweet (swēt) *adj.* **sweeter, sweetest. 1.a.** Having a sugary taste. **b.** Containing or derived from a sugar. **2.** Pleasing to the senses, feelings, or the mind; gratifying: *"Sin was yet very sweet to my flesh, and I was loath to leave it"* (Bunyan). **3.** Having a pleasing disposition; lovable: *a sweet child.* **4.** Not saline; fresh: *sweet water.* **5.** Not spoiled, sour, or decaying; fresh: *This milk is still sweet.* **6.** Free of acid. **7.** *Music.* **a.** Designating jazz characterized by adherence to a melodic line and to a time signature. **b.** Performing jazz in this way: *a sweet combo.* —*n.* **1.** The quality of being sweet; sweetness. **2.** Something that is sweet or contains sugar. **3.** *Usually plural.* Candy, preserves, or confections. **4.** *British.* Anything relatively sweet served as a dessert. **5.** A dear or beloved person. [Middle English *swe(e)te;* Old English *swēte.* See **swād-** in appendix.] —**sweetly** *adv.* —**sweet′ ness** *n.*

Sweet (swēt), **Henry:** 1845–1912. British philologist and phonetician.

sweet alyssum. A widely cultivated plant, *Lobularia maritima,* native to the Mediterranean region, having clusters of small, fragrant white or purplish flowers.

sweet basil. A species of **basil** *(see).*

sweet bay. A small tree, *Magnolia virginiana,* of the southeastern United States, having large, fragrant white flowers.

sweet birch. A tree, the **black birch** *(see).*

sweet·bread (swēt′brĕd) *n.* The thymus gland of an animal used for food [SWEET + BREAD (euphemism for the food).]

sweet·bri·er (swēt′brī′ ə) *n.* Also **sweet·bri·ar.** A rose, *Rosa eglanteria,* native to Europe, having prickly stems, fragrant leaves, and pink flowers. Also called "eglantine."★

This reprint from *The American Heritage Dictionary* provides substantial information about *sweet* as an adjective and noun. Additional entries reveal how the word *sweet* appears in other words and word combinations. If you were to go on reading, you would come across entries for *sweet cherry, sweet cicely, sweet cider, sweet clover, sweet corn, sweeten, sweetening, sweet fern, sweet flag, sweet gale, sweet gum, sweetheart, sweetie, sweeting, sweet marjoram, sweetmeat, sweet pea, sweet pepper, sweet pepperbush, sweet potato, sweetsop, sweet sultan, sweet tooth,* and *sweet William.* Such a collection of word entries should indicate the vast amount of information that a good dictionary provides not only about parts of speech but about other matters as well.

Teach yourself the more common abbreviations from the table of abbreviations (or elsewhere) in your dictionary. The following is a partial list of commonly used abbreviations:

VOC

39c

act. for active	p.p. for past participle
adj. for adjective	pred. for predicate
adv. for adverb	prep. for preposition
auxil. for auxiliary	pres. for present
conj. for conjunction	prin. pts. for principal parts
fut. for future	pron. for pronoun
n. for noun	sing. for singular
part. for participle	subj. for subjunctive
perf. for perfect	v. for verb
pl. for plural	v.i. for verb, intransitive
poss. for possessive	v.t. for verb, transitive

★By permission. From *The American Heritage Dictionary of the English Language.* © 1979 by Houghton Mifflin Company.

This list is a reminder that some knowledge of grammar and grammatical terms is necessary for intelligent and successful use of the dictionary.

5. Meanings

For any given word, choose the meaning that fits your writing or reading purpose, since words may have one or more of the following meanings; historical meaning, traditional meaning, figurative meaning, or new meaning.

Hyphenated words and two or more words forming phrases that have idiomatic, specialized, or figurative meanings are explained in the regular alphabetical listing, either entered separately or put under the main word.

lock away, to store or safeguard in a locked box, container, etc.

lock out, 1. to shut out by or as by locking the door against. 2. to keep (workers) from a place of employment in an attempt to make them accept the employer's terms.

lock, stock, and barrel, [Colloq.], completely.

lock up, 1. to fasten the doors of (a house, etc.) by means of locks. 2. to enclose or store in a locked container. 3. to put in jail.

under lock and key, locked up; safely put away.★

6. Levels of usage

Your dictionary enables you to judge the acceptability of a word by the absence or presence of a restrictive label. Any word that is not accompanied by a restrictive label or explanatory comment is appropriate in formal and informal English, and any word or phrase that is labeled "colloquial" or "informal" is generally acceptable in *all* informal speech and writing. All other labels are guides to special use.

Four types of restrictive labels are common:

1. *Geographic,* indicating a country or section of a country where the word is common: *Chiefly U.S., British, Scotch, New England, Southern, Southwest, Western U.S., dialect.* It is not surprising that geographic labels are necessary, for English is the

---

★By permission. From *Webster's New World Dictionary,* Second College Edition. Copyright © 1980 by William Collins Publishers, Inc.

native language of some 300 million people in various parts of the world, and it is a second language of one-third to one-half as many more.

2. *Time,* indicating that the word is no longer used, is disappearing from use, or is still used but has a quaint form or meaning: *obsolete, archaic.*

3. *Subject,* indicating that a specialized word or a specialized meaning belongs to a restricted department of knowledge such as science, technology, a trade, a profession, a sport, and the like.

4. *Cultural,* indicating whether the word or a special use of a word is substandard or acceptable as informal or formal English: *illiterate, slang, dialect* (may be geographic also), *colloquial, poetic, literary.* A foreign word or phrase that has not been Anglicized will also bear its language label.

No Supreme Court of language exists to which a final appeal can be made. Lexicographers use their best judgment in compiling and interpreting language data. Dictionaries may differ, therefore, in the labels they attach to certain words or meanings. For example, the same word in several dictionaries may have the label "obsolete," "archaic," or "dialect," or no qualifying label at all. Remember also that some dictionaries are more permissive than others, and hence differ; their makers tell us that it is often difficult to apply a label like "colloquial" or "informal" or "slang" to a word or phrase out of context.

Some dictionaries carry comments on levels of meaning and the usage problems involved. Here, for example, is such an entry:

Usage: *Like,* as a conjunction, is not appropriate to formal usage, especially written usage, except in certain constructions noted below. On other levels it occurs frequently, especially in casual speech and in writing representing speech. In formal usage the conjunctive *like* is most acceptable when it introduces an elliptical clause in which a verb is not expressed: *He took to politics like a fish to water. The dress looked like new.* Both examples, which are acceptable on a formal level to 76 percent of the Usage Panel, employ such elliptical, or shortened, expressions following *like.* If they were recast to include full clauses containing verbs, *like* would preferably be replaced, in formal usage, by *as, as if,* or *as though: took to politics as a fish takes to water; dress looked as if it were new.* The examples that follow illustrate the difference. All employ *like* to introduce full clauses containing verbs; all are termed unacceptable by more than 75 percent of the Usage Panel, and in every case a more desirable construction is indicated: *He manipulates an audience like* (preferably *as*) *a virtuoso commands a musical instrument.*

The engine responds now like (preferably *as*) *good machinery should. It looks like* (preferably *as if*) *they will be finished earlier than usual. He had no authority, but he always acted like* (preferably *as if*) *he did.* The restriction on *like* as a conjunction does not affect its other uses. Fear of misusing *like* often causes writers to use *as* in its place in constructions where *like* is not only acceptable but clearly called for. It is always used acceptably when it functions prepositionally, followed by a noun or pronoun as object: *works like a charm; sings like an angel; looking for a girl like me* (not *I*); *spoke like one who had authority* (but not *like he had authority*). Used prepositionally, *like* indicates comparison; in modern usage *as,* in place of *like,* would imply the assumption of another role: *he behaved like* (not *as*) *a child. She treated him like* (not *as*) *a fool. John, like* (not *as*) *his grandfather earlier, chose to ignore politics.*★

7. Derivation (origin)

The derivation or origin of a word—linguistically speaking, its *etymology*—is usually one of two types: (a) whenever known, the ancestral or foreign languages from or through which the word attained its English form (Old English, Latin, Greek, German, and French have been heavy contributors, but some 150 other languages have had a part), or (b), less commonly, a narrative account of how the word was formed or received its meaning (see in your dictionary, for example, *derrick, burke, macadam, radar*).

Find in your dictionary the page or pages giving the language or word origin abbreviations and symbols used and apply them to a random sampling of words. This information, usually entered between brackets, may come either near the beginning or at the end of the vocabulary entry.

8. Synonyms

Synonyms are words that in one or more of their definitions have the same or similar meanings. Frequently these approximate equivalents have differences in both denotation and connotation that enable you to choose words that are precise and emphatic. So necessary is this study that entire volumes have been compiled to aid speakers and writers: *Webster's Dictionary of Synonyms, Crabb's English Synonyms, Roget's International Thesaurus of English Words.*

★By permission. From *The American Heritage Dictionary of the English Language.* © 1979 by Houghton Mifflin Company.

Your dictionary includes at the end of many of its entries a listing and frequently a brief discussion of synonyms, showing the differences in meaning of apparently similar words; it may indicate by a number which usage is part of the synonymous meaning. Virtually every page offers one or more examples.

9. Antonyms

Antonyms are pairs of words that have opposite or negative meanings: *man–woman, man–boy, man–beast, man–God, holy–unholy,* and so on. These opposite meanings are not all-inclusive: A word may be an antonym of another only in a certain limited meaning. One antonym of *man* concerns sex; another, age; another, biology; another, religion. Your dictionary suggests antonyms for many words.

VOC

39c

10. Other information

Other information that may appear as part of an entry or as separate entries in the main part of your dictionary includes abbreviations; biographical names; capitalized words and words spelled with both capitals and small letters; cross-references to words listed elsewhere; examples of word use in phrases and sentences; foreign words and phrases (usually so labeled or given a special symbol); geographic names; homographs and homonyms (respectively, words spelled alike but having different meanings and words spelled differently but pronounced alike); the meanings of idiomatic phrases; prefixes, suffixes, and other combining word-elements; and, for appropriate words, pictorial or graphic illustrations.

The wealth of information included under each vocabulary entry is supplemented, in reliable dictionaries, by other material in the front and back pages. Become familiar with it. In addition to a discussion of spelling (orthography), pronunciation, usage levels, and the like, there may be sections that offer guidance on punctuation, grammar, letter writing, proofreading, and rhyming; a list of American colleges and universities; and other useful information.

39d. Vocabulary building and dictionary use

Each of us has three vocabularies. First, we have an active *speaking* vocabulary, a working supply of words that we use daily. Second, we have a *writing* vocabulary, some of whose words we do not usually use in speech. In addition to these active vocabularies, each of us has a *potential, recognition,* or *reading* vocabulary, which is the largest of the three. This potential vocabulary consists of the many words that we recognize and partly understand, possibly from the context, but would not be able to use in our own speaking and writing. Until we use such words—start them working *for us*—they are not really ours. (Of course, some words that we have to look up while reading will have no real use value in our own speaking and writing.)

Real effort is needed to move words from your potential vocabulary to your active vocabulary. It is, however, the best way to begin vocabulary improvement, for the good reason that these words are already somewhat familiar to you.

You should constantly try to expand your vocabulary, not only because doing so will improve your reading, writing, and speaking, but also because a good vocabulary will be increasingly important in your life. As Johnson O'Connor, a scientific investigator, has stated,

An *extensive knowledge of the exact meanings of English words* accompanies outstanding success in this country more often than any other single characteristic which the Human Engineering Laboratory has been able to isolate and measure.

The most important element in vocabulary growth is the *will* to learn new words. But wide reading and intelligent listening should lead straight to a good dictionary.

If in reading you dislike breaking your chain of thought by looking up words in a dictionary (although the very need to use a dictionary has already broken that chain), jot down unfamiliar words and look them up as soon as possible. Keeping a notebook nearby is a good idea. And be sure, after you have thoroughly studied an appropriate and useful new word, to use it in speaking and writing until it is yours.

39e. Synonyms and antonyms

Collecting lists of synonyms and distinguishing among their meanings is an effective way to enlarge your vocabulary. Many dictionaries include listings and explanations of hundreds of synonyms. When looking up a word, carefully study the synonym entries. If you do this, you may be able to choose a more exact and effective word and at the same time enlarge your active vocabulary.

For example, after becoming aware of synonyms, will you have to write that the baby is *cute,* the game *thrilling,* the idea *interesting,* the dress *glamorous* or *chic,* the play *exciting?* A study of synonyms for *old* might add to your vocabulary these words, among others: *immemorial, aged, ancient, aboriginal, decrepit, antique, hoary, elderly, patriarchal, venerable, passé, antiquated, antediluvian.*

Studying antonyms will also contribute to vocabulary growth. For example, seeking antonyms for *praise* may add to your vocabulary such words as *vilify, stigmatize, lampoon, abuse, censure, blame, deprecate, condemn, impugn, denigrate, disparage,* and *inveigh against.* Even such a simple word as *join* has numerous approximate opposites, among them *uncouple, separate, sunder, unyoke, cleave, disconnect,* and *dissever.*

VOC

39f

39f. Prefixes and suffixes

Another method of adding to your vocabulary is to make a study of prefixes and suffixes. A *prefix* is an element placed *before* a word or root to make another word; a *suffix* is placed *after* a word or root. You can add to your vocabulary by learning the meanings of several prefixes and suffixes. Here is a brief list of the most common ones:

Prefixes

ad-	"to, against"	adverse, adjective
ante-	"before"	antedate, anteroom
anti-	"against"	antisocial, antiwar
circum-	"about, around"	circumstance, circumflex
hyper-	"beyond the ordinary"	hypercritical, hyperactive
il-, in-,	"not"	illogical, indefinite,

im-, ir-		impossible, irresponsible
poly-	"many"	polygon, polysyllable
post-	"after"	postseason, postwar
un-	"not, reverse of"	unfair, unbend

Suffixes

-ful	"characterized by" or "as much as will fill"	beautiful, spoonful
-hood	"state, condition, character"	childhood, falsehood
-less	"without"	faultless, hopeless
-ly	"like"	saintly, bravely
-meter	"measure"	speedometer, thermometer
-polis	"city" or "resident of"	metropolis, cosmopolitan
-ship	"condition, character, skill"	friendship, statesmanship
-some	"tendency"	loathsome, meddlesome

voc

39g

39g. Combining forms

Combining form is a term for a word element that rarely appears independently but does form part of a longer word. *Graph,* for example, although it is a word by itself, appears most frequently as a combining form in such words as *photograph* and *lithography.* Knowing the meanings of forms like the following will help increase your vocabulary:

anima	"life, breath"	animal, animation
aqua	"water"	aquarium, aqualung
bios	"life"	biopsy, biosphere
culpa	"fault"	culprit, culpable
domus	"house"	domicile, domestic
ego	"I"	egoism, egocentric
facilis	"easy"	facile, facilitate
gramma	"letter"	grammar, grammatical
lex	"law"	lawyer, legal
liber	"book"	library, libretto
locus	"place"	locality, local
navis	"ship"	navigate, navy
opus	"work"	opera, operation
populus	"people"	population, populate
sanctus	"holy"	sanctuary, sanctify

sophia	"wisdom"	sophomore, sophisticated
tacitus	"silence"	tacit, taciturn
thermo	"heat"	thermometer, thermal
umbra	"shade"	umbrella, umbrage
vita	"life"	vital, vitamin

EXERCISE 21

Read carefully every word on *one* page of your dictionary. As your instructor directs, prepare an oral or written report concerning three or four of the interesting items that you found.

EXERCISE 22

Answer the following questions:

1. Give the full title, the edition, and the copyright date of your dictionary.
2. Is there a section explaining how to use the dictionary? Where?
3. Is there a guide (key) to pronunciation? Where?
4. What is orthography? Does your dictionary have a section on orthography? Where?
5. Is there an explanation of the abbreviations used in the dictionary? Where?
6. In the definitions of words with more than one meaning, in what order are the meanings arranged?
7. Does your dictionary give biographical facts about famous people? Where?
8. Does your dictionary explain foreign words and phrases? Where?
9. Is there a discussion of punctuation? Where?
10. What is an etymology? In the word entries in your dictionary, where are the etymologies placed?

EXERCISE 23

Give the derivation (origin) of these words:

1. telescope
2. panic
3. manufacture
4. professor
5. nicotine
6. April

EXERCISE 24

What restrictive label, if any, is attached to each of the following in your dictionary?

1. baloney
2. cocky
3. disremember
4. jiffy
5. pesky
6. renege

EXERCISE 25

With the aid of your dictionary, answer the following questions:

1. When did P. T. Barnum die?
2. Who was called the Iron Duke?
3. *Fast* occurs as what parts of speech?
4. What is the length of the Red River?
5. What is the Solent?
6. What is the population of Des Moines?
7. What is "the white man's burden"?
8. How is *Gloucester* pronounced?
9. Who was Saint Dunstan?
10. Does Missouri have a larger area than Illinois?
11. Where is The Hague?
12. What is the plural of *moose?*
13. What was the NRA?
14. What is the status of the word *eftsoons?*
15. What was William Sidney Porter's pen name?

EXERCISE 26

Write the words in the following list. Select for each word the letter of the group of words in the second column that defines it. Use your dictionary when you are uncertain.

1. ambidextrous
2. assiduous
3. cacophony
4. elucidate
5. grandiose
6. innocuous

a. a hater of humanity
b. haughtily disdainful
c. cowardly
d. disgrace or reproach incurred by conduct considered shameful
e. formal expression of praise

7. invective
8. misanthrope
9. ostentatious
10. supercilious
11. vicarious
12. encomium
13. concatenation
14. abscond
15. fallacious
16. nebulous
17. pusillanimous
18. sophistry
19. incognito
20. opprobrium

f. logically unsound
g. able to use both hands equally well
h. constant in application
i. false argument
j. not harmful
k. affectedly grand
l. make clear
m. experienced in place of another
n. having one's identity concealed
o. harsh sound
p. to run away to avoid legal process
q. vague, hazy, cloudy
r. an utterance of violent reproach or accusation
s. state of being linked together
t. characterized by show

EXERCISE 27

List the synonyms given in your dictionary (or in a thesaurus) for each of the following words. Prepare for class a written (or oral) presentation of the likenesses and differences among the synonyms given for *two* of the words.

1. street
2. opposite
3. frank
4. answer
5. trite

6. defame
7. yield
8. magic
9. tolerant
10. effort

EXERCISE 28

Give one or more antonyms for each of the following words. Use your dictionary or a thesaurus.

1. professional
2. solicitous
3. huge
4. repudiate
5. dark

6. decrease
7. grave
8. sophisticated
9. fine
10. arrogant

EXERCISE 29

Give the meaning of each of the following prefixes and suffixes and list five words containing each. Your dictionary will help.

1. mono-	6. micro-	11. –est	16. –let
2. non-	7. auto-	12. –able	17. –ness
3. pseudo-	8. sub-	13. –ment	18. –like
4. semi-	9. bi-	14. –graph	19. –er
5. over-	10. multi-	15. –ish	20. –ine

EXERCISE 30

Give the meaning of each of these combining forms. Use a word containing this form in a sentence.

1. aristos	3. causa	5. hostis	7. pedi
2. beatus	4. decem	6. meter	8. petra

**gl/
dict**

40

40. A glossary of diction

The following glossary contains words and expressions that may cause problems in writing. The list is not exhaustive but does include some of the more often raised points of word usage. If this material does not apply to your problems, if you wish more detailed information, or if you do not find the particular word or phrase you are seeking, consult your dictionary.

A few of these expressions are nonstandard, but many are unacceptable only in formal English. Remember especially that no stigma attaches to the labels "informal" and "colloquial." They indicate that a given expression is more appropriate in conversation and informal discourse than in formal writing.

Usage is constantly changing. Expressions that are now restricted in some way may later be considered standard. Furthermore, because no dictionary or textbook (including this one) is a final authority, some usages are disputed. Probably no two experts would agree on all the comments that follow. But this illustrative list should serve as a starting point; you may add other words and expressions to it from time to time.

This glossary is not intended to hamper or restrict your speech. It should acquaint you with what is generally considered the usage of educated persons when they are writing formally. It should also serve as a guide on those occasions when you need to be on your best behavior and to speak or write as correctly as you can. Several of the nonrecommended words and expressions in this glossary will be considered acceptable in the daily speech of almost everyone, but not in carefully prepared formal writing.

Standard English, so-called, has nothing to do with character, intelligence, morality, or even aesthetics. Yet all of us should remember that there are more people with power, money, jobs to hand out, and grades to assign who speak and write standard English than those who do not. Anyone who speaks "unacceptably" is all too often an object of regional, racial, or national prejudice. This harsh fact and unfortunate truth should be squarely faced.

a, an The choice between *a* and *an* depends on the initial sound of the word that follows. *An* should be used before a vowel sound, *a* before a consonant sound: *an* adult, *a* picture; *an* honor, *a* historian.

ability, capacity *Ability* means the power to do something, physical or mental (*ability* to speak in public). *Capacity* is the ability to hold, contain, or absorb (a room filled to *capacity*).

above As an adjective, preposition, adverb, and noun, *above* has many uses. As an adjective, it means "as written or mentioned previously." As a noun, (In light of the *above,* my suggestion is this), its use is frowned upon by some authorities. *For these reasons* and *therefore* can often be substituted for *above.*

absolutely This word means "completely," "perfectly," "wholly." In addition to being overused as an intensifier, it is both faulty and wordy in an expression such as "absolutely complete." Avoid using *absolutely* or any other such modifier with words like *complete, perfect, unique.* (See *unique* and Section 19e.)

accept, except *Accept* means "to receive" or "to agree with"; *except* means "to omit" or "to exempt." (I will not *accept* your offer. The men were punished, but Ned was *excepted.*) As a preposition, *except* means "other than." (Everyone *except* me was on time.)

ad A colloquial abbreviation, much used, for *advertisement.* In strictly formal writing, avoid such abbreviations as *ad, auto* for *automobile, phone* for *telephone, exam* for *examination.* (See Section 32.)

A.D. It's wordy to write "in the year 1066 A.D." because A.D. means "in the year of our Lord." A.D. should always come before the date: A.D. 1975.

adapt, adept, adopt To *adapt* something is to adjust or modify it. (He *adapted* the rules to fit his convenience.) *Adept* is an adjective meaning "skilled" or "expert" (Pancho is *adept* in pastry making). To *adopt* something is "to choose for or take to oneself" (Marta has *adopted* the basketball team as her pet project").

advise This word, meaning "to counsel," "to give advice to," is overused in business letters and other forms of communication for "tell," "inform." (I am pleased to *inform* [not *advise*] you that the check has been received.)

affect, effect As a verb, *affect* means "to influence" or "to assume." (This book has *affected* my thinking.) *Effect* as a verb means "to cause" and as a noun "result." (Your good work will *effect* an improvement in your mark for the term. This play will have a good *effect* on youth.)

again, back Certain words prefixed with *re-* already contain the sense of "again" or "back": *rebound, regain, reconsider, reply, refer, revert.* It's wordy to write, for example, "refer back" and "revert again." (See Section 38i.)

ain't This contraction is considered illiterate, dialectal, or colloquial and is cautioned against in standard English, both written and spoken. The word, which stands for *am not,* is often used informally even by educated people, but it has not been accepted in the sense that *isn't* (for *is not*), *aren't* (for *are not*), and *weren't* (for *were not*) have been.

all, all of. The *of* in *all of* should be omitted before nouns (*all* the players, *all* the doughnuts) but used before pronouns (*all of* us, *all of* them).

all right, alright The former expression is correct but has been overworked to mean "satisfactory" or "very well." *Alright* is analogous to *altogether* and *already* (both standard words) but is not yet an acceptable word in standard usage.

all that This expression is informal in statements such as "I don't dislike him *all that* much." Omit *all.*

allude, refer To *allude to* is to refer to indirectly; to *refer to* is to call attention to. (When she spoke of her difficulties, we knew that she was *alluding to* her recent illness, but she did not *refer to* it specifically.)

allusion, illusion An *allusion* is a reference. An *illusion* is a false impression, a deception. (The speaker made several *allusions* to plays by Shakespeare. Cesar had the *illusion* that he was a great jai alai player.)

almost (See *most, almost.*)

already, all ready The former means "earlier," "previously." (When she arrived, her friend had *already* left.) *All ready* means "all are ready." (They will leave when they are *all ready.*)

altogether, all together *Altogether* means "wholly," "completely." (He was not *altogether* pleased with his purchase.) *All together* means "all in company" or "everybody in one place." (The family was *all together* for the holidays.)

alumnus, alumna An *alumnus* is a male graduate; an *alumna* is a female graduate. The respective plurals are *alumni* and *alumnae*. To refer to graduates of a school as *alum* or *alums* is to use slang.

A.M. (midnight to noon), **P.M.** (noon to midnight) Both of these abbreviations are clear indicators of time; therefore, "in the morning," "in the afternoon," or "o'clock" are unnecessary when A.M. or P.M. is used. Figures, not words, are conventionally used; omit 00 with on-the-hour figures. (We left here at 8 A.M. and arrived in Detroit at 3:45 P.M.) Make "12 o'clock" clear by saying "12 noon" or "12 midnight."

among, between The former shows the relationship of more than two objects; *between* refers to only two or to more than two when each object is considered in its relationship to others. (We distributed the candy *among* the six children. We divided the candy *between* Jill and Gray. Understanding *between* nations is essential.)

amount, number The former is used of things involving a unified mass—bulk, weight, or sums. (What is the *amount* of the bill?) *Number* is used of things that can be counted in individual units. (I have a *number* of hats and coats.)

and etc. *Etc.* is an abbreviation for the Latin phrase *et cetera,* meaning "and so forth." Omit the *and* in *and etc.*

and/or Primarily a business and legal expression, *and/or* is objected to by purists and other especially fastidious users of English. It is somewhat vague and also has business connotations that are objectionable to some people. Although it is a useful timesaver, you should avoid using it in strictly formal English.

and which, that, who; but which, that, who Conventional sentence structure provides that these phrases should appear in clauses only if they are preceded by clauses that also contain *which, that,* or *who.* ("This is the first book *that* I bought *and that* I treasure," not "This is the first book I bought and *that* I treasure.")

ante-, anti- *Ante* means "before" as in "antedate" and "antebellum." *Anti* means "against," "opposed to" (*antifreeze, antibiotic*).

anyway, anyways *Anyway* means "in any case," "anyhow." (She was planning to go *anyway.*) *Anyways* has the same meaning as *anyway,* but it is considered either dialectal or colloquial when used to mean "in any case."

anywheres, nowheres, somewheres These are dialectal words. Omit the *s.* (That morning I could not find my car keys *anywhere.* When we were ready to leave, her briefcase was *nowhere* to be seen. *Somewhere* in the dormitory we must have a good guitarist.)

gl/
dict

40

apt, liable, likely *Apt* suggests fitness or tendency. (She is *apt* in arithmetic.) *Liable* implies exposure to something burdensome or disadvantageous. (You are *liable* for damages.) *Likely* means "expected," "probable." (We are *likely* to have snow next month.) *Likely* is the most commonly used of the three terms. These distinctions in meaning have broken down somewhat, but *apt* and *liable* used in the sense of "probable" are sometimes considered colloquial or dialectal.

as One of the most overworked words in the English language. It is a perfectly good word, but *since, because,* and *when* are more exact and effective conjunctions. (*Since* [not *As*] it was snowing, we decided to stay indoors.) *As* is often misused in place of *that* or *whether.* (I doubt *that* [not *as*] I can go.) In negative comparisons some writers prefer *so* . . . *as* to as . . . *as.* (He is not *so* heavy *as* his brother.) In general, use *as* sparingly; nearly always a more exact and effective word can be found.

as good as, if not better than A correctly phrased but awkward and mixed comparison. A statement will be more effective when *if not better* is put at the end.

AWKWARD: My work is as good as, if not better than, your work.
IMPROVED: My work is as good as yours, if not better.

(See Section 41h.)

awful, awfully, abominably These and such other expressions as *terrible, ghastly,* and *horrible* are loose, overworked intensifiers. If you really need an intensifier, use *very.* (See *very* and Section 38c.)

bad, badly, ill *Bad* is an adjective meaning "not good," "not as it should be." *Badly* is an adverb meaning "harmfully," "wickedly," "unpleasantly," "inefficiently." *Ill* is both an adjective and an adverb and means "sick," "tending to cause harm or evil," or "in a malevolent manner," "wrongly." (She was very *ill.*) *Bad* and *badly* are often incorrectly used with the verb *feel.* ("I feel *bad* today"—not *badly,* unless you mean that your sense of touch is impaired.)

be sure and This expression is considered both colloquial and unidiomatic. (When you get there, be *sure to* [not *sure and*] write to me.)

being as A colloquial or nonstandard substitute for *since, because, inasmuch as,* and so on. (*Since* [not *Being* as] I have some money, I'll lend you some.)

beside, besides *Beside* is normally a preposition meaning "by the side of." *Besides* is an adverb meaning "moreover" and, infrequently, a preposition meaning "except." (The old man sat *beside* the stove. I can't go because I have no money, and *besides* I don't feel well.)

between (See *among, between.*)

bug *Bug* as a noun is used informally to mean both a germ or virus and an enthusiast or fan.

INFORMAL: I have a nasty *bug* that will keep me in the house a day or two.
Phil is a *bug* about diesel motors.

As a verb, *bug* is a slang term for "annoy" or "bother." (That teacher *bugs* me.)

but, nevertheless Redundant when both are used, since each means a contrast. (The team played well, *but* it can play better. The team played well; *nevertheless,* it can play better.)

but which (See *and which.*)

can, may, might *Can* suggests "ability," physical and mental. (He *can* make good progress if he tries hard enough.) *May* implies permission or sanction. (The office manager says that you *may* leave.) The distinction between *can* and *may* (ability vs. permission) is illustrated in this sentence: Lee thinks that you *can,* and you *may* try if you with. *May* also expresses possibility and wish (desire). (It *may* snow today [possibility]. *May* you be happy in your new work [wish, desire].) *Might* is used after a governing verb in the past tense, *may* after a governing verb in the present tense. (She *says* that you *may* try. She *said* that you *might* try.) (See Section 16b.)

cancel out Omit the *out.* This wordy expression is often used, perhaps by analogy with *cross out* or *strike out.*

cannot help, cannot help but The first of these expressions is preferable in such statements as "I *cannot help* talking about my trip." The *but* should be omitted, since its addition can result in a double negative: Use *cannot help* and *can but. Can't hardly* is a double negative. The expression, however, appears frequently in the speech (but rarely the writing) of well-educated people in all walks of life.

capital, capitol The first of these words may be employed in all meanings except that of "a building." A *capitol* is an edifice, a building. (He raised new *capital* for the company. The sightseeing bus passed the state *capitol.* Sacramento is the *capital* of California.)

case This word (other than indicating the forms of pronouns and nouns) has many vague meanings. *Case, phase, factor, instance, nature,* and *thing* are prime examples of jargon. *To case* in the sense of "examine carefully" (*case the joint*) is slang.

center around Objected to by some authorities as illogical. They insist that objects or people surround the center, not vice versa. Alternatives are *center on, center upon,* or *concentrate.*

coed An institution can be "coeducational," but it is somewhat demeaning to refer to a woman as a "coed." One does not refer to men students in a predominately female college as "coeds." Women in any educational institution are as much "eds" as men are, and vice versa.

common, mutual The former means "belonging to many or to all." *Mutual* means "reciprocal." (Airplanes are *common* carriers. Our respect and love were *mutual*.) Avoid the wordiness of this kind of statement: He and I entered into a *mutual* agreement.

compare, contrast *Compare* is used to point out similarities (used with the preposition *to*) and to examine two or more objects to find likenesses or differences (used with the preposition *with*). *Contrast* always points out differences. (The poet *compared* his lady *to* a wood thrush. The teacher *compared* my paper *with* Henry's and found no signs of copying. In *contrast to* your work, mine is poor.)

complement, compliment *Complement* implies something that completes. (This jewelry will *complement* your dress.) A *compliment* is flattery. (Beulah enjoyed the *compliment* paid her.)

compose, comprise, constitute *Compose* and *constitute* mean "make up," "form the basis of." (She *composed* her speech from many notes. Tennis *constitutes* both his exercise and his recreation.) *Comprise* means "embrace," "include," "contain": (The Soviet Union *comprises* several different so-called republics.)

contact, contacted Each of these words has perfectly proper uses, but as verbs, especially in business terms, they have been overworked. Possible substitutes are *communicate with, call, call upon, telephone, meet, meet with*.

continual, continuous In some uses these words are interchangeable. A subtle distinction is that *continual* implies "a close recurrence in time," "in rapid succession," and *continuous* implies "without interruption." (The *continual* ringing of the doorbell bothers me. The ticking of the watch was *continuous*.)

contrast (See *compare, contrast*.)

convince, persuade The former means "to overcome the doubts of." *Persuade* implies "influencing a person to an action or belief." (I am *convinced* that you are right and you have *persuaded* me to help you.) *Convince to* is not idiomatic.

> WRONG: I *convinced* him *to* see the play.
> RIGHT: I *persuaded* him *to* see the play
> I *convinced* him *that* he should see the play.

council, counsel *Council* means "an assembly," "a group." (This is a *council* of citizens.) *Counsel* is both a noun and a verb and means "advice" or "to advise." (The physician gave me expensive *counsel*. The manager will *counsel* fast action by the board of directors.)

gl/ dict

40

cute This is an overworked and vague word that generally expresses approval. Probably *charming, clever, attractive, winsome, piquant, pleasing, vivacious,* or one of a dozen other adjectives would come nearer the meaning you have in mind.

data This word was originally the plural of the Latin *datum* and means "facts and figures from which conclusions may be drawn." Purists consider the word to be plural and use it with a plural verb, but its use with a singular verb is widespread. (*These data are* not reliable. *This data is* not reliable.)

des′ert, desert′, dessert′ These three words involve problems in spelling, pronunciation, and meaning. The first, with accent on the first syllable, means "barren ground." (The *desert* is 100 miles wide.) *Desert* (with accent on the second syllable) means "to abandon." (Don't ever *desert* your true friends.) *Dessert* (note the double *s*) is "the last course of a lunch or dinner." (Apple pie is his favorite *dessert*.)

different from, than, to *Different than* and *different to* are considered colloquial by some authorities, improper and incorrect by others. Even so, these idioms have long literary usage to support them and are widely used. No one ever objects on any grounds to *different from*. Use *different from* and be safe, never sorry.

disinterested, uninterested The former means "unbiased," "impartial," "not influenced by personal reasons." *Uninterested* means "having no interest in," "not paying attention." (The minister's opinion was *disinterested*. I was completely *uninterested* in the play.) As a colloquialism (a somewhat inexact one), *disinterested* is often used in the sense of "uninterested," "indifferent."

disregardless (See *irregardless, disregardless*.)

done, don't The principal parts of this verb are *do, did, done. Done* is frequently used incorrectly as the past tense of *do*. (We *did* [not *done*] our work early today.) *Don't* is used incorrectly for *doesn't*. (It *doesn't* [not *don't*] make much difference to me.)

due to Some authorities label this phrase "colloquial" when it is used to mean "because of." Nevertheless, it is widely used in this sense by capable speakers and writers. Purists prefer such expressions as *owing to, caused by, on account of,* and *because of*. If you wish your English to be above any possible criticism, avoid using *due to* as a preposition. (Tension there was *caused by* [not *due to*] racial unrest that had been building for decades.) Most important, remember that *due to the fact that* is a wordy way of saying the short and simple word *since*.

each . . . are *Each*, even if not followed by *one*, implies "one." Any plural word used in a modifying phrase does not change the number. (Each

gl/
dict

40

is [not *are*] expected to contribute *his* or *her* time. *Each one* of you *is* a fraud.)

either . . . or, neither . . . nor The former means "one of two." *Neither* means "not one of two." *Or* is used with *either,* *nor* with *neither.* The use of *either . . . or* and *neither . . . nor* in coordinating more than two words, phrases, or clauses (as in "Neither Raquel, Carlos, nor Lionel is present") is sanctioned by some authorities but not by others. (*Either* of you *is* satisfactory for the role. *Neither* the boys *nor* the girls wished to dance.)

emigrate, immigrate The former means "to leave"; the latter means "to enter." (Our janitor *emigrated* from Poland in 1958. Many people have tried to *immigrate* to this country in the last decade.) The corresponding nouns, *emigration* and *immigration,* are similarly distinguished in meaning.

enthuse This word is a formation derived from "enthusiasm." Most dictionaries label *enthuse* as colloquial, although it is shorter and more direct than *be enthusiastic about* or *become enthusiastic over.* Even so, the word is overused and somewhat "gushy"; do not use it in formal English.

envelop, envelope The verb *en-vel'op* (accent on the second syllable) means "to cover," "to wrap." (Fire will soon *envelop* the entire block.) *En'-vel-ope* (accent on the first syllable) is a noun meaning "a covering." (Put a stamp on this *envelope.*)

except (See *accept, except.*)

farther, further These words are interchangeable in meaning, but unusually precise writers and speakers prefer *farther* to indicate space, a measurable distance. *Further* indicates "greater in degree, quantity, or time" and also means "moreover" and "in addition to." (We walked two miles *farther.* Let's talk about this *further.*)

feature As both verb and noun, *feature* is overworked in the sense of "emphasize" or "emphasis." *Feature* is slang in the expression "Can you *feature* that?" meaning, presumably, "Can you imagine that?"

fewer, less Both of these words imply a comparison with something that is larger in number or amount. Although *less* is widely used in place of *fewer,* particularly in informal writing and in speech, the distinction between them seems useful. *Fewer* applies to number. (*Fewer* horses are seen on the streets these days.) *Less* is used in several ways: *less* material in the dress, *less* coverage, *less* than a dollar. (The *less* money we have, the *fewer* purchases we can make.)

figuratively This word means "metaphorically," "representing one thing in terms of another," "not literally." (*Figuratively* speaking, you acted like a mouse.) (See *literally.*)

firstly, secondly These words are acceptable, but most skilled users of the language prefer *first* and *second* because they are just as accurate and are shorter. *First of all* is a wordy expression.

fix This is a word of many meanings. In standard English it means "to make fast." As a verb, it is informal when used to mean "to arrange matters," "to get revenge on," "to repair." As a noun, it is used colloquially for "difficulty" or "predicament" and is a slang term for an injection of a narcotic.

flaunt, flout To *flaunt* is to display, to parade. (She *flaunted* her new fur coat.) To *flout* is to defy, to scorn, to scoff at. (Those drivers *flout* all rules for safe driving.)

folks This word is colloquial when it is used to refer to "relatives" and "family." Both dialectal and colloquial is the expression *just folks,* meaning "simple and unassuming people." *Folksy* is a colloquial word for "sociable," "casual," or "familiar."

foreword, forward A *foreword* is a preface or introduction. *Forward* suggests "movement onward." (This book needs no *foreword.* The crowd surged *forward.*)

formally, formerly The first term means "in a formal manner," "precisely," "ceremonially." The latter means "in the past." (The defendant bowed *formally* to the judge. Betty was *formerly* an employee of that company.)

former, latter *Former* and *latter* refer to only two units. To refer to a group of more than two items, use *first* and *last* to indicate order.

free gratis *Gratis* means "without payment," "free." Use either *free* or *gratis,* not both.

funny A common and useful word, but one that is vastly overworked. Use of *funny* to mean "strange," "queer," "odd," "remarkable" is considered informal. Its primary meaning is "humorous" or "comical."

further (See *farther, further.*)

genius, genus The former refers to great ability. (Bach was a man of *genius.*) *Genus* refers to class or kind. (What is the *genus* of this plant?)

good, well The former is an adjective with many meanings: a *good* time, *good* advice, *good* Republican, *good* humor. *Well* functions as both an adjective and an adverb. As an adjective, it means "in good health"; as an adverb, it means "ably" or "efficiently." (I feel *well* once again. The sales force worked *well* in this campaign.)

got, gotten The principal parts of *get* are *get, got, got* (or *gotten*), all of which are acceptable words; your choice will depend upon your speech habits or on the rhythm of the sentence you are writing or speaking. *Got* is colloquial when it is used to mean "must," "ought," "own," "possess," and the like. (I *ought* [not *got*] to go.) (See *have got to.*)

gl/
dict

40

301

gourmand, gourmet These words have to do with eating, but they differ in meaning. A *gourmand* is a large eater. (Diamond Jim Brady was a *gourmand,* often eating for three hours at a time.) A *gourmet* is a fastidious eater, an epicure. (As a French chef, he considers himself a *gourmet.*)

graduate This word has several meanings, all of which are in some way related to marking in steps, or measuring. Idiom decrees that one *graduate from* (not *graduate*) a school. Careful writers prefer "was graduated" to "graduated" in a sentence such as "Tim was graduated from college."

gratis (See *free gratis.*)

hang, hung The principal parts of *hang* are *hang, hung, hung.* However, when the word refers to the death penalty, the parts are *hang, hanged, hanged.* (The draperies are *hung.* The murderer was *hanged.*)

have got to A colloquial and redundant expression for "must." (I *must* [not *have got to*] do my laundry today.) (See *got, gotten.*)

healthful, healthy These words are often used interchangeably, but *healthful* means "conducive to health" whereas *healthy* means "possessing health." In other words, places and foods are *healthful,* people and animals *healthy.* (I wonder whether she is a *healthy* person because she lives in a *healthful* climate.)

highbrow (See *lowbrow, highbrow.*)

hopefully In the meaning of "let us hope" or "it is hoped," the use of *hopefully* is debatable. Preferably, do not use the word in a sentence such as "*Hopefully,* we shall have finished our work by then."

human, humane The word *human* refers to a person. Some especially careful writers and speakers do not use the word alone to refer to members of the human race; they say or write *human being.* However, the practice of using the word alone as a noun has a long and respectable background. *Humane* means "tender," "merciful," "considerate." (His treatment of the prisoners was *humane.*)

i.e., e.g., viz., N.B., P.S. These and many other abbreviations commonly appear in writing. Although abbreviations are not recommended for formal writing, many of them are useful shortcuts. For "that is" we use the abbreviation *i.e. E.g.* is an abbreviation meaning "for example." *Viz.* is an abbreviation meaning "namely." *N.B.* stands for Latin *nota bene,* meaning "note well." P.S. is the abbreviation for *postscript;* P.SS. stands for *postscripts.* (See Section 32.)

if, whether In standard English *if* is used to express conditions; *whether,* usually with *or,* is used in expressions of doubt and in indirect questions expressing conditions. (*If* it doesn't snow, we shall go [simple condition]. We have been wondering *whether* we would reach our sales quota [doubt]. I asked *whether* the doctor had arrived [indirect question].)

immigrate (See *emigrate, immigrate.*)

imply, infer To *imply* is to suggest a meaning that is hinted at but not explicitly stated. (Do you *imply* that I am not telling the truth?) To *infer* is to draw a conclusion from statements, circumstances, or evidence. (After that remark, I *infer* that you no longer agree.)

impractical (See *unpractical*.)

in, into The former is used to indicate motion within relatively narrow or well-defined limits. (She walked up and down *in* her room for an hour.) *In* is also used when a place is not mentioned. (The airplane came *in* for a landing.) *Into* usually follows a verb indicating motion to a place. (When Marion strode *into* the room, everyone fell silent.)

in back of This phrase is colloquial for "behind." However, *in the back of* and *in front of* are considered standard terms, although both are wordy. *Behind* and *before* are shorter and nearly always will suffice. (*Behind* [not *in back of*] the office was the storeroom. *Before* [or *in front of*] the house was a tree.)

individual (See *party, person, individual*.)

inferior than, to The former is not standard idiom; the latter is. (This oil is *inferior to* [not *than*] that.)

ingenious, ingenuous *Ingenious* means "talented," "clever," "resourceful," or "inventive." (This is an *ingenious* computation device.) *Ingenuous* means "innocent," "frank," or "naive." (Sally is an *ingenuous* little girl.)

inside of, off of, outside of The *of* in each of these expressions is superfluous. (*Inside* [not *Inside of*] the barn the horses are eating hay. The boy fell *off* [not *off of*] his tricycle.) When *inside* and *outside* are not prepositional, the *of* should be included: the *outside of* the house, the *inside of* the tent.

irregardless, disregardless Each of these words is an illiteracy. (See Section 38a.) That is, neither is a standard word and neither should be used under any circumstances, formal or informal. The prefixes *ir-* and *dis-* are both nonstandard and superfluous in these constructions. Use *regardless*.

is, was, were These are parts of the verb *to be*. It may help you to remember that *is* is singular in number, third person, present tense. (He [or *She* or *It*] *is* in the room.) *Was* is singular, first or third person, past tense. (I [or *He* or *She* or *It*] *was* in the room.) *Were* can be either singular or plural, second person in the singular, and all three persons in the plural, and is in the past tense. (*You* [both singular and plural] *were* in the room. We [or *You* or *They*] *were* in the room.) The two most frequent errors in using *to be* are employing *was* for *were*, and vice versa, and using *is* in the first or second person instead of in the third, where it belongs.

is when, is where These terms are frequently misused, especially in giving definitions. Grammatically, the fault may be described as using an adverbial clause in place of the noun phrase or clause that is called for. "A subway *is where* you ride under the ground" can be improved to "A subway *is* an electric railroad beneath the surface of the streets." "Walking *is when* you move about on foot" can be improved to "Walking *is the act of* [or *consists of*] *moving* about on foot."

it's me (Please turn immediately to Section 14b.)

kind of a, sort of a In these phrases the *a* is superfluous. Logically, the main word (which can be *kind, sort,* or *type*) should indicate a class, not one thing. (What *kind of* [not *kind of a*] party is this?) Although *kind of* and *sort of* are preferred in this construction, these phrases are often used colloquially to mean "almost," "rather," "somewhat." (She was *rather* [not *kind of*] weary. Martha was *almost* [not *sort of*] resigned to going.)

later, latter The spelling of these words is often confused. They also have different meanings. *Later* refers to time. (He arrived at the office *later* than I did.) (For *latter,* see *former, latter.*)

lead, led These words show the confusion that our language creates by using different symbols to represent one sound. *Lead* (pronounced *lēd*) is the present tense of the verb and causes little or no difficulty. *Led* (pronounced like the name of the metal) is the past tense and is often misspelled with *ea*. (*Lead* the blind man across the street. He *led* the blind man across the street yesterday.)

learn, teach Standard English requires a distinction in meaning between these words. (I'll *learn* the language if you will *teach* me.) *To learn* someone something is an illiteracy.

least, lest The former means "smallest," "slightest." The latter means "for fear that." (He did not give me the *least* argument. Give me your picture *lest* I forget how you look.)

leave, let Both words are common in several idiomatic expressions implying permission, but *let* is standard whereas *leave* is not. (Let [not *Leave*] me go with you.)

legible, readable These terms are synonymous in the meaning of "capable of being read with ease." *Readable* has the additional meaning of "interesting or easy to read." (Your handwriting is *legible*. This book is *readable*.) *Legible* refers to penmanship; *readable* has to do with content and structure.

lend (See *loan, lend.*)

less (See *fewer, less.*)

lest (See *least, lest.*)

let This word, with a primary meaning of "allow," "permit," has many uses. Phrases like the following, however, are colloquial and should not be used in formal English; *let on* (in the sense of "pretend"), *let out* (as in "school *let out*"), *let up* (meaning "cease"). *To let one's hair down* is both colloquial and trite. (See also *leave, let*.)

liable (See *apt, liable, likely*.)

like (See Section 20c.)

literally This word not only is overused but also is confused with *figuratively*. It is an antonym of the latter and really means "not imaginatively," "actually." (See *figuratively*.)

loan, lend Many careful writers and speakers use *loan* only as a noun (to make a *loan*) and *lend* as a verb (to *lend* money). Because of constant and widespread usage, *loan* is now considered a standard verb but one to be avoided in strictly formal English.

loose, lose, loss *Loose* means "not fastened tightly." (This is a *loose* connection.) *Lose* means "to suffer the loss of." (Don't *lose* your hard-earned money.) *Loss* means "a deprivation," "a defeat," "a reverse." (The coach blamed me for the *loss* of the ball.)

lots of, a lot of, a whole lot These terms are informal for "many," "much," "a great deal." The chief objection to their use is that each is a vague, general expression.

lowbrow, highbrow These terms are used so much in both writing and speaking that presumably they will, in time, be accepted as standard usage. Their status now is that of either slang or colloquialisms, depending on the authority consulted. *Lowbrow* refers to a person who lacks, or is considered to lack, cultivated and intellectual tastes. Naturally, *highbrow* is applied to those who do have such attainments.

luxuriant, luxurious The former term refers to abundant growth; *luxurious* pertains to luxury. (The undergrowth was *luxuriant*. The furnishings were *luxurious*.)

mad This short word has many acceptable meanings, such as "insane," "frantic," and "frenzied." Most authorities consider *mad* to be colloquial when it is used to mean "angry" or "furious." (I was *angry* [or *furious*] *with* [not *mad at*] him.)

may (See *can, may, might*.)

maybe, may be The former means "perhaps." (*Maybe* you will finish your task early today.) *May be* (two words) is used to express possibility. (It *may be* going to rain today.)

memorandum This word, which is of Latin origin and means "short note" or "record of events," has two plurals, both of which are acceptable in standard English: *memoranda* and *memorandums*. Abbreviations are *memo* (singular) and *memos* (plural).

might of An illiteracy. (If you had asked, I *might have* [not *might of*] accompanied you.) (See *would of*.)

gl/
dict

40

moral, morale As an adjective, the former has a meaning of "good," "proper." (Frances' *moral* code was high.) *Morale* refers to a condition, state of being, or attitude. (The *morale* in this college is excellent.)

most, almost *Most* is the superlative of *many* and *much* and means "greatest in amount, quality, or degree." *Almost* means "very nearly," "all but." *Most* is colloquial when used for *almost*. (He has *almost* [not *most*] finished his assignment.)

muchly An illiteracy. Despite the fact that you may often hear this word, it really doesn't exist—at least not in standard English. Use *much* instead.

must As a noun, this word is no longer considered slang by most authorities, but it is tiresomely overused to mean something essential or necessary, as in "This movie is a *must*."

myself, yourself, himself, herself *Myself* is often used in informal speech for "I" or "me." Reserve its use for emphasis (I *myself* will do this) or in a reflexive sense (I hurt *myself*). The same usage applies to *yourself, himself,* and *herself.*

neither . . . nor (See *either . . . or.*)

nice This is a word with many meanings, including "agreeable," "pleasant," "attractive," and "delightful." Its overuse suggests the need for more specific substitutes.

no place, nowhere The former is a perfectly sound phrase (There's *no place* like home), but in standard English it cannot be a synonym for *nowhere*. (She could find her purse *nowhere* [not *no place*].) Be certain to spell *nowhere* correctly; *nowheres* is dialectal.

O, oh The former is usually part of a vocative (direct address), is normally capitalized, and is rarely followed by any mark of punctuation. *Oh* is an interjection, may be followed by a comma or an exclamation point, and is capitalized according to the usual rules. (O Mickey! You don't really mean that. Yet, *oh,* what hatred we had for him! *Oh,* what a chance!)

off of (See *inside of.*)

O.K. This everyday term is colloquial or business English for "all right," "correct," "approved." It is occasionally spelled *OK, okay, okeh.* The terms *oke* and *okeydoke* are slang. For the debatable origin of O.K., see any standard dictionary.

oral, aural, verbal *Oral* means "spoken." (The order was *oral,* not written.) *Aural* means "received through the ear," or "pertaining to the sense of hearing." (After the concussion, Jane's *aural* sense was below normal.) *Verbal* means "of, in, or by means of words." In such a sentence as "Our contract was *verbal*," it may mean "unwritten." *Oral* and *verbal* are often confused in everyday use.

outside of (See *inside of.*)

paid, payed *Paid* is the past tense and past participle of the verb *pay.* (He *paid* all his bills promptly.) *Payed* is used only in the sense of *to pay out* a cable or line. (He *payed out* the anchor line slowly.)

party, person, individual Except in telephone and legal language, *party* implies a group and should not be used to refer to one person. *Individual* refers to a single, particular person. As nouns, *individual* and *person* are synonymous. As an adjective, *individual* means "single," "separate," and is therefore repetitious when used to modify *person* or when "each" has been used. Thus, both *individual person* and *each individual member* are wordy.

passed, past The former is the past tense of the verb *to pass;* in its use as a verb, the latter is the past participle. (The car *passed* us at 70 miles an hour. Your troubles are now *past.*) *Pass* is not only a verb but a noun as well. In one or the other of these categories, it appears in many expressions that are either colloquial or slangy, among them *a pretty pass, make a pass at, pass out, pass up, pass the buck.*

percent, percentage Both of these words mean "rate per hundred," but the former (also written *per cent*) is used with numbers (twenty *percent*, 30 *percent*). *Percentage* is used without numbers: Madelyn wants a small *percentage* of the profits.

personal, personnel The former means "private," "individual." (The employer granted me a *personal* interview.) *Personal* is a much overused word. Perhaps because we wish to belong, to show a close relationship with someone, we say or write such sentences as "He is a *personal* friend of mine." The *personal* should be omitted. *Personnel* means "a body of persons," usually a group employed in any work, establishment, enterprise, or service. (The *personnel* of this firm *was* [or possibly *were*] carefully chosen.)

plan on going, plan to go Both of these expressions are in everyday use, but the former is considered less idiomatically sound than *plan to go.*

plenty Informal for "very" or "fully." (The weather is *very* [not *plenty*] hot today.) Better still, omit *very.*

principal, principle The former means "a sum of money" or "a chief person." As an adjective, *principal* means "main" or "chief." *Principle* is always a noun meaning "a governing rule or truth," "a doctrine." (The *principal* of that school was a man of *principle.*)

prof. In formal writing, use *professor.* Privately, you may wish to use terms that are less respectful than either *prof.* or *professor.* (See Section 32.)

proposition A mathematical term colloquially overused for *affair, offer, project, undertaking, proposal,* and similar words.

provided, provided that, providing. *Provided* and *providing* are in good use as conjunctions with the meaning "if," "on condition," "in case," or "it being understood." They are often followed by *that,* although *that* is not required.

quiet, quit, quite *Quiet* means "still" or "calm." (It was a *quiet* meeting.) *Quit* means "to stop," "to desist." (Did you *quit* working?) *Quite* means "positively," "entirely." (I am *quite* certain there is a burglar in the house.)

quite a This phrase is informal when used to mean "more than." In formal English avoid using such phrases as *quite a few, quite a bit,* and *quite a party.*

raise, raze, rise *Raise* means "to elevate," "to lift." (Please *raise* your eyes and look at me.) *Raze* means "to tear down." (The wreckers will *raze* this building.) *Rise* means "to get up." (When the chairperson enters, everyone should *rise.*) Strictly, the word *raise* is never a noun; a few purists therefore consider it colloquial to refer to a *raise* in wages. When referring to bringing up children, *rear, raise,* and *bring up* may all be used. *Rear* is preferred in this connection, although *bring up* is also standard; *raise* is colloquial. *To raise Cain, raise the roof, raise a rumpus,* and *raise the devil* are all slang. *To get a rise out of* someone is also slang.

rang, wrung *Rang* is the past tense of the verb *ring,* meaning "to give forth a sound." (He *rang* the bell for ten minutes.) *Wrung* is the past tense of the verb *wring,* "to press or squeeze." (Roberto *wrung* out the clothes before hanging them on the line.)

real In the sense of "really" or "very," *real* is nonstandard. (Are you *really* [or *very*—not *real*] certain of your figures?) Adverbial use of *real* is increasing steadily in everyday speech but not in formal writing.

reason is because In standard English, the construction beginning "the reason is . . ." is followed by a noun or a noun clause, usually introduced by *that.* Yet we often hear such a sentence as "I couldn't go; the *reason was because* I had to work." In spite of its form, the construction introduced by *reason was* is more a noun clause than an adverbial one. But such a use should appear only in informal speech. Standard writing requires "I couldn't go; the *reason was that* I had to work.

reason why A redundant expression. Omit *why* and, in most constructions, also omit *reason.* "The *reason why* I like this job is the salary I get" can be improved by writing, "I like this job because of the salary."

refer, refer back *Refer* means "to direct attention" or "to make reference"; therefore, *back* is not needed. (Please *refer* [not *refer back*] again to my statement.) The same kind of faulty diction is evident in *repeat again* and *return back.* (See *again, back.*)

repeat again (See *refer, refer back*.)

respectfully, respectively The former means "in a respectful manner." (My detailed statement is *respectfully* submitted.) *Respectively* means "severally" or "in specified order." (*Farewell, au revoir,* and *auf Wiedersehen* are ways of saying good-by in, *respectively,* English, French, and German.)

return back (See *refer, refer back*.)

rise (See *raise, raze, rise*.)

said, same, such As an adjective, *said* is used in legal writing but is considered jargon in standard English. Unless you're a lawyer (or a lawyer's assistant), avoid such expressions as *said party, said person,* and *said proposal. Same* as a pronoun is also characteristic of legal and business use. Lawyers may insist on its retention, but you should avoid such expressions as "check enclosed in payment for *same.*" *Such* may be an adjective, an adverb, or a pronoun—all with standard uses. It is considered colloquial, however, when used in place of a demonstrative. (I could not tolerate *that* [not *such*].) *Such* is also colloquial when used as an intensifier. (She is *a very* [not *such a*] charming person.)

saw, seen The principal parts of *to see* are *see, saw, seen. Seen* is improperly used as the past tense; *saw* is incorrect as the past participle. (I *saw* [not *seen*] you yesterday. I *have seen* [not *have saw*] you every day this week.)

sensual, sensuous The former refers to the gratification of appetites. *Sensuous* suggests the appeal of that which is pleasing to the senses. (In his abandon he indulged in every *sensual* excess he could imagine. Elvira loved the *sensuous* music.)

set (see *sit, set*.)

shall, will Distinctions in the use of *shall* and *will* have largely broken down. A few careful writers (and even fewer speakers) still observe them, but most of us make no effort to choose between them—except for using *shall* in questions (*Shall* I leave now?). (See Section 16b.)

should of (See *would of*.)

should, would In general, use *should* and *would* according to the rules for *shall* and *will*. (See Section 16b, items 13 and 14.)

sit, set *Sit,* predominantly an intransitive verb, not requiring an object, has the meaning of "to place oneself." *Set,* predominantly a transitive verb, requiring an object, means "to put" or "to place." (*Set* the book on the table and come *sit* here.) *Set* used for *sit* in the meaning shown is dialectal or an impropriety. However, both words have several special meanings. For example, *set* has an intransitive use: The sun *sets* early tonight.

so *So* is correctly used as a conjunctive adverb with a semicolon preceding it, and it is frequently used as a coordinating conjunction between independent clauses with only a comma before it. The chief objection to

gl/
dict

40

so in such constructions is overuse. In constructions like the following, *so* can often be replaced by *therefore, thus, accordingly,* and the like, or the sentence can be altered.

INEFFECTIVE: The bridge was out on Route 8, *so* we had to make a long detour on Highway 20.

IMPROVED: Since the bridge was out on Route 8, we had to make a long detour on Highway 20.

In correcting the overuse of *so,* guard against a worse error, that of using another conjunctive adverb with a comma before it and thus writing an unjustifiable comma splice: The bridge was out on Route 8, *therefore* we had to make a long detour on Highway 20. (Use a semicolon or a period.)

Sometimes *so* is vaguely used when the writer means *so that* or *in order that.*

INEFFECTIVE: Do people want the legislators to spend more money *so* they themselves can pay higher taxes?

IMPROVED: Do people want the legislators to spend more money *in order that* they themselves can pay high taxes?

so as (See *as.*)

sort of a (See *kind of a.*)

stationary, stationery The former means "having a fixed or unmoving position." (This rock is *stationary.*) *Stationery* means "paper for writing." (This is new *stationery.*)

statue, stature, statute A *statue* is a sculptured likeness. (This is a *statue* of Robert E. Lee.) *Stature* is often used figuratively (as in *a man of moral stature*). A *statute* is a law. (This *statute* forbids kissing in public.)

sure This word is used as adjective or adverb, but it is colloquial in the sense of "surely," "certainly," "indeed." (He was *certainly* [not *sure*] angry with the policeman.) *Sure* is also colloquial in such expressions as *sure enough* (meaning both "certainly" and "real") and *sure-fire* (meaning "certain to be successful"). (See *be sure and.*) *Sure* does have correct adverbial uses in expressions such as "as sure as night follows day" and "Sure, I'll go," but normally it should be employed only as an adjective.

tasteful, tasty The former means "having or showing good taste, sense, or judgment." *Tasty* means "flavorful," "savory," "having the quality of tasting good." (The reception was a *tasteful* affair, and the food served at it was *tasty.*) *Tasteful* for *tasty* is in rare or archaic use; *tasty* for *tasteful* is colloquial.

that, this As adverbs, used with some adjectives and adverbs of quantity and extent: *that much, this much, that far, this far.* Informal with other adjectives and adverbs, as in the following:

I didn't realize you were *that* good.
The runner was *that* tired he could not finish the race.
How can any test be *this* difficult?

(For *that* introducing restrictive relative clauses, see Section 13e.)

their, there, they're These simple and common words cause difficulty, but they are easy to keep straight. *Their* is a possessive pronoun. (This is *their* house.) *There* means "in or at that place." (Were you *there* when she arrived?) *They're* is a contraction of *they are.* (We are disappointed because *they're* not coming.)

then, than These words are often confused in writing and sometimes in pronunciation. *Than* is a conjunction used in clauses of comparison. (He worked better today *than* he did yesterday.) *Then* is an adverb of time. (We *then* went to a restaurant.)

these kind, those kind, these sort, those sort *Kind* and *sort* are singular nouns; *these* and *those* are plural modifiers. Use *this kind, this sort, those kinds, those sorts.*

till, until, 'til Each of these words means "up to the time of." *Till* and *'til* (a shortened form of *until*) have the same pronunciation and are used more often within a sentence than at the beginning. *Until* appears more often at the beginnings of sentences and is sometimes considered somewhat more formal than its two synonyms. All three terms are correct in standard English.

to, too, two Correct use of these words is a matter of careful spelling. *To* is a preposition (*to* the store) and the sign of an infinitive (*to* work). *Too* is an adverb meaning "also" or "overabundance of." (We *too* are working, but Jack is *too* lazy *to* get up.) *Two* is the number after one. (The *two* men were *too* tired *to* go.)

try and, try to The correct idiom is *try to.* However, *try and* is in everyday use and has been for a century. Conventional formal English would have you write, "*Try to* [not *try and*] finish your work early."

uninterested (See *disinterested.*)

unique This word means "having no like or equal" and expresses absoluteness, as do words like *round, square, perpendicular.* Logically, the word *unique* cannot be compared; something cannot be "more unique," "less unique," "more round," "less round." If a qualifying word such as *nearly* is used, the illogicality is removed. "This is the *most unique* painting in the museum" is not standard, but "This is the *most nearly unique* painting . . . " is. See Section 19e.

unmoral, amoral, immoral *Unmoral* means "having no morality," "nonmoral," "unable to distinguish right from wrong." Thus we may say that an infant or a mentally disordered person is *unmoral. Amoral* means "not concerned with moral standards," "not to be judged by criteria or standards of morality." Morons and animals, for example, may be called *amoral. Immoral* means "wicked," "contrary to accepted principles of right and wrong." The acts of thieves, murderers, and embezzlers may be called *immoral.*

gl/
dict

40

unpractical, impractical, impracticable The first two of these terms are interchangeable, although *impractical* is considered more formal by some writers. Each means "not practical," "lacking practical usefulness or wisdom." *Impracticable* means "not capable of being carried out, used, or managed." (The piccolo player was a good man but thoroughly *impractical*. The manager considered my plan *impracticable*.)

until (See *till*.)

up Often redundant when used with verbs that already include the ideas, such as *rise up, stand up, end up,* and the like. But *up* is needed in many idiomatic expressions, such as *bring up, keep up, lay up, move up, sit up, tie up*.

used to, used to could In the phrase *used to,* the *d* is often elided in speaking so that it sounds like *use to*. In writing, the *d* must be included. *Used to could* is an illiteracy; write *used to be able*.

very *Very*, like *so, surely, too, extremely,* and *indeed,* has been so much overused that it has lost value as an intensifier. Consider whether your meaning isn't emphatic without an intensifier: (You are [*very*] positive about the matter.) *Very* is used colloquially to qualify participles; formal use has adverbs like *much* or *greatly*. Do not substitute *plenty* or *mighty* for any use of *very*.

COLLOQUIAL: I was *very annoyed* with myself.

FORMAL: I was *much annoyed* with myself.

COLLOQUIAL: I am *very torn* between the desire to speak my mind and the desire to keep out of trouble.

FORMAL: I am *greatly torn* between . . .

BETTER: I am *torn* between . . . [After all, isn't one either *torn* or *not torn*?]

wait on In the sense of "serve," this is an acceptable phrase. (I have to *wait on* the customers now.) In the sense of "await" or "wait for," the phrase is dialectal or colloquial. (Please hurry; I don't want to *wait for* [not *wait on*] you.)

well (See *good, well*.)

where This is a useful word, but it should not be substituted for *that* in standard English. (We noted *that* [not *where*] the umpire made a mistake.)

where at As two words, this phrase is redundant for *where*. In standard English avoid such a statement as "Janet did not know *where* she was *at*."

whether (See *if, whether*.)

while As a conjunction, *while* means "during or at the same time that," "as long as." (I read *while* you slept). In expressing contrast or opposition it is considered less exact than "although" and "whereas." (Al-

though [preferably not *while*] I agree with you, I do not like your conclusion.)

who, whom The former is the nominative case; the latter, the objective. When in doubt, try as a memory device the substitution of *he* or *she* for *who* and *him* or *her* for *whom,* since the proper use for *he* or *she* and *him* or *her* is more easily recognized: I wonder *who* [or *whom?*] I should invite. I should invite *him* or *her.* Therefore: I wonder *whom* I should invite. (See Section 14h.)

who's, whose The former is a shortened form of *who is.* (*Who's* ahead in the office pool?) *Whose* is in the possessive case of *who.* (*Whose* toes did I step on?)

will, would (See *shall, will; should, would.*)

wise This word is an acceptable adjective but is slangy in such expressions as *wise guy, get wise to, get wise, put wise to, wise up, wisecrack.*

-wise This suffix has many standard uses and appears in such fully acceptable words as *clockwise* and *sidewise.* Unfortunately, it has been greatly overused in recent years and appears in scores of awkward and strained neologisms: *ideawise, travelwise, saleswise, timewise, moneywise.*

worst kind, worst sort, worst way Slang terms for *very much, greatly, intensely,* and the like.

would (See *should, would.*)

would of, could of, might of, should of These terms are nonstandard expressions that probably result from attempts to represent what is pronounced. That is, in rapid and informal speech *would have* (*would've*) has the sound of *would of.* In each phrase, *have* should replace *of.*

you all In the sense of "all of you," this phrase has a recognized and standard plural meaning. When used to refer to one person, it may be considered dialectal.

you know This is a tiresomely overused expression, a conversational filler that adds nothing to most statements in which it is used.

gl/ dict

40

V.
The Sentence

All writing of whatever kind—paragraphs, whole compositions, reports, research papers, personal and business letters, and answers to most examination questions—depends on a basic unit of expression, the sentence. Effective sentences, in turn, depend on (1) knowledge of sentence structure, what might be called "sentence sense," and (2) experience and practice in reading effective sentences and phrasing them.

Talking about the qualities of sentences is an artificial activity. Actually, good sentences are as much a matter of personality and judgment as of rules and requirements. Good sentences will come when you know what you want to say, have some interest in what you know or think, and want to share that knowledge and understanding with readers.

Naturalness and ease should be primary goals in sentence writing, but it will help to review three major characteristics of good sentences. A sentence should be *correctly punctuated, clear,* and *effective.*

Punctuation

First, what in the form of a sentence can prevent its being considered correct by customary standards? The three faults usually considered most glaring are *incompleteness* (the sentence fragment), the *comma splice,* and the *fused sentence.* Each of these flaws in punctuation is explained and illustrated in Sections 41 and 42. Learning what these three faults are and how to correct them will make a good start toward writing effective sentences.

Clearness

Second, what in the structure, the phrasing of sentences can come between you and your reader, preventing communication and leaving your reader confused or annoyed? Clearness in sentence structure is discussed in following sections under such headings as *misplaced modifiers, faulty coordination* and *subordination,* and *consistency.* Each of these terms is fully discussed and illustrated.

Effectiveness

Appropriate punctuation and clearness are only minimum characteristics of effective sentences. To achieve a varied, pleasing, flexible style that will be appropriate to your purposes and readers, you should consider other qualities that make sentences more than just correct, inoffensive, and understandable. Major violations of effectiveness are discussed under such headings as *wordiness, lack of unity,* and *choppiness* (corrected at times by *sentence combining*).

These requirements may be expressed in seven statements that cover the basic qualities of structurally correct, clear, and effective sentences:

1. A sentence should be *complete.*
2. A sentence should be *properly punctuated.*
3. A sentence should have its *words in proper order.*
4. A sentence should be *logical in structure.*
5. A sentence should be *consistent in structure.*
6. A sentence should be *unified.*
7. A sentence should be *concise.*

Before beginning study of Sections 41–50, make certain that your knowledge of grammatical terms and principles of usage is adequate. If your grasp of such details as parts of speech, phrases, clauses, verbals, subjects, predicates, and the like is shaky, turn to Section 10 from time to time for a brief refresher. If what you find in that section is insufficient for your needs, consult the index of this book for the location of fuller explanations. The sections that follow cannot be fully meaningful unless you *know* what the terms of reference mean.

41. Completeness

The word *sentence* can mean "a stated opinion." By this definition, all words, or groups of words, that "make sense" to your reader or listener can be called sentences. But remember these two requirements for a *complete* sentence: (1) It must have both a subject and a verb operating as a verb that actually appear or are clearly implied (understood); (2) it must not begin with a connecting word such as *although, as, because, before,* and *while* unless an independent clause follows in the same construction.

Sentence fragments

Here is a sentence acceptable in any variety of written English: "Carrying a large package, the spy approached the house with furtive steps." Had the history of printing and the development of our punctuation system been different, it is possible that we might have been taught to write the sentence like this: "Carrying a large package. The spy approached the house. With furtive steps." But a sentence punctuated in this way differs from what readers expect. Whether or not you could explain what the trouble is, you would sense that these three groups of words belong together and should be attached to main clauses or provided with subjects and predicates.

41a. A phrase is not a sentence.

The phrases that appear as sentence fragments are usually participial, infinitive, absolute, appositional, and prepositional. This list of names may sound like a fearsome five, but you have only to recognize their incompleteness and correct the punctuation of such fragments.

To correct them, (a) attach the phrase to the sentence to which it belongs, or (b) make the phrase a sentence by adding a subject and predicate.

Each of the following illustrations has three parts: The first contains a sentence fragment with a label identifying its kind; two corrected versions follow, using each of the methods just suggested.

FRAGMENT: *Having worked in the sewers for six months.* Doris began to dream of lurking alligators. [Participial phrase]

REVISED: 1. Having worked in the sewers for six months, Doris began to dream of lurking alligators. [Phrase attached to sentence]

2. Doris had worked in the sewers for six months now. She began to dream of lurking alligators. [Phrase made a sentence]

FRAGMENT: Gus now has two goals in life. *To pass freshman composition* and *to find a roommate who doesn't mind his spider collection.* [Infinitive phrases]

REVISED: 1. Gus has two goals in life: to pass freshman composition and to find a roommate who doesn't mind his spider collection.

2. Gus now has two goals in life. He wants to pass freshman composition and to find a

sen
frag

41a

roommate who doesn't mind his spider collection.

FRAGMENT: *Fearless roommates being short that year.* Gus flushed away his collection. [Absolute phrase]

REVISED: 1. Fearless roommates being short that year, Gus flushed away his collection.

2. Fearless roommates were in short supply that year. Gus therefore flushed away his collection.

FRAGMENT: Alligators dead from spider bites began to turn up at Sludgemont. *The city water purification plant.* [Appositional phrase]

REVISED: 1. Alligators dead from spider bites began to turn up at Sludgemont, the city water purification plant.

2. Dead alligators began to turn up at the city water purification plant. Their spider-bitten bodies clogged the intake filters at Sludgemont.

FRAGMENT: *After weeks of decreasing alligator dreams.* Doris began to have nightmares about spiders. [Prepositional phrase]

REVISED: 1. After weeks of decreasing alligator dreams, Doris began to have nightmares about spiders.

2. After a few weeks, Doris' dreams about alligators gradually ceased. Then she began to have nightmares about spiders.

41b. A dependent clause is not a sentence.

Adverbial, adjective, and noun clauses can never stand alone. They always depend on something else for completeness. A sentence like "Clara was only 12" is complete, but if we add certain words to it the sentence becomes part of a larger construction: "*Although* Clara was only 12." The reader asks, "Although Clara was only 12, *what?*" *Although* signals a relationship that would be fulfilled by a sentence such as "Although Clara was only 12, she was readily admitted to college."

FRAGMENT: I had no money for the ticket. *When suddenly Pedro paid me what he had borrowed.* [Adverbial clause]

sen frag

41b

REVISED: I had no money for the trip. Then suddenly Pedro paid me what he had borrowed. [Clause made into a sentence]

I had no money for the trip, but suddenly Pedro paid me what he had borrowed. [Clause attached to a sentence]

FRAGMENT: *Because the course is difficult.* We do not advise you to enroll in it. [Adverbial clause]

REVISED: Because the course is difficult, we do not advise you to enroll in it.

The course is difficult. We do not advise you to enroll in it.

FRAGMENT: Jason has talked with Coach Barnett. *Who thinks Jason's chances of making the team are good.* [Adjective clause]

REVISED: Jason has talked with Coach Barnett. He thinks Jason's chances of making the team are good.

Jason has talked with Coach Barnett, who thinks that Jason's chances of making the team are good.

FRAGMENT: She said. *That she no longer loved me.* [Noun clause]

REVISED: She said that she no longer loved me.

She said, "I no longer love you."

41c. Some sentence fragments are justifiable.

Many statements convey a full thought without an actual or implied subject or verb. Such expressions as *Ouch, Hello, Good-by, Never again, But to continue* can and do make clear, often effective, statements. Fragments appear in plays, short stories, and novels because they are mirrors of normal conversation.

Context is important in asking and answering questions and in providing details after a general statement:

"Where did you get those shoes?"
"At Finchley's."
"On sale?"
"But of course."
"How much?"
"None of your business."

Similarly, a descriptive phrase following a complete statement or question is a commonly seen fragment (the fragments are italicized in the following example):

What was [Stonehenge]? What purpose did it serve, this monument and memorial of men whose other memorials have all but vanished from the earth? Was it a city of the dead? *A druid place of horrid sacrifice? A temple of the sun? A market? A pagan cathedral, a holy sanctuary in the midst of blessed ground?* What was it—and when?

—GERALD S. HAWKINS, *Stonehenge Decoded*

How effective or appropriate a sentence fragment is in a particular context is often more a matter of taste than of fixed rule. Your safest course is to use an occasional fragment only after you have proved your knowledge of sentence completeness.

Incomplete constructions

41d. A construction once begun should not be left unfinished.

You may begin a statement and then, forgetting where you and your thoughts are, keep adding words but stop before you have given meaning to the words with which you started. In such an unfinished construction, examine carefully what you have written to discover what is missing.

INCOMPLETE: Some of the students from abroad, not being used to central heating, and also wearing heavy clothes.

REVISED: Some of the students from abroad, not being used to central heating, and also wearing heavy clothes, were often uncomfortably warm.

41e. Repeat a main verb or an auxiliary verb for completeness.

Most of us have a natural and commendable desire not to repeat ourselves, a desire that should carry over into our writing. A sentence such as "Ed plays a better game of tennis than my room-mate" is complete without a verb following the word *roommate*. We write the sentence as it is to avoid repeating the word *plays*.

But in the following sentence a word that is necessary for completeness has been omitted: "The lawn was mowed and the hedges neatly trimmed." The verb in the second clause should be *were*, not *was*, to agree with the plural *hedges*. The difficulty can be removed by repeating the main verb or by changing the second subject:

REVISED: The lawn *was* mowed and the hedges *were* neatly trimmed.

The lawn was mowed and the *hedge* neatly trimmed.

Here is a similar problem with auxiliary verbs:

ORIGINAL: I never have and probably never will learn to play the sitar.

Again, the word that is omitted after *have* is not the same in form as the verb *learn* later on in the sentence; the omitted word would be the past participle form *learned*.

REVISED: I never have *learned* and probably never will learn to play the sitar.

41f. Repeat prepositions where needed to make meaning clear.

The following sentence can have two meanings:

ORIGINAL: Tomorrow morning I have classes in Spanish literature, history, and philosophy.

The ambiguity lies in the modifier *Spanish*: are the classes in Spanish literature, Spanish history, and Spanish philosophy, or in history and philosophy of some unspecified kind *and* Spanish literature? In other words, does the adjective *Spanish* modify just the word following it or all three nouns? The problem is resolved by repeating the preposition or by changing the order of the objects of the preposition:

REVISED: Tomorrow morning I have classes in Spanish literature, *in* history, and *in* philosophy.

Tomorrow morning I have classes in history, philosophy, and *Spanish literature*.

Another problem requires not repetition of a preposition but the inclusion of omitted prepositions.

ORIGINAL: Even a prisoner like Ivan Denisovich could take pride and have respect for his work.

The omitted preposition in this sentence is not a repetition but a different word. The sentence results from combining two verb phrases for each of which idiomatic usage requires a different preposition:

. . . could take pride *in* his work.
. . . could have respect *for* his work.

The repeated *could* can be omitted, but no preposition is repeated. To correct, simply include both prepositions:

REVISED: Even a prisoner like Ivan Denisovich could take pride *in* and have respect *for* his work.

41g. Repeat words where needed to avoid confusion in comparisons.

The following sentence can have two meanings:

ORIGINAL: Mathematics interested Charlene more than Angelo.

As a result of omissions, we are not sure whether the sentence has the first or second of the following meanings, either of which would be acceptable:

REVISION: Mathematics interested Charlene more than *it did* Angelo.
Mathematics interested Charlene more than *Angelo did*.

Words such as *very, so,* and *really* (called *intensifiers*) are often used in comparisons:

Bucephalus is a stupid person. [Without an intensifier]
Bucephalus is a *very* stupid person. [With an intensifier]
Bucephalus is a *really* stupid person. [With intensifier]

Each of these three sentences is acceptable in both informal and formal writing. But difficulties arise when such intensifiers are used in making comparisons in the comparative and superlative degrees. (See Section 19d.) The following sentences would be acceptable in only informal speech and writing:

Bucephalus is *so* stupid. [*so* as intensifier]
Bucephalus is the *stupidest* person. [superlative degree as intensifier]

For clarity in writing, limit the use of *so* and the superlative degree to actual comparisons, making certain that the standard of comparison is included:

ORIGINAL: Bucephalus is so stupid. [So stupid that what?]
REVISION: Bucephalus is so stupid that he thinks the Mexican border pays rent.

ORIGINAL: My grammar textbook has the dumbest jokes. [Compared to what else?]
REVISION: My grammar textbook has the dumbest jokes I've ever seen in print.

Finally, make sure that you are comparing similar things: persons to persons, occupations to occupations, objects to objects, and so on:

ORIGINAL: American diners eat more hamburgers than any other country.
REVISION: American diners eat more hamburgers *than* diners in any other country.
More hamburgers are eaten in America than in any other country.

ORIGINAL: A computer programmer makes more money than teaching.
REVISION: A computer programmer makes more money than *a teacher*.
Computer *programming* is a better-paying *job* than teaching.

41h. Repeat words needed in double comparisons.

Double comparisons are those in which the writer includes two comparisons in the same statement. Sometimes both positive and comparative degrees of an adjective or adverb are used in the same sentence, as in the two examples that follow:

sen
frag

41h

ORIGINAL: J. Paul Getty was *as* rich, if not richer, *than* I am.

Betty Cook's powerboat is *as* fast, if not faster, *than* Joel Halpern's.

If we separate the two comparisons and put them in their full forms, we can see the problem more clearly:

. . . as rich *as* I am.   . . . as fast *as* Joel Halpern's.
. . . richer *than* I am.   . . . faster *than* Joel Halpern's.

No word is repeated in the two comparisons: The positive has *as*, the comparative has *than*. No omission is justified; use both *as* and *than* in the comparisons:

FIRST REVISION: J. Paul Getty was as rich *as,* if not richer *than,* I am.

Betty Cook's powerboat is as fast *as,* if not faster *than,* Joel Halpern's.

But we are not finished with these sentences. The double comparison can be an effective way of expressing your intention, but it can lead to long constructions before the second half of the comparison is revealed. Unless you have some reason, such as suspense, for postponing the second half of the comparison, the sentence will sound smoother if the first comparison is completed before the second begins:

SECOND REVISION: J. Paul Getty was *as rich as I am,* if not richer.

Betty Cook's powerboat is *as fast as Joel Halpern's,* if not faster.

sen frag

41i

41i. Complete any constructions that have been confused by word omission.

Most omissions of words not resulting from a desire to avoid repetition are like slips of the tongue—that is, they are human errors rather than misperceptions of structure. But they still cause misunderstanding:

ORIGINAL: The capo and hitman of the mob resented Senator Frink's bill to create a federal Department of Slot Machines.

The sentence makes it sound as though one man is both capo and hitman, a result of the omission of an article before *hitman*.

REVISION: The capo and *the* hitman of the mob resented Senator Frink's bill to create a federal Department of Slot Machines.

Both the capo and the hitman resented Senator Frink's bill . . .

EXERCISE 1

Make each of the following sentences sound sensible and complete. Revise in more than one way if you wish.

1. Mackinac Island, which rises out of the Straits of Mackinac between Lake Huron and Lake Michigan.

2. I must do much better than I have been doing. If I am going to achieve my many objectives in life.

3. I should like to go back to New York State for a visit. To the country where the air is fresh, the waters are clear, and the people are friendly.

4. And so it goes, summer vacation after summer vacation. The mountains one year, the lake the next.

5. Carefully I listened to every word of advice that my parents gave me. How always to keep a sharp eye on my luggage. When to ask for information from the driver and when not to. Different methods to use for passing the time.

6. Good students need to take challenging courses. Courses where students know they will have to work for grades.

7. Now that I have determined what some people remind me of. I wonder what I remind people of.

8. I hope to travel through most of Europe. And finally wind up my travels by visiting the countries to the south of us.

9. I have ended the semester learning a great deal. Even though my papers are still filled with many serious mistakes.

10. The most important thing about spring is that the sun is out most of the time. No more walking to class or work in the darkness of early morning.

EXERCISE 2

Make each of the following sentences sound sensible and complete. Revise in more than one way if you wish.

1. It's not like going for miles to fish, and then after fishing all day and night, and still going home without any fish.

Completeness/sentence fragments

2. My room, I was told, when, after what seemed like running through a maze, I set my eyes on what was to be my home for the coming months.

3. There are many people who are out to achieve a particular goal, and even though they do not come up to our individual standards.

4. While a good driver, one who obeys all traffic signs and signals, who drives courteously and carefully at all times, is demonstrating one of the important marks of a good citizen.

5. Superstitious beliefs are started by people who assume something that has happened to them as a result of another event, which had taken place prior to the time of whatever happened to them.

6. Without my high school reputation as a football player I would not have received an offer to attend college on a scholarship, and therefore never having the opportunity to continue my education.

7. In one letter, the letterhead had only the name and address of the company, while in another letter the name of the company, home address, addresses of branch offices, and officers of the company.

8. You soon learn, and after these simple instructions about borrowing books from the library.

9. Would appreciate an early reply. Anxiously awaiting to meet you then.

10. I have come to the conclusion that since literature takes up time that high school teachers could spend in teaching writing.

EXERCISE 3

Necessary words are omitted in the following sentences. Either supply the words or rearrange the sentences.

1. An extensive search of the literature has been made, and the results compiled.

2. Portable typewriters are similar but smaller than other typewriters.

3. Two years ago I took and passed a lifesaving course was offered at the "Y."

4. No famous people reside in my hometown, and never have.

5. They were glad that their garage had not been painted as many of their neighbors had been.

6. His nationality is Austrian and is proud of having a degree from University of Vienna.

7. The pay is good, surroundings pleasant, and opportunities excellent to meet successful men and women.

8. I thought of leaving immediately but decided that action would be childish.

9. This is a very casual style that has and will not decline in popularity for some time.

10. I am enclosing a collection of letters which I think you will be inte
ested.

EXERCISE 4

Rewrite the following sentences so that they are clear and complete.

1. There are many aspects to having a cabin, family gathering, fishing, avoiding work and parties, all of these amount to fun and relaxation.
2. John wondered is he one of those strange people who enjoy watching the sun rise.
3. When someone breaks a mirror and exclaims that he will now have seven years of bad luck doesn't really believe it.
4. The development of the individual into an independent, self-respecting person can be furthered by these books and, through them, a better world.
5. Since there are many opportunities for someone with a college education and can apply them to today's living.
6. Colorful Colorado is the highest and one of the most scenic states in the United States.
7. In her portrayal of characters, Jane Austen was just as successful and more so than many of our present-day novelists.
8. Over the years our basketball team has been one of the best.
9. I can handle cars better than Mother.
10. Many small cities and rural communities are plagued with as much or sometimes even more crime than the big city.

comp

42

42. Compounds

Writing correctly is difficult now and always has been. You are expected to write complete sentences with no unjustifiable fragments. (See Section 41.) But you are also expected to write full sentences *one at a time*. When your mind is racing or wandering, this is no simple task.

Even if you succeed in this task, possibly after careful revision of a first draft, most of your sentences may turn out to be short, simple, and jerky. A short sentence can be effective, but a series of short sentences will sound monotonous and give unwanted emphasis to comparatively unimportant ideas. Careful, thoughtful writing will contain many examples of coordination and subordination—the combining of short sentences and clauses into longer sentences that suggest the comparative importance of thoughts, that provide variety, and that mark a mature style. (See Sections 43, 44.)

Not all sentence combinations, however, are effective. Two kinds that not only are ineffective but are usually considered incorrect are the *comma splice* and the *fused sentence*.

42a. The comma splice

The *comma splice* (also called the *comma fault*) is an error in punctuation and sentence construction. It consists of using a comma to combine what really are two sentences. That is, a comma splices (joins) statements that should be separated by a period or joined by a semicolon, a colon, or a conjunction and a comma. (See Sections 21–25.)

The comma splice, or "comma fault," appears in several writing situations:

1. Two statements that are related by content but have little or no actual grammatical relationship:

> A meeting of the club is scheduled for tonight, many important items are on the agenda.

REVISION: A meeting of the club is scheduled for tonight. Many important items are on the agenda.

> A meeting of the club is scheduled for tonight; many items are on the agenda.

2. Two related statements, the second of which begins with a personal pronoun the antecedent of which is in the first:

> The ambulance driver examined the victim carefully, he did not say a word.

REVISION: While the ambulance driver was examining the victim he did not say a word.

> The ambulance driver examined the victim carefully, but he did not say a word.

3. Two related statements, the second of which begins with a demonstrative pronoun or adjective (*this, that, these,* etc.):

> Drive carefully when you approach the bridge, this is very narrow.

REVISION: Drive carefully when you approach the bridge. It is very narrow.

Drive carefully when you approach the bridge because it is very narrow.

4. Two statements, the second of which contains, or begins with, a conjunctive adverb. (*however, then,* etc.):

I was late for the lecture, however, Ms. James did not scold me.

REVISION: Although I was late for the lecture, Ms. James did not scold me.

I was late for the lecture, but Ms. James did not scold me.

As you will have noted from the revisions just given, the comma splice can be corrected in several ways:

1. Use a period after the first statement and a capital letter at the beginning of the second.
2. Use a semicolon between the statements.
3. Subordinate one of the statements and use a comma.
4. Insert a conjunction between the statements, or as a substitute for the conjunctive adverb, and retain the comma.

Although comma splices can be corrected in several ways, you should avoid trying to show a cause-and-effect relationship between two unrelated items. Unjustifiable comma splices are always confusing to readers, and many writers and editors avoid them altogether. Even so, an occasional comma splice can be both suitable and effective in such short and closely knit sentences as these:

I worked, I struggled, I failed.

That is Alice, this is Michele.

We are not going to the library, we are going to a movie.

42b. The fused sentence

A sentence must usually be followed by a terminal mark, a full stop: period, question mark, exclamation point. A fused sentence results when two sentences are run together with no mark of punctuation between them. Such a construction confuses readers be-

comp

42b

cause they do not know where one thought ends and another begins:

> Late that same month the dam broke thousands of people were left homeless in the resulting flood.

REVISION: Late that same month the dam broke. Thousands of people were left homeless in the resulting flood.

Late that same month the dam broke; thousands of people were left homeless in the resulting flood.

> After two days they left London for Copenhagen this city is the capital of Denmark.

REVISION: After two days they left London for Copenhagen; this city is the capital of Denmark.

After two days they left London for Copenhagen, the capital of Denmark.

> Rollo Royce is demanding a five-million-dollar contract from the Philadelphia Seizures he claims the fans pack the park to see him strike out.

REVISION: Rollo Royce is demanding a five-million-dollar contract from the Philadelphia Seizures. He claims the fans pack the park to see him strike out.

Rollo Royce is demanding a five-million-dollar contract from the Philadelphia Seizures because he claims the fans pack the park to see him strike out.

Both the fused sentence (42b) and the comma splice (42a) are serious flaws in sentence construction that result from inadequate punctuation and careless thinking. Each results in compounds that are ineffective and cause confusion. But certain forms of sentence combining can be both effective and desirable.

42c. Effective sentence combining

We smile when we hear a child say, "That's my train. That's a blue car. This is a yellow one. That one is the engine. It's red." In such an exaggerated series of choppy sentences, the monotony of the structure is readily apparent. Although you are not likely to write a childish series like this one, remember that a good writer is notable for frequent and efficient use of subordination (sections

43, 44). It is not brevity that is ineffective—quite the contrary; choppiness, jerkiness, and lack of indication of thought relationships are the problems to be overcome. As you revise your papers, make certain that you have not written a series of choppy sentences and that you have linked your thoughts with the proper connectives, most notably *subordinating conjunctions* (Sections 5, 20) and *relative pronouns* (Sections 2, 13).

Consider these seven correct and complete sentences:

1. A patient swallowed a pill.
2. It contained only a little milk sugar.
3. He had been told it was a powerful drug.
4. Within ten minutes he was suffering severe reactions.
5. His lips swelled.
6. His skin broke out.
7. Other patients displayed physical reactions after taking the same drug.

These seven sentences can be effectively combined into three:

A patient swallowed a pill that contained only a little milk sugar. He had been told that it was a powerful drug, and within ten minutes he was suffering severe reactions: his lips swelled and his skin broke out. Other patients also displayed physical reactions after taking the same drug.

comp

42c

For another illustration, consider these three series of jerky sentences and independent clauses:

It was dark. She was afraid to enter the room. She called her brother. He did not answer her. She was more terrified than ever.

REVISION: Because it was dark, she was afraid to enter the room. When she called her brother, he did not answer her, and consequently she was more terrified than ever.

We have an 80-acre farm located in southern Missouri. Besides the 80 acres, we lease a neighbor's farm of 50 acres. Our farm is in the rolling country. We have to terrace our land. On our farm we have a small wood. The wood has a creek running through it. There are two hills on both sides of our farm. We therefore call our farm "Green Valley Farm." Our farm is shaped like the state of Texas. The creek we call the Little Rio Grande.

REVISION: In southern Missouri we have an 80-acre farm, to which we have added 50 more acres leased from a neighbor. The rolling land, which we have to terrace, is flanked by two hills; hence the name "Green Valley Farm." Running through a small wood on our property is a creek, which, because the farm is shaped like the state of Texas, we call the Little Rio Grande.

I work in a supermarket, and my job is stocking shelves. I have many friends there, but perhaps my best friend is Warren. He has a good disposition, which I don't.

REVISION: I work in a supermarket where I stock shelves. Of all my friends there, Warren, who has the good disposition I lack, is perhaps the best.

For still another example of sentence combining, study these two sentences:

1. The pitcher lost the game in the thirteenth.
2. He had pitched twelve perfect innings.

The sentences can be effectively combined:

After he had pitched twelve perfect innings, he lost the game in the thirteenth.

or

The pitcher, *who* had pitched twelve perfect innings, lost the game in the thirteenth.

Mature writing avoids the faulty combining of sentences in comma splices and fused sentences and exhibits effective combining in properly coordinated and subordinated related thoughts. If these principles are not fully clear to you, pay special attention to the exercises that follow and also turn to Sections 43 and 44, which deal with faulty coordination and subordination.

EXERCISE 5

Correct any unjustifiable comma splices in the following sentences. Revise each by one or more of the methods suggested in Section 42a.

1. I have found most of the information which you requested, if you should desire any additional information, do not hesitate to write me.
2. This scene reminded me of a miniature scale model, the only clue to the contrary was the movement of traffic.
3. I left out many important facts about camp, the singing, discussion groups, and games all played a large part in my camp experience.
4. One common error in writing is incorrect spelling, the other is the occasional use of faulty diction.
5. The risks associated with keeping money at home are many, one must guard against fire, flood, tornadoes, and thieves.
6. Good letters are rarely "dashed off," usually they are the result of careful planning and writing.
7. In high school it is the teacher's job to educate students, in college it is up to students to achieve their own education.
8. There is no doubt about it, Yellowstone National Park is well worth an extended visit.
9. Before you come to college, no one tells you what to expect, you have to find out the hard way.
10. People don't care if it is raining or snowing, they still want to watch a football game.
11. There is just one problem, there isn't enough parking space for all the people who come to shop.
12. These are real championship cars, many are used at this speedway only.
13. It seems only yesterday that I was a youngster, now I am a member of the senior class.
14. My teacher was no longer interesting, Latin became cut-and-dried material.
15. On the ground it was 100° F., in the plane it was a comfortable 65° F.

EXERCISE 6

Supply punctuation in these fused sentences.

1. I grew up on a small farm not far from town thus I have experienced both country and town life.
2. We opened the door of the house and looked around the house was empty except for a couple of chairs covered with sheets.
3. We first lived in Massachusetts then my father's business made us move to the Midwest.
4. Some people don't worry about their country they worry only about themselves.
5. I did not see anything very funny in having a flat tire in fact I wanted to forget about it as soon as possible.

6. In Wisconsin there are many farms throughout the countryside most of these are dairy farms.

7. Some students tell their parents they must have a new car otherwise they will quit college.

8. "John" is a simple name for a boy probably it is the most common boy's name in existence.

9. The date and time of the interview are all right however I am not sure where the interview is to take place.

10. Knowing how to use a dictionary is no problem each dictionary has a section in the front of the book telling how to use it.

EXERCISE 7

Each of the following problems contains a main clause (the A sentence) and a clause that will become subordinate (the B sentence). Join each pair by placing one of the subordinating conjunctions in front of the B sentence; then join it to the beginning or the end of the A sentence. If you place it at the beginning, separate it from the A sentence by a comma. (If Exercises 7, 8, and 9 present difficulties, look ahead to Sections 43 and 44.)

comp

42c

1. A. The Modocs lost only five warriors in action.
   B. At least 168 whites were killed or wounded in the six-month conflict. [*although*]
2. A. Jack found white homesteaders had moved into his homeland.
   B. The treaty had not yet been ratified by the Senate. [*although*]
3. A. The tribe had lost the few crops it cultivated.
   B. Women and children, continually badgered by the Klamaths, had failed to gather enough food to last through the winter. [*when*]
4. A. Indian Bureau officials agreed that the Modocs could remain off the reservation.
   B. No complaints were made against them. [*as long as*]
5. A. Jack's entire band was accused by settlers of general lawlessness.
   B. Most acts of thievery and eventually murder were committed by a shaman's small group of rowdy youths. [*although*]
6. A. Several incredulous warriors emerged from huts carrying rifles.
   B. Jackson informed the awakened Modocs that they must move immediately. [*as*]
7. A. Sagebrush served as fuel.
   B. Small patches of grass afforded grazing for cattle. [*while*]
8. A. The attack stalled.
   B. Modocs scurried from boulders to fissures in the enshrouding fog. [*as*]

9. A. Demoralized volunteers headed homeward.
   B. Footsore troopers set up dismal winter bivouacs in the snow. [*while*]
10. A. Jack continued to hope for a peaceful solution.
   B. The dissidents used ridicule to humiliate him. [*until*]

EXERCISE 8

This exercise in sentence combining involves the use of relative pronouns.

EXAMPLE: A. *Transistors* revolutionized the electronics industry.

B. *Transistors* are made from a small piece of germanium.

Transistors, *which* are made from a small piece of germanium, revolutionized the electronics industry.

Each of the following problems consists of two sentences; the sentences have a noun phrase in common (*transistors* in the example). Replace the repeated noun phrase in the B sentence with *who* or *which,* depending on whether the noun phrase refers to a human or to a nonhuman. Then insert the B sentence into the A sentence immediately following the first occurrence of the noun phrase. Separate the clause that was the B sentence from the A sentence by commas.

comp

42c

1. A. The most apparent parallel between the Harlem Renaissance and the present must be *the cult of the Exotic Negro.*
   B. *The cult of the Exotic Negro* disgusted Langston Hughes.
2. A. Alain Locke's essay entitled "*The New Negro*" brought the issues into focus.
   B. "*The New Negro*" appeared in his epoch-making volume of the same name.
3. A. Influences of the Beat poets can be seen in the work of *Bob Kaufman.*
   B. *Bob Kaufman* is considered by some to be the greatest innovator among the poets of that generation.
4. A. Virtuoso naming overwhelms *the listener.*
   B. *The listener* assumes that the speaker really must know what he is talking about.
5. A. While Imamu Baraka was employing the dozens in poetry, *Stokely Carmichael and H. Rap Brown* employed it as a mode of attack and of entertainment.
   B. *Stokely Carmichael and H. Rap Brown* were engaged in direct political action.

6. A. Charles Keil points out the black oratorical technique of *repetition*.
    B. *Repetition* characterizes both the preacher and the blues singer, in this case, Martin Luther King and B. B. King.

In the next group of problems, there is one additional step. First, as before, replace the repeated noun phrase in B with a relative pronoun, *which* or *whom*. Next, move that relative pronoun to the beginning of the B sentence. Finally, insert the B sentence into the A sentence as before.

7. A. One early group of Black poets wrote in dialect and took for their subject matter *the lives of the common folk*.
    B. They sometimes caricatured *the lives of the common folk* in the manner of white writers like Thomas Nelson Page.
8. A. The hallmark of successful use is *wit*.
    B. Listeners and readers instantly recognize and respond to *wit* in a manner similar to their response to metaphysical imagery.
9. A. *George Moses Horton* can be studied in William Robinson's excellent anthology, *Early Black Poets*.
    B. The traditional English hymn influenced *George Moses Horton*.
10. A. The poet works with a group of images drawn from *the spirituals and the blues*.
    B. He builds his free but disciplined associations upon *the spirituals and the blues*.

comp

42c

EXERCISE 9

This exercise in combining is concerned with compound sentences.

EXAMPLE: A. Glassmaking is one of the earliest American industries.
          B. It began in New York and Pennsylvania in Colonial times (;)

          Glassmaking is one of the earliest American industries; it began in New York and Pennsylvania in Colonial times.

EXAMPLE: A. Phil expects to finish by five o'clock.
          B. I think he's optimistic. [, *but*]

          Phil expects to finish by five o'clock, but I think he's optimistic.

Each of the following problems contains two sentences (A and B) that are to be joined in a compound sentence. Following each B sentence is a connector in brackets, sometimes with a comma: [;], [*and*] or [, *and*], [*but*] or [, *but*], [*or*] or [, *or*], and [*yet*] or [, *yet*]. To join the sentences, place the connectors in parentheses at the beginning of the B sentence, as shown in the examples. Use no punctuation except that given in parentheses.

1. A. Ursula K. Le Guin's Earthsea Trilogy was one of her earliest works.
    B. It remains one of her most popular pieces of writing. [, *but*]
2. A. The first volume is titled *A Wizard of Earthsea.*
    B. Its hero is a boy called Sparrowhawk. [, *and*]
3. A. Sparrowhawk lives on Gont, an island in an archipelago.
    B. Travel between the islands is often dangerous and difficult. [;]
4. A. As a young child, Sparrowhawk lives in a poor village, herding goats.
    B. He feels a yearning and a power within himself. [, *yet*]
5. A. He uses magic to defeat a pirate raid.
    B. A wizard hears of his feat. [*and*]
6. A. Eventually Sparrowhawk travels to Roke, the island of magicians.
    B. His education begins. [, *and*]
7. A. *A Wizard of Earthsea* brings Sparrowhawk to manhood.
    B. It is only the first of three novels of his adventures. [, *but*]
8. A. *The Tombs of Atuan* tells of his struggle with old gods.
    B. *The Farthest Shore* brings his adventures to a close. [, *and*]
9. A. Each novel can be read and enjoyed as a separate story.
    B. Each continues the story of a complex and fascinating character. [, *yet*]
10. A. The Earthsea Trilogy was both a popular and a critical success.
    B. It stands as a major work of twentieth-century fantasy. [;]

co-
ord

43

43. Coordination

The adjective *coordinate* means "of equal rank or importance." As pointed out in Section 42c, you can effectively express your ideas in constructions that show their varying importance, and you can also subordinate less significant thoughts so that important ones can be emphasized.

Coordination, the process of making compound sentences, can be an effective tool for the writer. The ideas of balance or contrast lend themselves especially well to the form of the compound sentence:

> It was cold in the fall in Milan *and* the dark came very early.
> —ERNEST HEMINGWAY

> The road we have long been traveling is deceptively easy, a smooth superhighway on which we progress with great speed, *but* at its end lies disaster.
> —RACHEL CARSON

Compound sentences come naturally because we have been using them since we were very young. A child might say, "We went to the ballpark and we saw the players and there was a big crowd and we ate hot dogs." It is not important whether such sentences are a normal stage of language development or are fostered by some of the kinds of prose children are given to read. Whatever their source, compound sentences come easily, but the skillful writer will use them not automatically but effectively.

In combining coordinate phrases, clauses, and sentences, you may make one or more of the following errors.

43a. Stringy, run–on compounds

A string of short compounds has an immature sound to it; but more seriously, such a string can obscure the relationships between the ideas in the component sentences. Changing one or more of the independent clauses in the string into dependent clauses can make the relationships between them explicit:

ORIGINAL: John dropped the Ming vase and broke it and the museum director fired him.

REVISION: Because John dropped the Ming vase, breaking it, the museum director fired him.

ORIGINAL: There are many reasons for unhappy marriages and one of them is the husband is the domineering type and he believes the woman's place is in the home, but his wife wants a job and she is always telling him how bored she is, and this always ends with one of them getting mad and one of them may say something that he or she doesn't really mean, and then the fight is on.

REVISION: Many reasons exist for unhappy marriages, and one is a domineering husband who believes that the wife's place is in the home. His wife, however, wants a job, and finds housework boring. Before long, both husband and wife are angry and say things that they don't really mean. Then the fight is on.

Common causes of stringy sentences are the *and habit,* the *but habit,* and the *so habit,* illustrated by these immature sentences:

The carpenter placed the tools in the box, *and* she climbed up the ladder; *and* then she took the tools from the box and placed them on the roof.

I asked him to go, *but* he said that he didn't want to, *but* when I insisted, he said that he would.

It is getting late *so* we will have to leave now *so* as to be on time.

43b. Seesaw sentences

"Seesaw" sentences take their name from the familiar playground device. Such sentences move alternately up and down and quickly become monotonous:

We thought of going to a park, but we didn't have enough money. Next we decided to take a walk, but a heavy rain prevented that. We bought some soft drinks, and we went to John's house to watch TV. Soon John started snoring, and I became bored and restless.

Closely related and fully as ineffective is the so-called "accordion" sentence, one that contains a series of overlapping subordinate clauses introduced by *who, which, that.* Example: "The kind of dessert that he likes is one which has plenty of whipped cream and that contains chopped nuts." The remedy? Reduce predication: "He likes desserts that have plenty of whipped cream and chopped nuts."

43c. False coordination

Coordinating conjunctions serve to join parts of equal rank: adjective to adjective, verb to verb, or, of concern here, clause to

co-
ord

43c

339

clause and sentence to sentence. Remember that independent main clauses coordinate with independent main clauses, dependent clauses with dependent clauses, direct questions to direct questions, indirect questions to indirect questions, and so on.

ORIGINAL: I asked him if he needed a ride [indirect question] and what time did he want to go [direct question]?

REVISION: I asked him if he needed a ride and what time he wanted to go.

A common problem with the principle of joining equal parts is the "and which" construction, which should not be used to join a relative clause to an independent clause:

ORIGINAL: The members of the team at first showed some racial prejudice, *and which* eventually disappeared.

The simplest and best method of correcting this problem is to omit the conjunction:

REVISION: The members of the team at first showed some racial prejudice, which eventually disappeared.

Never use *and which, but which, and who, but who,* unless you have written a preceding *which* clause or *who* clause.

This is a beautiful tennis court, *and which* we enjoy using.

The simplest method of correcting this sentence is to omit *and* and also the comma, since the clause is restrictive. Or you can supply a preceding *which* clause:

This is a beautiful tennis court which is open to all and which we enjoy using.

Even better, cut out some of the deadwood:

We enjoy playing tennis on this beautiful court.

EXERCISE 10

Rewrite the following sentences in order to eliminate various kinds of confusing or improper coordination:

1. Decisive action is to be taken at the meeting, and at which everyone is urged to be present.
2. I met my brother yesterday and who asked me how my first week of college had been.

3. I would like to teach in a small consolidated school, but I am also taking speech therapy as a minor.
4. We went on a tour of our library and it proved to be very interesting.
5. On Christmas afternoon we went to church, and where a beautiful Christmas program was presented.
6. My history teacher became ill for a short time but there was no substitute teacher to replace him and we did not have any history classes for a week.
7. The road out of the City of Destruction to the Celestial City is filled with temptations and misleading paths upon which one is likely to stumble, and if he is misled.
8. All the cadets standing in formation are an impressive sight and which will not be forgotten soon.
9. When I looked out the night the snowstorm ended, I saw a world that was truly beautiful, and the trees had ice all over them, and the light made them sparkle, and the snow on the ground was as white as white could be.
10. It is seldom that such an insect is found, so great pains must be taken not to destroy it.

44. Subordination

The term *subordination* means "the act of placing in a lower class or rank." When writers select one idea for primary emphasis in a sentence, they automatically decide to subordinate others in the same sentence. If they don't, their sentences will appear in primer style and will fail to emphasize central ideas.

Subordination in English serves to specify the logical relationships existing between clauses; relationships such as time, place, manner, condition, cause, concession, and the like are easily made clear by beginning the dependent clause with the appropriate subordinating conjunction:

TIME: *Whenever black attendants understood the idea of my search,* documents I requested reached me with miraculous speed.
—ALEX HALEY

CONDITION: *If you want to combine different varieties of flowers of varying heights,* study the catalogs.
—HAMILTON MASON

CLAUSE: *Because they help to set a style of expression,* public opinion polls have become one of the great institutional bores of our time.

—EDWIN NEWMAN

Careful use of subordination can improve the ease with which a reader grasps a series of ideas and can effectively express the relationships you intend.

44a. Subordination expresses and clarifies the relationships among short sentences in a series.

As noted in Section 42c, a series of short sentences may express the information you wish to convey without showing which of that information is being selected for emphasis and which is not. Select the main point of the series and place it in an independent clause. Put the subsidiary information in an appropriate dependent clause:

ORIGINAL: Ritual, emotion, and reasoning are significant aspects of human nature. But one ability is almost unique to humans. This is the ability to associate abstractly and to reason.

REVISION: While ritual, emotion, and reasoning are all significant aspects of human nature, the most nearly unique human characteristic is the ability to associate abstractly and to reason.

—CARL SAGAN

If an idea of less importance is put into an independent clause and an important idea is put into a dependent clause, the result is called an *upside-down* subordination. Usually, the most dramatic event and its effect are major elements; preliminaries such as time and place usually form minor (subordinate) elements.

ORIGINAL: Val was nearly out of breath when she spied a light in the distance.

REVISION: When Val was nearly out of breath, she spied a light in the distance.

ORIGINAL: I was halfway across the field when the bull charged.

REVISION: Just as [or *when*] I was halfway across the field, the bull charged.

44b. Excessive subordination

Sometimes the most effective way to make your point may require you to subordinate a dependent clause to a dependent clause:

Soccer will grow ever more popular in the United States, partly because football injuries will continue to mount until some real rule changes are made.

In this example, the dependent clause "until some real rule changes are made" is attached to another dependent clause, "because football injuries will continue to mount." Such subordination is not excessive.

Yet subordination can become excessive, especially when three or four dependent clauses descend from the main clause like a flight of stairs, as they do in these sentences from student papers:

ORIGINAL: I have been in the student show which has affected my grades because it has taken a lot of my evening time, when I should have been in my room studying since my assignments have become longer and more difficult. [Note the vague reference of *which* in the second clause.]

REVISION: Being in the student show has affected my grades because it has taken much of my evening time. Instead of rehearsing, I should have been in my room studying, since my assignments have become longer and more difficult.

ORIGINAL: These are orchids that were grown in Hawaii, where there is an excellent climate, and which were flown here today. [Note that this sentence is also wordy and contains a faulty "and which" construction.]

REVISION: These orchids, grown in Hawaii where there is an excellent climate, were flown here today.

These orchids, grown in Hawaii's excellent climate, were flown here today.

sub-ord

44b

EXERCISE 11

Rewrite the following sentences, correcting excessive or illogical or otherwise faulty subordination.

1. We were almost home before our car skidded into another car and caused a wreck.

2. As the lightning struck the house, Mother was talking on the telephone.

3. The following day I was driving down the highway at a reasonable speed, when suddenly a car whipped past me.

4. Whitefish Bay is eight miles north of Milwaukee, having a population of about 12,000 people.

5. Our town is a purely residential town having its own school district consisting of a high school and a grade school which total about 900 students.

6. In my senior year we reached the finals, where we won our semifinal, the final, and the state championship.

7. After being here a week, I discovered that one works all day in classes which seem to be so placed that I must run from one end of the campus to the other before I can attend them.

8. During my freshman year I am living in a rooming house which is owned by an elderly lady whose father was a college professor for some 50 years at Marion, which is another college in the state supported by public funds.

9. It was so dark that I had to turn on a light to read the clock in the kitchen that is directly opposite a large window which is on the east side of the house that is hidden from the street light by a large oak tree.

10. Of course we cannot always help everyone, but what I am saying is that when people ask for help from someone who could within his own limitations be of great help, when he doesn't.

45. Unity

Unity means "oneness, singleness of purpose." It applies not only to papers and paragraphs but also to sentences. Unity in the sentence is not necessarily related to length or complexity—long and complex sentences may be unified as well as short and simple ones. The important consideration is that the ideas of the sentence be related to one another. For example, this is a unified sentence:

> Although Fritz claims to be interested in the simple things of life, he plays his records on a quadraphonic stereo system and drives a supercharged Triumph; in fact, he seldom comes to class without his pocket cassette recorder and a hundred-dollar calculator.

The sentence is long and refers to several things, but it is unified because its ideas support a single point—the contrast between Fritz's beliefs and his possessions.

Another sentence could be packed with information and details and still be unified because it focuses on one individual:

> Much of the credit for a new Carter image belonged to Gerald Rafshoon, 44, the well-tailored, curly-haired, New York-born adman who had worked in every Carter campaign since 1966.

Unity in a sentence is weakened by (1) introducing unrelated details and (2) combining unrelated ideas.

45a. *Details* in a sentence should support the point of the sentence.

ORIGINAL: The class registration moved with agonizing slowness, stranding in the stuffy gym a line of students dressed in jeans, shorts, cutoffs, tanktops, sandals, or no shoes at all.

What the students were wearing has little to do with the registration procedure. In revision, shorten any long, rambling sentences and omit unrelated details. This advice does not mean you should omit details; rather, select supporting ones, ones that are related to the point of the sentence. Instead of telling what the students wore, tell what they did as a result of their long wait:

REVISION: The class registration moved with agonizing slowness, stranding in the stuffy gym a line of students who shuffled, groaned, sweated, or even stretched out full length on the floor.

Consider another example.

ORIGINAL: We accepted the invitation to have the golf tournament at Moose Junction, a small town in Minnesota, which has only 5000 inhabitants but which contains several supermarkets, a number of churches, two good hotels, a number of motels, being on the junction of one United States highway and two state roads, and, since 1975, a drive-in restaurant as well as a golf course owned by a wealthy man named Putt.

un

45a

After deciding to keep the golf tournament as the central idea, one could revise this series of apparently unrelated details so that they have unity:

REVISION: We have accepted the invitation to have the golf tournament at Moose Junction, Minnesota, because of the facilities it offers. It is easily accessible by railroad and by several highways, United States Route 39 and two state roads, 138 and 139, which intersect there. The city has two good hotels and several motels; in addition, quite a number of the city's 5000 inhabitants have agreed to open their homes to us. Restaurants are adequate, including a new large drive-in near the golf course. Naturally, the deciding factor in choosing Moose Junction has been this golf course. One of the best, in every sense, in the Midwest, it is owned and maintained by a golf enthusiast and wealthy man named, appropriately, Mr. Putt.

What has happened in this revision is that the writer has *shown* how each of the details related to the decision that was made. Still another method of revision would be to remove all details that are not directly related to the tournament and the golf course.

45b. The *ideas* in a sentence should support a single point.

Unrelated ideas can occur in the same sentence. When unrelated ideas obscure the point of the sentence, achieve unity by placing the conflicting ideas in separate sentences or supplying words that will make clear the relationship that was not apparent in the original version. Of course, if no relationship at all exists, omit the unrelated ideas.

ORIGINAL: Bagpipes sound like plain noise to many people, and I enjoy playing them.

REVISION: Bagpipes sound like plain noise to many people. Nevertheless, their distinctive wail appeals to me, and I enjoy playing them.

ORIGINAL: Juana was a good student, and she had a TV set in her room.

REVISION: Juana was a good student, and since her grades were high, she felt that some time spent watching the TV set in her room was not a serious distraction.

EXERCISE 12

Revise the following sentences to give them unity. Add words when necessary.

1. I enjoyed our Halloween party very much, but it was a cold night.
2. John is a very fine dancer and plays the clarinet well.
3. The farmer who is superstitious will always expect rain three days during the week when it rains on Monday, and pioneers and early Americans would always check the husk on the corn for thickness; if the husks were thick, they prepared for a long and cold winter.
4. My oldest brother, James, is 25 years old, and he is married to an English teacher.
5. The town of Aurora has a population of 7000, and no farmers live in the town.
6. One hundred years ago John E. Sherman was elected mayor of our city; however, the present mayor is Wendell G. Orson.
7. We feel that our club is the best at State College, which was founded in 1899 by two brothers, George and Daniel Slate; they founded the club, not the college, which was established by an act of the State Legislature in 1870, and the moving spirit there was Morton Dowhill, the Speaker of the Senate.
8. For our evening meal we have to wear a shirt, tie, jacket, and suitable trousers and shoes, but the food is really special: roast lamb, beefsteak, roast beef, and pork chops are some of the main dishes that we have.
9. As I grew older, my desire to play basketball grew also, and when I entered high school I was too small to play my first two years of school, being only five feet tall, so I had to sit on the bench, but later in high school I began to grow, and before I graduated my senior year I was playing center on the first team, for I had grown 13 inches in two years.
10. If I had a million dollars, I would buy me a new car and a new suit and a new pair of shoes and go all around the world and see it all and when the car got something wrong I would not wait to get it fixed. I would buy me another new car and give the old one to some kids and keep going and if it was water I would buy me an airplane and just keep going. [Schoolboy's theme on "What I Would Do With a Million Dollars"]

un

45b

46. Word order

Words in an English sentence have meaning largely because of their position. That is, they have one meaning in one position, another meaning in another position, and little or no meaning in still another position. Some linguists maintain that the true basis of English grammar is word order. "My *first* roommate's name was Angela" has a different meaning from "My roommate's *first* name was Angela." Again, changing the position of only one word results in ideas that are quite dissimilar: "I was invited to a party *tonight*" and "I was *tonight* invited to a party"; "the best *possible* result" and "the best result *possible*."

Try to keep related words together so that your readers can see the connection you have in mind; try to place every modifier so that it is associated with the word or phrase it modifies.

46a. The squinting modifier

A modifier "squints" when it "looks both ways" and may refer to either of two parts of a sentence. In a sentence containing a squinting modifier, a reader is unable to judge which of two meanings is intended.

Consider this sentence: "The person who can do this well deserves praise." *Well* may modify either *can do* or *deserves*. One way to clear up the confusion is to add *certainly* after *well*. Now the adverb *well* modifies *can do,* and the adverb *certainly* applies to *deserves*. Such a construction involves *juncture*. (See *juncture* in Section 10.) Removing *well* would clarify the sentence but also change its possible meaning.

46b. Position of modifiers

The position of certain words will alter the meaning of a sentence. These words include *only, even, hardly, scarcely, merely, nearly, seldom, never, not, almost, just, quite,* and still others. The chief offender, however, is *only.*

Here is a sentence containing 11 words: "Only the manager told me to finish the job before noon." In it the word *only* can appear in every position from 1 through 11: "The *only* manager told me . . . ," "The manager *only* told me . . . ," "The manager told *only* me . . . ," and so on. The position of *only* determines what the sentence means: 11 somewhat different meanings are possible. [Note that placing *only* in the sixth position causes a split infinitive, perhaps not an effective construction. (See Section 46e.)]

For another example involving *only,* notice how its position can affect the meaning of these sentences:

The New York *Times* reviewer criticized Professor Hiatus' book.

Only the New York *Times* reviewer criticized Professor Hiatus' book. [The reviewers for other papers liked it.]

The New York *Times* reviewer *only* criticized Professor Hiatus' book. [He didn't punch the professor in the nose.]

The New York *Times* reviewer criticized *only* Professor Hiatus' book. [He liked the other books.]

The New York *Times* reviewer criticized Professor Hiatus' *only* book. [The professor has written just one book.]

Remember that words like *only* and the other modifiers mentioned earlier are usually associated with the following word. Occasionally they apply to the preceding word: "The meeting was for incoming freshmen *only.*"

modf

46c

46c. The position of phrases and clauses

Like words, modifying phrases and clauses should be placed next to, or near, the words they modify to eliminate any chance of confusion. In the following, the writers obviously did not mean what their sentences indicate:

ORIGINAL: Stash's Hamburger Palace is closed for repairs to customers.

I decorated our Christmas tree with our family.

We put our presents under the tree, which we had wrapped the night before.

As these sentences show, rephrasing is necessary.

REVISION: Stash's Hamburger Palace is closed to customers
while repairs are being made.

My family and I decorated our Christmas tree.

We put our presents, which we had wrapped the
night before, under the tree.

46d. Dangling modifiers

Any misplaced word, phrase, or clause "dangles" in the sense
that it hangs loosely within a sentence. Writers should never assume that readers will know which words other words are intended to modify; the relationship should be expressed, and the
modifiers should be placed so that your readers can easily make
the intended association.

Dangling verbal phrases

Sentences containing dangling verbal phrases may be corrected
in three ways: (1) by expanding the verbal phrase to a dependent
clause; (2) by supplying the substantive (noun or pronoun) that the
dangling phrase *should* modify; (3) by placing the construction so
near the supplied substantive that no confusion is possible.

ORIGINAL: *Walking down the aisle,* the curtain rose. [Participial
phrase]

To play tennis well, a good racquet is needed.
[Infinitive phrase]

By exercising every day, your health will improve.
[Gerund phrase]

REVISION: While we were walking down the aisle, the curtain
rose.

Walking down the aisle, we saw the curtain rise.

A good racquet is needed if you wish to play tennis
well.

To play tennis well you need a good racquet.

Your health will improve through daily exercise.

If you exercise every day, your health will improve.

Each of the ineffective sentences given may be improved by one
or another of the three methods suggested. (Most of us don't mind

modf

46d

making an error, but we do dislike being thought incoherent or ludicrous.)

In the following sentence The words *approaching the campus* seem to describe the tower:

Approaching the campus, the tower of University Hall was seen.

The writer of the sentence changed an active voice sentence to a passive. It might have started out like this:

Approaching the campus, we saw the tower of University Hall.

When the main clause was put in the passive voice, the two noun phrases, *we* and *the tower of University Hall,* changed position:

Approaching the campus, the tower of University Hall was seen by us.

Perhaps because that passive clause sounded awkward, the writer dropped *by us,* leaving the modifier *approaching the campus* to dangle, that is, leaving it stranded far from the construction it is supposed to modify.

As the following example suggests, sentences using the passive voice often invite dangling modifiers.

modf

46d

ORIGINAL: Caught without his shotgun, a grouchy bear was aroused by Grandpa Walton.

Sometimes all that is necessary is to put the sentence back in the active voice.

REVISION: Caught without his shotgun, Grandpa Walton aroused a grouchy bear.

ORIGINAL: After seeing Niagara Falls, other falls seemed small by comparison.

REVISION: After one has seen Niagara Falls, other falls seem small by comparison.
Seeing Niagara Falls makes other falls seem small by comparison.

When a verbal phrase denotes a general action rather than a specific one, it is not a dangling modifier:

Considering everything, his suggestion was reasonable.
The action is considered general because no particular event or individual is mentioned in the verbal phrase.

Dangling elliptical clauses

Ellipsis means "an omission." An *elliptical clause* is one that lacks an expressed subject or predicate, or both. It dangles unless the implied subject is the same as that of the main clause.

ORIGINAL: *When 19 years old,* my grandfather died.
While working last night, the lights went out.
Before thoroughly warmed up, you should not race a motor.

To correct such confused sentences, insert in the dangling clause the needed subject and verb, or change the subject (or subject and verb) in the main clause.

REVISION: When I was 19 years old, my grandfather died.
When 19 years old, I lost my grandfather through death.
While I was working last night, the lights went out.
Before it is thoroughly warmed up, you should not race a motor.
You should thoroughly warm up a motor before you race it.
You should not race a motor before it is thoroughly warmed up.

46e. Split constructions

Separating, or splitting, closely related parts of a sentence is not always a mistake. Yet splitting the two parts of an infinitive, parts of a verb phrase, a verb and its subject, and a preposition and its object often causes confusion for a reader. Wherever possible, keep logically related parts together.

The split infinitive

When a word, phrase, or clause comes between the sign of the infinitive, *to,* and a verb, the construction is called a *split infinitive.* Reputable speakers and writers occasionally split an infinitive; consequently, this practice is no longer considered a grave error. Also, on rare occasions, you must split an infinitive to make clear what

modf

46e

you have in mind. For example, in this sentence, "Martha wants *to really see* Tod in person," moving *really* to any other place in the sentence would change the meaning or weaken the effectiveness of the sentence.

Normally, however, no sound reason exists for putting an adverb or phrase or other group of words between *to* and a verb. "He requested us to *as soon as possible* leave the building" would be clearer and more natural if the italicized words were moved to the *end* of the sentence. (If the italicized words were moved to the *beginning* of the sentence, meaning would be altered.)

Separating the parts of a verb phrase

An auxiliary verb with a main verb forms a frequent pattern in English. (See Section 16.) Splitting such a verb phrase is rarely effective and usually results in an awkward construction. In sentences such as the following, the italicized words should be brought together:

> There was the boy we *had* before we left *seen* in the park. [There was the boy we *had seen* in the park before we left.]
>
> This building *has,* although it is hard to believe, *been* here for more than a century. [This building *has been,* . . . Although it is hard to believe, this building *has been* . . .]

modf

46e

Unnecessary separation of subject and verb, preposition and object

Separation of a subject and its verb and a preposition and its object is occasionally justifiable. For example, such words as *not, never,* and *always* frequently come between the parts of a verb phrase and between a subject and a verb: "Muriel has never in class raised her hand." The justifiable separation of subject and verb and preposition and object occurs when only a few words are involved, never in lengthy phrases and complete clauses. In awkward and generally ineffective sentences like the following, the italicized elements should be brought together:

> *Muriel,* as soon as she heard the question, *raised her hand.* [Subject and verb; revise the sentence to begin, "As soon as she heard . . ."]

Mabel crept *into*, although she was terrified, *the frail canoe*. [Preposition and object; begin the sentence with "Although."]

Antonia *asked*, even before I could finish, *what I really meant*. [Verb and object; begin the sentence with "Even before . . ."]

Placing coordinate elements together

When two clauses or phrases of approximately equal strength and importance are used in a sentence, avoid putting one at the beginning of the sentence and the other at the end. The italicized phrases and clauses in these sentences should be brought together and joined by *and:*

Although she was an ardent golfer, she could never break 90, *although she practiced daily.*

With fair weather, we should have a pleasant journey, *with good luck.*

EXERCISE 13

Change the word order of each of the following sentences:

1. Each day I see a new building going up from my study window.
2. In this book the author tells of roving around Europe in an autobiographical manner.
3. Some courses in composition require you only to write frequently and to speak occasionally.
4. I don't think certain articles in our book of readings are interesting.
5. Each spring my father and I pull the machinery out of the shed that we will need for sowing oats.
6. In the poem the heroine relates the story of her marriage to one of her girlfriends.
7. In some courses the student is more required to work and think than just to copy and memorize.
8. As we interpret your directions, whenever it is possible, we should keep to the superhighways.
9. I have never had a shot hurt as this shot did before.
10. There are some instructors who cannot really explain what they want their students to know in a clear manner.

EXERCISE 14

Change the word order of each of the following sentences:

1. She nearly laughs with each word she speaks.

2. Today I registered as a freshman, and it almost took the whole day.
3. I hope to work in a mentally and physically handicapped clinic.
4. If I spend half an hour on the courses I have the next day, the night before, I find that I can get a better grade.
5. Everyone at the ceremony was impressed by the 63-year-old baby's christening dress.
6. Looking out my window, many red lights from emergency vehicles could be seen.
7. After traveling farther, the signs began appearing more regularly.
8. The article is not written in technical language, thus making it easy for the layperson to understand.
9. Being unmarried, all the girls in Fairfield Junior High School loved the handsome young chemistry teacher.
10. Enclosed with this letter you will find your membership card.

EXERCISE 15

Change the word order of each of the following sentences:

1. If writing a letter by hand, a good fountain pen or ball point pen should be used.
2. This report is filed with the Federal Aviation Agency, thereby completing the pilot's preparation for a trip.
3. After walking for 50 yards, the land gradually began to slope downward.
4. To enjoy poetry it should be read slowly and carefully.
5. At the age of 2 my father bought a small farm near this college town.
6. Upon checking into the hospital, a cute nurse of about 18 showed me to my room.
7. Going east, the main object of the trip will be visiting Maine.
8. Shortly after entering Germany, the inns and hotels became more attractive.
9. When boiled, Mother would shell and slice the eggs for the salad.
10. Many interesting topics are to be found browsing through the dictionary.

EXERCISE 16

Revise the word order of each of the following sentences:

1. Hanging from the ceiling, you will see a beautiful, old-fashioned chandelier.
2. After a quick walk through the crowds, the New York Public Library offers a haven from the hustle-bustle of the street.
3. Coming toward the house, the white fence posts can be seen, no matter what the direction of approach.

modf

46e

4. As a college professor, I am sure you can give me advice about the electives I should take as a high school senior.

5. I have seen the sun come up over the beautiful mountaintop many times, sitting around a nice warm fire with the odor of frying bacon drifting through the air.

6. It, as I have found, seems sometimes an almost impossible task.

7. The way it looks now, during vacation I should have gotten everything I planned to do, done.

8. I would, since I worked for you three summers ago, like to use your name as a reference in my job hunting.

9. It is my fondest wish to go back to Washington to once again and with more time at my disposal view those memorable sights.

10. In fact, every day would find me out on the pier, which seemed to extend an endless distance into the ocean, fishing.

47. Parallelism

In writing, the word *parallelism* suggests "similarity," "close resemblance." When two or more ideas in a sentence are related in function and purpose, they can and should be phrased in the same grammatical form (words, phrases, etc.).

The baby is *sweet* but *noisy*. [Words]
Pierre loves to read both *at home* and *at school*. [Phrases]
Susan was shocked when she discovered *that one tire was flat* and *that the jack was missing*. [Clauses]

For additional illustrations of effective parallelism, consider these sentences:

PHRASES: Every afternoon Punch is on the corner *telling lies about his love life* or *listening to equally outrageous yarns from his friends.*

DEPENDENT CLAUSES: I was desperate *when I arrived late at the motel* and *when I found that no rooms were available.*

INDEPENDENT CLAUSES: Lincoln said, "*You can fool all of the people some of the time* and *some of the people all of the time,* but *you can't fool all of the people all of the time.*"

As an effective test of parallelism, draw lines under the parallel elements. Then draw a corresponding number of lines in parallel form and write the underlined words on them. Note that the example from Lincoln contains parallel phrases within parallel clauses.

Every afternoon Punch is on the corner
<u>telling lies about his love life</u>
or
<u>listening to equally outrageous yarns from his friends.</u>

I was desperate
<u>when I arrived late at the motel</u>
and
<u>when I found that no rooms were available.</u>

Lincoln said,
<u>"You can fool</u>
<u>all of the people some of the time</u>
and
<u>some of the people all of the time,</u>
but
<u>you can't fool</u>
<u>all of the people all of the time.</u>

47a. Sentence elements that are coordinate in rank should be parallel in structure.

ORIGINAL: Louise liked to row and playing tennis.

REVISION: Louise liked *to row* and *to play* tennis.

or

Louise liked *rowing* and *playing tennis.*

ORIGINAL: The Washington Dirigible plays at many school functions, engagements in nearby towns, and concert tours.

REVISION: The Washington Dirigible *plays* at many school functions, *has* engagements in nearby towns, and *performs* on concert tours.

or

The Washington Dirigible plays at many school

functions, at gatherings in nearby towns, and on concert tours.

ORIGINAL: Clyde would like to wield enormous power and that he might have fabulous wealth.

REVISION: Clyde would like to wield enormous power and *to have* fabulous wealth.

or

Clyde has two ambitions: enormous power and fabulous wealth.

Absolute parallelism is not always necessary. In the following sentences, the form is not parallel, but the functions are. In the first example, the italicized parallel elements are all adverbial; in the second, three nouns (two proper, and one common noun with modifier) are parallel.

The speaker talked *slowly* and *with a slight stammer.*

Into Mordor walked *Frodo, Sam,* and *a creature of doubtful identity.*

47b. Partial or misleading parallelism

Each element in a series should be similar in form and structure to all others in the same series. But the same structural form should *not* be used for sentence elements of *unequal* value. Watch out for elements that may appear to modify the same element when they are not actually parallel.

Steve has worked as a camp counselor, tennis coach, and has served as a bank teller. [Revise this sentence to read, "Steve has worked as a camp counselor, tennis coach, and bank teller."]

That TV play was dramatic, exciting, and had an involved plot. [Revise this sentence to read, "That TV play was dramatic, exciting, and involved in plot."]

ORIGINAL: They left quickly, and they had a good automobile.

For your sake, for $25 I will assist you.

We bought that set from a local dealer and with a good walnut finish.

REVISION: They left quickly in a good automobile.

For your sake, I will assist you to the extent of $25.

We bought that set from a local dealer; it has a good walnut finish.

47c. Place parallel elements immediately after correlative conjunctions.

The four pairs of correlative conjunctions (*both . . . and, either . . . or, neither . . . nor,* and *not only . . . but also*) should be followed immediately by the same grammatical form: two similar words, two similar phrases, or two similar clauses.

ORIGINAL: I *neither* have the time *nor* the inclination to play rollerball.

REVISION: I have *neither* the time *nor* the inclination to play rollerball.

ORIGINAL: *Either* you can cash your check at the bank *or* at the student union.

REVISION: You can cash your check *either* at the bank *or* at the student union.

ORIGINAL: The ushers require that you be *either* seated before the beginning of the show *or* that you wait outside until after the first number.

REVISION: The ushers require *either* that you be seated before the beginning of the show *or* that you wait outside until after the first number.

II

47c

EXERCISE 17

Make a parallelism diagram for all parallel elements in the following passage:

The world will little note nor long remember what we say here, but it can never forget what they did here. It is for us, the living, rather, to be dedicated here to the unfinished work which they who fought here have thus far so nobly advanced. It is rather for us to be here dedicated to the great task remaining before us; that from these honored dead we take increased devotion to that cause for which they gave the last full measure of devotion; that we here highly resolve that these dead shall not have died in vain; that this nation, under God, shall have a new birth of freedom; and that government of the people, by the people, for the people, shall not perish from the earth.

—ABRAHAM LINCOLN, *"Address at Gettysburg"*

EXERCISE 18

Make a parallelism diagram for all parallel elements in the following passage:

Studies serve for delight, for ornament, and for ability. Their chief use for delight, is in privateness and retiring; for ornament, is in discourse; and for ability, is in the judgment and disposition of business. For expert men can execute, and perhaps judge of particulars, one by one; but the general counsels, and the plots and marshalling of affairs, come best from those that are learned. To spend too much time in studies is sloth; to use them too much for ornament, is affectation; to make judgment wholly by their rules, is the humour of a scholar.

—FRANCIS BACON, *"Of Studies"*

EXERCISE 19

Correct all errors in faulty parallelism in the following sentences. Except where correlative conjunctions are involved, (1) change the structure of the first element to agree with that of later ones or (2) change the structure of later elements to agree with that of the first.

1. The morning was dark, cold, and there was a little snow in the air.
2. This could be the reason why I did not like my teacher and she not liking me.
3. Mr. Bennet was not only a failure as a husband, but as a father as well.
4. Mary is an attractive 5 feet, 5 inches tall, auburn hair, blue eyes, and full of enthusiasm.
5. My father said that I could drive the car and to be careful because the tires were in bad shape.
6. In registering, the student often finds that the classes she wanted are either full or cannot be fitted into her time schedule.
7. There are girls in my dorm who got average grades in high school and getting above-average grades now.
8. St. Francis intended to found a society of men desiring to return to the manners of the primitive church and who would profess absolute poverty.
9. Since it was Easter, and because of the many flowers in bloom, the explorer decided to give the area the name of Florida.
10. In careless driving, the driver not only risks the life of his own passengers, but also the lives of others.

cons

48

48. Consistency

Consistency means "holding together," "retaining form," "agreement among themselves of the parts of something." Consistency in a sentence means that its parts are in agreement, that they are similar in structure, and that they remain so unless there is a clear reason for changing (shifting) them. That is, for example, if one part of your sentence uses the present tense of a verb, other parts of that sentence should also use the present tense if the time element is unchanged.

To write effectively, be consistent in *tense, voice, mood, pronoun reference* (number and person), and *diction*. (If necessary, refer to these terms in other sections.)

48a. Unnecessary shifts in tense

Tense is the time of the verb (present, past, future, present perfect, etc.; see Section 17). Consistency in the use of tense may be a pitfall because it is easy to shift unnecessarily from present to past or from past to present or back and forth between the two. Note the switches in this example:

NONSTANDARD: Claire *was walking* briskly along the sidewalk when suddenly a riderless horse *came charging* around the corner. At a full gallop, it *races* down the middle of the street, then *veers* abruptly and *heads* directly for her. In panic, Claire *leaped* to the nearest doorway.

STANDARD: Claire *was walking* briskly along the sidewalk when suddenly a riderless horse *came charging* around the corner. At a full gallop, it *raced* down the middle of the street, then *veered* abruptly and *headed* directly for her. In panic, Claire *leaped* to the nearest doorway.

cons

48a

Again, you may sometimes be confused when writing about literature whether the tense should be past or present. For instance, the writing of *Macbeth* occurred almost 400 years ago; on the other hand, the play exists and is frequently performed. Either tense (past or present) may be used, but do not shift from one to the other; be consistent in your use throughout the paper—or at least in a given paragraph.

ORIGINAL: Macbeth *leaves* [present tense] Lady Macbeth and *goes* to King Duncan's room. There he *took* [past tense] a dagger from a sleeping guard and *murdered* the king.

REVISION: Macbeth *leaves* Lady Macbeth and *goes* to King Duncan's room. There he *takes* a dagger from a sleeping guard and *murders* the king. [Or change to the past tense: *left, went, took,* and *murdered.*]

Also, do not allow the fact that you are narrating a past event allow statements that apply now to be drawn to the past tense:

ORIGINAL: On our way home, we visited Bath, North Carolina. The houses there *were* old and picturesque.

Does this mean that the houses are no longer there? Since the second sentence describes something not on the past time-line of the narration, do not let the desire for consistency lead to a false or misleading statement.

REVISION: On our way home, we visited Bath, North Carolina. The houses there *are* old and picturesque.

48b. Consistency in the use of voice

cons

48b

Do not shift needlessly from active to passive or from passive to active voice unless good reason exists for the shift. (See Section 3b, subsection 6.) Not only is such shifting annoying to the reader; it causes a distracting change. It's good advice to use the active voice whenever possible because doers and agents are usually more appealing than those who sit and do nothing.

ORIGINAL: His advice to us lawyers was to follow an ambulance and much money will be earned.

REVISION: His advice to us lawyers was to follow an ambulance and earn much money.

ORIGINAL: When tourists approach Cape Canaveral, the enormous assembly building can be seen in the distance.

REVISION: When tourists approach Cape Canaveral, they can see the enormous assembly building in the distance.

ORIGINAL: During the test, Gus prayed for help, but no answers were received.

REVISION: During the test, Gus prayed for help, but he received no answers.

One reason for shifting from active to passive, or vice versa, is to keep the same subject in consecutive sentences. Notice in the following examples that both verbs are in the active voice in each pair of sentences or clauses. But use of the active voice requires either that other verbs be substituted or that one be placed in the passive if the subjects of both sentences are to be the same.

ORIGINAL: His advice to us lawyers was follow an ambulance and much money will follow you.

REVISION: His advice to us lawyers was follow an ambulance, and you will be followed by much money.

ORIGINAL: When tourists approach Cape Canaveral, the enormous assembly building impresses them in the distance.

REVISION: When tourists approach Cape Canaveral, they are impressed by the enormous assembly building in the distance.

48c. Inconsistent use of mood

Be consistent in use of the subjunctive, indicative, or imperative moods in compound predicates and in parallel dependent clauses. (See Section 18c.) Do not shift needlessly from one to another.

ORIGINAL: If I *were* in your position and *was* able to afford it, I would buy a home computer.

REVISION: If I *were* in your position and *were* able to afford it, I would buy a home computer.

48d. Unnecessary shifts in number

A common error in the use of number is a careless shift from plural to singular or from singular to plural, or failure to make pronouns and antecedents agree in number.

A small child can be a joy, but *they require* constant attention. [Change *they* to *it* or *he* or *she,* and *require* to *requires.*]

If men really try their best, *he is* bound to succeed. [Change *he* to *they* and *is* to *are.*]

48e. Unnecessary shifts in the class or person of pronouns

A shift in pronoun reference violates the general principle that pronouns and antecedents agree in person. (See Sections 2, 13.) The most common occurrence of this problem is the shift from the third person to the second-person *you*.

ORIGINAL: If *one* studies hard enough in high school, *you* will have no trouble in the first year of college.

REVISION: If people study hard enough in high school, they will have no trouble in the first year of college.

If *you* study hard enough in high school, *you* will have no trouble in the first year of college.

48f. Inconsistency in diction

Keep in mind the general level and tone of your writing, the kind of reader you are writing for, and the characteristics of your subject. For example, do not mix slang with formal language and constructions. (See Section 38g.) On the other hand, in an informal essay, do not use the longest and most studied words you can find.

ORIGINAL: After judicious consideration and polling the opinions of my fellows, I concluded that Professor Hiatus' class was the pits.

REVISION: After judicious consideration and polling the opinions of my fellows, I concluded that Professor Hiatus' class left much to be desired.

or

After thinking it over and checking with my friends, I decided that Professor Hiatus' class was the pits.

Also, avoid changing suddenly from literal speech to figurative language or vice versa. When you do use a figure of speech, you should not suddenly shift the figure. (see Section 37f). By not sustaining one figure of speech, we obtain such an inconsistent and confused statement as this:

She got into a rut and felt all at sea when she lost her job. [Whoever *she* is has trouble. Perhaps this will be an improvement: "She felt depressed and uncertain when she lost her job."]

EXERCISE 20

Rewrite the following sentences, making them conform to principles of consistency:

1. Taking drugs to keep awake retards rather than quicken the mind.
2. Finally our destination was reached, and, as the bus door opened, all 20 of us eagerly climbed out.
3. After I had several tranquilizing pills, three men came in with one of those beds to transport you to the operating room.
4. Offices of advertising agencies began at 23rd Street; the garment industry begins at 37th street.
5. Today I began preparing to leave, and several tasks had to be performed in preparation for my leaving.
6. When I feel bitter, taking your spite out on a golf ball is better than taking it out on your friends.
7. He was a far different man when he returns than he was when he started.
8. When people have the same likes and dislikes, more fun can be had by all.
9. In high school or college, a student should not take easy courses if they want to get the best education possible. Besides, you learn more from the more difficult courses if you work at it.
10. When one enters Colorado from the east, he would think it to be another state of plains.
11. A student may spend too much time in activities, and before long college will become an obligation that has to be met by him.
12. The British middle class was conscious of their social position and were constantly trying to improve it.
13. There is no sense in a person's buying a dictionary that does not meet your needs.
14. I must regulate myself with a strict schedule so that valuable time will not be lost.
15. If one were not fortunate to be born in the upper classes in ancient Rome, you did not have a life of much promise.

49. Transition

Individual sentences may be clear, effective, and appropriate and yet not be suitably related when put together in a paragraph. Any lack of clearness probably is due to faulty transition. Remember that *transition* means passing from one place, state, or position to another, and that *evidence of transition* consists of linking or bridging devices.

Three kinds of transition apply to writing: between paragraphs (see Section 56), within the sentence, and between sentences. When used within the sentence, transitional devices usually come between clauses; when used between sentences, they come near or at the beginning or end of the sentences they link. Not only should thoughts progress logically; a reader must be able to grasp both them and their interrelations.

49a. Make sentence transitions clear by using transitional words and phrases.

Between dependent and independent clauses, evidence of relationship is expressed by (1) subordinating conjunctions such as *if, since, because, as, while, so that, although, unless, before,* and by (2) relative pronouns:

> Only human beings use language, *unless* the signing taught to chimps can be considered a language.
> The book that Tolkien wrote first was the last *that* was published.

Between independent clauses and between sentences, transition is accomplished by personal pronouns, demonstrative pronouns, and coordinating conjunctions such as *and, but, or, yet:*

> Maureen felt ill in the first set. *She* came alive in the second. [Personal pronoun]
> We had little success at first, but *this* did not stop us. [Demonstrative pronoun]
> Garo Yepremian added the extra point for the Dolphins, *but* then he usually does. [Coordinating conjunction]

Correlative conjunctions such as *not only . . . but also, either . . . or,* etc. can be used:

> In your first year, *either* you pass the swimming test *or* you register for Beginning Swimming.

Conjunctive adverbs such as *again, also, anyhow, however, moreover, on the other hand, for example, therefore,* and *finally* can also be used for this purpose:

tran

49a

In "demand-pull" inflation, too many buyers are chasing too few goods; *consequently,* the price of the goods rises.

Although transitional devices between sentences usually come at the beginning or end of linked sentences, sometimes they can be more effectively placed as second or third words, following the subject they introduce:

John's motorcycle gets seventy-eight miles to the gallon; my moped, *by contrast,* gets more than one hundred.

A mechanical skill can be an intellectual aid. Typing, *for instance,* has improved the composition of many a student.

49b. Make transitions between sentences clear by repeating nouns and using pronouns.

An effective kind of repetition for transition from one sentence to another is the use of pronouns referring to preceding nouns and pronouns:

A writer whose fast-paced novels easily convert to movies is Alistair MacLean. *He* wrote *The Guns of Navarone, Ice Station Zebra,* and *Where Eagles Dare.*

Synonyms are also effective:

A writer whose fast-paced stories easily convert to movies is Alistair MacLean. *The British adventure novelist* wrote *The Guns of Navarone, Ice Station Zebra,* and *Where Eagles Dare.*

Occasionally, too, key or important words can be repeated in succeeding sentences:

One of the required *courses* in an engineering student's first semester is E101, Introduction to Engineering Procedures. This *course* . . .

In the following sentences, from the first two paragraphs of Huxley's "The Method of Scientific Investigation," italicized words illustrate various devices for sentence transition.

The method of scientific investigation is nothing but the expression of the necessary mode of working of the human mind. *It is simply* the *mode* at which all phenomena are reasoned about, rendered precise and exact . . .

You will understand *this better,* perhaps, *if* I give *you* some familiar example. *You* have all heard it repeated, *I* dare say, that *men of science* work by means of *induction and deduction, and* that by the help of *these operations, they,* in a sort of sense, wring from nature certain *other* things which are called natural laws and causes, and that out of *these,* by some cunning skill of *their* own, *they* build up hypotheses and theories. *And* it is imagined by many that the operations of the common mind can be by no means compared with *these processes, and* that *they* have to be acquired by a sort of special apprenticeship to the craft. To hear *all these* large words *you* would think that the *mind* of *a man of science* must be constituted differently from *that* of *his* fellow men; *but if you* will not be frightened by terms, *you* will discover that *you* are quite wrong, *and* that *all these* terrible apparatus are being used by *yourselves* every day and every hour of *your* lives.

49c. Labored and artificial transition

tran

49c

The major purpose of transitions is to show relationship and the direction of relationship; a secondary aim is to make this relationship evident smoothly and unobtrusively.

In this example, transitions are needed between short, choppy sentences and clauses:

Baseball is said to be the national game; I do not like it. If it is the national game, thousands must enjoy watching it, or playing it. I know people who do not ever attend a game; I know people who see as many as fifty games a year. I should not make a dogmatic statement about the appeal of the sport; I have never witnessed a game.

In a first revision, the writer inserted conspicuous transitional words and phrases (here italicized) at the beginning of each sentence or independent clause:

Baseball is said to be the national game; *however,* I do not like it. *Yet* if it is the national game, thousands must enjoy watching it, or playing it. *To be sure,* I know people who do not ever attend a game; *on the other hand,* I know people who see as many as fifty games a year. Perhaps I should not make a dogmatic statement about the appeal of the sport; *you see,* I have never witnessed a game.

In a second revision, the writer varied the position of transitional words and let pronouns and repetition achieve this more effective passage:

> *Although* baseball is said to be America's national game, I do not like *it*. *Yet* if *it* is the *national game,* hundreds must enjoy playing the *game* and thousands must enjoy watching *it*. I know people who see as many as fifty or sixty *games* a season and who drive many miles to see *them;* on the other hand, I know people who never attend a *game* and who wouldn't walk across the street to see *one*. Perhaps it is all a matter of *sporting* taste, *and* perhaps I should not make a dogmatic statement about the appeal of *baseball*. *You see,* I have never seen a *game, and* I prefer a *sport* that I can take part in, peacefully, quietly, badly perhaps, and without "fan"-fare. I *prefer* golf.

EXERCISE 21

Copy one long or several short paragraphs of prose (without conversation) from a book of readings. Underline the various devices for transition between sentences and between clauses. Write a paragraph (approximately 100 words) commenting on the methods used.

EXERCISE 22

Apply the directions in Exercise 21 to an article in a current magazine.

EXERCISE 23

Apply the directions in Exercise 21 to one of your own papers.

50. Conciseness

Concise means "expressed in few words; brief and to the point." Logically, therefore, *conciseness,* the noun form, is primarily a problem in diction, and as such it is discussed in Section 38i. But conciseness is also a problem in writing sentences.

A sentence may be complete and unified and yet be ineffective because it is wordy. A sentence of 100 words may be concise, and one of 20 may be wordy. No sentence can be effective when it contains too many words or ideas—or too few.

Do not use so many words that meaning is lost in a forest of verbiage, or so few that your meaning is obscured through brevity. Your aim should be effectiveness; wordiness, like long-windedness in speech, is never effective.

The best way to achieve conciseness is to develop the habit of examining your sentences carefully, looking for places where words can be cut. Two suggestions apply specifically to sentences.

50a. Reduce predication.

Reducing predication means reducing the number of words in an assertion, cutting out unnecessary words by making one word serve the purpose of two or three or more. The purpose of reducing predication is to subordinate detail within a larger structure. For example, one synonym can replace several words without altering in any way the intended meaning. Consider these steps:

1. Combine two short sentences into one.

ORIGINAL: I am a freshman in the School of Design. I am specializing in Landscape Architecture.

REVISION: I am a freshman in the School of Design, specializing in Landscape Architecture.

2. Reduce a compound sentence to a complex or simple sentence.

ORIGINAL: Gus' parrot is a vicious and ill-tempered brute, and there is not a person here who doesn't fear and avoid it.

REVISION: Gus' parrot, a vicious and ill-tempered brute, is feared and avoided by every person here.

3. Reduce a complex sentence to a simple sentence.

ORIGINAL: Henry H. Abbott, who has been a leader in campus activities and scholarship, is admired and respected by every other student.

REVISION: Henry H. Abbott, a leader in campus activities and scholarship, is admired and respected by every other student.

4. Reduce clauses to phrases.

ORIGINAL: The voters balked at approving a stadium which cost 250 million dollars.

REVISION: The voters balked at approving a stadium costing 250 million dollars.

5. Reduce clauses and phrases to single words.

ORIGINAL: When the train stalled on the crossing, a line of motorists waited in a frantic state.

REVISION: When the train stalled on the crossing, a line of motorists waited frantically.

ORIGINAL: Rocky Top was shrouded in a haze like the color of smoke.

REVISION: Rocky Top was shrouded in a smoke-colored haze.

conc

50a

6. Reduce two or more words to one.

. . . a member of a club.

. . . a club member.

. . . an instructor in the Department of Mathematics.

. . . a mathematics instructor.

. . . are going to attend.

. . . will attend

7. Change nouns into related verbs.

Many verbs change to related nouns (so-called *nominals*) by adding suffixes: *approve* becomes *approval,* *consider* becomes *consideration,* and so on. When these nominal forms follow *have, be,* and some other verbs, words can be cut by removing the verb and replacing it with the verb form of the noun.

ORIGINAL: Sula *had hopes* that the dean would *give approval* to the plan she had *brought to completion.*

REVISION: Sula *hoped* that the dean would *approve* the plan
she had *completed.*

8. Where possible, eliminate *there is, there are.*

It is often possible to shorten sentences beginning with these
words.

ORIGINAL: *There are* three genders in English.

REVISION: English has three genders.

ORIGINAL: *There were* four students nominated for class
president.

REVISION: Four students were nominated for class
president.

ORIGINAL: In the library *there are* many reference books to
help you.

REVISION: The library has many reference books to help
you.

Study the following series of reductions. The first statement
contains nineteen words; the last contains seven words. Has the
last omitted any essential information included in the first?

1. In the distance we could see the tops of the Rocky Mountains.
   These mountain tops were covered with snow.

2. In the distance we could see the tops of the Rocky Mountains,
   which were covered with snow.

3. In the distance we could see the Rocky Mountains, which
   were covered with snow.

4. In the distance we could see the Rocky Mountains, covered
   with snow.

5. In the distance we could see the snow-covered Rocky Mountains.

6. In the distance we saw the snow-covered Rocky Mountains.

7. We saw the distant, snow-covered Rocky Mountains.

conc

50b

50b. Cut unnecessary details and superfluous words.

Some comedy shows include a long-winded character whose
speeches, full of unnecessary details, amuse the audience but irritate

other characters. Don't put your readers in the position of those characters; if your sentence extends to tedious length, its details obscure or weaken its point:

> We want to thank you for your communication letting us know about your change of address, and we are pleased to tell you that we have made the necessary changes on the company records so that we shall send you all future mail at the correct address. [From a life insurance company letter]

Freed of unnecessary wordiness and detail, this sentence says:

> Thank you for sending us your new address. We've noted the change on our mailing lists.

EXERCISE 24

Look up in a good dictionary the following nouns: *brevity, circumlocution, curtness, diffuseness, periphrasis, pleonasm, prolixity, redundancy, sententiousness, succinctness, tautology, terseness, verbiage, verbosity*. Write definitions and give examples of any five.

EXERCISE 25

Look up in a good dictionary the following adjectives: *compendious, concise, diffuse, laconic, pithy, prolix, redundant, succinct, summary, terse*. Write definitions of any five.

EXERCISE 26

Study several of your own recent papers. Can you make one of them more concise and effective by following the recommendations given in Section 50? Suggestion: Select five wordy sentences and make them more concise.

EXERCISE 27

Make the following more concise:

1. I remember two things I did that first night of college. They were getting acquainted with my new roommate and watching TV in the dormitory lounge.
2. I waited for the signal which would indicate that the hunt had begun. I did not hear it, however. The dogs were all barking and the horses

were stamping their feet. Between the barking of the dogs and the stamping of the horses all other sounds and noises were drowned out.

3. There are two main highways leading into and going through Brookville. They are Highway 41, running south from Chicago to Florida, and Highway 28, running northeast and southwest.

4. When I arrived at the doctor's office, I noticed that he had a beautiful reception room. The room was furnished with modern furniture and with a warm-colored carpet on the floor and with soft, soothing colors on the walls.

5. Our city now has a new park that was opened not long ago. The land which it occupies was, not long ago, just a piece of swamp and wasteland which has since been drained, filled in, and leveled off.

VI.
The Paragraph

A *paragraph* is a group of sentences that seem to belong together. As a *unit of thought,* a paragraph can present a single, clear purpose that is more or less complete in itself, or it can serve as one of a series of sentence-bundles developing a larger thought. The paragraph is also a *visual unit.*

Good paragraphing is essential for clarity and effectiveness. Logically separated groups of sentences help you plot your course and see the progress you are making. They also help your readers by making the structure and development of your ideas clear and readily understandable.

Paragraphing is visual in that it separates certain ideas from others, thus furnishing readers with signposts or road markers. A series of carefully constructed paragraphs develops separate ideas in such a way that readers, following signs laid out, can quickly and clearly grasp the parts and the whole that they constitute.

Readers easily tire unless a page of writing is broken up into smaller units. The sign of the paragraph, *indentation,* is a helpful visual lure to readers. They feel that they have completed a section of writing and can go on to another unit. Some books, magazine articles, and even short stories are divided into chapters or sections, not so much to keep closely related ideas or parts of the action together as to furnish a "breathing space."

The following list presents eight desirable characteristics of paragraphs. If your paragraphs possess these qualities, they will show that you have carefully checked your writing. If they do not, they will reveal that you have been guilty of insufficient or careless thought and revision. Note, however, that these characteristics apply only to *expository* paragraphs, the kind that you will most likely be writing. In published prose, especially short stories, novels, and much descriptive writing, paragraphs appear that do not exhibit these characteristics, or at least show only some of them.

Each of these characteristics of effective expository paragraphs is explained and illustrated in later sections. As you study Sections 51–60, refer to this list from time to time.

1. A good paragraph concerns itself with *a single controlling idea,* one that is either expressed or implied.

2. A good paragraph contains a *body of thought,* not a mere fragment. The well-developed paragraph is never sketchy or incomplete.

3. A good paragraph must be unified. *Singleness of purpose* is essential; irrelevant detail must be removed.

4. A good paragraph contains full material in *proper order.* The sentences in it are so arranged that they clearly develop a controlling idea in a logical, understandable progression.

5. A good paragraph is *well proportioned.* If the thought of the paragraph is important, the paragraph should be so completely developed that the reader can readily understand the significance of the thought. If the paragraph discusses an idea, or a group of related ideas, of comparatively less importance, the size of the paragraph reveals the difference in weight.

6. Good paragraphs are of *varying length.* This statement implies what was just said about proportion; it also means that a series of short, choppy paragraphs, or a group of very long ones, should usually be avoided. It does *not* mean that all your paragraphs should be of "medium" length.

7. A good paragraph contains *transitional aids.* The thoughts within a paragraph should be linked to show orderly progress, and the passage from one paragraph to another should be clear.

8. A good paragraph is *mechanically correct.* It is conventionally indented; it contains the words that belong with it, not with the preceding paragraph; in dialog, it correctly represents every change of speaker.

51. The topic statement

51a. The central idea of a paragraph is usually stated in a single sentence.

Most expository paragraphs contain a topic sentence that sets forth or sums up the central idea of that paragraph. This *topic sentence,* although so called, may not be a "sentence" at all. It is the statement containing the controlling idea, which may be expressed in various forms: (1) as one of the clauses in a compound sentence; (2) as the main clause of a complex sentence; (3) as a phrase within the sentence; (4) as a single word; or (5) as a short, simple sentence—usually the most effective kind of topic sentence.

Not every well-constructed paragraph contains an expressed topic sentence, but every good expository paragraph either contains or implies one. The reader, reflecting, can sum up the central thought of the paragraph in his or her own "topic sentence." However, consideration for the reader is an argument in favor of actually expressing the topic.

When you begin a paragraph with a topic sentence, you make a commitment about what you are to discuss and you arouse the reader's expectations. If your paragraph is successful, it will fulfill the promise in your initial sentence and satisfy the reader. Consider how the following paragraph achieves both objectives. The topic sentence is shown in italics.

With his telescope Galileo made some important astronomical discoveries. For instance, he discovered that there are satellites around the planet Jupiter. He saw that the moon was not flat, as people commonly believe, but that it had high and low areas, and he even calculated the height of some of its mountains. The Milky Way revealed itself to him as a vast collection of stars, and by studying sunspots he reached the conclusion that the sun rotates. [After the topic sentence, the remainder of the paragraph *tells what* important discoveries were made.]

51b. The position of the topic sentence can be varied.

The usual position of the topic sentence, as in the foregoing example, is at the beginning of the paragraph. In a paper of three or four paragraphs, each could begin with a topic sentence. But a topic, or thesis, sentence can be moved around to afford variety. It would be easy to put the topic sentence about Galileo's telescope at the end of the paragraph:

Galileo was the first man to discover that there are satellites around the planet Jupiter. He saw that the moon was not flat, as people commonly believe, but that it had high and low areas, and he even calculated the height of some of its mountains. He perceived the Milky Way as a vast collection of stars, and by studying sunspots he reached the conclusion that the sun rotates. *Thus, with his telescope Galileo was able to make some important contributions to astronomy.*

Notice that here the topic sentence is used to sum up the paragraph rather than to introduce it.

When the topic sentence is placed within the paragraph, the sentence or sentences before it are usually introductory:

Many people have heard about the famous Leaning Tower of Pisa, but few know that Pisa also has a university of ancient origin. In about the year 1580 its most illustrious student was

¶
top

51b

a mathematical genius named Galileo Galilei, who was soon to invent the hydrostatic balance, a thermometer, and a proportional compass. *But Galileo's greatest invention was his telescope, which enabled him to make some significant contributions to astronomy.* It was this instrument that made it possible for Galileo to discover satellites around Jupiter, the unevenness of the moon's surface, and the fact that the Milky Way is a vast collection of stars. By studying sunspots, he was also able to infer the rotation of the sun.

Here is a paragraph in which the topic "sentence" is a noun clause in the first sentence, is repeated in the third sentence, and is stated again, in different words, in the sixth:

What makes an airplane fly is not its engine nor its propeller. Nor is it, as many people think, some mysterious knack of the pilot, nor some ingenious gadget inside. *What makes an airplane fly* is simply its shape. This may sound absurd, but gliders do fly without engines and model airplanes do fly without pilots. As for the insides of an airplane, they are disappointing, for they are mostly hollow. No, *what keeps an airplane up* is its shape— the impact of the air upon its shape. Whittle that shape out of wood, or cast it out of iron, or fashion it, for that matter, out of chocolate and throw the thing into the air. It will behave like an airplane. It will *be* an airplane.

—WOLFGANG LANGEWIESCHE

¶
top

51c

51c. A paragraph may be built around an implied central idea.

It is sound advice to phrase a topic sentence for every paragraph you write, but occasionally you can omit it provided the paragraph tracks around a central idea. Here is such a paragraph:

Among the great men of the Renaissance, many were artists, like Raphael, Titian, Michelangelo, Van Dyke, and Rembrandt. Others were poets, such as Spenser, Shakespeare, Tasso, and Ronsard. Still others were pioneers in science: Galileo and Kepler in astronomy, for instance, and Vesalius and Harvey in medicine.

The implied topic sentence here is, "The Renaissance produced many creative people in different fields."

EXERCISE 1

Select an essay from one of your textbooks and pick out the topic sentence (or state the implied topic sentence in your own words) of each of the *first three* paragraphs. What is the position of each in the paragraph? If the sentence does appear, what kind of sentence or partial sentence is it? If it doesn't appear, explain how you determined what it was.

EXERCISE 2

Write two expository paragraphs of between 75 and 100 words each, choosing any *one* of the following topic sentences. In your first paragraph, put the topic sentence at the beginning. In your second, place it toward the middle or at the end. Be sure to use the *same* topic sentence for both paragraphs.

Jorge is a backseat driver.

Here's the best way to buy a secondhand car.

Going steady has its disadvantages.

Student government in this college is [is not] a farce.

Failing to protest injustice is a form of cowardice.

The Hippocratic Oath might better be called the hypocritical oath.

52. Development

¶
dev

52

The secret of effective writers—if they may be said to have a secret—is their ability to form a thought, no matter how vague or fragmentary, and then to develop it so that it is clear, helpful, and meaningful to readers. In other words, *the heart of effective expository writing is paragraph development.*

Haven't you frequently made a statement or written a sentence and then halted, aware that the thought needed expansion and that it seemed bare and incomplete? Discovering what to say or write in order to complete a thought is the core of the writing process. It's what first-year English is all about. It's what any course in expository writing and most courses in speaking are all about.

Suppose, for instance, that in thinking about a job you recently had, this idea comes to mind: "Break time is the most important part of the worker's day." This is a satisfactory topic sentence, but it can hardly stand alone without some explanation and expansion. After some thought, you might develop a paragraph with enough substance to explain to your readers what you mean:

> *Most employees* work toward a paycheck, but on a daily basis they *work toward break time.* A few minutes off changes the rhythm of the workday, breaks tedium into pieces, and contains a measure of civility that separates people from the machines they operate and the paper they handle. Some rush to the coffee machine; some to the nearest pizza place; some trade news and gossip; some spread their coffee and cake on tables in a restroom. No matter what individuals do, everyone relishes a brief chance to be a person and not a cog in an industrial machine.

Paragraphs are most often ineffective not because their central ideas are weak but because their substance, their content, is thin, meaningless, or just plain uninteresting. Getting something to say about an idea, to flesh it out, requires mental activity. "Robin is fun loving and good natured" is an adequate central thought, a satisfactory topic sentence. Developing the idea in that sentence is something else again. Neither repetition of the idea nor vague generalizations will build a good paragraph of solid substance upon it and around it. What to do? Look at Section 52a.

52a. Gather material from your own thoughts and experiences.

Your own curiosity, observation, imagination, and reflection can provide useful developing details. You may think your experiences and thoughts are unimportant and worthless, but actually they are alive and significant precisely because they belong to you. They are not the secondhand comments and impressions of someone else but are really a part of the essential you. Only *you* know how, and in what ways, "Robin is fun loving and good natured." Your observations of Robin in action, your thoughts about her, can and will help you develop this concept. For example, you can *relate* how Robin "picked up" a dull party that seemed to be dying, how through sheer good spirits she got everyone into a receptive mood, ready and eager to enter into the spirit of a lively evening. Or you can *contrast* the good-natured reaction of Robin when made the butt of a practical joke with the angry or sour attitude of Lucile in a similar situation. Or you can *define* what you mean by "fun loving" or "good natured" or both, making specific references to Robin's mannerisms and personality as you do so.

52b. Draw upon the experiences of others.

Your own immediate resources will be insufficient for developing certain ideas with which you have had little or no experience and about which you may have thought not at all. But you can draw upon the experiences and observations of others as revealed in conversation, television and radio programs, books, motion pictures, newspapers, magazines, and lectures. You probably have had little direct contact with, say, the problems of emerging nations in Africa. But you can put others' ideas about these nations through the hopper of your own mind. Phrased in your own words, ideas picked up from outside sources will put flesh on the bare bones of a basic thought.

Suppose that a friend has just returned from a trip abroad and has told you of the difficulties in keeping straight the various currencies needed to buy postage stamps of varying denominations. A thought flickers in your mind: Why not an international postage stamp? A student recently wrote the following paragraph, one developed by stating the advantages suggested in the italicized topic sentence:

> *Wouldn't it be a good idea to have an international postage stamp, available for purchase and use at any post office anywhere in the world?* Such a stamp would save travelers both time and money, not to mention the relief it would provide in dealing with strange currencies. Businesses with foreign connections would find it a boon. Most importantly, such a stamp might be helpful in bringing more closely together scores of countries in this troubled world.

52c. Avoid already obvious statements.

You will accomplish nothing more than boring your readers if you tell them what they and everyone else know. One student, asked to write about a magazine he read regularly, wrote this paragraph:

¶
dev

52c

This magazine has several kinds of articles. Among them are articles about sports and food. Each article is by a different writer. Some articles are more interesting than others. Most of them are pretty good.

Instead of interesting his readers, he evoked yawns by writing choppy sentences, failing to provide details, and not revealing what the topic sentence stated.

52d. Avoid needless repetition of the topic sentence.

Repetition that adds nothing to the main idea is merely thought going around in circles. No matter how varied the words you use, meaningless repetition is flabby and monotonous. Notice how the topic sentence is echoed again and again in this ineffective paragraph:

> *Some people pay too much attention to material things.* They spend hours thinking about ways to make money and more hours about ways to spend it. Their greatest concern is clothes, meals, travel, and the money required to get these things. Giving so much attention to food, shelter, and clothing is plain silly. They should pay attention to more important matters.

That "some people pay too much attention to material things" is probably a fact, but it is also a generalization. Badly needed for the development of this general idea are specific *details* and definite *facts* (statements of occurrences that can be, and possibly have been, verified by others). For example:

1. A woman spends several days a week shopping for the latest styles and designs in imported clothes.
2. A man frankly says that he "lives to eat" and is more interested in a city's restaurants than in its libraries, museums, religious centers, sports spectacles, concerts, or anything else it has to offer.
3. A group of people, the so-called "jet set," wander from country to country in search of the latest and the smartest in clothes, food, and entertainment.

Each of these three statements of facts and details can be developed into an effective paragraph or series of paragraphs.

EXERCISE 3

Develop *one* of the following topic sentences into a substantial paragraph (about 100 words) based wholly on your own experience:

1. Anyone can learn to —— [dance, swim, skate, or whatever].
2. I am accident prone.
3. During the game last Saturday my most embarrassing experience occurred.
4. Once I scored a minor triumph.
5. Junk food can cause trouble.
6. I was not fit, mentally or physically, to take any kind of examination.

EXERCISE 4

Develop *one* of the following topic sentences into a substantial paragraph (about 100 words) based on material drawn from the experiences of others or from what you have read:

1. Alcoholism is an illness, not a moral weakness.
2. Tailgating is a dangerous practice.
3. Jumpy starts affect a car's mileage rating.
4. The packaging of a product plays an important role in its sales.
5. Most of the country is still served by a handful of TV stations.
6. The boundaries of power between Congress and the President have always been disputed.

EXERCISE 5

¶
dev

52d

What are the weaknesses of each of the following paragraphs? How would you revise each to give it more substance and interest?

1. The police force is made up of brave people. They have to risk their lives every day. Several in this city are killed each year in the line of duty. They have to work in all kinds of weather. They get good pay and deserve all they get.
2. When I'm awakened by a fire siren, I don't get angry. I realize that the fire might be in a tenement where people are desperate, and the sound of the alarm lets them know that help is coming. Besides, when I'm in the country, I don't get upset when frogs and birds wake me up early.
3. The government ought to help everyone who wants to go to college and hasn't enough money. The government should give needy high school graduates money for books and tuition and also for room and board if they go to college away from home. By helping them get

through college, the government would have more educated people to help run things in future years. Because this is a great advantage, the government should help everyone who wants further education.

53. Methods of development

Paragraphs may be developed in several ways. No one way is necessarily better than another. All should have one purpose in common: to make the reader see exactly and fully the point made in the topic sentence or implied by the paragraph as a whole. Often writers can achieve this purpose best by using a combination of methods. When they begin a paragraph, they do not tell themselves that they will use this or that method but let their central idea determine the best way to make the reader visualize and understand it.

The only sure test of the substance of a paragraph is that of communication. *Define,* if the terms you use are not clear; *give instances and examples* of the concept you have in mind that will relate to your reader's experience and understanding; *compare or contrast* the idea expressed in your topic sentence with something that you can be reasonably sure the reader already comprehends; *explain in detail* if the idea is difficult to understand.

An illustration: A student was recently reading about attempts of scientists to launch people into interstellar travel. In the article he read, plans and preliminary steps to this end were being ridiculed, and it occurred to the student that, throughout history, daring thinkers and discoverers have been laughed at or disregarded by their contemporaries. He also recalled that many of those who have been ridiculed have later come to be accepted as great because of their eventual success. Such reflection enabled him to come up with a topic sentence: *Shortsighted people ridicule what they cannot understand.* After further thought and much reading, he developed the following paragraph. It uses a series of *instances and examples* to convey the idea expressed in the italicized topic sentence and ends with a sentence that is both a summary and a transition (see Section 56) to a following paragraph.

History follows a pattern of first denouncing great discoveries only to honor them after the discoverers themselves have been destroyed or ridiculed by their detractors. For centuries, men have honored the

meth

53

teachings of Socrates as preserved in the *Dialogues* of Plato, but the man himself was condemned to death for corrupting youth with his novel ideas. Lee de Forest was prosecuted for using the mails to defraud because he wrote that his vacuum tube "would transmit the human voice across the Atlantic." And this was as recent as 1913! Daguerre, the creator of photography, was committed to an insane asylum for insisting that he could transfer a likeness to a tin plate. The automobile was opposed because agriculture was felt to be doomed by a vehicle that ate neither oats nor hay. Stephenson's locomotive was denounced on the grounds that its speed would shatter men's minds and bodies. The eminent Sir Walter Scott called William Murdoch a madman for proposing to light the streets of London with coal gas, and the great Emperor Napoleon laughed off the idea as a "crazy notion." Some churchmen argued against the plan as being blasphemous, since God had divided the light from darkness. And some physicians insisted coal-gas lights would induce people to stay out late and catch cold. Who are the heretics and madmen of today who will be honored and acclaimed a decade or century from now?

Paragraphs are most frequently developed by the use of

1. instances or examples
2. particulars and details
3. division
4. definition
5. comparison or contrast
6. reasons or inferences
7. cause and effect
8. combination of methods

¶
meth

53a

Each of these methods is explained and illustrated in the sections that follow.

53a. Develop a paragraph by instances or examples.

Writing a series of sentences that provide instances or examples of the more general statement in the topic sentence is a common and effective method of developing a paragraph. The following paragraphs illustrate this plan:

Actually, there is no evidence that people who achieve much crave for, let alone live, eventful lives. The opposite is nearer the truth. One thinks of Amos the sheepherder, Socrates the stonemason, Omar the tentmaker. Jesus probably had his first revelation while doing humdrum carpentry work. Einstein worked out his theory of relativity while serving as a clerk in a Swiss patent office. Machiavelli wrote *The Prince* and the *Discourses* while immersed in the dull life of a small country town where the only excitement he knew was playing cards with muleteers at the inn. Immanuel Kant's daily life was an unalterable routine. The housewives of Königsberg set their clocks when they saw him pass on his way to the university. The greatest distance Kant ever traveled was sixty miles from Königsberg.

—ERIC HOFFER

The italicized thesis sentence is clear and understandable, but Hoffer uses seven instances or examples to make his central thought not just understandable but memorable. Anyone reading this paragraph is certain to relate to one or more of the persons mentioned: Amos, Socrates, Omar, Jesus, Einstein, Machiavelli, and Kant. Enough is said of each person to nail down the thought of the topic sentence: that not one of these great achievers either wanted or lived an eventful life.

The latest aberration in the American pursuit of happiness is the feelgood movement. The country is swarming with swamis from Asia, quacks from California, and evangelists of sexual joy, narcotic paradise, communal contentment, and dining ecstasy. Psychologists who can whip off a quick volume of tips on how to feel good 24 hours a day adorn the best-seller lists. In the warm baths surrounding Disneyland West, gurus of feelgood preside over group gropes aimed at squeezing the nasty wrinkles out of psyches yearning for a peace ineffable.

—RUSSELL BAKER

Notice that the second sentence of this paragraph names three kinds of people (swamis, quacks, evangelists) and mentions four ways of seeking happiness (sexual joy, narcotics, communal living, dining pleasure). The third and fourth sentences each name another group of people who attempt to profit from a desire of persons to "feel good." Instances and examples fulfill the promise of the topic sentence.

The odd ways in which checks have been written are a reflection of the foibles of those who make them out. This was symbolized a few years ago when a check for $1,000, painted on the side of a 134-pound watermelon, was drawn against the account of the Parker County (Texas) Melon Growers Association to pay a contestant on a television show with the appropriate title, "People Are Funny." Then there was the sailor stationed at San Diego who was plagued with requests for money from home. In desperation he engraved a check on a piece of battleship plate with a blow torch and sent it home, confident that the annoying requests would now stop. At the end of the month, though, the steel check came back with his other canceled checks, with a proper endorsement on the back—also made with a blow torch. And recently a Connecticut perfume company drenched its checkbooks with samples of its product, printed the word "scent" instead of "cent," and the words "pay to the odor of" the customer.

—"TOPICS," *The New York Times*

This paragraph offers three examples to justify the statement of the topic sentence. They provide sufficient detail to enable the reader to agree that the checks written were indeed "odd."

53b. Develop a paragraph with particulars and details.

This method of development involves naming and explaining specific details relating to the topic sentence.

Of course, men have endocrine problems. They may suffer thyroid disease, infertility, impotence, Addison's disease, diabetes, pituitary disease, and a host of other endocrine ailments to which we are all heir. But they often serve effectively in high jobs and high office. John Kennedy had a serious hormonal disorder, adrenal insufficiency. Everyone who lives long enough deteriorates physically. By the time a man is old enough to be within hailing distance of the Presidency, you can be sure he has something the matter with him. His blood vessels, his stomach, and anything else aren't what they were when he was sixteen.

—ESTELLE RAMEY

This paragraph of *particulars and details* does not differ greatly from those supplying *instances and examples*. The author follows up the topic sentence with a list of *particular* illnesses and then cites the *example* of President Kennedy. The last three sentences supply *details* about the common physical plight of aging males.

¶
meth

53b

In the first of the following paragraphs, the author is discussing football. The paragraph is taken from an essay entitled "Freudian Football," a satirical comment on what may be called "football fever" and the enormous pageantry displayed at "big" games.

In the second paragraph, Packard is discussing "serial mating," one suggested way of meeting the challenge of changing social and sexual attitudes. Notice that the basic term given in the topic sentence is supplied with synonyms; then particulars and details are provided about this kind of "modern" marriage.

> *In these rites the egg of life is symbolized by what is called "the oval,"* an inflated bladder covered with hog skin. The convention of "the oval" is repeated in the architectural oval-shaped design of the vast out-door churches in which the services are held every Sabbath in every town and city, also every Sunday in the greater centers of population where an advanced priesthood performs. These enormous roofless churches dominate every college campus; no other edifice compares in size with them, and they bear witness to the high spiritual development of the culture that produced them.
>
> —THOMAS H. FERRIL

> *Sometimes it is called serial monogamy, sometimes serial polygamy, sometimes consecutive polygamy.* But the basic idea is pretty much the same for all. It would assume a turnover of partners over the 50-odd years that a man and a woman can expect to live after they first consider marriage. Swedish sociologist Joachim Israel suggested that 4 or 5 marriages might be about par for a lifetime. The mood behind such proposals was summed up by a New York model when she said, "Why lie to yourself? We know we're not going to love one man all our lives." Among others, a psychologist–social worker in California, Virginia Star, has advocated the adoption of renewable marriage contracts. She suggests the contract lapse unless renewed every 5 years.
>
> —VANCE PACKARD

meth

53c

53c. Develop a paragraph by analyzing the divisions suggested by the topic sentence.

In this method, a writer calls attention to two or more parts of the topic. If each part is expanded in considerable detail, separate paragraphs would be advisable.

For the last few years I've noticed two trends in literature about the future. Journals like *Audubon Magazine, Sierra Club Bulletin,* and *Cry California* are generally concerned about imminent ecological disaster—the death of canyons and valleys, the end of whales, big cats, eagles, falcons, pelicans, and even man. The magazines popularizing science, such as *Popular Science* and *Popular Mechanics,* speak of the technological Utopia of the future—a television screen attached to every telephone, a helicopter on every rooftop, and sleek supersonic transports for the fortunate few within them who cannot hear their sonic boom. The two kinds of journal seem oblivious of each other and mutually exclusive. Yet there is a connection: The more we strive to reach the popular science future, the more likely we are to achieve the ecological disaster.

—GARRETT DE BELL

The italicized topic sentence makes it clear that the paragraph will be developed by a discussion of the *two* trends in futuristic literature that De Bell has noticed.

In the next two extracts, the first is fleshed out by comment on *two* kinds of snobbishness, the second by details concerning the *three* New Yorks that the author has discerned.

There are two kinds of snobbishness. That of the man who has a good many opportunities and looks down on those who lack them is recognized by all. The other kind of snobbishness is rarely understood, yet it is real. It is that of the self-made man who glories in his success in overcoming difficulties and admires greatly people who have achieved the things he considers of importance.

—ELEANOR ROOSEVELT

¶ meth

53c

There are roughly three New Yorks. There is, first, the New York of the man or woman who was born here, who takes the city for granted and accepts its size and its turbulence as natural and inevitable. Second, there is the New York of the commuter—the city that is devoured by locusts each day and spat out each night. Third, there is the New York of the person who was born somewhere else and came to New York in quest of something. Of these three trembling cities the greatest is the last—the city of final destination, the city that is a goal. It is this third city that accounts for New York's high-strung disposition, its poetical deportment, its dedication to the arts, and its incomparable achievements. Commuters give the city its tidal restlessness; natives give it solidity and continuity; but the settlers give it passion. And whether it is a farmer arriving from Italy to set up a small grocery store in a slum, or a young girl arriving from a small town in Mississippi to escape the indignity of being observed by her neighbors, or a boy arriving from the Corn Belt with a manuscript in his suitcase and a pain in his heart, it makes no difference: each embraces New York with the intense excitement of first love, each absorbs New York with the fresh eyes of an adventurer, each generates heat and light to dwarf the Consolidated Edison Company.

—E. B. WHITE

53d. Develop a paragraph by definition.

This way of developing a paragraph involves answering the implied question of a reader, "What do you mean?" A conventional definition has three parts: the *term,* the *genus,* and the *differentia.* That is, a term is placed in the class or kind to which it belongs (genus) and is then distinguished from other members of its genus: "Braille (the term) is a system of printing or transcribing (genus) in which the characters are represented by raised letters (the differentia)."

Most definitions are less formal and exact than this. You can define something that you are discussing by using synonyms, by mentioning examples or instances of the term, by telling what something is not, or by comparing and contrasting the term with something known and familiar.

Here are three examples of paragraphs that define, that tell what is indicated in the topic sentence. In the first, Tigner defines *science* by listing the steps of scientific discovery. In the second, Fischer defines *ecology* by telling what studying it can do for you. In the third, Keller defines *love* by comparing it with well-known aspects of nature.

Science is a method of knowledge that arose and first proved its usefulness within the realms of mechanics, physics, and chemistry. In essence it is remarkably simple. The first step is to discover the pertinent facts. Next, you make a guess as to the law which accounts for these facts. And finally, you test the correctness of this guess by experiment. If your experiments do not verify the first guess, you admit that you were wrong, and make another guess. And so on, until you have found a piece of demonstrable knowledge, or demonstrated that the truth with regard to that particular matter is so far unknown.

—HUGH STEVENSON TIGNER

All these courses are really branches of a single science. *Human ecology* is one of the youngest disciplines, and probably the most important. It *is the study of the relationship between man and his environment,* both natural and technological. It teaches us to understand the consequences of our actions—how sulfur-laden fuel oil burned in England produces an acid rain that damages the forests of Scandinavia, why a well-meant farm subsidy can force millions of Negro tenants off the land and lead to Watts and Hough. A graduate who comprehends ecology will know how to look at "what is going on in the world," and he will be equipped to do something about it. Whether he ends up as a city planner, a politician, an enlightened engineer, a teacher, or a reporter, he will have had a relevant education. All of its parts will hang together in a coherent whole.

—JOHN FISCHER

"*Love is something like the clouds that were in the sky before the sun came out,*" she replied. Then in simpler words than these, which at that time I could not have understood, she explained: "You cannot touch the clouds, you know; but you feel the rain and know how glad the flowers and the thirsty earth are to have it after a hot day. You cannot touch love either; but you feel the sweetness that it pours into everything. Without love you would not be happy or want to play."

—HELEN KELLER

¶ **meth**

53e

53e. Develop a paragraph by comparison or contrast.

An idea can be made clear by showing the likeness or unlikeness of the topic to something that is already familiar to the reader. In practice, comparison and contrast are often combined in the same paragraph; in the third of the following paragraphs, cause and effect is added to comparison and contrast.

The method of scientific investigation is nothing but the expression of the necessary mode of working of the human mind. It is simply the mode at which all phenomena are reasoned about, rendered precise and exact. There is no more difference . . . between the mental operations of a man of science and those of an ordinary person than there is between the operations and methods of a baker or of a butcher weighing out his goods in common scales and the operations of a chemist in performing a difficult and complex analysis by means of his balance and finely graduated weights. It is not that the action of the scales in the one case and the balance in the other differ in the principles of their construction or manner of working; but the beam of one is set on an infinitely finer axis than the other and of course turns by the addition of a much smaller weight.

—THOMAS H. HUXLEY

Men will have to give up ruling-class privileges, but in return they will no longer be the only ones to support the family, get drafted, bear the strain of power and responsibility. Freud to the contrary, anatomy is not destiny, at least not for more than nine months at a time. In Israel, women are drafted, and some have gone to war. In England, more men type and run switchboards. In India and Israel, a woman once ruled. In Sweden, both parents take care of the children. *In this country, come Utopia, men and women won't reverse roles; they will be free to choose according to individual talents and preferences.*

—GLORIA STEINEM

White America is basically a middleclass society; the middle class sets the mores and the manners to which the upper class must, when it wishes influence, seek to conform, at least in appearances, and which the lower class struggles to attain or defensively rejects. *But dark America,* of the rural and of the urban Negro, *has been automatically assigned to be a lowerclass society;* the lower class sets the mores and manners to which, if the Negro upper class wishes influence, it must appeal; and from which the Negro middle class struggles to escape. As long as this chasm between white and dark America is allowed to exist, racial tensions and conflict, hatred and fear will spread. The poor are always alienated from normal society, and when the poor are Negro, as they increasingly are in American cities, a double trauma exists—rejection on the basis of class and race is a danger to the stability of society as a whole. Even though Negroes are a minority in America—approximately one-tenth of the population—a minority that is sick with despair can poison the wellsprings from which the majority, too, must drink. The social dynamics of the dark ghettos can be seen as the restless thrust of a lower-class group to rise into the middle class.

—KENNETH B. CLARK

53f. Develop a paragraph by reasons or inferences.

When a topic sentence states a general opinion, particularly a debatable one, it is good sense to support that statement by (1) giving reasons for the assertion or (2) drawing inferences from facts that are presented.

> *Our citizens will have to learn at least one foreign language.* The reason is not so they can sell things to Brazilians, or study German medical books, or appreciate those beauties of Homer which are lost in translation. Nor is it because they will gain satisfaction in recognizing the Latin roots of the word *satisfaction.* It is not even because grubbing for roots is good discipline. It is because they cannot understand their own language unless they have studied another. The native of any country is immersed in his own language and never sees it as a linguistic structure. He cannot learn what he ought to know about language from talking about his own.
> —ROBERT M. HUTCHINS

> *Sexual stereotypes are not to be identified with sexual or innate differences, for we know nothing about these matters.* John Stuart Mill was the first man (since Plato) to affirm that we could know nothing about innate sexual differences, since we have never known of a society in which either men or women lived wholly separately. Therefore, he reasoned, we can't "know" what the pure "nature" of either sex might be: What we see as female behavior, he maintained, is the result of what he called the education of "willing slaves." There is still no "hard" scientific evidence of innate sexual differences, though there are new experiments in progress on male hormones of mice and monkeys. Other hormonal experiments, especially those using adrenaline, have indicated that, for human beings at least, social factors and pressures are more important than physiological ones.
> —FLORENCE HOWE

¶
meth

53f

If we look at the world around us, we see that *love has become a rare commodity, spontaneous warmth all but quenched, laughter is heard only through the television tubes.* We are bound together by our humanity yet dare not look one another in the eye for fear we will see some part of ourselves reflected there, some part in need that frightens and repels us. We give our help to the children in the form of gadgets, our help to one another in the form of alcohol, trinkets, and gestures. Why is it that we can no longer be human and love and weep and laugh and relish making fools of ourselves? For we long to do these things, we long to be more human, to put more into life, get more out of life. It is as if we are going through life on tiptoe, never really experiencing it; life passes by like a painless and bland movie when we long to sink our teeth into its being. Why can't we? What has happened to us? What has been done to us?

—LISA HOBBS

53g. Develop a paragraph by cause and effect.

In this kind of paragraph development the topic sentence suggests a conclusion (effect) drawn from data. These data make up the supporting material of the paragraph. Or, conversely, if the topic sentence states a cause, developing material deals with the effects or results of that cause.

Tragedy was a Greek creation because in Greece thought was free. Men were thinking more and more deeply about human life, and beginning to perceive more and more clearly that it was bound up with evil and that injustice was of the nature of things. And then, one day, this knowledge of something irremediably wrong in the world came to a poet with his poet's power to see beauty in the truth of human life, and the first tragedy was written. As the author of a most distinguished book on the subject says: "The spirit of inquiry meets the spirit of poetry and tragedy is born." Make it concrete: early Greece with her godlike heroes and hero–gods fighting far on the ringing plains of windy Troy; with her lyric world, where every common thing is touched with beauty—her twofold world of poetic creation. Then a new age dawns, not satisfied with beauty of song and story, an age that must try to know and to explain. And for the first time tragedy appears.

—EDITH HAMILTON

The central thought of this paragraph is that tragedy began in ancient Greece when thinking people came to believe that evil is an essential part of all life. This realization was the *cause* of the writing of tragedy.

Women in our society complain of the lack of stimulation, of the loneliness, of the dullness of staying at home. Little babies are poor conversationalists, husbands come home tired and sit reading the paper, and women who used to pride themselves on their ability to talk find on the rare evening they can go out that their words clot on their tongues. As the children go to school, the

¶
meth

53g

mother is left to the companionship of the Frigidaire and the washing machine. Yet she can't go out because the delivery man might come, or a child might be sent home sick from school. The boredom of long hours of solitary one-sided communication with things, no matter how shining and streamlined and new, descends upon her. Moreover, the conditions of modern life, apartment living, and especially the enormous amount of moving about, all serve to rob women of neighborhood ties. The better her electric equipment, the better she organizes her ordering, the less reason she has to run out for a bit of gossipy shopping at the corner store. The department stores and the moving-picture houses cater to women—alone—on their few hours out. Meanwhile efficient mending services and cheap ready-made clothes have taken most sensible busy work out of women's hands and left women—still at home—listening to the radio, watching television.

—MARGARET MEAD

In the thesis sentence the author states a general *effect:* In our society, dullness, loneliness, and lack of stimulation are the lot of women. She then develops this thought by listing specific *causes,* dividing these causes into those connected with husbands and children and those associated with what the author calls "conditions of modern life."

The birth of a volcanic island is an event marked by prolonged and violent travail; the forces of the earth striving to create, and all the forces of the sea opposing. The sea floor, where an island begins, is probably nowhere more than fifty miles thick—a thin covering over the vast bulk of the earth. In it are deep cracks and fissures, the results of unequal cooling and shrinkage in past ages. Along such lines of weakness the molten lava from the earth's interior presses up and finally bursts forth into the sea. But a submarine volcano is different from a terrestrial eruption, where the lava, molten rocks, gases, and other ejecta are hurled into the air through an open crater. Here on the bottom of the ocean the volcano has resisting it all the weight of the ocean water above it. Despite the immense pressure of, it may be, two or three miles of sea water, the new volcanic cone builds upward toward the surface, in flow after flow of lava. Once within reach of the waves, its soft ash and tuff are violently attacked, and for a long period the potential island may remain a shoal, unable to emerge. But, eventually, in new eruptions, the cone is pushed up into the air and a rampart against the attacks of the waves is built of hardened lava.

—RACHEL CARSON

¶ meth

53g

397

53h. Develop a paragraph by a combination of methods.

Each of the methods explained so far is useful, and examples of all of them can be found in every published essay or article. Many paragraphs, however, do not follow a single method but use a combination of methods. The following is one example of methods in combination. For the sake of reference, a number is assigned to each sentence: (1) topic sentence; (2) amplification by contrasting statement; (3) cause; (4) effect, again contrasting statement; (5) illustration. As a whole, the paragraph supplies reasons to support the topic statement, but, as you can see, it does so in more than one way.

(1) The people have no tradition of outsiders and no procedures for handling them. (2) They are not hostile, but they are suspicious and afraid of them. (3) History has proved that to talk to strangers sooner or later leads to trouble or ends up costing money, and so history has rendered them incapable of telling truths to outsiders. (4) They don't lie, but they never of their own will provide the truth. (5) There are people in Santa Vittoria who are capable of denying knowledge of the town fountain when it can be heard bubbling behind their backs.

—ROBERT CRICHTON

Actually, each of the illustrative paragraphs in Sections 53a–g uses more than one method of development. For example, look at the first illustrative paragraph in Section 58e. The major means of development is *comparison* and *contrast*, but notice that the paragraph also uses *definition, instances* and *examples,* and *reasons* and *inferences.* (Check back through this section if your understanding of these terms is not clear.)

Now that you are aware of the various ways of developing the central idea of a paragraph, turn again to the student-written illustration near the beginning of Section 58: "History follows a pattern . . ." Does this excellent paragraph make use of more than one method of development?

EXERCISE 6

Develop *one* of these sentences into a paragraph through the use of *instances* or *examples:*

Driving on icy roads is dangerous.

Parents can make mistakes, too.

A professional person who is agreeable can get away with not knowing very much about his or her profession.

EXERCISE 7

Develop *one* of these sentences into a paragraph through the use of *particulars* and *details*. (Use instances or examples, too, if you wish. And at least two of the sentences will require comparison and contrast.)

I've found that high school and college are quite different.
Professional ice hockey resembles mayhem more than it does sport.
Jim is the most prejudiced person I know.

EXERCISE 8

Develop *one* of these sentences into a paragraph through the use of *division:*

At least these three important qualities a good teacher should have.
There is more than one reason for getting enough rest and recreation.
Solar energy has several advantages.

EXERCISE 9

Develop *one* of the following sentences into a paragraph through the use of *definition:*

What do I mean by "common sense"?
What you just did was not a practical joke; it was a mean trick.
Habit is everyone's flywheel.

¶ **meth**

53h

EXERCISE 10

Develop *one* of the following sentences into a paragraph by using *comparison* or *contrast:*

My life today is very different from what it was a year ago.
Luella and I have different goals in life.
Getting a good job is one thing; getting ahead on the job is another.

EXERCISE 11

Use *reasons* or *inferences* in developing *one* of these sentences:

Admitting to college everyone who wants to go can create many problems.

Selling military hardware to undeveloped nations is a debatable policy. Lending money to friends can turn them into enemies.

EXERCISE 12

The following paragraph by Joyce Cary develops the topic sentence "Every age, they say, has its special bit of nonsense" by concentrating on "modern nonsense" about "the mass man." Development is primarily through the use of particulars and details.

Every age, they say, has its special bit of nonsense. The eighteenth century had its noble savage and the nineteenth, its automatic progress. Now we have this modern nonsense about the "mass man." We are all told constantly that people are becoming more and more standardized. That mass education, mass amusements, mass production, ready-made clothes, and a popular press are destroying all individuality—turning civilization into a nice, warmed, sterilized orphan asylum where all the little lost souls wear the same uniforms, eat the same meals, think the same thoughts, and play the same games.

Write a paragraph explaining yet another bit of modern nonsense by means of a different set of particulars and details. Consider such ideas as our absorption in automobiles *or* addiction to TV *or* desire to look young *or* reliance on patent medicines.

¶
meth

53h

EXERCISE 13

The following paragraph by George Orwell is developed by means of cause and effect:

But this sense of guilt and inevitable failure was balanced by something else: that is, the instinct to survive. Even a creature that is weak, ugly, cowardly, smelly, and in no way justifiable still wants to stay alive and be happy after its own fashion. I could not invert the existing scale of values, or turn myself into a success, but I could accept my failure and make the best of it. I could resign myself to being what I was, and then endeavour to survive on those terms.

Phrase a topic sentence about some failure that you have experienced socially or at school or work. In a developing paragraph, indicate the causes of that failure or its effects, or both.

54. Unity

No matter how you build a paragraph, every sentence in it should contribute to its central thought. Paragraphs should possess singleness of thought and purpose.

The key to paragraph unity is the controlling idea. When you develop a paragraph, concentrate on the topic in hand and don't let it slip away. However pleasing a momentary thought may seem, if it leads you into any sentence, or even so much as a phrase, that has nothing to do with where you began, put it out of mind or save it for a different paragraph.

54a. Omit material that is unrelated to the main thought of the paragraph.

Lack of unity is ineffective. Why? Readers who have been following you down one line of thought will be puzzled and annoyed to come across a statement that has no relationship to what they have just been reading.

One way to test for unity is this: ask yourself how each sentence relates logically to the central thought. If you can't explain the connection, discard the idea. If you discard too much, find other material that does show a relationship. If you can't bear to throw away material, save it for a paragraph in which it will make a unified fit.

In this student-written paragraph, the italicized sentence destroys unity. The offending sentence is a perfectly good one; it simply doesn't belong here and should be placed elsewhere.

Our government is primarily one of lawyers and bureaucrats who seem to feel that any attempt to root out gobbledygook is an attack upon their own livelihood. The present tax law, a creation of lawyers, is gleefully enforced by bureaucrats. *The Social Security Act was passed in 1935 and has had several major amendments since then.* Since nobody, including lawyers, knows exactly what our tax code means, lawyers can enjoy never-ending litigation.

The following paragraph illustrates careless violation of paragraph unity. The first two sentences deal with patent examiners; the last four deal with patent office models. Suggested improvement: The two paragraph topics might have been expanded, each in its own paragraph.

(1) One thousand examiners, trained both in science and in law, examine some 80,000 patent applications in Washington each year. (2) This work is done in an atmosphere of academic calm behind the tall white columns at the north end of the U.S. Department of Commerce, of which the Patent Office is a part. (3) The Office no longer has its great tourist attraction, the collection of models. (4) Since 1870, models have not generally been required to accompany applications. (5) However, there are 200,000 of the models in a museum at Plymouth, New Hampshire, and others in the Smithsonian. (6) The Patent Office itself displays only a handful, such as a keyboard violin, an earlier air conditioner with miniature blocks of ice, and a burglar alarm shaped like a watchdog.

Carefully analyze this paragraph:

There are many superstitions all over the world. In some foreign countries like New Guinea, superstitions have more meaning to the people than they do here in the United States. Many people believe in superstitions to the extent that they would stake their lives on them. However, the other group of people disbelieve in superstitions. I am one of these people who disbelieve them, and I am proceeding to tell why I do.

The first sentence states the controlling idea, the *topic* of the paragraph. Each of the following four sentences deals in some way with superstitions, but not one of them bears on the topic itself. Not only that; no one sentence is directly related to any of the others. Each of the five sentences might well be used in a paper on superstition, but not all in the same paragraph.

¶
un

54a

EXERCISE 14

How and why do the following paragraphs lack either unity or full development or both? Which sentences in each paragraph don't belong?

1. (1) My father tried to tell me when I bought the car that I would have trouble with the engine, but I did not listen. (2) I had so much trouble with the engine that I decided to sell my car.

2. (1) Greater New York City contains several main divisions. (2) Orig-

inally, the city was confined to Manhattan Island, but it has enlarged through consolidation of other divisions. (3) The city consists of five boroughs—Manhattan, Brooklyn, Queens, Richmond, and the Bronx. (4) Manhattan is the heart of New York and contains its great commercial, financial, and mercantile institutions, and also its famous museums, libraries, cathedrals, railway stations, and imposing apartment houses. (5) Brooklyn is a residential district with a large number of industrial establishments. (6) Staten Island is mainly residential, while Queens, containing more than one-third of the total area of Greater New York, is the "home" borough. (7) Running through some of these divisions are many famous thoroughfares. (8) The best-known is Broadway, which is lined with fashionable shops, beautiful churches, elegant clubs, and immense hotels. (9) Most of the great transatlantic lines have their piers in the Hudson River.

3. (1) Thanksgiving is always a happy time at my home. (2) This is the time of year to be thankful for all the things we have in this country. (3) Thanksgiving was first started by the Pilgrims during the time of the foundation of our country. (4) The Pilgrims left England in September 1620 and arrived at Plymouth in November. (5) They had a long, hard winter; many died. (6) But the following year was prosperous, and in gratitude to God they celebrated the first Thanksgiving with prayers and a bountiful feast. (7) They invited many Indians to the feast. (8) At Thanksgiving our family is always together for at least one time during the year. (9) Sometimes we have friends in for dinner; at other times we have a large family reunion. (10) When all of the relatives are present, everyone has a wonderful time.

55. Order

¶
ord

55

Hasty and inaccurate thinking causes not only a lack of paragraph unity but also a disorderly arrangement of sentences. Because our minds do not always work logically, we may write ideas as they occur to us, as they flow or drift into our stream of consciousness; we may place ideas ahead of the place where they belong or forget them and add them later in the paragraph. Anyone who has attempted to tell a long story or has heard one told ("Oh, I should have said . . ." or "I forgot to say . . .") knows how easy it is to get ideas in the wrong order.

In a well-written paragraph each sentence leads clearly to the one that follows. Related parts are kept together; one part of the thought is finished before another is begun.

55a. Arrange sentences in a clear, orderly sequence.

Sentences in a paragraph, like chapters in some books, should show clear progress or a readily understandable forward movement of some sort. Several kinds of arrangement are possible: Which one to use depends on the subject of a paragraph and the effect you are trying to create. Four major kinds of arrangement (order) are available: time order (chronology), space order, general to particular, and particular to general.

1. Arrangement by chronology (progress through time).

Sentences follow one another in the order of the events narrated, the steps of a process, or the description of something that involves passage of time, as, for example, a sunrise, a sunset, or the approach of a storm. For instance, if you are writing a paper about a typical day, you might begin with what you do upon getting out of bed and proceed with an account of eating breakfast, going to school, and attending classes. This material would be followed by mention of lunch, afternoon classes and sports, outside work, return home, an evening meal, and before-bedtime activities.

Explanations of a process also tend to arrange themselves in time order. The following paragraphs, written by an enterprising student who worked after school hours as a plumber's apprentice, contain sentences written in time order:

> When a sink, bathtub, lavatory, or shower drains slowly or not at all, the cause is an accumulation of grease, hair, or other debris lodged somewhere in or near the drain.
>
> First, try cleaning with a rubber force cup. This device also goes by the name of "plunger" or "plumber's friend." It should have a flat, wide face so as to make contact with the almost flat fixture bottom.
>
> Run an inch of water into the basin. Remove the stopper (if there is one).
>
> Stop the overflow outlet with a wet cloth. (This will keep the plunger pressure from bypassing the clogged area and escaping through the outlet.) Place the force cup directly over the drain. Plunge it down and then pull it up, firmly and rhythmically building up force. Then pull the plunger off the opening to draw up the stoppage.

If plunging has not worked after several tries, use a chemical drain cleaner. If this does not remove the debris, use an auger, also known as a "plumber's snake." Rotate the auger into the drainpipe so that it can cut its way through the stoppage.

If the drain is still clogged, remove the plug at the bottom of the trap. Insert the snake at the trap. If the trouble persists, remove the entire trap to locate the clog.

And then—and then—telephone for a plumber.

2. Space order (arrangement by physical point of view).

In space order, details are arranged from near to far, left to right, inside to outside, top to bottom, and so forth. Many descriptive paragraphs follow this order: descriptions of a building, a landscape, a painting, and many other objects. If, for example, you are describing a building, you should not shift carelessly and without warning from the back to the front of it, or from the outside to the inside, or from one floor to another. Your readers will be confused if they think you are writing about the front of a building and suddenly, without proper transitional aids, you begin to comment on a picture in one of the rooms or TV antennas on the roof.

In the following paragraph, the author is standing on an elevation from which she can overlook a valley. The description moves *right,* then *left,* then *straight ahead* and then *farther and farther away* from where she is standing:

> *On my right* a woods thickly overgrown with creeper descended the hill's slope to Tinker Creek. *On my left* was a planting of large shade trees on the ridge of the hill. *Before me* the grassy hill pitched abruptly and gave way to a large, level field fringed in trees where it bordered the creek. *Beyond the creek* I could see with effort the vertical sliced rock where men had long ago quarried the mountain under the forest. *Beyond that* I saw Hollins Pond and all its woods and pastures; then I saw in a blue haze all the world poured flat and pale between the mountains.
>
> —ANNIE DILLARD

¶
ord

55a

3. General to particular or particular to general order.

Employing this form of order, a writer makes a general statement and follows it with details, or states an effect and then cites causes, or names a term and then explains it. Look once again at the illustrative paragraphs in Section 53. Note especially those that illustrate paragraph development by the use of reasons or inferences (Section 53f); those that mention a cause and follow with an effect (Section 53g); and those that start off with a general statement and follow with details (Section 53b).

Consider this paragraph by Joyce Cary:

> *What I suggest is that no kind of education, however narrow, can produce the mass mind.* The reason is that minds are creative, that thoughts wander by themselves and cannot be controlled by the cleverest police. All education is free in this sense; it cannot be shut up within walls. To teach people to think, if only to make them more useful as soldiers and mechanics, is to open all thoughts to them—a whole world of new ideas. And though the dictator may wish to think of them as a proletariat, they have already begun to leave the proletariat.

The first sentence makes a general statement and is followed by clearly logical supporting details: an inference drawn from reasons.

In the following paragraph from James Harvey Robinson's essay "On Various Kinds of Thinking," specific details lead from supporting details to a general statement:

> On the 28th of October, 1831, three hundred and fifty years after Galileo had noticed the isochronous vibrations of the lamps, creative thought and its currency had so far increased that Faraday was wondering what would happen if he mounted a disk of copper between the poles of a horseshoe magnet. As the disk revolved an electric current was produced. This would doubtless have seemed the idlest kind of experiment to the stanch businessmen of the time, who, it happened, were just then denouncing the child-labor bills in their anxiety to avail themselves to the full of the results of earlier idle curiosity. But should the dynamos and motors which have come into being as the outcome of Faraday's experiment be stopped this evening, the businessman of to-day, agitated over labor troubles, might, as he trudged home past lines of "dead" cars, through dark streets to an unlighted house, engage in a little creative thought of his own and perceive that he and his laborers would have no modern factories and mines to quarrel about if it had not been for the strange, practical effects of the idle curiosity of scientists, inventors, and engineers.

¶
ord

55a

EXERCISE 15

What sentences seem out of order in the following paragraph? What sentences don't belong here? How would you rearrange the sentences?

(1) Since this is a theme on dictionaries, I have looked up some material on dictionaries and their background. (2) The first dictionary aiming to give a complete collection of English words was published in 1721 by Nathan Bailey, and was called *The Universal Etymological English Dictionary*. (3) This book was also the first in English to trace the derivation of words and to mark the accents as an aid to pronunciation. (4) The greatest American lexicographer was Noah Webster. (5) His dictionary was published in 1828 and has been repeatedly revised. (6) It provided features such as illustrations, synonyms, abbreviations, and other helpful additions. (7) The earliest Greek and Latin dictionaries did not contain all of the words of the language, but instead contained the more difficult words and phrases. (8) Samuel Johnson published a dictionary in London in 1755; he had married a woman some twenty years older than he was. (9) A pronouncing dictionary was prepared by Thomas Sheridan; he was the father of Richard Brinsley Sheridan, who wrote a number of plays and gave some speeches in Parliament. (10) The earliest dictionary was written in the seventh century B.C. and was printed on clay tablets. (11) The dates and specific information about these dictionaries were taken from a reference book I have.

EXERCISE 16

Arrange the sentences in the following paragraph to make them more effective.

(1) A hot rod can also be called a custom-made car. (2) It has a custom-made engine and a special body. (3) Most hot rods are built around stock parts from standard model cars. (4) Hot rods can do 90 to 100 miles an hour and get 20 or more miles on a gallon. (5) The car that holds the speed record can go 189 miles an hour. (6) Some of the parts used are found in auto graveyards. (7) Souping up the engine is the most important step. (8) This means tearing down the engine and adjusting the block for an easier flow of gas to the combustion chamber.

¶
ord

55a

EXERCISE 17

Rearrange the following sentences to make the paragraph more effective:

(1) The view at Lookout Point was spectacular. (2) As far as one could see were mountains. (3) Closer by, off to our right, rose enormous cliffs, from one of which cascaded a waterfall that disappeared

into the chasm below. (4) It was amazing to think that we had driven up so high along that winding road. (5) It was so quiet that we could hear the roar of the water. (6) To our left was a deep, wooded gorge. (7) Way down below we could see the roof of the hotel we had left that morning. (8) As it was midsummer, I was surprised to see there was still snow on some of the highest peaks.

EXERCISE 18

For each of the following paragraphs indicate the kind of *order* and principal *method* of development used.

Nature is a wonderful artist. Along with April's showers in the spring of the year, she shows her first hint of the fantastic and beautiful show that is to come. Early flowers burst into color and early birds begin tuning up for the symphony that will soon be summer. Then, as suddenly as if it were turned on, summer arrives. A tree with a "nest of robins in its hair," a brook babbling its light air, the wind rustling its feet in the grass—all make a symphony scored thousands of years ago. Yet this song has never grown old. In the fall of the year, however, nature shows her real colors. The leaves on the trees turn shades from red to violet, and the pace of nature's song quickens as the winds expand her summer life. Then, more suddenly than when she came on the stage in April, she becomes passive. With the first snow of winter, animate Nature goes to sleep to rest for the next year's show.

—STUDENT THEME

Much of the slang in common use today comes ultimately from characters on the other side of the law. This will be recognizable, for example, in words relating to American money. For "money" in general we have such terms as *dough, lettuce, the green* or *the big green, folding stuff,* and various others. The different denominations all have their slang terms: *singles* or *fish* for one-dollar bills; *fin* for a five; *sawbuck* for a ten and *double sawbuck* for a twenty; *C-note* or *century* for a hundred; *grand* for a thousand. All of these are old, well-weathered terms and are familiar to many people who wouldn't dream of holding up a drugstore. But it is clear that they have their highest frequency in those districts where policemen would prefer to go in pairs. —PAUL ROBERTS

¶
tran

56

56. Transition

Transition means "passage or change from one position or stage to another." In writing, transition involves showing evidence of the links between related units (sentences and paragraphs). This evidence—a word, phrase, clause, or sentence—may link sentences and even paragraphs. A paper is coherent when its parts are tied together.

Even though a paragraph contains plentiful substance, it will not make sense to a reader if the sentences are loosely joined or disconnected. It is easy to assume that a reader will understand our shifts in thought, whereas we ought to be aware that if we fail to express the hidden connectives that appear in our thinking we are causing confusion.

Relating one sentence in a paragraph to another often requires the use of transitional words. Have you noticed that some teacher or other speaker is particularly easy to understand because he or she constantly relates one thought to another by using such transitional devices as *however, on the other hand, for example, similarly, conversely,* and the like?

Transitions resemble highway signs: "Detour: 100 Yards"; "Sharp Curves Ahead"; "Slow Down: End of Pavement"; "Form Single Lane"; "End of Construction." Such signs prepare one for changing conditions. Transitional expressions have precisely the same effect on the reader. For example, when you complete a paragraph, you can use a transitional word or phrase to let the reader know what is coming next. When you finish a group of paragraphs dealing with one phase of a topic, you can inform the reader that another topic is being taken up. Sometimes, you can sum up what has been written; more often you can point out the road ahead. Such indications are a help to the reader and a major aid to clearness and effectiveness.

¶
tran

56a

56a. Use transitional expressions when they are needed within a sentence, between sentences, and between paragraphs.

Important as transitions are, they should be brief and inconspicuous. Largely a mechanical feature of style designed to make the machinery run smoothly and easily, any transitions that are used should not distract the reader's attention from ideas. Since transitions reveal relationships, transitional devices are inherent in the material, should grow out of the nature of the material, and need to be put into words that are adequate to show already existing relationships. In a well-constructed paragraph, few transitional devices are needed.

Devices that accomplish bridging or linking include the following:

TO ADD AN IDEA: besides, also, moreover, in addition, another way, a second method, further, furthermore, similarly, and then, again

TO CONTRAST IDEAS: but, yet, nevertheless, still, however, in contrast, on the contrary, instead, otherwise, on the other hand, whereas, unlike, yet

TO COMPARE IDEAS: like, similarly, equally, correspondingly, in like manner, likewise.

TO SHOW RESULT: therefore, thus, consequently, as a result, hence

TO SHOW TIME: then, afterwards, later, meanwhile, at last, thereafter, now, earlier, immediately, henceforth, before, formerly, at the same time, simultaneously

TO SHOW FREQUENCY: often, frequently, sometimes, now and then

TO INDICATE SUMMARY: in conclusion, to sum up, to conclude, in brief, finally

An entire sentence may be used transitionally. Also, coherence may be gained by repeating words at the close of one paragraph and the beginning of another. Note the italicized expressions in the following examples:

. . . This concludes the author's comments on taxation. *But taxation* is not the only problem she discusses. [Repetition]

. . . Thus we may say that he is a splendid specimen, physically. *On the other hand,* his mentality is of a low order. [Entire sentence]

. . . The valence of certain elements varies in different compounds. *But let us first discuss the valence of two common elements,* oxygen and hydrogen. [Repetition]

Sometimes the shift in thought between two paragraphs, or two groups of paragraphs, is so marked that a word, phrase, or sentence is not sufficient to indicate the transition. In such a situation a short transitional paragraph may be used to give a summary of what has been said and suggest what is to follow. Note the italicized paragraph in the following example:

> There are three primary essentials to the good composition: correctness, clearness, and effectiveness. If a theme lacks any one of these elements, it is not a good theme; if it lacks more than one, or lacks any one to an unusual degree, it is a very poor paper.
>
> *These elements, then, are the* sine qua non *of the good theme. It now remains for us to define each of these terms and apply them to such matters as diction, punctuation, and sentence structure.*
>
> A good theme must be correct in its diction. Correct diction implies . . .

Paragraph connection may be faulty because the writer fails to give needed information. For example, in a descriptive paper, one paragraph may end with a description of the exterior of a house, and the next may begin with a discussion of the view from an upstairs room. What happened? Did the writer move? Or one paragraph may discuss the industry of the Belgians, and the next may begin: "Thus, we see that they are a warlike nation of people." The reader properly asks why. Does industry cause a martial spirit? A gap has been left in the thought and must be filled in with, perhaps, a statement that industry has resulted in a need for raw materials and that this need has fostered a desire to acquire territory containing these materials.

Good writing is always characterized by skill in the revelation of thought relationships. Transitional aids are indispensable to writers who wish fully to communicate their thoughts, and the exact shadings of their thought, to readers.

¶

tran

56b

56b. Repeat a key word or a variation of a key word.

Repetition of a word in successive sentences or even in the same sentence can effectively link the parts of an idea. Linking can also be accomplished by using a closely related word or a different form of the word a second time. Notice the italicized words in these passages from John Steinbeck's *The Grapes of Wrath:*

One of the greatest disappointments of *childhood* is a *broken* promise. An adult who *breaks* his word never fully regains a *child's* confidence.

They knew it would take a long time for the *dust* to settle out of the air. In the morning the *dust* hung like fog, and the sun was as red as ripe new blood. All the day the *dust sifted* down from the sky, and the next day it *sifted* down.

Here are other examples of effective repetition of key words:

There is tolerable *traveling* on the beaten *road,* run how it may; only on the new *road* not yet leveled and paved and on the old *road* all broken into ruts and quagmires is the *traveling* bad or impracticable.

—CARLYLE

Raphael paints wisdom, Handel sings *it,* Phidias carves *it,* Shakespeare writes *it,* Wren builds *it,* Columbus discovers *it,* Luther preaches *it,* Washington arms *it,* Watt mechanizes *it.*

—EMERSON

56c. Certain adjectives and pronouns may be used as transitional aids.

The demonstratives *that* and *this* can be effective transitional aids when used sparingly and accurately. [Be especially careful to use *this* to refer not to an entire previous statement but only to a clearly identified noun. (See Section 13h.)] Pronouns are common transitional aids in all kinds of writing, especially that in which people are involved (short stories, novels, biographies). Notice the use of demonstratives and pronouns in these student paragraphs:

Abraham Lincoln once remarked that people do not have a satisfactory definition of the word "liberty." That statement is true. Lincoln pointed out that for some people the word meant doing what one pleased with oneself and one's labor. Others, he commented, thought it meant doing whatever one pleased with other men and their labor. What one group would call *liberty* another would call *tyranny.* This is the kind of confusion that we have today with words such as "freedom," "progress," and "license."

Plants are organisms of the vegetable kingdom. They may be as complex and large as a tree or as simple and small as one of the algae. Plants perform photosynthesis, and therefore they are the source of food and of most oxygen. For their growth, all plants need light, water, oxygen, carbon dioxide, and varying amounts of other elements and substances. Organic matter from many of them is found in coal and petroleum. These facts about plants suggest why they are essential to all of us.

EXERCISE 19

Pick out all the transitional expressions in one of your recent compositions. How do they compare with those listed in Section 56a?

EXERCISE 20

List the transitional devices used in each of the following paragraphs:

The snow began to fall in tiny, hard flakes that nestled on the roof of the car. At first we paid little attention; however, we realized before long that we were in for trouble. In the first place, my worn rear tires began to lose traction. Of course, this was not serious yet, but it would be in time. The snow, as I said, was hard and made sand-like drifts on the road, which we began to slide in. Moreover, the fall was so heavy that my headlights seemed to be shining against a dazzling white wall. This blindness, fortunately, was not as serious as it would have been were the road not deserted. We would, as a matter of fact, have been glad to risk hitting an occasional car just to have some company. As a result of our loneliness and increasing nervousness, Jim and I chatted away like a couple of old gossips. But we were not fooling each other one little bit. Just the same, the idle conversation was better than plowing along in tense silence. Perhaps it made me drive better. Fortunately, the lights of the Greenville gas station suddenly glowed through the whiteness. We were, in short, safe again.

The method of scientific investigation is nothing but the expression of the necessary mode of working of the human mind. It is simply the mode at which all phenomena are reasoned about, rendered precise and exact. . . .

You will understand this better, perhaps, if I give you some familiar example. You have all heard it repeated, I dare say, that men of science work by means of induction and deduction, and that by the help of these operations, they, in a sort of sense, wring from nature certain other things which are called natural laws and causes, and that out of these, by some cunning skill of their own, they build up hypotheses and theories. And it is imagined by many that the operations of the common mind can be by no means compared with these processes, and that they have to be acquired by a sort of special apprenticeship to the craft. To hear all these large words you would think that the mind of

¶
tran

56c

413

a man of science must be constituted differently from that of his fellow men; but if you will not be frightened by terms, you will discover that you are quite wrong, and that all these terrible apparatus are being used by yourselves every day and every hour of your lives.

—THOMAS H. HUXLEY

57. Length

No definite rule for paragraph length can be given. About the average length, however, something can be said. Length should always vary with an author's subject. If the subject is analytical, philosophical, or scientific—one that demands full concentration from readers—the paragraphs will tend to be longer than those in a popular magazine designed to be read rapidly. In the former, the average length of paragraphs might be 400 words; in the latter, the longest rarely exceeds 150 words. In "The Talk of the Town" section of *The New Yorker,* paragraphs vary in length from 40 to 400 words. *The National Geographic Magazine* uses numerous one-sentence paragraphs.

¶
len

57a

57a. Avoid short, underdeveloped paragraphs.

At times short paragraphs are necessary, effective, and appropriate. As a general rule, however, a short paragraph is usually an underdeveloped paragraph. Too often, writers are unwisely content with two or three short sentences. Each of the following, telling little about the key word or paragraph topic (italicized), is an example of a short, underdeveloped paragraph:

The *curriculum* in the School of Home Economics is largely basic, for students follow the same plan of study for the first two years. At the beginning of the third year, one has the opportunity to choose the option in which he or she is most interested.

We met several *interesting people* as we walked up and down the Miami beach. Often we would meet someone from home. Once we met the daughter of the mayor of Caracas.

Note the choppy effect of these short paragraphs:

As we drove north after spending Christmas vacation in Florida, the whole country seemed to take on a different atmosphere.

While the ground farther south was green, the ground near Louisville was covered with a soft blanket of snow.

The trees and bushes glittered in the sun like a jeweler's window. The telephone wires drooped with their heavy weight of ice.

The sun, as it shone on our car windows, struck the ice on the windows and seemed to send rays of light in every direction.

The failure here is not so much underdevelopment as lack of combining, (See Section 42c.) If the four short paragraphs were put together, a satisfactory paragraph would result.

57b. Avoid overly long, rambling paragraphs.

A series of long paragraphs, each running to a page or more, is likely to strain your readers' attention. Why not furnish an occasional paragraph break that will afford readers an opportunity to catch their breath and summarize the thought? Moreover, long paragraphs may contain material not belonging in them; they thus violate the principle of unity. (See Section 54.) Usually, it is difficult to write an effectively unified paragraph of over 250 words.

Variety in paragraph length is as important as variety in the length and structure of the sentences making up a paragraph. (See Section 58.) In a paper of, say, six paragraphs, two might run to 100–150 words, two might contain about 50 words, and two 75 words. Such proportions are arbitrary; in a given paper the content might call for three long paragraphs and three short ones. No paper, however, should contain any undeveloped paragraphs or a steady series of lengthy ones.

¶
len

57b

EXERCISE 21

Count the number of words in five consecutive paragraphs of some essay. How many words does the longest contain? The shortest? What is the average? Repeat this exercise for another essay by another writer on a different subject. Make a comparison of the two. What does this comparison teach about variety in the length of paragraphs?

var

58

EXERCISE 22

Compare the average length of paragraphs in an article in *The Atlantic Monthly* or *Harper's Magazine* with the average length of those in an article in *Time, People, Us, Newsweek, Esquire,* or *Reader's Digest.*

EXERCISE 23

Count the number of words in each paragraph of one of your own recent papers. How does your average compare with your findings for Exercises 21 and 22? What ideas do you get from this comparison?

58. Variety

Paragraphs are built with many kinds of sentences, but a series of similarly constructed sentences may make any paragraph seem monotonous.

No rule can be set down about how much variety the sentences in a given paragraph should have. Good writers neither count the number of words in their sentences nor consciously mix simple and compound sentences with complex ones. But they do achieve variety in sentence structure. They vary length and, occasionally, word order. They use declarative, imperative, interrogative, and exclamatory sentences. They enliven a series of sentences by using various kinds of words, phrases, and clauses as beginnings or endings.

Sentences also involve sound and rhythm. Read your paragraphs aloud to yourself. Often the ear will detect what the eye has passed over. If some of them seem halting and jerky, perhaps you have broken your thought into several short sentences that need to be combined. If the pace seems slow and lumbering, you may have combined ideas that should be expressed in shorter sentences. Your ear may also detect awkward or jarring sound combinations. If you don't trust your own voice, have a friend or family member read your paper to you.

58a. Avoid using a string of short sentences.

In the following paragraph, short sentences beat like hailstones. Not even transitional devices and the correction of a lack of unity could relieve the jerkiness and monotony of this paragraph:

> Henry Adams embarked on an intellectual career. He toured all of Europe. He gained the friendship of many great men of his time such as John Hay and St. Gaudens. All the time he was seeking reasons and rules for the actions of life. He was influenced by Darwin and Marx. He was constantly being disappointed by seeing one of his theories disproved. Adams was sincere in all the inquiry he made into the meaning and culture of humanity. His philosophy is simple and understandable. It is often untrue.

58b. Avoid using a series of lengthy sentences.

A sequence of overloaded sentences makes heavy reading. Besides crowding unrelated ideas together, prolonged sentences are difficult to read and understand. Here is how the illustrative paragraph in Section 58a would look (and not be improved) if the sentences were overloaded:

> Henry Adams embarked on an intellectual career and toured all of Europe, gaining the friendship of many great men of his time such as John Hay and St. Gaudens; all the time he was seeking reasons and rules for the actions of life, being influenced by Darwin and Marx. He was constantly being disappointed by seeing one of his theories disproved, but Adams was sincere in all the inquiry he made into the meaning and culture of humanity; his philosophy is simple and understandable, although it is often untrue.

¶
var

58c

58c. Do not begin several successive sentences in a paragraph with the same word or phrase.

Especially to be avoided is beginning a sentence with the words that end the sentence before it. Also to be watched out for are a series of sentences all beginning with *there is, there are, it was, this, that,* or *I.*

There is a large elm outside my window. There is one branch that brushes the window itself when the wind blows strongly. There is even danger that the tree will topple in a heavy wind.

I have decided to find a job. I have asked around to find out about work. I have also read the want ads. I think I'll find something before long.

Having decided to go back for more schooling, I have written to various colleges nearby. Having little money, I will have to settle on one which I can attend from home. Having this in mind, I shall probably go to a community college only five miles from home.

58d. Not every sentence in a paragraph need begin with its subject.

It is natural to begin every sentence, whether written or oral, with the subject. Occasionally departing from this practice will add variety and provide interest. For instance, if each of six sentences in a paragraph begins with the subject, switch one or two around. A sentence such as "I leaped onto my moped and pursued the speeding car down the street" can be altered to read, "Leaping onto my moped, I pursued the speeding car down the street." "Celestial navigation embraces many fields of science" can be changed to "Embracing many fields of science is celestial navigation."

Variety in paragraphs is largely a matter of variety in sentences because paragraphs are built with sentences. Yet you can also attain paragraph variety by varying the length of successive paragraphs (Section 57) using different methods of paragraph development (Section 53), and employing different kinds of order (Section 55).

¶
var

58d

EXERCISE 24

Rewrite the paragraphs given in Section 58a and 58b so that the sentences will vary appropriately in length.

EXERCISE 25

Revise the following paragraph so that it will exhibit greater variety in sentence length and structure:

When my mother bought the encyclopedia set and the bookcase to hold it, I was disappointed because it meant that I would not get the new bicycle I wanted. When I first showed Mother the picture of the bicycle in the mail order catalog, she said I could have it, as my old one, which I had bought secondhand, had a wobbly front wheel, rusty handlebars, and most of the paint chipped off the frame, but after she paid for the encyclopedia she said she couldn't afford to buy me a new bicycle and that I had to make out as best I could with the old one. When I saw my mother and my older sister taking volumes of the encyclopedia out of the bookcase and looking up different things in them, I was still annoyed about the bicycle, but after a while my curiosity got the best of me and I began to look up some things I'd wanted to know, like where Guadalcanal is and how General Custer made his last stand. When I later got my newspaper route, I saved up enough money to buy the new bicycle anyway, and I was never sorry again that we had a good encyclopedia, because I get a lot of use out of it.

59. Mechanics

The conventions of mechanical correctness in paragraphs are few and easily learned.

59a. Indent the first line of every paragraph.

¶
mech

59a

Indentation, although mechanical, is important. Indent the first line of every paragraph about an inch (or, if you type, 5 or 10 spaces). Exception: Business letters using block form usually do not indent paragraph beginnings. (See Section 78.)

The break of distinct paragraph indentation is a clear, effective aid to writer and reader in recognizing divisions of thought within the whole composition. It also aids in reading; the break serves as a signal that a distinction between separate parts of the composition is about to be made.

Use indentations of equal length for all the paragraphs in the same paper. Make no exception for numbered paragraphs.

Avoid frequent use of the marks ¶ and no ¶, meaning, respectively, "a new paragraph intended" and "no new paragraph." Preferably, recopy the entire page.

Do not indent the first line of the second page or succeeding pages unless the indentation is the beginning of a new paragraph.

59b. Do not leave part of a line blank within a paragraph.

Unless a new paragraph begins on the next line, do not leave part of a line blank within a paragraph. Blanks in lines that are not last lines of paragraphs mislead your reader, who expects such a break to finish the discussion of one phase of a subject. Margins at the left of the page should always be uniform.

59c. When writing dialog, use a new paragraph for each new speaker.

In recording conversation and writing dialog, use a separate paragraph for each speaker's words. Most of these paragraphs will be short, sometimes very short, but starting a new paragraph for each change of speaker enables the reader to keep track of who is talking to whom. When only two people are speaking, the routine speaker identifications, such as *James said, Joan asked, Bill replied,* can be kept to a minimum.

Consider the following excerpt from Poe's *The Cask of Amontillado:*

> "How?" said he. "Amontillado? A pipe? Impossible! And in the middle of the carnival!"
>
> "I have my doubts," I replied; "and I was silly enough to pay the full Amontillado price without consulting you in the matter. You were not to be found, and I was fearful of losing a bargain."
>
> "Amontillado!"
>
> "I have my doubts."
>
> "Amontillado!"
>
> "And I must satisfy them."
>
> "Amontillado!"
>
> "As you are engaged, I am on my way to Luchresi. If anyone has a critical turn, it is he. He will tell me—"
>
> "Luchresi cannot tell Amontillado from Sherry."
>
> "And yet some fools will have it that his taste is a match for your own."

60. Revision

The preceding nine sections have treated the paragraph as something separate from a composition. This distinction is artificial: A paragraph may be a complete paper in itself or part of a longer composition. Even if a composition extends for several paragraphs, its effectiveness depends largely on the effectiveness of individual paragraphs.

No matter how carefully you have prepared a paragraph, it may be faulty in some respect. Paragraph revision is important. In fact, it is essential if the completed paper is to be clear, interesting, and effective.

Before you decide that a paragraph is adequate, ask yourself these questions:

1. Is it too short?
2. Is it fully developed?
3. Does it lack support for the topic sentence?
4. Does it provide enough specific details?
5. Does it contain aids to interest, such as examples, particulars, illustrations, and dialog?

60a. Give time and thought to the revision of every paragraph.

¶
rev

60a

If time permits—and it usually does—check carefully every paragraph that you complete. You may find nothing to change. In most instances, however, you will probably wish to do some revising. You can make any or all of four kinds of revisions when you are reworking a paragraph:

1. You can *add* material.
2. You can *delete* material.
3. You can *substitute*.
4. You can *rearrange* sentences.

Even minor revisions can improve a paragraph. Consider how one student revised this paragraph:

ORIGINAL: Living in a clique may lead to prejudiced thinking. The fraternity may not allow foreign students, minority students, or students having a certain religion to pledge the fraternity. The fraternity member will not get a chance to meet these students and may get the wrong ideas about them. These rejected students will tend to cling together and worsen the problem by getting false ideas.

REVISION: The most important disadvantage of living in a fraternity is the effect that it may have on a person's mind. Living in a clique may lead to prejudiced thinking. The fraternity may not allow foreign students, minority students, or students having a certain religion to pledge the fraternity. The member will not get a chance to be in close contact with these people and may misinterpret their ideas and beliefs. The rejection of some students may lead to rejection of others of the same race, nationality, or religion and thus instill in the student an intolerant attitude for the rest of his life.

An instructor was dissatisfied with the paragraph that follows. So was the student who wrote it. After a talk with her teacher, she revised it.

ORIGINAL: Ancient peoples probably knew a lot that has been forgotten. In our rush for new discoveries, we overlook the wisdom of our forefathers and thereby lose much that might be useful.

REVISION: Knowledge once lost is all too rarely regained. We seize upon new discoveries and follow after the latest fads and notions like so many stupid sheep. For instance, we spend hundreds of millions of dollars every year for patent medicines of little value. We ought to remember that the original inhabitants of this continent knew a great deal about the curative value of herbs and medicinal roots, many of which might be more useful than drugstore potions and pills. But what North American Indians knew really died with someone's great-grandmother, and present-day scientists have to learn all over again—if they ever do. For another example, most ancients seem to have had full heads of hair. Isn't it possible that they knew a cure for baldness that has escaped modern–day scalp experts? Instead of always seeking the new, mightn't it be wise occasionally to try to rediscover what knowledge of the past could still be useful to us?

EXERCISE 26

The following paragraphs are ineffective for various reasons outlined in Sections 51–60. Try to make them more effective.

He is now a physician, but it took him many years to become one.

He was a poor boy and had to work his way through high school, college, and medical school.

He worked in a department store in St. Louis for four years while he was going to college. He made good grades while he was in college and had no difficulty in gaining entrance to a medical school.

He made his tuition money at medical college by tutoring some high-school students who lived near his room.

He is now a successful practitioner of medicine. He says that his own son wants to become a doctor and he is willing for him to do so, provided money is plentiful enough. His own experience was rather bitter, and he has no desire for his son to have to earn money while attending school.

EXERCISE 27

The following selection lacks unity, order, and suitable transitional devices. Rewrite it so that it is more effective. You may wish to add, delete, or substitute material, or rearrange the sentences.

Several hundred years ago, it was customary for European towns to hold annual fairs in their market places. To these fairs came farmers who wished to sell their products and peddlers who wished to sell their wares. Only small businessmen went to customers' homes to make sales. Large business houses hire men and women to sell wares from door to door. One day a young man came to my home. When the lady of the house appeared, he began to talk rapidly. I answered the doorbell and let him into the house. "How do you do, Mrs. Johnson? Any of the articles I have may be bought for one dollar. Each is worth more. Which would you prefer?" And he kept on and on. Finally my mother had a chance to say, "I am very busy and, furthermore, do not wish to buy anything. Please go at once." But the sale was eventually made, and the canvasser left for the next house. This type of canvasser can never amount to much, for he relies more upon the appeal of sympathy than upon salesmanship. I was sitting in a friend's home one afternoon when one of these dynamic salesmen appeared. It was a very cold day, and I had gone to see my friend in preference to playing football. He carried a small vacuum cleaner in one hand and a valise in the other. He rang the doorbell and made himself at home. He demonstrated the machine, explaining its mechanism clearly. He was close to 60 years of age, and his hair was graying around the temples. Then he compared his prospect's machine with his new one and made a trade-in offer. The gentleman's sales argument was perfect. He departed as soon as the sale was made. She accepted the offer and bought a new vacuum cleaner. He did not give the customer time to regret the purchase. Modern canvassers are indeed different from the peddlers who sold their wares in medieval times. Today in all parts of the world, especially in thickly populated districts, these modern peddlers can be found.

VII.
Composing

No one can be said to write well until he or she can compose a completed whole, an entire paper. An automobile is more than the sum of its parts: motor, electrical system, body, wheels, and so forth; a composition is more than the sum of its words, sentences, and paragraphs. Dependent though it is on its units of construction, a paper is dependent on more than these.

The first 60 sections of this book, important though they are, are primarily intended to help you write effective compositions as they are discussed in Sections 61–75. As you write whole papers you will wish to refer again and again to these first 60 sections but will wisely concentrate on the preparation of complete compositions.

Actually, you may have had little experience in writing, although you have been speaking since infancy. What you *say* and how you say it may sometimes be neither clear nor effective, yet such shortcomings rarely result from lack of practice in talking. But few students entering college have made more than infrequent *writing* efforts. The slim total may consist of an occasional composition or book report or "research" paper, a few letters, a job application or two, answers on school examinations, and the like.

When physical scientists test theories, they turn to the laboratory. When social scientists translate theories and formulas into techniques and tools, they resort to fieldwork. Chemists and biologists and sociologists and engineers and home economists use retorts, microscopes, case studies, testing machines, and demonstration homes to relate theory to reality. For those who wish to use English clearly and effectively, the prescribed laboratory work is writing papers.

Many beginning students of biology or chemistry or physics have been appalled at how rapidly their instructor set them to performing laboratory work. Such students, feeling inadequate in both knowledge and technique, might wonder how they will learn or remember hundreds of immediately needed facts.

Similarly, some beginning composition students feel unprepared to write papers because they have many facts about grammar, usage, punctuation, diction, spelling, and structure to learn or relearn, many details to keep in mind. Yet the only way to learn to write is to write; and the sooner the process is started, the quicker the design and purpose of writing become clear. When you begin to write whole compositions, you are on the way to becoming a practical and effective handler of language.

The Three Steps in Writing

If you think of writing as a single process, it will seem a difficult task. But writing is *not* a single process. The writing of anything—a letter, a composition, a report, even a memorandum—consists of three parts. Each of these parts, or steps, is dependent on the other two, but the problem of getting words on paper is simplified and made more manageable if you will approach these operations one at a time.

These three parts are (1) planning, (2) writing, and (3) revising.

Planning

If you could sit down to write *what you have thought* and not to *think what you will write,* your difficulties would be greatly reduced. That is, approach writing gradually by "prewriting," by planning ahead.

The simplest kind of prewriting may be referred to as "writing on the hoof." This form of prewriting means writing much of the time as you go about your daily activities. You are constantly tossing about ideas while walking, talking, eating, working, reading, and even sleeping. If you can pull together some of these ideas for your writing, you will be doing precisely what professional writers do constantly.

Actually, you have engaged in this type of prewriting since early childhood. Have you ever muttered any remarks to yourself before saying them aloud? Have you planned what you were going to say to someone when next you met him or her? Have you written a letter in your head many times before putting it on paper? You may not have thought of this kind of activity, this thinking ahead, as a kind of writing. And yet it is, and an essential kind, too.

It is an excellent and helpful idea to form the habit of jotting down in a notebook or diary some of the random thoughts that come to you every day. From these jottings may come solid material that you can use in papers that you write.

Prewriting in a full sense involves getting ideas, selecting something to write about, and shaping that something into a manageable topic. Prewriting also means considering what you hope to achieve, your purpose in writing. Prewriting is further concerned with the reader or readers you have in mind. A major part of the before-actual-writing stage is gathering material to develop the topic you intend to discuss. This developing material may come from many sources, *yourself most important among them.* Then comes the final step in prewriting: organizing (shaping, outlining) the ideas you have assembled.

Writing

When the basic decisions involved in prewriting have been made, you can concentrate on putting words on paper. If you have done your planning well, the writing will not be easy, but it will be much easier than you may ever have found it before. The act of writing will consist of carrying out preplanned decisions through a draft that may or may not be complete and satisfactory but will nevertheless represent a substantial achievement no matter how much your original plans are altered while you write.

In writing, you will be concerned with the beginning and ending of a paper, with its title, with the proportions of its paragraphs, with its unity and consistent tone. These matters require care and thought, but they will seem far less difficult if your preplanning has been adequately done.

Revising

When your first draft is completed, you will be ready for the final step. This step requires that you examine carefully what you have put on paper. You may wish to add a sentence here or take one out there. You may feel that the order of paragraphs should be altered. A word doesn't seem "right"; what would be a better term?

In everything anyone writes, errors or shortcomings of some sort are inevitable. No one—including skilled professional writers—can preplan, write, and revise all at one time. Even when a paper has been thoroughly preplanned and "written in one's head" many times, it is still likely to exhibit problems in thinking, in organization, in logical and sensible development, and in sentence and paragraph structure. And even if your first draft contains no flaws of these kinds, it is almost certain to reveal a few errors in spelling, punctuation, and mechanics.

Good writing is never easy, but it becomes less difficult and much more manageable if you approach it one step at a time. Keep in mind, however, that the writing process does not always occur in a linear fashion—arranged in a line. Instead, writing often involves constant repetition of the three steps of planning, writing, and rewriting. One starts with planning and then proceeds to writing and rewriting, but effective papers usually result from all three phases occurring at some point, or several points, during their composition.

In the pages that follow, Sections 61–64 will provide specific help in *planning* papers. Sections 65–72 will assist in the actual *writing* process. Sections 73–75 deal with the problems of *revision*.

"If at first you don't succeed . . ."

Sometimes during the course you may begin to lose heart. Don't be discouraged, for writing is difficult—difficult for everyone regardless of training and experience. The French essayist and philosopher Voltaire wrote:

The necessity of saying something, the embarrassment produced by the consciousness of having nothing to say, and the desire to exhibit ability, are three things sufficient to render even a great man ridiculous.

Disappointments may come as often as triumphs during first-year English. Try to accept both as a part of the effort, excitement, and, yes, fun, involved in mastering a worthwhile skill.

Also, try not to think of writing as a complicated series of *do's* and *don'ts,* a long list of *thou shalt not's.* Instead, approach writing as what it is: a useful medium that will help you communicate clearly and interestingly to and with others. What activity could be more important to you or to anyone?

61. Finding something to write about

Four basic problems are involved in all writing: getting ideas, getting material, writing, and rewriting. These steps are closely related, so closely that they may be expressed as two steps: (1) discovering what we think (or think we think) about people, places, events, and ideas; and (2) communicating our thoughts to readers. The first step is *thinking;* the second is *writing.* The two are always linked.

61a. Think about yourself.

Before writing comes thinking. Thinking itself should begin with *self-evaluation,* a basic approach to all self-expression. We need to do what a good shopkeeper does periodically: take stock.

It is difficult to get at the truth about oneself. Unearthing the facts requires digging, thinking, and careful reflecting. And when you have arrived at some truth about yourself, or what you believe is the truth, when you have evaluated what some experience or person has done to shape your thought and life, it may take courage to put on paper what you have found. All of us keep a curtain between ourselves and others; we hide behind masks; we keep to ourselves some secret part of self—even when we think we are being open. Such caution (or self-preservation) is normal; in some areas of thought and experience, it is both wise and necessary.

But how refreshing to both writer and reader to discover an honest revelation rather than a set of standard pretenses! Many papers about character and attitudes are predictable because they attempt to express what their writers think is expected rather than

comp

61a

what they really think or feel or believe. One freshman English teacher has remarked that if you remove the pronouns in most compositions, it is impossible to tell whether the writer is a man or a woman. Even if some of your innermost thoughts and feelings must be kept sacred, you should be able to reveal others without incriminating yourself.

A good place to start with self-analysis is to think about what the members of your family mean and have meant to you, what friends you have and what kind of people they are, what you have obtained from your schooling thus far, and what your ideas (or lack of them) are about religion, money, drugs, politics, love, marriage, recreation, sports, work, morals, and hobbies. The ideas you have now may change in a few months or even in a few days, but that does not matter. What is important is that you take the first step in becoming a writer, the first step in learning to communicate thoughts and feelings effectively: Find out things about yourself that, perhaps, you have never realized before.

Ten Questions to Ask Yourself

1. What are my *social* beliefs? (Do I really like people? What kinds of people? What qualities do my friends have? Do I like men better than women or women better than men? Do I like children—as a general rule, occasionally, never? Why do I hold these attitudes?)

2. What are my *religious* beliefs? (Do I believe in God? If so, am I a transcendentalist, a Baptist, a Roman Catholic? Or do I simply believe in some sort of Supreme Mind? If not, am I agnostic or atheistic? Why do I hold these beliefs?)

3. What are my *political* beliefs? (Am I interested in national and international politics? Am I a reactionary, a conservative, a liberal, a radical, or an extremist in politics? What do I mean by these terms? Why do I hold these attitudes?)

comp

61a

4. What are my *moral* beliefs? (Do I subscribe to, and practice, the "Golden Rule"? Do I believe that "Honesty is the best policy" or that "The end justifies the means"? What do I really think of the Ten Commandments as a guide for human conduct? Do I know all ten? Do I believe in the single or double standard? Do I believe in the sanctity of marriage? in romantic love? in free love? Why do I hold these attitudes?)

5. What do I want to be, and to be doing, five (ten) years from now? Why?

6. What do I expect to be, and to be doing, five (ten) years from now? Why?

7. What, for me, is the single major problem facing the world today? Why have I selected this from many possible choices?

8. What would constitute for me the greatest happiness I can imagine? the greatest disaster? Why?

9. Am I an observant person, alert to what is going on about me? Am I capable of self-analysis and criticism? Am I open-minded—tolerant of other people and their ideas? Am I capable of reflection and meditation? Am I aware of my limitations?

10. How did I get to be the way I am? What were (or are) the principal events, persons, and places that have molded my life thus far?

What you find out about yourself in considering such questions as these may disappoint, disgust, or excite you. But it is impossible to give them serious thought without having dozens of ideas occur. These ideas may be unformed and shaky, but many of them may suggest topics about which you could write with some interest and possibly some pleasure.

1. Use your mind and memory

Many people feel that their own ideas and experiences are not significant or interesting. Others show false modesty and refuse to consider subjects in terms of their own experience. Actually, personal experience provides a freshness and interest that are hard to equal. The writer's own *observation, curiosity, imagination,* and *reflection* provide material that can capture the reader's attention as very little "secondhand knowledge" is able to do.

Indeed, it is impossible for people to write wholly objectively; writers necessarily put something of themselves into everything they write. The more of themselves they put into their writing— that is, their own ideas, reactions, and observations—the more likely they are to write with interesting detail.

It is likely that your powers of observation, your curiosity, your imagination, and your willingness to reflect have not been developed fully. Freshman English gives you a chance to develop these assets and to use them in your writing.

Observation

Accurate, clear, and usable *observation* means looking at something long and carefully enough really to see what you are looking at. Most of us settle for fleeting observations, for just a surface view. We fail to pay close attention. The only person who should have difficulty in observing is one who is blind and deaf and without the ability to taste, touch, or smell. Yet many of us go through life half-dead, not really seeing and hearing what is going on around us. Without this ability to observe, we can never describe fully or effectively. With it, we have only the problem of selecting from a mass of details those that will most accurately indicate what we wish to convey. Guy de Maupassant, in telling of his apprenticeship as a writer and the assistance Flaubert gave him, wrote the following:

> Talent is enduring patience. It is a matter of looking at that which one wishes to express long enough and with sufficient attention to discover in it an aspect no one has seen. Everything has its unexplored elements, because we are accustomed to see things with the eyes of others. The least thing contains something of the unknown. Find it! To describe a blazing fire or a tree on the plain, let us live with that fire or tree. . . . This is the way one becomes original.
>
> Furthermore, having laid down the truth that in the entire world there are no two grains of sand, two flies, two hands, or two noses exactly alike, he [Flaubert] compelled me to describe an object so particularized as to distinguish it from all others of its species and class. He used to say, "When you pass a grocer seated on his doorstep, or a concierge smoking his pipe, or a cab stand, show me that grocer and that concierge in all their physical appearance and in all their moral nature so that I shall not mistake that grocer and that concierge for any other, and make me see by a single word wherein a cab horse differs from the fifty others that go before and come after him."

comp

61a

Curiosity

As children, each of us had a desire to learn and to know, but as we grew older our *curiosity*, our inquisitiveness, lessened. Most of us tend to accept (or reject) people and situations and ideas without really digging into them, without asking questions and seeking specific details. We fall back on general impressions. First-year English provides excellent opportunities for getting rid of these faulty habits.

Imagination

In a workaday, practical existence, few of us use *imagination*—our ability to form mental images of what is not actually present in real life. No workable sets of exercises exist for training the imagination of writers, yet this capacity is a rich source of writing material. Everyone daydreams, but imagination can be more immediately useful and practical than daydreaming because it can be applied to real-life people, situations, and circumstances. Try following through on such speculations as "what would happen if . . ." and "I wonder why . . ."

Reflection

Reflection is another name for careful thinking. Don Marquis, an American writer and humorist, once remarked: "If you make people *think* they're thinking, they'll love you. If you really make them think, they'll hate you." Careful thinking is hard work, but it has no peer as a source of writing material. If you give solid, prolonged thought to events in your life, to situations that surround you every day, to people whom you know and see regularly, an astonishing amount of material will appear.

2. Four idea-provoking sources

In addition to the suggestions about where to look for ideas that have already been mentioned, the following items deserve attention.

Memories

Can you recall how someone, or some place, or some idea seemed to you at an earlier time in your life? What can you remember about the day you entered first grade? the first (or most memorable) Christmas you can recollect? the most cruel (or kindest) thing anyone ever did to you? your first date? your first serious illness?

People and Places

Who is the most entertaining (or dullest or most arrogant) person you have ever known? What one person did you admire most when you were 10 years old? Whom do you admire most today?

comp

61a

What is the most beautiful (or appealing or restful) place you have ever seen? What is, or once seemed, the most shocking sight in your hometown?

Incidents and Events

What is the most appalling accident you have ever witnessed? What event in your life provided the greatest excitement? sense of achievement? biggest disappointment? worst embarrassment? Of all the incidents in your life, which one do you remember with the greatest pleasure? the most shame? If you could relive one day (or one hour) in your life, what would that day (or hour) be?

Imagination and Daydreaming

If you could be any person in the world for a day (or month), whom would you choose to be? With what one person who has ever lived would you most like to have an imaginary conversation? If you had free choice and unlimited resources, in what city or century would you most like to spend a week or a year? What is your idea of a perfect day?

None of these topics and questions is guaranteed to produce workable ideas, but your mind will probably be triggered by a few of them. What remains to be done is to test an idea to see if it is usable and then to get hold of material for its development.

61b. Get ideas from others.

Although every writer, including you, obtains material from observation, curiosity, imagination, and reflection, no one can afford to neglect the ideas and materials that can be obtained from others—unless the writer is a recognized authority on a particular topic. And even authorities discuss ideas with other experts.

1. Reading

Thoughtful *reading* will expand and intensify your own ideas and may suggest entirely new lines of thought. When thoughts and information are obtained from others, they can be reflected upon, put into the hopper of your own mind, and used with whatever original details you can add to them. True originality is not so much a matter of substance as of individualized treatment. Passing

comp

61b

on the ideas of others without acknowledgment or change is pla-giarism. Absorbing the ideas of others and expressing them in your own way is sensible and productive.

2. Listening

Every day our ears are bombarded with talk of one kind or another. If we really learn to listen, especially to people who have something to say, our own ideas will be stimulated and our knowl-edge increased. It's important to *learn to listen* as we listen to learn.

3. Conversation

Meeting and talking with others is valuable as a social activity. It is also worthwhile as a learning device because *conversation* stocks our minds and helps us develop knowledge about human nature. Conversation with a fellow student, a college employee, a propri-etor of a nearby store, a bus driver, or a cashier at a movie theater may produce useful ideas and materials for writing.

4. Interviewing

A form of conversation often overlooked is *interviewing*. You do not need to have access to famous people in order to conduct interviews. The formal interview has gradually gone out of fashion even in newspapers and magazines, but a sort of clipped version forms the basis of many television and radio talk shows. Inter-viewing a person and accurately recording what you hear is diffi-cult, but it is excellent training for the ear, the eye, and the mem-ory. It is also a prime source of material and topics for papers and reports.

5. Miscellaneous sources

Still other suppliers of ideas and information are the audiovisual media: radio and television programs, tape recordings, films, phonograph records, and works of art such as paintings and sculp-tures. Each of these is an expression of the thoughts and experi-ences of others and an excellent source of material. Using these media, you can write your opinion of and reaction to them and even why you agree or disagree with what they express. Always remember, however, to make the experiences and reflections of others your own by assimilating them thoroughly and by expressing the result in your own words. Once again; don't steal, because stealing is plagiarism. And if you borrow, be certain to mention your source or else take care to express yourself *in your own words,* not in those of the lender.

EXERCISE 1

Make a list of five incidents in your life that you think might be interesting to your instructor and the members of your class.

EXERCISE 2

List five general subjects about which you think you know specific details that are not known to your classmates.

EXERCISE 3

Prepare a brief description (written or oral) of some personal experience or of some incident that you have witnessed that could be used in developing a paper based on one of the following topics:

The Value of a Time Budget
My First Afternoon in Chemistry (or Biology) Lab
Social Clubs Should (Should Not) Be Abolished
Few Athletes Are Outstanding Students
The Library Is (Is Not) a Poor Place for Studying
Eating at a Quick-Lunch Counter
My Idea of Boredom
Why Smoking in Public Should (Should Not) Be Banned
My Town's Overuse of Energy

comp

61b

EXERCISE 4

Name a book, movie, TV show, novel, play, or magazine article from which ideas might be drawn for a paper dealing with one of the following subjects:

Underprivileged Children
Social Injustice

The Plight of Cities
Alcoholism
Safe Automobile Driving
Drug Abuse
Child Abuse
Buying on the Installment Plan
Stealing in Supermarkets
Living One Day at a Time
Sex Without Marriage

EXERCISE 5

Name and briefly describe someone you know who would be able to provide information on the subject you selected for Exercise 4.

62. Choosing a topic

The first requirement in writing a paper is to have something
to write about. But even if you have a general idea of what you're
going to develop, you need to select a specific topic. A *general
subject area* is one thing; a *topic* is another; and a *thesis* (or *purpose*)
is a third.

A *subject area* consists of a wide range of ideas, one that is too
large and unwieldy to be considered a topic. For instance, if your
assignment is to "describe an embarrassing experience," you have
been given a subject area but not a specific topic. The *topic* of a
paper is its specific subject—the question to be answered, the specific incident to be narrated, the particular person or event to be
described. The *thesis* of a paper is its point, its main idea. Thesis
and purpose are discussed in Section 63.

62a. Select an interesting topic.

This somewhat vague suggestion can be made specific. First,
does the topic interest you? It is difficult to write effectively unless
you are actually interested in the material. Vagueness, aimlessness,

dullness, and sketchiness are the hallmarks of uninterested writing; force and vigor come naturally when you like your subject.

You may not be interested in labor unions, for example, but if you have a friend who has lost her job as a result of joining or not joining a union, you are likely to write about unions with genuine interest. Perhaps you have seldom even thought about South America, but if you become friends with a Brazilian, you may discover that that continent and that country have a new interest, meaning, and appeal for you.

Of course, you will be required to write papers on topics in which you are not really interested; but when you are *choosing* a topic, select one that appeals to you. Then ask yourself, will the topic interest my readers, that is, classmates and instructor? A writer needs to spend considerable time analyzing readers' likes and dislikes, planning ways to interest them in ideas or to present ideas in which they are already interested.

It is shortsighted to argue that what seems clear and interesting to you as a writer will always appeal to your readers, for in writing to please only ourselves we frequently are too easily pleased. Most professional writers and editors have undergone an apprenticeship that has made them reasonably certain that their tastes reflect those of their readers—yet they always keep their readers in mind. If you lose sight of your reader, you may fail to communicate.

As a writer, you will never be judged by your private vision, only by that part of it which shows on paper. It is a mistake for a writer to sit around admiring his or her mental processes, extraordinary insights, and captivating ideas. Readers are not likely to be sitting around in any such admiring state. Their demand is "show me," and they are justified.

Men and women are first of all interested in themselves. This belief is not cynical so much as it is part of the law of self-preservation. Readers are constantly looking for, and interested in, ideas to which they can relate and by which they can measure themselves. We identify nearly everything that we see and hear with ourselves if we possibly can. What, for example, does anyone look for first in a photograph of a meeting that he or she has attended? What does one think about upon seeing an advertisement for a dress or suit other than "How will that look on me?" or "Can I afford it?" or "Will I like it?"

What are some other compelling ideas and interests, matters to

comp

62a

which your readers are nearly always attracted and to which their responses will usually be quick and strong? The late Joseph Pulitzer, a famed newspaper publisher and editor, once stated that the most effective topics for front-page treatment are murders, sex, wills, and how the rich spend their money. The newspaper with the largest circulation in the United States, *The New York Daily News,* adheres fairly closely to this somewhat sensational formula. In freshman English, however, you and your instructor will probably settle on other topics. The following list may suggest ideas and provide tests for measuring the appeal to others of what you have already chosen to write about:

1. Timely topics—either new ideas or recent facts, or the development of some old idea by emphasizing its relationship to recent developments.
2. People—unique, prominent, or familiar.
3. Important matters—those that involve the life and property of others and are related to the reader's own welfare.
4. Conflict—contests between people, those between individuals and nature, and internal conflicts (within the person).
5. Amusements and hobbies.

An examination of current popular magazines will provide further evidence of what apparently interests people in general. Many topics that are constantly treated in periodicals will not be good topics for you, but they do provide insights into people's tastes and concerns: health (how to get and keep it), catastrophes (everything from accidents to obituary columns), self-improvement, religion and religious or ethical experiences, relationships between the sexes, money (who has it, how it was gotten, what was done with it). With such clues to readers' interests, it should not be difficult to select appealing ideas, topics that are appealing to both you and your readers.

comp

62b

62b. Select a topic about which you know something.

Ideas and materials derived from personal experience, observation, and thought can be developed as parts of compositions or as papers complete in themselves. If you write about something you actually know, something you have thought or seen or heard, you have a head start on presenting your material effectively.

Just as one cannot expect to handle a tool or machine expertly without some previous experience, so one cannot expect to write effectively without some experience or firsthand acquaintance with the topic of the composition. John R. Tunis' books and articles on sports are based on many years of direct observation and study; Kenneth Roberts' stories of Arundel—*The Lively Lady, Arundel, Captain Caution*—came out of his personal familiarity with the Kennebunk, Maine, area; his considerable study and research; and careful observation of people. Herman Melville shipped as a sailor in 1839. Two years later he sailed around Cape Horn in the whaler *Acushnet,* and the following year he was "captured" by cannibals in the South Seas. These experiences—and his keen observation of men and the sea—he used in *Typee,* in *Redburn,* and in his great novel *Moby Dick.*

Good writers resort to their own experience for ideas—to things they know or have thought or seen or heard. Remember, however, that your own special experiences (hobbies, jobs, personal relationships, dates, parties, volunteer work, travels, and the like) are quickly exhausted as writing materials unless you can develop from them some fresh thoughts, new insights, and novel conclusions and judgments. Almost any of your particular experiences will quickly become wearisome even to you unless you can develop some awareness that has meaning above and beyond the incident itself.

Assigned the general subject of "a good friend," a freshman wrote the following account of a long-dead relationship such as you and I and millions of others have experienced. Because each of us recognizes the universality of the happening, this nostalgic account has a meaning and purpose beyond the narrative itself.

comp

62b

When I began to take stock of all the friends whom I have had, I quickly came to the conclusion that Jerry was the most important and had exerted the greatest influence upon my life. His family moved to my block when I was only 10. Jerry was 15 at the time, but the fact that he was so much older than I seemed to make no difference to him. I was highly flattered that he seemed to like me, and I haunted his house day after day. We took long walks together, on which he would tell me stories he had picked up from TV and radio programs. I suppose he changed the plots a lot and added twists of his own, but he knew what would appeal to the active imagination of a 10-year-old.

Jerry never seemed to mind giving me so much of his time and, although he had many other friends, he always made me feel that I was his special crony. He taught me all I still know about birds and flowers; he came over to read to me every day when I broke my leg and had to stay in the house for weeks. His ideas about people and moving pictures and even food and clothes were my ideas. I gradually came to feel that Jerry meant more to me than either my father or mother did. During that whole first year of our acquaintance he never said or did an unkind thing to me, and I began to look up to him as I would have to a god.

But as months rolled by, a change came in our friendship. Jerry almost stopped coming by the house, and every time I went to his or telephoned, he put me off with some excuse such as "I'm studying now" or "I've got some jobs to do for Mom." When we passed on the street, he'd still give me a warm smile and friendly wave with a "Hiya, kid," but he would hardly ever stop to talk. Finally it dawned on me that he was no longer really interested in me and that his tastes had changed. I noticed him with a girl once in a while and several times saw him all slicked up going out in his family's car on a Friday or Saturday night. I simply couldn't understand what was so great about girls, parties, dances, and big social affairs.

But what I could understand was my hurt when he finally made me know that our closeness as friends was at an end. Of course he didn't really mean to hurt me, but it was a long time before I realized that it was an age problem that caused the break. There's a world of difference between the attitudes and interests of a teenager and a twelve-year-old. Now that I'm over sixteen myself, I realize this, and the hurt I felt then has given way to happy memories of the good times we once had together.

I wonder if millions of other boys and girls have had a similar experience.

62c. Select a topic that you can handle adequately.

Make certain that the topic you choose is sufficiently limited to allow for effective development in the time you have and the length you are allowed. It is difficult, even impossible, to write an effec-

tive 500-word paper on a subject that actually would require perhaps 5000 words. If you choose a big idea and fail to limit it, you
will inevitably write sketchily and without the concreteness discussed in Section 62d. You may select a topic that is interesting to
both you and your reader and that you know something about;
yet it may not be a good paper simply because you cannot develop
it adequately within the limits prescribed. "Civil Demonstra-
tions," "Professional Football," and "The History of My Hometown" are examples of such subject areas. They cannot be treated
in a short paper; even if the paper is to be lengthy, they will require
more extended research than you can undertake.

"Aviation," for another example, is a hopelessly broad subject.
Limited to "Aviation in the United States," it would still be so
broad as to require book-length treatment. You might be able to
develop adequately a topic such as "The Career of Wilbur Wright,"
but such a composition would require considerable research and
several thousand words. If you are interested in a recent airplane
accident, you might be able to handle effectively a topic such as
"The Last Flight of ——." This problem of limiting a topic is
partly a matter of basic idea and partly one of selecting the kind
of material discussed in the next section.

62d. Select a topic that is concrete and specific.

Concrete describes something that can be perceived through the
senses: seen, heard, felt, smelled, tasted. Its opposite is *abstract,*
something that exists only in the mind. Compare the following
topics, which are divided into concrete and abstract groups, and
decide which seem more interesting to you and, more important,
would be easier to write about:

comp

62d

Abstract	Concrete
Self-Sacrifice	What Dr. Tom Dooley Did in Indochina
Working for Peace	Why Betty Williams and Mairead Corrigan Received the Nobel Peace Price
Nuclear War	Hiroshima After the Blast
Welfare Problems	Trying to Feed a Family of Six on $58 a Week

Specific means "restricted to a particular individual or situation."
Its opposite is *general,* something that applies to many things. Once

again, compare the following examples; ask yourself which you are more likely to know something about or could research in a reasonable amount of time.

General	Specific
Problems in College Athletics	Under-the-Table Payments to Athletes at State Colleges
Industrial Pollution	The Lethe River: No Swimming Allowed
Mandatory Retirement	Watching My Grandfather Sit and Stare
Buying on Credit	What the Time Payments on My Car Taught Me

EXERCISE 6

With which of the following general subject areas or topics are you comfortable? What do you know about them?

1. Effective Measures for Preventing Skyjacking
2. Government Aid to Private Schools
3. The Funding of Symphony Orchestras
4. The Funding of Rock Groups
5. The Disposal of Radioactive Wastes
6. Local Censorship of X-rated Movies
7. The Dangers of Nuclear Energy
8. Athletic Scholarships on the Basis of Need
9. The Intellectual Level of Prime-Time Television
10. Dating Customs in This Community
11. The Handling of Public Drunkenness
12. Water Pollution
13. The Selling of Armaments to Third World Countries
14. The Law and Marijuana
15. Driver-Training Courses

comp

62d

EXERCISE 7

Change each of the following abstract or general ideas to a more specific, concrete topic by focusing on a particular individual or situation. (Take another look at Section 62d.)

1. Spectator Sports
2. Property Taxes
3. Modern Life Styles
4. The Exploration of Space

5. Guerrilla Warfare
6. Animal Life
7. Slum Clearance

8. Conservation
9. College Organizations
10. Historic Places

EXERCISE 8

Apply the four suggestions for selecting topics given in this section to the following and, if requested, present your findings in an oral or written report.

An interview with a well-known personality.

An account of a visit to a law court during a criminal trial.

A history, including a description, of one of the buildings in your hometown.

A description and character sketch of one of the best-known employees of the college.

A description of a local cafeteria during the lunch hour.

A description of college "types": the athlete, the aesthete, the iconoclast, the bluffer, the grind.

A description of, and commentary on, a popular television program.

A critique of a motion picture that is currently being shown.

An account of the conversation among a group of friends after a party.

A commentary on the "easiest" and the "most difficult" courses and professors in the college.

EXERCISE 9

Examine a recent issue of some magazine that is widely circulated. You might make your choice from such periodicals as *The Atlantic Monthly, Reader's Digest, People, Us, Seventeen, National Review, Playboy, Esquire, The New York Times Magazine, Ebony,* and *Cosmopolitan.* Make an analysis (written or oral) of the different topics treated. What does your study reveal about reader interests?

EXERCISE 10

From the study you made for Exercise 9, mention one article that was most interesting to you; one dealing with a topic about which you already knew a good deal; one that developed a topic that you feel you could handle yourself. Be prepared to discuss them in class.

comp

62d

EXERCISE 11

From the following list of American holidays and special occasions, select *two* about which you have (or can easily find) detailed information that is probably not shared by your classmates. For each of the two, phrase a limited topic that interests you and that possibly will appeal to readers whom you designate.

New Year's Eve   April Fool's Day
New Year's Day   Halloween
Lincoln's Birthday   Hanukkah
International Women's Day   Christmas Day
Armed Services Day   Yom Kippur

63. Shaping and developing a topic

Getting a reasonably limited, concrete, and specific topic is an indispensable beginning. But it is only a beginning. Several tasks remain: gathering specific information about the topic, deciding exactly the purpose and the central point or thesis of the paper, and considering how best to communicate that controlling thesis to a specific reader or readers.

There should be an objective for your paper other than the completion of a required assignment, for there can be no such thing as good *purposeless* writing. How you determine your purpose will control and direct your selection of material. Every composition is a means of communicating to some clearly defined person, or group of persons, a series of thoughts, facts, or emotions. Thus, writing can be either a search for ways to accomplish a central aim or, as dull writing usually is, a setting down of words according to mechanical requirements. Simply completing a routine assignment will neither bring credit to you nor provide any pleasure for your readers.

Ask these four questions about any idea (topic) you select:

1. What special characteristics distinguish my topic?
2. What am I trying to do with it?

comp

63

3. For what specific reader(s) am I developing it?
4. How can I best convey my purpose and meaning to my reader(s)?

Your answers to these questions may be vague at first, but stick with them. Thinking about them is a form of prewriting, a valuable part of the process of self-expression. Also keep in mind three other considerations:

1. What is the required length of the paper?
2. How much do I really know about the topic?
3. Where can I get more information about it?

Your task will become simpler if you restrict the topic to some phase that can be handled properly in the number of words assigned. As has been pointed out, some topics are too general or too large to be handled in brief space.

Think the topic through in the prewriting stages and then sit down to begin writing what you have thought. If this sounds like a vague suggestion, consider the following specific ideas.

63a. Determining purpose

In a single sentence (which may or may not be included in the actual paper), state your central purpose, your controlling idea. That is, what is the *theme* of the composition? A *thesis sentence* will help you to grasp, identify, and state your central purpose. On the general subject of "Part-Time Employment," for example, you might try a plan like this:

Limited subject: "How I Got a Summer Job"
Possible title: "I Earn and Learn"
Reader: a next-door neighbor one year younger than I am
Length: 500 words
Thesis sentence: Those who plan ahead and apply early can get a summer job.

This subject is too broad to be treated fully in a brief composition, but your purpose is clearly stated: You can, through an account of your own experiences, show your neighbor how to get the summer job that he or she wants. Your basic decision has now been made; your purpose will control the choice of material to be used in your paper and the effect that that material will have on your reader. For further comment on the thesis sentence, see Section 64a.

63b. Listing details

In determining your purpose, make an inventory, an accounting, of what you know and what you will need to find out. Your list might consist of ten or more items that could be used, arranged in no particular order:

1. Qualifications for getting a job
2. Timing the campaign
3. Discovering job opportunities (want ads, government bulletins, high school or college employment office)
4. People who can help
5. Making applications
6. Preparing for an interview
7. Carrying out the interview
8. Difficulties in being interviewed
9. Following up job prospects
10. Use of supporting letters

Such a listing provides an overview of your subject. After thinking about such a list, you may decide to limit your previously stated central purpose even further and settle on the topic, "How to Find Out About Summer Jobs." You would then concentrate on item 3 and eliminate the others. Or you might concentrate on items 6–8 and confine your paper to "Being Interviewed Is Frightening" or "Tough Interviewers I Have Known." A valuable result of listing developing material is limiting a subject to manageable proportions.

63c. Consistent method of development

For the paper suggested here (a summer job), an informal narrative approach is probably best. But such a method will not work for all topics. Some ideas require definition of terms and a serious,

comp

63c

critical approach. Some require argument, reasons for and against this or that cause or action.

Some topics require humorous details; some require descriptive details; some require comparison and contrast. Whatever method you select—and remember that that is determined largely by topic and reader—be consistent in its use. Also, when you have finished writing, check to see that you have consistently maintained the method you selected. This is not to say that a paper cannot contain both humorous details and descriptive comments but that each should contribute consistently to the central purpose of the composition.

Be steadfast in your primary aim: to inform, or amuse, or persuade, or convince, or ridicule, or whatever. One purpose is enough for any one composition.

Decide on the basic form of writing you will use. If you wish to argue, omit narrative detail that adds nothing to your central purpose. If you wish to tell a story, use little argument and exposition—and none that has no direct relationship to your aim.

Try to make your paper unified in tone and mood. Tragedy and comedy, dignity and farce, pathos and ridicule are difficult to mingle in a short paper. A solemn page on Robert F. Kennedy's assassination should not contain references to his lively undergraduate days. A farcical paper on nightclub humor will lack unity if you add serious thoughts about the plight of minority groups.

63d. Considering your readers

Always keep your prospective reader in mind. Usually, your readers will be your instructor and classmates, but you may be asked to write for someone else. Whoever your readers are, how much do they already know about your topic? What can you write that will be freshly informative? interesting? appealing? If you are writing on a subject about which your reader knows little or nothing, what background information should you supply? What terms need to be defined? What technical material had best be omitted to avoid confusing your reader? What kinds of illustrations, examples, and descriptive details will help make the subject as clear to your reader as it is to you?

You can save yourself time and trouble by *always* deciding in

comp

63d

advance just whom you are writing for. It's wasteful to unearth material that is not needed for your central purpose. It's even more wasteful to gather material that is already well known to your readers. Regardless of who your readers are, however, you will need specific details to shore up the purpose, the thesis, that you have in mind. You will need concrete material and factual evidence to support a position or idea. No writer can be effective without ample substance, more than is needed or can be used.

Try to remember that "the general reader" does not exist. Suppose that the runoff of chemical fertilizers from farmlands is polluting downstream waterways, and your aim is to analyze the situation and recommend changes. It is simple to identify the readers who will have a strong interest in the subject: farmers are one group; those who fish, swim in, or sail the waterways are another; a town or city that gets its drinking water downstream is a third; consumers of the crops the farmers grow are a fourth, and still others could be named. If you recommend that the farmers cut down the amount of fertilizer they use, they and the consumers of their produce may be opposed, as well as manufacturers of fertilizers. If you recommend that the town build a purification plant, people whose taxes will go up may oppose your solution. Whatever your recommendation, some groups will support it and others will oppose it. Your job will therefore be easier or more difficult depending on which particular group you address.

Even the arguments you use and the way you present them may differ depending on the audience. In the example just presented, we supposed that people who fish might be affected. But there are distinctions even within this group that could change the way you write. A family that fishes for sport might lose one of its favorite spots if the pollution continues, but family members have probably visited that spot on a weekend or a vacation; they may have a number of places they choose among, and the loss of this one area is for them simply an inconvenience. But what about a family that fishes commercially? It stands to lose a means of making a living, and a resulting move to some other area may mean the loss of a home as well. Clearly, the problem is more serious for those who fish commercially than for those who fish for sport.

Many essays are not nearly as effective as they might be simply because the writer has no clear concept of the audience. Always ask yourself: Why would readers care about my topic? How important is the subject to them? What readers are likely to support or oppose the arguments I present?

If you decide as clearly as you can who your readers will be, the organization and the writing of your paper will become simpler.

63e. Conveying an actual sense of fact

As you preplan your essay, keep jotting down facts, details, incidents, anecdotes, records of conversation, and the like that can be helpful in developing the specific topic you are shaping from the general subject area of your paper.

Good writing is definite, concrete; it contains specific details that arouse interest. In other words, it either contains facts or conveys an impression, a sense, of fact. A composition on taxation will hardly be effective as long as you abstractly discuss the theory of taxation; but when you make a specific, concrete statement you make your work come alive. For example: "Whether or not you own real property, you pay taxes. According to a recent estimate, everyone in our town paid an average tax of $850 this past year."

Specific answers to the questions Who? What? Where? When? Why? How? always achieve effectiveness. They furnish realistic touches and clear imagery, which the reader has a right to expect. Note the difference in effectiveness between these two excerpts from student essays:

My roommate was selfish. He cared nothing for me or anyone else and was completely absorbed in looking out for his own interests.

John was selfish. He borrowed my neckties and razor blades, sometimes without asking permission, but he hated for me to borrow even a sheet of paper from him. When he had to get up for an early class, he walked around noisily and made no effort to keep from waking me. But he grumbled for ten minutes one morning when I accidentally dropped my history book and waked him.

comp

63e

These suggestions can help you convey an actual sense of fact: (1) Enumerate specific details; (2) narrate specific incidents; (3) use comparison and contrast; (4) show definite relationships between causes and effects. Turn to Section 53 for examples of these and other ways of getting a sense of fact into your writing.

63f. Getting movement into your paper

Writing that is studded with facts may be dull and lifeless. History books are sometimes considered dull, for example, but they are not thin in facts or supposed facts. Neither are stock market statistics, insurance reports, or legal briefs. But none of these is interesting, effective, *alive*. They have little dramatic effect, human interest, humor, satire, or any of the other qualities that make writing more than merely readable. Not every writer can be humorous or satirical or urbane, but everyone can make occasional use of dialog, of a series of questions or exclamations, or of active verbs and narrative details. Study the following:

1. She was not certain that she should have stopped payment on the check. She thought she might be sued for nonpayment.

   Should she have stopped the check? What could Mr. Jones do to her? What would he do? Oh, if only she could get her father's advice!

2. The house had been freshly painted and shone in the afternoon sun.

   "I see you have had your house painted, Mr. Dodge."
   "Yes, Lem and I decided a fresh coat of green and white would help, so we bought paint and brushes and did the job ourselves."
   "Did you, indeed? Well, the house certainly does look lovely in the afternoon sun."

3. A friend of mine was talking to a theatrical agent who was not particularly distinguished for the range or choice of his vocabulary. He was therefore a little startled to hear the word *eclectic* suddenly pop out.

   "Joe! Where did you get hold of that elegant word?"
   "*Eclectic*? Oh, I just happened to come across it in the dictionary."
   "What do you mean you *just* happened to come across it in the dictionary?"
   "Well, you see, I was looking up the word *egregious* and on my way to *egregious* my eye caught the word *eclectic* and I liked it."
   "O.K. But how did you *happen* to be looking up the word *egregious*?"
   "I always look up the word *egregious*!"

4. Startled by a cop, this same comedian might grab his hatbrim with both hands and yank it down over his ears, jump high in the air, come to earth in a split violent enough to telescope his spine, spring thence into a coattail-flattening sprint and dwindle at rocket speed to the size of a gnat along the grand, forlorn perspective of some lazy back boulevard.

—JAMES AGEE, *Agee on Film*

63g. Avoiding plagiarism

As you are preplanning a paper, trying to shape a topic and gathering material for its development, you are likely to get from some source one or several ideas that are new to you. This is a hopeful sign that you are really searching, thinking, and reflecting.

But taking the ideas and words of another and passing them on as your own is *plagiarism,* a form of thievery. Sometimes you can acknowledge a source with a mere phrase: "As Salinger suggests, . . ." Sometimes you will need to make fuller acknowledgment in a footnote. But borrow, don't steal, and do indicate who the lender is.

It is equally important that in gathering material from others you think about it and try to state in your own words what you have learned. It is unnecessary to acknowledge every item of information you glean: you do not need to cite some authority if you write that water is wet or the earth is round or war is destructive. But you should always put information of whatever kind through your own thought processes and usually should express it in your own words. (See Section 80j for suggestions on what to footnote.)

comp

63g

EXERCISE 12

Consider each of the following as a core (thesis) sentence. Choose *one* of them, limiting it to specific details and instances from your own observation. With a specific, named reader in mind, list five items from your experience, imagination, and reflection that could be used in developing material for a composition of 300–500 words.

Movies Are (Are Not) Better Than Ever

Television Programming Does (Does Not) Reflect Our Cultural Levels and Tastes

All Forms of Social Dancing Are (Are Not) a Waste of Time
Intercollegiate Sports Are (Are Not) a Racket
What Inflation Has Done to My Spending Habits

EXERCISE 13

For *one* of the following general subjects, list ten or more items that might be used in one phase of its development:

College Politics
The Peaceful Uses of Atomic Energy
Weekend Fun
Suicide, Pro and Con
Compulsory Inspection of Motor Vehicles
Pill Popping
Alcoholics and Heavy Drinkers
Offshore Drilling for Oil and Gas
Problems of Divorced Women
State Highway Regulations
My Philosophy of Life
Day People and Night People
Country and City Living
Living on Campus and Off
Health Foods and Junk Foods
The Appeal of Foreign Films

EXERCISE 14

For the topic selected in Exercise 13, indicate how items of developing material would differ for each of the following imagined readers:

my English teacher
my parents
my best friend
my elderly aunt
my mother's best friend
the person I live with

EXERCISE 15

Clip a political cartoon from the editorial page of your daily newspaper. Attach it to a sheet of paper. Below it list the information a reader would need in order to understand it and the attitudes a reader would need in order to sympathize with it. Bring your results to class and see if your list meets with general agreement.

EXERCISE 16

Considering the three elements of newsstand price, advertisements, and articles, what are the differences among the readers of the pairs of magazines in the following list? (If you are not familiar with all the groups, select the ones you do know something about.)

Cosmopolitan and *Woman's Day*
Argosy and *Esquire*
National Geographic and *Holiday*
Seventeen and *Glamour*
Time and *Newsweek*
Sports Illustrated and *Sport*
Rolling Stone and *The National Review*
The New Yorker and *Mother Earth News*
House and Garden and *Good Housekeeping*
TV Guide and *Variety*

EXERCISE 17

For *one* of the following general subjects (1) phrase a thesis sentence; (2) list five details that might be used in development; (3) suggest the tone you propose to use; (4) name a specific reader or group of readers for whom you intend to write. Confine your treatment to *one* sharply limited phase of the subject you select.

The Costs of Hospital Care
Unemployment Insurance
America's Overuse of Energy
A Cure for Inflation
What's Wrong with This College
Mass Transit and Private Cars
The Control of Population
Air Pollution and Its Causes
Industry's Views on Ecology
Reverse Discrimination
The Supreme Courts of Warren and Burger
The Emergence of Black Studies

comp

63g

455

The Costs of Solar Energy
Home Energy Conservation
Criminal Justice in This State

64. Organizing and outlining a topic

After the selection and shaping of a topic comes the problem of organizing the material you have gathered so that it will fulfill the purpose you have in mind. That is, with a central purpose determined, details listed, and method of development decided, you face the task of whipping into shape a mass of accumulated ideas and details. Why is this step essential?

It is essential because no one—repeat, *no one*—can write an effective paper without some sort of plan for it. This plan can be formal or informal, sketchy or detailed, written or "just in one's head." It can be prepared in advance of writing or can be made from what has been written. But a plan of some sort, made and followed at some time, is essential in the preparation of any composition that is more than a paragraph in length.

One useful means of planning a paper is a formal outline. Some people object to outlining. They insist that preparing a formal outline steals valuable time from actual writing and that an outline acts as a brake on the free flow of their ideas. Both objections make some sense. But time spent on an outline will be more than repaid when one begins to write. Also, few of us always think logically. We *need* some control over the random ideas that pop into our heads.

An outline does not have to be detailed or elaborate. If you are writing a paper in class or an essay answer on an examination, only two or three minutes may be devoted to preparing a rough "sketch" outline that will certainly be informal and yet may pay dividends. Nor need an outline be followed slavishly; it should be your servant, not your master. As you write you may see that certain changes in plan are necessary and effective. Work *from* an outline, not *for* it.

It is as illogical to say that you can't prepare any kind of outline until after you read what you have written as it is to say that you can't tell what you're going to say until after you have said it. Making a comment first and not thinking about it until later gets people into trouble every day.

64a. Thesis sentence

Before attempting an outline of any sort, make certain that you have a central idea in mind. It usually helps to have one not only in mind but written down on paper. Such a summary statement, or plan of attack, is called a *thesis sentence* or *core plan.*

Because a thesis sentence indicates the central idea that you will develop in a paper, you should use one only in essays that really do have an idea to develop. Papers narrating an event, telling how to perform some activity, or describing a person or place have (or should have) a purpose but not necessarily a thesis, a controlling or dominant idea. Remember, however, that effective descriptions do have a dominant point of view and that good narratives make a point, often one that is not overtly expressed.

You need not always express a thesis sentence in the paper itself, although one should clearly control the development of any essay that requires one. If you do use such a statement, it should appear in the very first paragraph. Why? Because it works for the entire essay the way a topic sentence does in a paragraph. It tells the reader of your paper what the "big idea" is—and also helps you keep on track in developing that idea. As a summary statement of what is coming, it is a guide for both reader and writer.

In most instances, a thesis sentence can be phrased only after you have gone through the prewriting steps mentioned in earlier sections. Your preplanning will have led you to a conclusion and will have suggested some of the material required to develop it. That is, build a thesis sentence from the initial planning steps of a paper so that you will know how and with what you are going to develop it.

An effective thesis sentence should be stated so exactly that neither you nor your readers can misunderstand it. Also, it should indicate what *one* principal idea your essay intends to develop. A thesis sentence such as "The status of amateurs in athletics is being undermined because professionalism is increasing in nearly all sports" is not entirely precise or unified. It can be improved by

outl

64a

writing, "Increasing professionalism in sports is damaging the status of amateurism."

For instance, suppose that you wish to write an account of your first day of work on a new job. If you plan merely to write a personal experience, a story of what happened, you may not need a thesis sentence. But if you wish to draw a lesson from that experience, you might come up with a controlling idea. In any event, you jot down these ideas:

My First Day at Work

Sleeplessness the night before
Early-morning preparation
The trip to work
Getting started
How the day went

These five headings are a plan of some sort, one that proves any plan is better than none at all. It is a "sketch" or "scratch" outline that, if followed, will see to it that your paper stays on the track and at least follows a time sequence.

But if time permits—and it usually does—you can make this sketchy list of activities fit into a more elaborate and more helpful outline. In organizing and outlining material you have three choices: *topic, sentence,* and *paragraph* outlines.

64b. Kinds of outlines

1. The topic outline

My First Day at Work

THESIS SENTENCE: The first day at work is a nervous ordeal, but it can be endured because tension and worry pass away.

   I. Prework jitters
      A. The night before
         1. Setting the alarm clock
         2. Sleeplessness
         3. Thoughts of failing
      B. The next morning at home

      1. Hurried dressing
      2. A bolted breakfast
  II. The workday
    A. Getting to work
      1. A run for the bus
      2. My nervousness and other riders' composure
    B. The first hour
      1. Meeting the foreman
      2. Inability to understand
      3. Helpfulness of another worker
      4. Gradual easing of tension
    C. How the day went
      1. Slow passage of time
      2. Lunch hour
      3. Afternoon exhaustion
      4. Quitting time
      5. Satisfied feeling
      6. Readiness for tomorrow

2. The sentence outline

A sentence outline is made with sentences (usually topic sentences), not words and phrases. It is more elaborate than a topic outline and takes a little longer to make. It is, however, likely to be clearer to you as you proceed with your paper, and it is more helpful to a reader who wishes to make useful suggestions.

Here is how part I of the topic outline just presented could appear in a sentence outline:

My First Day at Work
  I. I was nervous and jittery the night before I was to begin work.
    A. I set the alarm clock and turned in early.
    B. I could not get to sleep and tossed restlessly.
    C. My mind was tortured with fears of not being able to do the job.
  II. The next morning I was tired and still nervous.
    A. I dressed hurriedly and clumsily.
    B. I did not feel like eating but bolted my breakfast.

3. The paragraph outline

A paragraph outline consists of groups of sentences (perhaps mainly topic sentences) that indicate the contents of entire para-

outl

64b

graphs. Such an outline may be used in planning your own composition, but it is even more helpful in setting down summary sentences to indicate the thought of successive paragraphs in a selection that you are studying.

In a paragraph outline, material is not classified into major headings and subheadings; rather, the topics of the paragraphs are listed in the order in which they are to appear. For illustration, here is a specimen paragraph outline of part II of the topic outline given earlier:

1. Dashing from the breakfast table, I made a run for the bus.
2. My inner fears and worries had me in a turmoil, but other riders on the bus seemed calm and casual.
3. The foreman was gruff, and my worries increased.
4. My hands were sweaty and my knees felt weak so that I couldn't catch on to what I was supposed to do.
5. A man nearby saw my confusion and kindly showed me, slowly and clearly, what my job was.
6. As I began to catch on, my hands stopped sweating and I began to feel easier in mind and body.
7. The morning passed slowly, and I thought lunchtime would never come.
8. During the afternoon, my muscles grew more and more tired, and I had to hang on until quitting time.
9. As I walked to catch the bus home, I felt satisfied that I had met the test of the first day and could meet the challenge of the next without fear.

4. The number system

The topic, sentence, and paragraph outlines just illustrated are widely used and often preferred to all other methods of indicating the organization of materials. In recent years, however, a different form of outline has been favored by some teachers and writers. An illustration of this *number system* follows:

THESIS STATEMENT: Although traditional domestic architecture disappeared in the second half of the nineteenth century, architects and designers now look to traditional forms to solve problems resulting from modern economic conditions.

1. The majority of American houses built between 1660 and 1860 fall into three types.
    1.1 The Pioneer style consisted of a one-room cabin with a loft and an all-purpose fireplace–hearth.
    1.2 The Pioneer style was replaced by the Old-World style house of two rooms: a large hall and a smaller parlor, perhaps with a loft or full second story.
    1.3 By 1850, the Old-World style house had been replaced by the American Folk Georgian style, with two rooms on either side of a central hall.
2. Technological innovations of the second half of the nineteenth century put an end to traditional domestic architecture of the Pioneer, Old-World, or Folk Georgian styles.
    2.1 The invention and widespread use of the stove made the specialization of rooms possible.
    2.2 The manufacture of cut nails meant houses could be built faster and cheaper.
    2.3 The invention of balloon framing made more rooms possible at less cost.

64c. Outline form

Any outline based on a thesis sentence that clearly indicates the structure of a paper is certain to be effective. The paper itself may be poor, but the outline for it will not be at fault.

It is true, however, that there are standardized forms for preparing outlines. Correctness in these forms is more a matter of convention than of logic, but you may wish to follow certain conventions. In fact, your instructor may insist that you do so.

1. Outlining is division. Subdivision means division into at least two parts.

If a single minor topic must be mentioned, express it in, or as part of, its major heading or add another coordinate minor topic.

The Case Against Cloning Human Beings

ORIGINAL: I. The idea of cloning humans is becoming a reality.

> A. Biologists have been able to clone some lower animals for years.
> II. Biological experimentation produces many failures before success is achieved.
>   A. Dr. Daniele Petrucci failed forty times before fertilizing a human egg *in vitreo.*
>   B. Many cloned frogs have been abnormal.
>   etc.

REVISION: I. Although biologists have been able to clone some lower animals for years, only now is the idea of cloning humans moving to reality.
II. Biological experimentation produces many failures before . . .

Do not artificially seek a subdivision B or 2 to correspond to every subdivision A or 1. Carry a single subdivision in your mind or make it part of a larger division, as in the example just given. Some instructors accept and advise a single subdivision serving as an example or illustration; however, such an example or detail can usually be made part of a larger division.

2. Avoid duplicating the title of the paper.

The first main heading of the outline should not repeat the title of the paper itself. If the idea expressed in the title logically must appear in the outline, rephrase it.

Preventing Suicide Among the Young

ORIGINAL: I. The best way to deal with suicide among the young is to keep it from happening.
II. The public needs to be educated about symptoms of an approaching suicide attempt.
III. The taboo on discussing suicide needs to be removed.
IV. Potential victims need understanding and support.

Since *to prevent* something means "to keep it from happening," the first point repeats the title. This outline could be improved by removing the first item:

REVISION: I. Teach the public the symptoms of an approaching attempt.

II. Remove the taboo on the subject of suicide.
III. Understand and support potential victims.

3. Try to achieve logical parallelism and appropriateness in developing a heading.

The Whale Versus Man

ORIGINAL: I. Whales provide commercially valuable products.
    A. Whale meat is a rich source of protein.
    B. Whale oil is used for several purposes.
    C. The whaling industry provides many jobs.
    D. Whale hunting has a long tradition.
  II. Whales should be saved for biological reasons.
    A. Whale species are becoming extinct.
    B. Other sources of protein could replace whale meat.
    C. Substitutes for whale oil are available.
    D. When whales disappear, there will be no jobs or tradition.
  III. The International Whaling Commission protects whales.

In this try at an outline are several errors. Under I, both C and D need revision. The whaling industry, although commercially valuable, is not a product, and a tradition is neither a product nor commercially valuable, although it may be psychologically important. Under II, only A is a "biological reason."

REVISION: I. People support the hunting of whales for several reasons.
    A. Whales provide some commercially valuable products.
      1. Whale meat is a rich source of protein.
      2. Whale oil is used for many commercial products such as soap, polish and waxes, and paints.
      3. Ambergris enhances the fragrance of expensive perfumes.
    B. The whaling industry provides many jobs.
    C. In cultures like that of the Eskimo, whale hunting is traditionally important.
  II. People's needs can be met without large-scale whale hunting.

outl

64c

463

      A. Substitutes for whale products are available.

      B. If whales become extinct, the whaling industry will collapse in any event.

      C. Native cultures could continue to hunt whales, but only at the cost of using traditional weapons such as the kayak and spear rather than powered boats and explosive harpoons.

  III. The International Whaling Commission should be empowered to enforce its decisions and should continue to ban hunting of endangered species and to lower the legal limit for all species.

4. Use parallel phrasing.

Topic, sentence, and paragraph outlines should be consistent in structure throughout. In a given outline, do not use a word or phrase for one heading and a sentence for another.

5. Avoid meaningless headings.

Few if any outlines require such headings as "Introduction," "Reasons," "Conclusions," and "Effects." If you feel that one or more such headings must appear, add specific explanatory sub-heads.

6. Follow conventional mechanics.

The mechanics involved in outlines concern *indentation, symbols,* and *punctuation.* Study the specimen outlines given earlier. Note the use of Roman numerals beginning flush left in a topic outline. Observe that capital letters indicate the first series of subdivisions. Study their indentation. If needed, the next series is indicated by Arabic numerals (1, 2, 3). If still further subdivision is needed, use small letters (a, b, c). A period follows each numeral or letter and, in sentence and paragraph outlines, each sentence.

Once again, no effective paper can be written without some sort of plan, organization of details, or formal outline. No matter how pleased you may be with the content and form of an outline, how-

outl

64c

ever, do not let it get in the way of the flow of development that should mark your paper. *If you pay more attention to following your outline than you do to the expression of your ideas, the paper you write will seem wooden, mechanical, undeveloped, and straitjacketed.* All that an outline can do—and it's a great deal—is to make certain that you can proceed from one point to another without worrying about whether you are covering the topic in an orderly, clear, and comprehensive manner.

EXERCISE 18

The following list consists of items that you might jot down if you decided to write a composition about a large, popular, year-round resort that you and your family have enjoyed. Put into proper outline form (*topic* or *sentence* as your instructor assigns) these unorganized details:

buildings	professional entertainment	indoor pool
dining hall	guest rooms	snowmobiling
location	archery	hiking
dramatics	volley ball	television room
movies	craft rooms	canoeing
badminton	horseback riding	theater
skiing	overnight camping	library
golf	swimming	water supply
ice-skating	nature study	reception area
sailing	tennis	lake

EXERCISE 19

Choose a subject, complete with thesis statement, in a class discussion. Compose an outline for an essay on that subject and compare it with those prepared by other members of your class. Discuss the good and bad features of the outlines presented. Revise yours in accordance with advice given in the discussion.

EXERCISE 20

Outline a complete short article from your favorite magazine.

EXERCISE 21

Revise the following outline so that items will follow the clearly thought out and approved form of a *topic* outline.

outl

64c

How Drivers Cause Accidents
I. By violating traffic regulations
   A. Passing a halted school bus
   B. Going through a stoplight
   C. Turning a corner without flashing a signal
II. By being selfish
   A. Not moving over for a passing car
   B. Blocking another car when parking
   C. Failing to dim lights when meeting another car
III. By being unfit to drive
   A. Driving while intoxicated
   B. Driving in wrong direction on one-way street
   C. Being too young or too old to drive
   D. Having poor vision
   E. Driving an unreliable car

EXERCISE 22

Make a suitable outline (*sentence* or *topic* or both, as directed) of these three "scratch" outlines:

Meet My Best Friend
Physical appearance
   Height and weight
   Complexion
Chief character trait
   Good-natured

My Favorite Restaurant
It serves two kinds of food
It serves Italian dishes
It serves American dishes
Its service is excellent
   The waiters are courteous
   They are also very efficient

Three 4-H Activities
Junior leadership
   age
   experience
   projects
Clothing
   age

outl

64c

experience
time
cost
Freezing
where purchased
cost

65. The first paragraph

"Well begun is half done," the old saying goes. Perhaps because everyone knows the truth of this maxim, many writers freeze at a blank sheet awaiting the first paragraph, no matter how carefully they have researched and outlined their material. The autobiographies of professional writers are filled with tales of their struggles with first paragraphs.

Remember that it is easier to keep writing than to start writing. Sometimes the best way to begin is *not* to start at the beginning. If you feel stumped for a beginning, start somewhere else. Begin by working on that part you feel most comfortable with—an argument in the body of the paper, for instance, or at its conclusion if you have a good ending in mind. Then, once the writing train has been set in motion, return to work on the beginning paragraph. Whether you approach the first paragraph immediately or return to it once you are rolling, here are some points to consider before writing it.

65a. Wordy beginnings

Beginning at the beginning, directly and clearly, is not easy. Many writers ramble for some time before they warm to their subject and come to grips with it. Examine your second and third paragraphs. If your paper really begins somewhere in those paragraphs, throw away everything that precedes that point.

Unless you are dealing with a highly controversial subject, avoid starting off with such expressions as "I think," "In my opinion,"

1st
¶

65a

and "It seems to me." Since you are writing the paper, it can be taken for granted that the thoughts and opinions are yours—unless you state otherwise.

Note the directness and clarity of purpose of these three opening sentences of student papers:

1. Of all forms of advertising, television commercials are the most blatant and least effective.
2. Although some of my fellow students think that telecasting is an unalloyed blessing, it should be pointed out to them that advertisers have usurped the supposedly free air for personal gain.
3. Everyone is familiar with television, but not everyone realizes that programs are used not only to give information and entertainment, but also to enrich those who prepare, present, and pay for them.

If your paper needs an introduction, write one. But remember that usually only long papers need to begin with a definition of terms, a history of the topic, or an explanation of your reasons for presenting a study. The shorter your paper is, the shorter your introduction should be. Most compositions can begin with a thesis, or core, sentence.

65b. Openings dependent upon the title of an essay

Title and the paper itself are independent. A first sentence should be self-explanatory without indirect or vague reference to the title. Avoid reference words like *this, that,* or *such* in beginning sentences.

Ineffective Beginnings
1. Someday I hope to follow my mother's footsteps in this profession.
2. Raising these has fascinated me since childhood.
3. I once endured the discipline of such an academy for a year.
4. In professional football this is the player to watch.

Improved Beginnings
1. Someday I hope to follow my mother's footsteps in the practice of law.

2. Raising tropical fish has fascinated me since childhood.

3. I once endured the discipline of a military academy for a year.

4. In professional football the linebacker is the player to watch.

Repeating the title but adding a thought to it, however, is not a faulty method of beginning a paper. When something is added and when reference to the title is not vague, repetition may be effective:

> This is a song of the once open road. Is there as much as five miles of highway left in the United States today without ten filling stations and at least one farmhouse called "Ye Willowe Inne"?
>
> —CHARLES MERZ, *The Once Open Road*

> I stand here ironing, and what you asked me moves tormented back and forth with the iron.
>
> —TILLIE OLSEN, *I Stand Here Ironing*

65c. Abrupt beginnings

The opening of a paper should not be wordy, but neither should it be abrupt. Instead of starting an essay with "The first step in building a bookcase is . . ." or "We must have better laboratory equipment because . . . ," the writer might better begin with a brief paragraph to prepare the reader for the process or argument to follow.

Although an abrupt opening with a quotation can sometimes be effective, such a device should be used sparingly. It should also be followed immediately by an explanatory passage to make the situation clear to the reader, as in this example:

> "Hey you, Slim."
> The boss at the cement plant, where I worked last summer, had given me the nickname my first day on the job. Now he was calling me to drive a truckload of bags to the freight yard.

Beginning with a definition can sometimes make an effective opening. For most readers, the term *extraterrestrial life* requires explanation. In "Of Life Beyond" Isaac Asimov explains the phrase so as to avoid both abruptness and reader confusion:

1st
¶

65c

469

If we are going to speculate about extraterrestrial life, we must first ask what we mean by the phrase. We can define "terrestrial life" without difficulty. That would include the millions of species of plants, animals, and microorganisms that now exist on Earth, or have existed on Earth in the past. We can then define extraterrestrial life as all forms of life that do not now exist on Earth and never have existed on Earth.

65d. Summary beginnings

Providing readers with a statement of the point of your entire paper can result in an effective first paragraph. Study this beginning of a long article on skiing by Eric Swenson:

> Late last autumn, when the first snow flurries dusted across the northern half of the United States, an estimated three million pairs of knees began to twitch. This mass flexing was the first symptom of a seasonal phenomenon that has progressed in twenty years from the status of a foreign foolishness to that of a national mania. Although still in early stages of development, this phenomenon has reversed migratory instincts, cut scars in the faces of ancient mountains, created an economic revolution in rural areas, upped the income of the medical profession, and released several million inmates of modern society into flights of ecstatic freedom.

The sentence that states your subject need not be the first one in the opening paragraph. As long as the paragraph makes it clear what the essay is about, the sentence that provides that information may be in the middle of the paragraph or even at the end, as this first paragraph from Arthur C. Clarke's "Where's Everybody?" shows:

> At this moment of time, when humanity stands upon the threshold of space and has already launched its first vehicles beyond the atmosphere, there is a centuries-old question which presses more and more urgently for an answer. In almost any astronomy book you will find a chapter devoted to the subject: "*Is there life on other worlds?*"—the answer given depending upon the optimism of the author and the period in which he is writing (for there are fashions in astronomy as in everything else).

1st
¶

65d

65e. Narrative and descriptive beginnings

Beginning with narrative or descriptive details or examples is a method aimed at engaging the reader's interest more effectively than might be possible with such opening sentences as "There are three points to be considered . . . ," "Hydrogeoflonics is composed of two separate fields . . . ," "My principal purpose in writing this paper . . . ," and so on.

The tall, black ships rode at anchor in the bay, the Stars and Stripes fluttering lazily at mastheads. A fleet of small cutters, white-clad sailors straining at their oars, moved swiftly toward the shore. There, stretching for a mile, thousands of armed Japanese warriors in colorful attire strained in silence to catch a glimpse of the oncoming Americans.

—DAVID LINDSEY

When the first European settlers arrived in this country, the passenger pigeon was the most abundant bird on the continent and probably the most plentiful creature ever to inhabit this earth. It was not at all uncommon for migrating flocks to number over a billion birds. Yet, by the early 20th century, they were gone from the face of America—every last one of them.

—DOREEN BUSCEMI

65f. Varied beginnings

Sections 65a–e cover the principal *don't's* and *do's* of writing first paragraphs, but several other methods of beginning a paper can be noted:

1. Beginning with a question

What is this democracy for which we fight?
—GEOFFREY CROWTHER, *The Citizen's Charter*

What is success? And how is it gained?
—JOHNSON O'CONNOR, *Vocabulary and Success*

2. Beginning with an exclamation

Something is wrong somewhere! That is the obvious thing to say about poetry in America today.
—EARL DANIELS, *Outline for a Defense of Poetry*

1st
¶

65f

471

3. Beginning with a quotation

"None can love freedom heartily but good men; the rest love not freedom, but license." That was Milton's opinion, and he had thought much about freedom and goodness.
—ELIZABETH JACKSON, *Of Goodness*

" 'That woman Estelle,' " the note reads, " 'is partly the reason that George Sharp and I are separated today.' "
—JOAN DIDION, *Slouching Toward Bethlehem*

4. Beginning by showing the divisions of the topic to be discussed

Two things become increasingly evident as the sickness of our American democracy approaches its inevitable crisis: one is the surpassing genius of the founders of this Republic; the other is the transience of even the greatest of political resolutions.
—ARCHIBALD MACLEISH, *Loyalty and Freedom*

5. Beginning with a general misconception that the writer intends to correct

Science is often defined inadequately as "an organized body of knowledge." This would make cookbooks, Sears, Roebuck catalogues, and telephone books science, which they are not.
—RALPH ROSS and ERNEST VAN DEN HAAG, *The Nature of Science*

Many people, if not most, look on literary taste as an elegant accomplishment, by acquiring which they will complete themselves, and make themselves finally fit members of a correct society.
—ARNOLD BENNETT, *Literary Taste: How to Form It*

1st
¶

65f

6. Beginning by directly addressing the reader

If you are an average reader you can read an average book at the rate of 300 words a minute. You cannot maintain that average, however, unless you read regularly every day. Nor can you attain that speed with hard books in science, mathematics, agriculture, business, or any subject that is new and unfamiliar to you.
—LOUIS SHORES, *How to Find Time to Read*

As we enter the new year, it is time to take stock of the fact that we are living through the greatest revolution in the history of mankind.

—CLARE BOOTHE LUCE, *A Vision of the Year 2000*

EXERCISE 23

Which of the following *beginnings* of papers are effective and which are not? Give reasons for your answers.

1. Have you ever thought what life was like on the earth ten million years ago?
2. Three important steps toward effective studying are selecting a definite place to study, planning ahead, and concentrating.
3. Naturally, the answer to the above question is *yes*. (Theme title: "Should Mothers Work?")
4. I think this is one of the most important questions a high school graduate can ask himself. (Theme title: "Am I Ready for College?")
5. I have known my roommate for only three weeks, but I wish I had never met him at all.

EXERCISE 24

Choose five articles from a book of readings or from current magazines (like *The National Geographic, Scientific American, Time, Glamour, Newsweek, Sports Illustrated, Mademoiselle*). Study their beginnings. What methods or combination of methods do they use to begin directly and clearly?

EXERCISE 25

From articles in magazines find examples of beginning paragraphs presenting an outline of the material to be covered. Find examples supplying some short detail, example, or illustration. Tell which method seems effective for the article in question and why.

fin
¶

66

66. The final paragraph

The important thing to remember in concluding is this: When you have said all you intend to say, *stop*. Do not write a conclusion simply for the sake of the conclusion. A short composition usually requires no formal conclusion; a summarizing sentence will suffice. A rambling and wordy ending will destroy the effect of what has been said. Except in argumentative writing, there can be little excuse for such phrases as "Thus we see" or "In conclusion, let me state." Do you remember the story of the guest who lingered at the door mumbling, "There was something else I wanted to say"? To this the hostess made the apt response, "Perhaps it was *good-by*."

Do not make the ending too abrupt, however; that is, leave an impression of completeness, of having rounded out a discussion and reached a goal. In other words, although short compositions do not usually require formal conclusions, they should end effectively. This means that the ending, because of its position, should contain a thought of such importance that it is a real contribution to the essay. For example, the closing statement generally should deal with the main thought of the composition, not with some minor detail of the discussion. In well-planned papers, after-thoughts are never so important as main thoughts. In many papers the beginning and ending are interchangeable.

Three kinds of ending, although not necessarily ineffective in themselves, have been overworked. The first of these is a *surrender to fate:* After exploring a problem for several pages, the writer figuratively throws up his or her hands with a statement like "What will happen? Only time will tell." Pay your reader the compliment of not saying what is already known and omit the obvious.

Closely related is the *surrender to the reader.* This is the ending that runs something like "The answer is in your hands." In persuasive writing, the reader expects you to suggest an answer to problems you have raised; if you give up and say that the responsibility is the reader's, the reader may mentally reply, "I'll be the judge of that."

Finally, avoid the *apologetic ending:* "Although I am not an expert on the subject, I hope you can understand me." If you have done an honest and thorough job of preplanning, writing, and rewriting your subject, you have done all that can be expected.

Numerous methods of ending a composition are available, including these:

1. Ending with a question

Or shall we really get down to the roots of good and evil and wrestle with our theories until we bring them into some kind of working conformity, not only with one another but with fact?

—ELIZABETH JACKSON

The miracle is that what he did in the little space of seventy years could have been done at all, even by a great genius. Is it any wonder that he had no time to be a man?

—DEEMS TAYLOR, *The Monster* (Richard Wagner)

Aren't there any flesh-and-blood women to be proud of anymore?

—ANNE BERNAYS, *What Are You Supposed to Do
If You Like Children?*

2. Ending with an exclamation

If present-day Louisiana has any claim to individuality, a color, a note of her own, it is lodged unmistakably in this sport-loving, sun-loving, unquenchable spirit which was and is New Orleans, Mistress of chivalry, cuisine, and the dance; cosmopolis of legend, caprice, and motley; the Columbine of the cities—New Orleans!

—BASIL THOMPSON

3. Ending with a direct or indirect quotation

But if he does remember poems pleasantly, no matter how few; even if there be only one, among those quoted here, which he has in the slightest degree liked, he is invited to continue in our common adventure after the peculiar pleasure of poetry, assured, in advance, of fun, and, I hope, of discovering in his experience

*life and food
for future years.*

—EARL DANIELS

fin
¶

66

There is still much to deplore about my education. I shall never read Latin verse in the original or have a taste for the Brontës, and these are crippling lacks. But all handicaps have compensations and I have learned to accept both cheerfully. To have first met Dickens, Austen, and Mark Twain when I was capable of giving them the full court curtsey is beatitude enough for any reader. *Blessed are the illiterate, for they shall inherit the word.*

—PHYLLIS MCGINLEY

4. Ending by bringing up and stressing a final important point

I will close with one last point. Science is fun, even for the amateur. Every scientist is himself an amateur in another field of science which is not his specialty, but the spirit is the same. Science is a game that is inspiring and refreshing. The playing field is the universe itself. The stakes are high because you must put down all your preconceived ideas and habits of thought. The rewards are great because you find a home in the world, a home you have made for yourself.

—I. I. RABI

Finally, it is a spirit of leadership seeking both courage and tolerance: the courage to search for truth and speak it even when, especially when, it pains; and the tolerance to understand that good and evil in human relationships, from the personal to the international, are not absolutes.

—G. GADDIS SMITH

5. Ending by summarizing the central thought or point of the theme or essay

Thus it is no mere transcript of life at a certain time and place that Hardy has given us. It is a vision of the world and of man's lot as they revealed themselves to a powerful imagination, a profound and poetic genius, a gentle and humane soul.

—VIRGINIA WOOLF

To assign unanswered letters their proper weight, to free us from the expectations of others, to give us back to ourselves—there lies the great, the singular power of self-respect. Without it, one eventually discovers the final turn of the screw: one runs away to find oneself and finds no one at home.

—JOAN DIDION

It is no longer good enough to blame man for keeping woman ignorant. For man himself is ignorant and in the sum total no more capable or enlightened than woman.

—LISA HOBBS

6. Ending with a prediction or a warning

A less commercial, more responsible America, perhaps a less prosperous and more spiritual America, will hold fast to its sentiment, but be weaned from its sentimentality.

—H. S. CANBY

fin
¶

66

476

Comfort is a means to an end. The modern world seems to regard it as an end in itself, an absolute good. One day, perhaps, the earth will have been turned into one vast feather-bed, with man's body dozing on top of it and his mind underneath, like Desdemona, smothered.

—ALDOUS HUXLEY

If women's lib wins, perhaps we all do.

—GLORIA STEINEM

EXERCISE 26

Examine the endings of three essays from a book of readings or from a favorite magazine. What methods or combinations of methods are used? Are they effective? Why?

EXERCISE 27

Which of the following endings of student papers are clear and effective and which are not? State reasons for your answers.

1. These facilities and many more like them make Oakdale a wonderful place in which to live.
2. Experiments in teaching tricks to animals are enjoyable for me. Why don't you try them? You might enjoy them, too.
3. Then the band began to play the recessional and the line of graduates began to move. I smiled as we walked forward to meet tomorrow. [Theme title: "Graduation Day at Junior High"]
4. From recent experiments in rocketry, we realize that a dream of yesterday is a possibility of today and will be a reality of tomorrow.
5. I have known her for only three weeks, but I wish I had never met her at all. (See Section 65, Exercise 23.)

prop

67

67. Proportion

Proportion requires that you develop each section of an essay according to its relative importance. For instance, you may have disposed of an introduction in a short paragraph, then devoted a longer paragraph to the next item (not one of major import), developed the most important item in three paragraphs, given two paragraphs to the next (of secondary importance), and used a brief paragraph for the ending. This could represent a well-proportioned paper.

Proportion concerns the amount of space, or details of treatment, for the various parts of a composition. It requires that the development given each division of a paper—each paragraph or group of paragraphs—coincide with the relative importance of the division. Note the word *relative;* importance is not absolute. In determining which parts of an essay should be developed at length and which less fully, you must be guided by your purpose and the readers for whom you are writing.

67a. Purpose

Elaborating on minor details either in the beginning or later in a paper may throw your essay out of proportion, obscure main points, and distract the reader.

For example, your purpose in writing may be to persuade fellow students to support the debating team. Your reasons are that debating is a more important activity than they think it is, that debating deals with significant issues of the day, and that debating is better preparation for adult life than are team sports. Proceed quickly to the heart of your argument. You need no long introduction about famous debates of the past, such as Lincoln versus Douglas or Darrow versus Bryan. Nor need you provide a long list of issues that might be worth debating; two or three examples will suffice.

Or suppose your purpose in writing a paper is to point out the silliness of much modern TV advertising. A paragraph on the origin and growth of advertising in general would not be too much, but if you were to put half the space of your essay into a discussion of historical backgrounds, the paper would be badly proportioned because your purpose is neglected. On the other hand, suppose your essay was historical in its purpose, showing how TV advertising became the way it is. In this instance the greater part of your paper might be devoted to its origin and growth.

67b. Your readers

Do not waste time and space defining common terms or describing objects that you can assume your readers know as well as you do.

Suppose your hobby is photography and that your purpose is to tell your readers how to enlarge snapshots for framing. Your topic presupposes that you are addressing yourself to readers who own cameras of one kind or another. You would be wasting their time and your own by explaining the difference between a positive print and a negative, describing a flashbulb, and defining time exposure. You can safely assume that your readers know such facts. What they want to learn is how to use an enlarger, how much one costs, whether it saves time and money to do one's own enlargements or whether it is advantageous to have them done commercially. Proceed to these points immediately and stress them throughout your paper.

Consider also how the readers will react to your arguments. An audience of college students may agree with a paper that argues that TV advertising is annoying and excessive; but an audience of advertising executives might be strongly opposed. For the second audience, your arguments would need strong support and great detail. Solely because of the audience's potential reaction, an essay for specialists would, in this instance, be longer than one for nonspecialists.

67c. Paragraph length

Planning in the outline stage may help you write a well-balanced paper, neither too long nor too short. If you do not follow some rough guide to proportion, you may find you have written a narrative of five pages, of which four deal with relatively insignificant matters and only one with the really important part of the story. Or, in an expository paper, you may find that you have written 400 words of introductory material and have only 100 left, into which you try to stuff important ideas that needed most of the 400-word space.

One way to avoid these problems is to place in parentheses after each part of your outline the tentative number of words you plan

prop

67c

to write on that division or subdivision. Of course, these amounts will be only estimates; you may find expansion or contraction necessary and desirable when you begin writing and rewriting. Preparing a paper is not a mechanical process, and one should never be rigidly held to some predetermined allotment of space. But when you are composing the final draft of an essay, check its proportions carefully.

EXERCISE 28

Count the number of words in each paragraph of *two* of your most recent compositions. Write a paragraph commenting on the proportions used, giving consideration to the topic, your reader(s), and your purpose.

EXERCISE 29

Study one of the essays in a book of readings or in a magazine. Does each paragraph seem to make a point the relative importance of which is proportionate to its length?

EXERCISE 30

Indicate the number of words proportionately suitable for each paragraph of a 400-word composition devoted to the explanation of a process: learning to dance, or playing bridge, or giving a party, or playing tennis, or some comparable activity, sport, or recreation. Select *one* subject and *adapt* or *alter* the following plan as necessary:

Learning to Swim
1. Correct mental attitude for the beginner
2. Correct body position
3. How to breathe
4. How to handle the arms
5. How to handle the feet and legs
6. Fears to overcome
7. Errors to be avoided
8. Summary

In a 400-word paper, is each of the 8 paragraphs worth exactly 50 words? Why? Why not? (Your answer should depend more on the needs and attitudes of your readers than on your particular interests, knowledge, or enthusiasms.)

prop

67c

68. Unity

Unity means "oneness, singleness of purpose," and applies to the whole paper, to the paragraph (see Section 54), and to the sentence (see Section 45).

The outlining procedure recommended in section 64 is designed to produce unified essays by requiring that at each stage minor points apply directly to the idea of the major point they develop. Similarly, each minor point should be developed with details that directly illustrate its idea. If that advice is followed, the composition will begin with a single subject, stick to that subject, and present concrete details to illustrate that subject. To achieve unity, your central question should not be, "What *else* can I say?" It should be "What *more* can I say about what I already have here?" (But when you have written all that is needed to make your point, *stop*. See the first paragraph of Section 66.)

68a. An essay should be devoted to only one phase of a topic.

No writer is likely to discuss completely unrelated subjects, such as a game of pro football in a paper whose topic is nuclear warfare. A more likely problem is that the topic may change from one phase of a subject into another that may be remotely related but has no real bearing on the central idea.

The unity of your essay may suffer from three weaknesses:

1. An irrelevant introduction or a useless conclusion is tacked on to meet a word quota. (See Sections 65 and 66 for help with beginnings and endings.)
2. Material that has little to do with the subject is included for its own sake or as padding. A writer with too few ideas for the required number of words may introduce material that is unrelated to the topic discussed. For example, some book reviews give much space to facts about the author and little space to the book. A student writing on "The Ingenuity of Robinson Crusoe on the Desert Island" began the paper: "Before giving a discussion of Robinson Crusoe's ingenuity on the deserted island, I think it well to give the main facts

of Daniel Defoe's life." Over half the paper was devoted to Defoe's biography.

3. Material is included that bears on the general subject but has little bearing on the *particular topic* being discussed. The paper shifts from one phase of the subject being treated to a related one. Sometimes this shift results from an incomplete analysis of the divisions of the outline or from a thesis statement that is broader than it should be. (See Section 64). For example, suppose a writer has the following brief outline to work with: Science fiction is an enormously popular field.

   I. Paperback SF novels published each year outnumber those of any other specialty genre.

  II. Professional magazines are increasing in number.

 III. Fan conventions are many and well attended.

 IV. Fans publish hundreds of amateur magazines.

The author writes an essay from the outline and notices (or has it pointed out) that the plan lacks unity. Upon reexamining the outline, the writer notices that all the points except III discuss publishing. Certainly, the idea of fan conventions is related to the popularity of science fiction, but the writer now sees that the topic is not just "popularity" but how the publishing of science fiction shows its popularity.

The simplest way to correct this lack of unity is to omit the distracting point and revise the thesis statement to describe more accurately what the essay actually discusses:
Science fiction publishing shows the popularity of the field.

   I. More paperback SF novels are published each year than those of any other specialty genre.

  II. Professional science fiction magazines are increasing in number.

 III. Fans publish hundreds of amateur magazines.

68b. An essay should have unity of tone.

Whether your purpose is to inform, to persuade, to amuse, to satirize, to ridicule, or whatever, be consistent in the way you handle the subject. The tendency of coaches to give preference to candidates according to height could be treated seriously as a questionable trend, or it could be treated humorously by speculating on how some schools might compete for a player who happened to be seven feet three inches tall. But to mix the two in the same theme would be equivalent to offering your reader oatmeal and dill pickles in the same dish.

In short, avoid mixing comedy and tragedy, satire and pathos, humor and stateliness, reverence and irreverence, absurdity and dignity in the same composition. It would, for example, be difficult to maintain unity of tone in a serious paper on international relations if you decided to add a comical anecdote or incident.

EXERCISE 31

Discuss violations of unity in the following plan (sketch outline) for an essay:

My Best Friend's Father
My friend's father is an excellent lawyer.
He studied hard when he was in college and law school and received many honors.
His parents died during his last year at law school.
My friend is not a good student; he is more interested in dancing, girls, and sports cars than he is in school subjects.
After he was graduated, my friend's father had a financial struggle for ten years.
He now has a large practice and substantial income.
He is getting older, is in poor health, and has hired a young lawyer as an assistant.
My friend and his father have many personality traits in common.

EXERCISE 32

Indicate how the following paper lacks unity and proportion. (See Sections 67 and 68.) If so directed, rewrite the composition by removing irrelevant ideas and adding appropriate material. To add detail you probably will have to visit a library.

THE INVENTOR OF THE AUTOMOBILE

Credit is usually given to a group of men who were said to have invented the automobile. These fifteen or twenty inventors each contributed something toward the invention of the automobile. The period of years for the contributions of these inventors fell between the years

un

68b

483

1880 and 1903. These inventors gained significance by the invention of a horseless carriage or a motor-driven vehicle. However, the latest facts prove that a man named Siegfried Marcus should receive full credit for the invention. In 1861, the first automobile chugged down the street in a small town in Germany. This information has been presented quite recently, and has startled many automobile fans.

In the first years of automobiles, people were decidedly against them. Automobiles were declared a menace to humanity. Farmers were constantly suing drivers for scaring their chickens and horses. A few states tried to obtain laws against automobiles but did not succeed.

As time went by, the public was gradually realizing that automobiles were becoming more useful. Roads and other conditions were now in favor of the automobile instead of against it.

69. Consistency

To be consistent, an essay must maintain a uniform point of view, mood, and tone. *Unity* is concerned primarily with content. *Consistency* is concerned with the writer's point of view and feeling toward subject matter.

Point of view has several different meanings. *Physical* point of view has to do with the position in time and space from which you approach or view material. *Personal* point of view concerns the relationship through which you narrate or discuss a subject, whether first, second, or third person. *Mental* point of view involves attitude and feeling toward a subject.

69a. Physical point of view

cons

69a

Whenever you write a paper involving physical point of view, choose some point in space or time from which to consider your subject. If you wish to describe a lake, for instance, choose a particular season of the year (obviously, this makes a considerable difference) and a specific spot from which you view it. Then use a consistent method of depicting scenic details. You could proceed clockwise or counterclockwise around the lake, from the nearby to the distant, or the reverse. Always let your readers know if and when you shift your point of view. They will be confused if you veer suddenly from the far shore of the lake to comment on the dock upon which you are standing.

Unless you know your material firsthand, your account of it may exhibit inconsistency, such as describing a garden with spring and autumn flowers in full bloom at the same time.

Aimless or abrupt shifts in time are also bewildering. Do not jump suddenly from one period in history to another or give the impression that it is morning and then unaccountably mention that it is evening.

Both space and time were ignored in the following; a thousand miles disappeared between the two sentences:

> Not long after dawn the four survivors were picked up by a French naval ship some thousand miles offshore. To their surprise, they were immediately seized by port authorities and clapped in jail.

Notice how, in this paragraph by John Updike, the author's position is the reference point for description; even sounds arrive where he is:

> But let me describe the music school. I love it here. It is the basement of a huge Baptist church. Golden collection plates rest on the table beside me. Girls in their first blush of adolescence, carrying fawn-colored flute cases and pallid folders of music, shuffle by me; their awkwardness is lovely, like the stance of a bather testing the sea. Boys and mothers arrive and leave. From all directions sounds—of pianos, oboes, clarinets—arrive like hints of another world. . . .

69b. Personal point of view

In most papers, you will choose one of four personal points of view. Which choice you make depends on your subject, your reader, and appropriateness in general. In relating a firsthand experience or in taking the reader into your confidence in a discussion, use the *first* person: *I, my, mine, me, we, our, ours, us.* In addressing the reader directly, use the *second* person: *you, your, yours.* When speaking about someone or about some group, use the *third* person: *she, her, hers, he, his, him, they, their, theirs, them.*

In writing explanatory or argumentative papers, you may have occasion to use the *impersonal: one, anyone, everybody,* and so forth, or nouns such as *a person, a student, a writer,* and the like.

Combinations of personal points of view (*I* and *you, we* and *they*) are frequently used by writers. But do not carelessly shift the point of view from *I* to *we* or *you* to *one* or from any one of these to another. If such a shift is necessary, as may happen, make sure that the reader will be prepared for the shift and will readily understand what you are doing.

69c. Mental point of view

Mental point of view may be considered in several ways. The first is the *objective* (or *subjective*) attitude taken in discussing or arguing an issue. You may weigh pros and cons, but it should be clear that you are consistently upholding a position, not changing it abruptly or being so ambiguous that the reader is confused about where you stand. For example, much can be said in favor of learning about science in a laboratory and learning about it in a general-science course. You could be consistent in pointing out the merits of each, or you could argue in favor of one or the other, but you should make clear to the reader at the outset what your point of view is, and you should uphold it throughout.

When you are *objective,* you refuse, or try to refuse, to let your own feelings, emotions, and prejudices control your attitude. You are impersonal; everything is seen as it is related to the object of thought:

> When a river ceases to flow because the water is deflected or dried up, there remains the river bed, sometimes cut deeply in solid stone. That bed is shaped by the flow and records as graven lines the currents that have ceased to exist. Its shape is static, but it expresses the dynamic form of the river.
>
> —SUSANNE K. LANGER

When you are *subjective,* you let your own feelings, emotions, and prejudices show in your writing; everything is seen through your eyes:

> Listening to music is such a muddle that one scarcely knows

how to start describing it. The first point to get clear in my own case is that during the greater part of every performance I do not attend. The nice sounds make me think of something else. I wool-gather most of the time, and am surprised that others don't. Professional critics can listen to a piece as consistently and as steadily as if they were reading a chapter in a novel. This seems to me an amazing feat. . . .

—E. M. FORSTER

Objectivity and subjectivity are not exclusive alternatives but, rather, opposite ends of a scale. A piece of writing may be more or less objective or subjective, but since the author is a human being, it will never be entirely objective. Since the author uses a language with common reference, it will never be entirely subjective either. As Henry David Thoreau said,

There is no such thing as pure *objective* observation. Your observation, to be interesting, i.e., to be significant, must be *subjective*. The sum of what the writer of whatever class has to report is simply some human experience, whether he be poet or philosopher or man of science.

Nevertheless, objectivity is a useful goal in some kinds of writing, even if complete objectivity is unattainable. Perhaps the worst offenders are those essays which pretend to be objective while using loaded words. (See Sections 37f, 38c). Essays that refer to businesspeople, for example, as either captains of industry or hucksters are misleading if they pretend to be objective.

Another aspect of the mental point of view is the frame of mind or mood in which a writer approaches a given subject. Going fishing on a fresh spring morning might bring forth a lighthearted mood. An expected failure on an upcoming examination might make you feel pessimistic. But if you merely told your reader, "I felt lighthearted" or "I was deeply pessimistic," you would be making an observation, not creating a mood. Establishing a mood requires choosing details that are consistent with it. Observe how the italicized words in the following example build up a dreary and solemn scene:

In outward appearance, the whole of the courtroom scene was *drab, ordinary*. There was the *stuffy* rectangle of a room, *half dark* in the *January dusk*. The electric lights glowed with *meager* in-

cons

69c

candescence. There was the judge, in his *robe,* at the desk of the court. There were the jurors, *solemn* as in church. There were the reporters from the daily journals, more *aloof,* more *judicial* than the judge. There were the police officers and court attendants, relaxed of body, concentrated of eye, jealous of the dignity of the court as a house dog of its master's room. Through the windows could be seen the *bulk of the Tombs, heavy, hopeless, horrible* as the things whence it takes its *chilly* name.

In the following passage by John Collier, the italicized words help to build a mood of unreality, a feeling that things are not what they seem:

> I was ready for anything when I came to the town of T—. It was already late in the year. *Dead leaves crawled like crabs* over the asphalt of the *deserted* esplanade. Winds *raced* along the corridors of the larger hotels, *barging into the wrong rooms.*
>
> It is at such a place, and at such a season, that one finds the *desperate* grass widow, or young things whose *natural credulity* snaps *starvingly* at the *grossest counterfeit.* The *illusion* of teeming possibilities had gone with the licentious *carnival* of summer, the *masks* of coarse sunburn, and *he who may be sitting alone* among the sand dunes. *Ravenous dreams pace* the *unvisited* sitting-rooms of villas, or *stalk* between rising waves and falling leaves.

In a passage like this, a statement about throngs of birds chattering gaily in the trees would be inconsistent in mood.

69d. Physical impression

In addition to maintaining a unified point of view, you may wish to create for your reader a distinct *physical impression,* a sense of being on the spot, present where the action is. To do so, try appealing to one or more of the senses: sight, sound, smell, touch, taste. The impression you create may be favorable, positive, and pleasant, or it may be unfavorable, negative, and unpleasant. Whatever it is, the impression should be developed consistently.

In the following paragraph the dominant physical impression is one of *smell.* Notice that the italicized words consistently appeal to that sense.

> Of all hours of the day there is none like the early morning

for *downright good odours*—the morning before eating. Fresh from sleep and unclogged with food, a man's senses cut like knives. The whole world comes in upon him. A still morning is best, for the *mists* and the *moisture* seem to retain the *odours* which they have *distilled* through the night. Upon a *breezy* morning one is likely to get a *single predominant odour* as of *clover* when the wind blows across a *hay field* or of *apple blossoms* when the wind comes through the orchard, but upon a perfectly still morning, it is wonderful how the *odours* arrange themselves in upright strata, so that one walking passes through them as from room to room in a *marvellous temple of fragrance*. (I should have said, I think, if I had not been on my way to dig a ditch, that it was like turning the leaves of some *delicate* volume of lyrics!)

—DAVID GRAYSON

In the following passage the writer uses the word *dry* only once, and the word *hot* not at all, but nevertheless gives an overwhelming effect of heat and dryness:

It was a breathless wind, with the furnace taste sometimes known in Egypt when a khamsin came; and, as the day went on and the sun rose in the sky it grew stronger, more filled with the dust of the Nefudh, the great sand desert of Northern Arabia, close by us over there, but invisible through the haze. By noon it blew a half-gale, so dry that our shrivelled lips cracked open, and the skin of our faces chapped; while our eyelids, gone granular, seemed to creep back and bare our shrinking eyes. The Arabs drew their head-cloths tightly across their noses and pulled the brow-folds forward like vizors with only a narrow, loose-flapping slit of vision.

—T. E. LAWRENCE

EXERCISE 33

What is the *physical* point of view (place, time) of some short story or other narrative that you have read? Does this point of view shift?

EXERCISE 34

What is the *personal* point of view in one of the essays or short stories that you have read?

cons

69d

EXERCISE 35

What is the *mental* point of view in some essay with which you are familiar?

EXERCISE 36

What is the *physical impression* created in one or more pieces of description that you have read?

EXERCISE 37

The Declaration of Independence is an outstanding example of effective, consistent prose. Compare the closing paragraph of the original and a version written by H. L. Mencken in what he called "American." Discuss the difference in tone between the two versions. Is each consistent in style and development?

We, therefore, the representatives of the United States of America, in general Congress assembled, appealing to the Supreme Judge of the world for the rectitude of our intentions, do, in the name and by the authority of the good people of these colonies, solemnly publish and declare that these united colonies are, and of right ought to be, free and independent states; that they are absolved from all allegiance to the British crown, and that all political connection between them and the State of Great Britain is, and ought to be, totally dissolved; and that, as free and independent states, they have full power to levy war, conclude peace, contract alliances, establish commerce, and to do all other acts and things which independent states may of right do. And for the support of this declaration, with a firm reliance on the protection of Divine Providence, we mutually pledge to each other our lives, our fortunes and our sacred honor.

Therefore be it resolved, That we, the representatives of the people of the United States of America, in Congress assembled, hereby declare as follows: That the United States, which was the United Colonies in former times, is now a free country, and ought to be; that we have throwed out the English King and don't want to have nothing to do with him no more, and are not taking no more English orders no more; and that, being as we are now a free country, we can do anything that free countries can do, especially declare war, make peace, sign treaties, go into business, etc. And we swear on the Bible on this proposition, one and all, and agree to stick to it no matter what happens, whether we win or lose, and whether we get away with it or get the worst of it, no matter whether we lose all our property by it or even get hung for it.

cons

69d

70. Coherence and transition

Coherence as applied to essays means a "holding together" of parts so that the relationships among ideas are immediately clear to the reader. In writing a paper you are trying to *transfer* thoughts from your own mind to the reader's and, at the same time, trying to show clear and orderly progress from start to finish. In a coherent composition, each paragraph is clearly connected to the preceding one and each group of paragraphs dealing with one section of a paper is closely related to other paragraph groups. A composition is coherent when its parts have been so carefully woven together that the reader is never confused about the relationships among ideas.

70a. Missing links in thought

Connections between ideas that seem sufficiently clear to you do not always strike the reader the same way. The fault may be that you have used an ambiguous reference word (*it* or *they,* for instance) that has one meaning to you and a different one to the reader. Or perhaps you have confused the reader by omitting an important connective detail.

For example, in one paragraph you write that you are at an airport intending to fly to Chicago, but fog has grounded all planes. In the next paragraph you describe having dinner at a Chicago restaurant with a friend. "How did you get there?" your reader wants to know. "Did the fog lift? Did you hitchhike? Go by train?" Only you know the answer, and it could easily have been supplied in a single sentence: "There was nothing to do but wait for the fog to lift (or resign myself to going by train, or undertake the hazards and uncertainties of getting a lift in such weather)." Then you proceed to relate how you actually got to Chicago.

70b. Transitional words, phrases, clauses, and sentences

Transition, by providing links between ideas, is an important means of achieving coherence in a paper. A writer who builds

coh/ tran

70b

491

transitional bridges between paragraphs is likely to see and to correct any missing thoughts.

Each new paragraph indentation is a signal to the reader to expect a changeover, a movement of some kind, in the writer's thought. The opening sentence of the paragraph must make this movement clear by transition—by the use of a transitional word, phrase, dependent clause, or sentence. Transitional expressions and devices are discussed in detail in Section 56a. Study that section to learn how transition applies to both paragraphs and complete essays.

Here is an example showing the opening sentences of five successive paragraphs concerning the early history of science, with transitions italicized:

1. There is no doubt whatever that our earliest scientific knowledge is of Eastern origin.

2. *For example,* as early as the middle of the fourth millenium, the Egyptians were already acquainted with a decimal system of numbers. [The writer then gives some additional examples.]

3. *These examples* will convince you that a considerable body of systemized knowledge was far anterior to Greek science.

4. *At any rate,* in the present state of our knowledge there is a gap of more than a thousand years between the golden age of Egyptian science and the golden age of Greek science.

5. *The spirit of Greek science,* which accomplished such wonders within a period of five centuries, was essentially the Western spirit, whose triumphs are the boast of modern scientists.

coh/
tran

70b

Skillful writers use transitional devices in surprisingly few ways. The first is the simplest, through the explicit use of *numbers.* In an essay by Edward Hallett Carr, a short sentence serves as a paragraph by itself as the writer moves to the conclusions of his study:

> This searching critique, though it may call for some serious reservations, brings to light certain neglected truths.
> *In the first place* . . .

The phrase with the number is itself an element of transition. The next paragraph begins with the words *The second point is* . . . and the next paragraph begins with *The third point is* . . .

A simple statement will serve for those papers that are organized by time, too:

> Such, *then*, would be my diagnosis of *the present condition* of art. I must *now*, by special request, say what I think will happen to art *in the future*.
> —KENNETH CLARK

Words like *next* and *then* and phrases like *another point* serve the same purpose.

70c. Transition through repetition

Transition may be shown by the repetition of key words, especially key nouns, at the close of one paragraph and the beginning of the next—a method that is especially effective if the key word is also the subject of the composition. In the next example, the author repeats such a word:

> . . . What [Thucydides] knew was *truth* indeed, with no shadow of turning and inexpressibly sad.
> But Xenophon's *truths* were true, too. . . .
> —EDITH HAMILTON

Writers may also repeat a word from the beginning sentence of one paragraph in the beginning sentence of the next paragraph. For example, William B. Willcox's subject is Sir Henry Clinton, a British commander during the Revolutionary War. Willcox gives one reason for choosing Clinton as his subject, then begins a new paragraph with

> Another consideration strengthened the case for *focusing* on Clinton.

Willcox picks up the italicized word and repeats it in the first sentence of the next paragraph:

> Clinton thus became the *focus* of my inquiry.

But he does something else, too. He connects to *focus* the word *inquiry,* which he then repeats at the beginning of the next paragraph:

Although my field of *inquiry* was established and its limits apparently set, I soon discovered that research can develop as unpredictably as if it had a life of its own.

Willcox shows new developments by linking a new word to a word from the first sentence of the preceding paragraph: *focusing on Clinton, the focus of my inquiry,* and *Although my field of inquiry.*

EXERCISE 38

From a book that you are reading or a current magazine, select an essay and study its transitional devices. Limit your study to transitions between paragraphs. Prepare for class a brief discussion of your findings.

EXERCISE 39

For another selected essay, list the transitional devices mentioned in Section 70 that occur both within and between paragraphs.

71. Choosing a title

You have learned that a well-phrased topic sentence can help you to keep on the track within a paragraph. (See Section 51.) Similarly, an effective thesis sentence aids in selecting materials for developing an essay. (See Section 64a.) Another useful device, this time for maintaining the steady focus of an entire composition, is a suitably chosen title.

A good title will serve as a constant reminder that all material included in a paper should bear on the subject. But since a really effective title often can be hit upon only after a composition has been completed, start with at least a tentative one that can help unify your writing while it is developing.

In addition to its unifying effect, a title can secure the attention of a reader. Most of us have been drawn to a particular motion picture, television program, book, magazine article, or short story by its attractive title. Giving a composition a good title is an important step in making an entire paper effective.

71a. Distinguish between a subject and a title.

The term *subject* is broader and more inclusive than the word *title*. "Eating Habits" makes an unsatisfactory title because it refers to a subject and is neither a specific topic nor a title. But if an actual title is assigned, then you must find out what subject is referred to. The most effective titles of papers indicate not a general subject but a specific topic with a stated theme (thesis sentence).

71b. Word the title clearly and effectively.

A title cannot mention everything that a composition contains, but it should provide at least a hint of the contents. Many effective titles provide a clear suggestion of what is to follow and are also catchy. If you cannot phrase a title that is both descriptive and arresting, settle for the former. These titles are effective, even though they are not unusually imaginative or intriguing: "Why a Classic Is a Classic," "How to Find Time to Read," "The Case for Greater Clarity in Writing," "What Happens in College," "College Athletics: Education or Show Business?" "A Windstorm in the Forest," "An Apology for Idlers," "How Americans Choose Their Heroes." As a working title for your first draft, try to come up with something accurate and clear; later you may be able to add appeal to accuracy.

Here are three suggestions for phrasing effective titles:

1. *Avoid long titles.* The most memorable titles usually, but not always, do not exceed six to eight words. "My Interview with Mr. Bixler" is not as attention getting as "The Time My Teacher in Seventh Grade Sent Me to the Principal's Office," but it is preferable because of its comparative brevity. Students of Wordsworth's poetry refer to a familiar poem as "Tintern Abbey" rather than by the title the poet gave it: "Lines Composed a Few Miles Above Tintern Abbey, on Revisiting the Banks of the Wye During a Tour, July 13, 1798."

2. *Avoid misleading or confusing* titles. A title such as "Watch the Birdie" might refer to a paper on photography, bird watch-

ing, golf, or badminton. Examine a title from a reader's viewpoint. Will it mean to him or her what it does to you?

3. *Avoid vague and commonplace titles.* Many a good composition has gotten off to a poor start because of an unclear, dull, or uninteresting title. A trite title such as "An Embarrassing Experience" can be altered to "My Face Was Red"; "A Trip to Washington" can be called "A Capital Journey"; "My Operation" is duller than "Proudly I Wear a Scar."

71c. Place and punctuate the title correctly.

A title should be centered on the page, on the first line of ruled paper or two inches from the top of unruled paper. Leave a space between the title and the first line of the essay.

Capitalize important words. (See Section 31.) Do not underline (italicize) a title or enclose it in quotation marks unless it is itself a quotation or unless you quote it in the paper. If the title is a question or exclamation, use a question mark or exclamation point, but never place a period at the end.

71d. The title and first sentence of a composition should be independent of each other.

The opening sentence of a composition should be self-contained. If readers see an opening sentence like "This subject . . . ," they will have to turn back to the title to find out what the subject is.

For further comment on this common mistake, see Section 65b. There it is suggested that the first sentence of an essay should always be self-explanatory without reference to the title of the paper. No exception to this requirement should be permitted unless additional comment is supplied in the opening sentence of the composition.

ti

71d

EXERCISE 40

Consult current copies of three or four magazines like *Esquire, The American Scholar, The Journal of Popular Culture, Us, Psychology Today,*

Field and Stream, Sports Illustrated, and *Seventeen.* Look at the titles of some ten articles; then skim through the content of the articles. (1) Are the titles commonplace? Are they appropriate? (2) Make a classification of the kinds of titles you find. Put in parentheses after each title the general subject of the article.

EXERCISE 41

Apply the directions of Exercise 40 to the titles of five essays or articles that you have chosen from one or more collections of essays.

EXERCISE 42

One of the most famous articles ever written was a study of automobile accidents and fatalities. It was called "—And Sudden Death." Try to phrase equally effective titles for articles on the following subjects:

1. Why an airplane flies
2. Advertisements designed to appeal to teenagers
3. A study of black American cowboys
4. American overconsumption of gasoline
5. How statistics can tell lies
6. Why money isn't everything in life
7. The story of Gettysburg National Cemetery
8. Sex in TV advertising
9. The problems of adopted persons
10. Burn it up, wear it out, throw it away

EXERCISE 43

What title (or titles) would you suggest to writers of papers developing these thesis sentences?

1. Whether a boy wants to grow a beard and wear his hair long is his own business and should not be regulated by any outside authority.
2. Young men and women are disillusioned about politics and politicians, and only a few of them want a career in government.
3. For a boy and girl to "go steady" may be convenient and economical, but how can they be sure they are meant for each other if neither ever goes out with anyone else?

Compare your suggestions with those of other students. Which do you like best? Why?

72. Writing and thinking (logic)

Education has been defined in many ways, but there is substantial agreement that it is the process of acquiring general knowledge and developing powers of reasoning and judgment. These aims are so connected that the first is completely dependent on the second. Thinking—or what we call thinking—directly causes, shapes, and influences our every act, emotional response, and attitude.

We rarely think about thinking and are constantly misled by the odd and faulty ideas we have about it. Much of what we call thinking is fixed habit, controlled response, daydreaming, and rationalization. Being human, each of us readily and consistently twists, ignores, or exaggerates evidence and established facts. Being human, we think what we want to think. We protect our beliefs. Being human, we flout both logic and common sense. We resent opposing ideas. As George Bernard Shaw once wrote, we use our reason only to support our prejudices.

This section provides hints and suggestions about thinking and logic that will help you think straight and avoid writing papers that contain illogical statements.

But what is *thinking* and what is *logic?* Briefly, *thinking* is judgment and reflection. *Logic* involves the principles of reasoning applied to any form of knowledge or study. When we engage in crooked thinking we are unreasoning; we are not logical; we are expressing ourselves in a way that is contrary to the rules and principles of logic. When we say "My ideas are all right but I can't seem to express them clearly," we are actually fooling ourselves. Clear, purposeful writing always reflects clear, logical thinking— that is, straight, not crooked, thinking.

Learning to think straight is a lifelong undertaking, but here are some suggestions that should help make your writing more understandable and possibly more acceptable to readers.

log

72a

72a. Try to make every statement reasonable.

It is all very well to recommend that every statement be reasonable, but this is a counsel of perfection. Reasoning is based on facts or what are considered facts. But facts change. For example, the facts of medicine or physics or chemistry even ten years ago are hardly the facts today. Reasoning is also based on conclusions drawn from facts. Yet the conclusions of one reasonable person from a given set of facts may differ widely from those of someone else.

Clearly, you cannot make every statement reasonable. But at least you can avoid making statements that are obviously questionable; if you do make such a statement, you should be prepared to prove it. You should attempt to make your meaning clear by offering evidence that might be considered factual. How logical are these statements?

All motor vehicles should have governors limiting their speed to 40 miles an hour. [What about police cars? ambulances? fire trucks?]

Since football is *the most dangerous of all sports,* my parents refused to allow me to play it when I was in high school. [Overlook the possible parental muddleheadedness: What about water polo? bullfighting? skin diving? Just how dangerous are these activities?]

Sue knows *all there is to know* about stocks and bonds. [All? Is there absolutely nothing that she doesn't know?]

Gambling is a bad habit; everyone should avoid it because habits are usually bad. [Can you prove that gambling is a bad habit? Are habits bad? All habits? What about the habit of obeying traffic rules? of paying your debts? of getting enough sleep? of telling the truth? of trying to live a good and decent life?]

How reasonable do you consider the twenty statements that follow, eighteen of which appeared in papers written by first-year college students? If any seem flawed, how would you explain their errors in logic?

1. Burning comic books is not censorship; it is planning the right kind of reading for children.

2. I think my new friend must be a native of France because she speaks French so well.

3. I'm convinced that money is not important because my family has very little and yet we live happily.

4. I had a slight accident with my car on my first date with Jerri, and she hasn't gone out with me since.

5. The United States should be a welfare state because the Fed-

eral Constitution says that the government must provide for the general welfare.

6. There were ten accidents at that corner last month. All the drivers in this town are crazy.

7. With so many UFO's being seen, there just must be other worlds than ours.

8. If inflation gets any worse, this country will be like Germany was after World War I.

9. I don't see how anyone can fail to believe in a Supreme Being.

10. No matter what others say, I believe that thought is possible without language.

11. There's nothing in nature that science can't explain.

12. Unemployed persons have no one to blame but themselves.

13. That's what I think, and nothing can make me change my mind.

14. You can't deny that private schools are snobbish.

15. Everybody knows that buying on time is bad business.

16. Nothing succeeds like success.

17. The careers of these twins prove that environment is more important than heredity.

18. Alcohol is a deadly drug and its use should be banned.

19. By definition, capitalism is a system that favors only wealthy people.

20. A pickpocket, as some writer has said, is a champion of free enterprise.

If you find no crooked thinking in each of these sentences, come back to them after you have studied the remainder of Section 72.

log

72b

72b. Define all terms that may not be clear.

You should never consider your reader entirely ignorant, but if you know enough to write about a subject you know details that your reader does not. Certain terms that are familiar to you may be unknown to your reader. Even in context, the reader may be unable to guess the meaning of certain expressions. Readers should look up words that they cannot define, but it is unwise to assume that they will always do so. Some slovenly readers never look up anything.

You should define technical words for the general reader. If you use such terms as *bibb, idocrase, pegmatite,* and *tufa,* you should define them immediately; not one reader in a thousand will know what you are writing about, although each of these words is included in standard desk dictionaries. In fact, not all readers will understand even more commonly used terms like *boldface, ecumenical, civil rights, exodontia,* and *logistics.* Always consider for whom you are writing: You need not explain *abscissa* if you believe your readers have studied trigonometry.

Words that are even more common than those just mentioned can cause confusion. What do you mean and what will your readers understand by *normal person, do-gooder, rugged individualism, affirmative action, vested interests, honest toil, low income, typical professor, freedom of speech, un-American, bleeding heart, brainwashing, welfarism, constitutional right, featherbedding, exploitation, extremist, collectivist, cancerous growth?* It won't do to assume that your readers are certain to have the same understanding of such terms as you have.

For instance, suppose you use the term *American Dream* in an essay. Would readers understand this expression precisely the way you do? Not likely. Your idea of the meaning and application of this expression should be explained. Here is how Arthur L. Anderson handled the term when he used it in a book entitled *Divided We Stand:*

> More than three quarters of the American people believe they are fulfilling the American Dream:
>
> The American Dream is the belief that Americans live in the freest society in the world—freedoms which are guaranteed by law. Though there is some discrimination based on racial, sexual, religious, and ethnic prejudice, each American has the opportunity individually to set his own goals within this framework of a free society.
>
> The American Dream is essentially materialistic, and "getting ahead" or "bettering oneself" usually means the increased acquisition of real estate, financial wealth, and material possessions. However, the Dream is not only materialistic; it also includes the pursuit of an individualized life-style, which frequently, if not always, centers in the family.
>
> The Dream also includes a belief in hard work as the legitimate means by which these goals can be achieved.
>
> The Dream finally includes the realization that both freedom

log

72b

501

and the pursuit of one's goals are best realized within a condition of national and international peace.

You may have a different idea of "the American Dream," but at least the author has made clear what *he* means.

For suggestions on methods of defining words and expressions that need clarification, see Section 53d.

72c. Avoid exaggeration.

As is pointed out in Section 38c, many of us tend to overuse emotion-packed words and intensifiers, words and phrases that we think will make our thoughts more dramatic and forceful. Excessive use of such expressions, however, lessens the acceptance and belief of our readers and causes them to assume that we are reasoning carelessly and thoughtlessly. Think carefully before you use such words as *abominable, appalling, astounding, atrocious, awe-inspiring, awfully, deathly, divine, dreadful, enormous, fantastic, fierce, fabulous, famished, frightful, ghastly, gorgeous, gruesome, hideously, horribly, horrifying, lethal, outrageous, petrified, scandalous, shamefully, shockingly, staggering, terribly, tremendous, viciously,* and *wonderful.* Such words have their place, but be sure in your own mind that their use is justified and that your readers will accept them in the context of what you're writing.

72d. Avoid logical loopholes.

log
72d

Offenses against straight and logical reasoning appear every day in the thought processes of each of us. What follows is brief comment on some of the crooked thinking suggested by what may be called *logical loopholes.*

1. Generalizations

A common error in reasoning is observing only a few instances and then jumping to a hasty conclusion. For instance, you know a few athletes whom you consider stupid. Does it follow that all, or even most, athletes are mentally deficient? What is the specific evidence for labeling certain groups "hippie freaks," "irresponsible women drivers," "dumb blondes," "male chauvinist pigs"? What is the evidence for "Every schoolboy knows . . ." or "All good Americans realize . . ." or "Statistics show . . ." or "Doctors say . . ."?

A sound strategy about generalizations is this: Never advance one unless you are prepared to support it with sufficient evidence to make your point clear. How much evidence? Sometimes you need to mention only three or four examples. On other occasions, you may need to comment on the evidence in considerable detail. The purpose of what you are writing will suggest the amount of evidence needed.

2. Cause-and-effect relationships

It is illogical to assume a cause-and-effect relationship between two facts or events simply because one follows the other in time. This logical loophole is known as *post hoc, ergo propter hoc* (Latin for "after this, therefore because of this"). This flaw, a variation of the hasty-generalization error, involves stating that a happening that precedes another must naturally or necessarily be the cause of the latter or that when one event follows another the latter event is a result of the first. The following statements illustrate illogical cause-and-effect relationships:

I have a cold today because I got my feet wet yesterday.

No wonder I had bad luck today; I walked under a ladder yesterday.

I won't say Jim is to blame, but his wife was not a spendthrift until after she was married.

The rise and spread of Christianity was the sole, direct cause of the fall of Rome.

3. *Non sequiturs*

A flaw in reasoning known as the *non sequitur* (Latin for "it does not follow") consists of confusing an inference and a sound conclusion. For instance, some professional writers admit to being poor spellers. Are you justified in concluding that you, who are also a poor speller, are destined to be a professional writer? Note these further examples of the *non sequitur* loophole:

He is the best backfield man I have seen this year. He will be

log

72d

chosen All-American. [Have you seen all the good backs in the country? Are you qualified to judge? Does it follow that because the player is the best you have seen, he should be recognized?]

This store has a new manager and a new price policy. Business and profits will pick up. [Maybe, but what if some other store in the neighborhood has made the same changes? What if the shopping public in the area is declining in numbers? What if the parking area is still inadequate?]

4. Biased or suppressed evidence

Facts that furnish grounds for belief and help prove an assumption or proposition constitute evidence. An obvious flaw in reasoning is the selection of evidence from questionable sources or the omission of evidence that runs contrary to the point you wish to make.

For example, the testimony of dedicated yoga disciples is in itself not sufficient to prove that practicing yoga promotes a peaceful mind or a healthful, happy life. What do those who do not practice yoga think? What do doctors and philosophers think? other authorities? recent converts? those who once practiced yoga and have given it up?

Figures and statistics can lie if evidence is biased or suppressed. Many of the so-called truths that we hear and read have been prepared by paid propagandists and directly interested individuals or groups. An individual who is seeking reelection to a town office may point to achievements in building codes, population growth, and improved schools but may omit any comment about increased taxes and faltering sewerage systems. An economist may deplore a rising unemployment rate but fail to mention that more persons are gainfully employed than ever before. Biased and suppressed evidence has caused everyone to recognize that "figures don't lie, but liars figure."

5. Begging the question

A common flaw in thinking consists of taking a conclusion for granted before it has been proved or assuming in the opening statement (proposition, premise) that which is to be proved in the conclusion. A question such as "Should a vicious man like Charles Grundy be allowed to hold office?" is "loaded" because it assumes what needs to be proved. Common forms of begging the question are *slanting, name calling,* and *shifting the meaning of a word.*

Using unfairly suggestive words to create an emotional attitude (as in the application of *vicious* to Charles Grundy) is a form of *slanting.* It is also a form of *argumentum ad hominem,* a Latin phrase meaning "argument against the person." That is, it is an argument aimed at the person who holds an opinion rather than against the opinion itself: "Only an idiot would believe that."

Guard against using or fully believing such suggestive words and phrases as *bigoted, saintly, progressive, reactionary, undemocratic ideas,* or *dangerous proposal.* Use them if you have supporting evidence; accept them if the proof offered seems valid. Otherwise, avoid slanting in writing and be on your guard when reading and listening.

Name calling is closely allied to slanting. It appeals to prejudice and emotion rather than to the intellect. It employs "good" words to approve and accept, "bad" words to condemn and reject. In writing and reading, be cautious in using such terms as *two-faced, yes man, angel in disguise, rabble rouser, benefactor, goon,* and so on.

Shifting the meaning of a word consists of using the same word several times with a shift in meaning designed to confuse the reader or listener. A *conservative* who is disposed to preserve existing conditions and to agree with gradual rather than abrupt changes is one thing; a conservative who is unswervingly opposed to all progress (i.e., a reactionary) is another. Student *unions* are one thing; labor *unions* are another. Should every citizen vote the Republican ticket because ours is a great *republic* or vote the Democratic ticket because this is a great *democracy?* Is there a difference between "doing good works" and being a "do-gooder"?

6. Testimonials

Citing statements from historical personages or well-known contemporaries is not necessarily straight thinking. In an attempt to bolster an argument, we are quick to employ such phrases as "authorities have concluded," "science proves," "hospitals say," and "laboratory tests reveal." Such expressions are sometimes no more than vague citations of unnamed authorities. Also, George Washington, Thomas Jefferson, and Abraham Lincoln—justly renowned as they are—might not have held economic, social, and political views necessarily valid in the twentieth century. Douglas MacArthur was an acclaimed military strategist, but something he said about internal combustion engines may be less convincing than the words of a good local mechanic. Are authorities in one field oracles of wisdom about any subject on which they speak or write? As a witness for or against an important educational policy, how effective would an eminent surgeon be? a football hero? a TV personality? If you were writing an attack on vaccination, would you reasonably expect the opposition of George Bernard Shaw to outweigh the pronouncements of the entire medical profession?

But even where there is little question of the validity of authority, be careful to see that neither bias nor the time element weakens your presentation. Some businesspeople and labor leaders are experts on economic problems, but their particular interests might prevent them from having the impartiality, the objectivity, of a disinterested observer. As for timing, remember that in many fields of human activity and knowledge, authorities soon become obsolete. Charles Darwin no longer has the last word on evolution; Sigmund Freud is not universally considered the final authority in psychoanalysis.

7. Distinguishing fact from opinion

A *fact* is based on actuality of some sort, a verifiable event or statement, whereas *opinion* is an inference that may be mingled with a supposed fact. That Ernest Hemingway was "an American writer" is a statement that can be proved. That Hemingway was "the greatest American novelist of the twentieth century" is only an opinion of those who hold it.

A favorite device of many writers and speakers is to mingle opinions with facts and thus obscure the difference between them.

8. Evading the issue

Evading the issue is most common in heated arguments. It consists of ignoring the point under discussion and making a statement that has no bearing on the argument. If you tell a friend that she drives too fast and she responds that you are a poor driver yourself, she has evaded the issue. She may be right, but she has neither met your objection nor won the argument. Such argument is especially common in political campaigns. It is easy to sidestep an issue and launch a counterattack, but such a method will not convince thoughtful readers.

9. Faulty analogy

Because two objects or ideas are alike in one or more respects, they are not necessarily similar in some further way. *Analogy* (partial similarity) can be both accurate and effective; otherwise we could not employ either similes or metaphors. But when we use figurative-language analogy (see Section 37f), we do not expect it to *prove* anything.

In the kind of writing most of us do most of the time, an analogy is useful chiefly as an illustration. But in many analogies the differences outweigh similarities: "Why do we need social security? Do we help trees when they lose their leaves in autumn winds? Do we provide assistance to dogs and horses in their old age? Don't some tribes kill people when they are too old to be useful?"

This analogy is obviously absurd, but even more literal analogies than this can be ridiculous. You may, for example, reason that since the honor system has worked well in many small colleges, it will work equally well in large universities. Are the similarities between the schools either superficial or less important than the differences? The whipping post was considered a deterrent to crime in seventeenth-century New England. Is it false analogy to suggest that similar punishment should be inflicted on twentieth-century criminals?

In itself, learning about the kinds of illogical or crooked thinking that everyone engages in occasionally will not materially improve anyone's thought processes. But becoming aware that many of the statements we make can be challenged on some logical ground should alert us to the need for straight thinking. Some answers to questions are obviously incorrect. Others may be partly right and partly wrong, with the "wrong" part caused by fuzzy thinking of some sort.

Straightening out crooked thinking is difficult. It may even seem a vague step toward better writing. But hazy and indefinite thinking will always prevent you from getting across to your readers precisely what you mean or think you mean.

log

72d

EXERCISE 44

Without paying too much attention to the exact, logical names, explain any errors in logical thinking in the following sentences or situations:

1. A student who is a scholar and nothing more will never get ahead in the world.
2. Two years of military training are included in the freshman year.
3. In my part of Arizona we have 365 days of sunshine every year, and that is a very conservative estimate.
4. A wife explained to her husband at breakfast that it was not her fault that the grocery was out of three-minute eggs.
5. [Three meanings] Headline on the garden page of the *Detroit News:* "Rose Fans Invited to Hear Insect Talk."
6. Jack became a great golfer because he was the son of an Ohio druggist.
7. Two women were in a restaurant: one, disliking smearcase, ordered cottage cheese instead; the other turned down horse mackerel salad in favor of tuna salad. How were these women fooled?
8. Can a man be a complete failure (success) because he never went to college except to accept honorary degrees?
9. To keep from hitting your thumb when driving a nail, you are advised to hold the hammer with both hands.
10. Did figures lie in the following? A college applicant was denied admission because he was not in the upper third of his class; he was only in the upper fourth.
11. A real estate agent recently sold a large quarter-acre wooded lot for $4000.
12. Since our grade schools and high school are located in a college town, we have the highest caliber of local education.
13. I have seen cars from almost every state in the Union, including Alaska and Canada, during my busy summer.
14. In national political campaigns, one party may send a "truth squad" to make speeches in cities where candidates of the other party have spoken. [What definitions of truth are suggested by "truth squad"?]
15. Henry Smith, 61 years old, a candidate for an important public office, was defeated by his rival, John Jones, aged 59. Throughout the campaign, Jones stressed in conversation and public speeches that Smith was a sexagenarian. Jones won easily.

log

72d

EXERCISE 45

In a biography entitled *Napoleon,* Emil Ludwig shows how Paris newspapers altered their news accounts from the time the deposed emperor escaped from the island of Elba on March 1, 1815, until he arrived in Paris three weeks later. Write a composition of 300–400 words as a commentary on this kind of name calling and on the weaknesses of human nature thus exhibited.

The monster has escaped from his place of exile.

The Corsican werewolf has landed at Cannes.

The tiger appeared at Gap, troops were sent against him, the wretched adventurer ended his career in the mountains.

The fiend has actually, thanks to treachery, been able to get as far as Grenoble.

The tyrant has reached Lyons, where horror paralyzed all attempts at resistance.

The usurper has dared to advance within 150 miles of the capital.

Bonaparte moves northward with rapid strides, but he will never reach Paris.

Tomorrow, Napoleon will be at our gates.

His Majesty is at Fontainebleau.

The Emperor has reassumed his imperial duties in Paris.

73. Revising

Writing an effective paper on the spur of the moment is a special skill, one that is useful chiefly at examination times. It is at least as difficult as the ability to speak extemporaneously and effectively. Rarely, however, will you be required to produce finished work on your first try. Almost always you have an opportunity to revise. And you should revise with care and attention. Most successful writers, professional and amateur, revise and rewrite not once but many times.

In commenting on the revising and rewriting that went into his famed novel, *The Sound and the Fury,* William Faulkner said, "I wrote it five separate times." Truman Capote, author of many works of fiction and nonfiction, including *In Cold Blood,* said of his work: "I write my first version in pencil. Then I do a complete revision, also in longhand."

Want more proof? The late Thornton Wilder, dramatist and novelist, once said, "There are passages in every novel whose first writing is the last. But it's the joint and cement between those passages that take a great deal of rewriting. Each sentence is a

rev

73

skeleton accompanied by enormous activity of rejection." The short story writer Frank O'Connor has stated that he rewrites "endlessly, endlessly, endlessly." He added "and I keep on rewriting after something is published."

Are you still unconvinced that all writing—repeat, *all*—requires careful checking, revision, and rewriting? Then listen to what James Thurber replied when asked if writing was easy for him:

> It's mostly a question of rewriting. It's part of a constant attempt to make the finished version smooth, to make it seem effortless." And when asked, "Then it's rare that your work comes out right the first time?" Mr. Thurber responded, "Well, my wife took a look at a first version and said 'That's high school stuff.' I had to tell her to wait until the seventh draft.

Alberto Moravia, a respected and popular writer, once commented:

> I like to compare my method of writing with that of painters centuries ago, proceeding from layer to layer. The first draft is quite crude, by no means finished. After that, I rewrite it many times—apply as many layers—as I feel to be necessary.

Such comments make writing seem like hard work. Well, it is. But *there is no such thing as good writing. There is only good rewriting.* If you are unwilling to revise and rewrite, you are skipping a major step toward becoming a better writer. True, you are not a professional writer and your work will not be judged by thousands or millions of readers. But if you realize that your work can be improved by revision, that such revision is necessary for all writers, and that your papers will be more effective in proportion to the amount of time you spend on them, then perhaps you can take heart and hope.

Also remember that the time spent in actually putting words on paper may be only a fraction of the time spent in preplanning. The writer of a good "one-hour" paper may well have composed it many times before setting it out on paper.

If this recommendation about rewriting seems grim, then relax over this amusing comment by the English poet Jonathan Swift:

> *Blot out, correct, insert, refine,*
> *Enlarge, diminish, interline.*
> *Be mindful when invention fails*
> *To scratch your head and bite your nails.*

73a. Carefully revise every composition.

If time permits—and it usually will if you allow for it—you can make any of four major kinds of revision when reworking a paper. You can

1. Add material
2. Delete material
3. Substitute material
4. Rearrange material

You might, for example, add a bit of dialog to increase the appeal of your paper. You might put in an example to reinforce your argument. You may discover that some paragraph is dull or that it repeats a point made earlier. Take it out. (True, eliminating words that were hard to come by and now seem precious is the most difficult phase of the entire rewriting process. Frequently, it is the most important.) You may discover that the paragraphs of your paper just don't seem to hang together, and you may wish to revise the structure of your entire paper. You may even find that you have not really written what you set out to write.

Consider this minor example of revision. An English instructor asked her students to write a brief paragraph with the topic sentence "Lying is bad policy." In ten minutes, one student wrote the following:

> Lying is bad policy. When you tell one lie, you usually have to tell a dozen more to cover up the first one. Even when you try your best to keep from getting caught, you usually wind up red-faced or red-handed. Sometimes the penalty for telling a lie can be severe. Telling the truth may hurt, but it's the only sure way to avoid trouble.

The instructor commented that the paragraph was free from obvious errors but that it was dull and repetitious. The writer improved it greatly in this simple revision:

> Lying is bad policy. A friend of mine applied for a summer job last year and told a lie about his previous experience when he filed his application. A week after he had started work, his supervisor discovered my friend's claim was false and fired him instantly. My friend not only lost his job, but he couldn't bear to explain what had really happened. Also, it was then too late

rev

73a

to get another good job and he was miserable all summer long. Now he knows, as I do, that lying can be both a bad and foolish policy.

This one paragraph—rewritten, the student said, in less than fifteen minutes—*adds, deletes, substitutes,* and *rearranges* material.

73b. Checklists for revising and rewriting

When revising a paper you should review its purpose, organization, development, sentence structure, diction, grammar, usage, and mechanics. The following checklists should serve as helpful guides to these matters:

Purpose
1. Does the paper have a clear, definite theme, a focus, a central point? Is it built around a stated or clearly implied thesis sentence?
2. Does it keep in mind the reader or readers for whom it is intended? Is the tone appropriate to the audience?
3. Does the paper seem likely to accomplish its purpose? If not, why not?

Organization
1. Does the plan of the paper follow a clear method of organization? For example, does it begin with a cause and proceed to an effect or begin with an effect and then develop the causes for that effect? Or, if the order is based on time, does the paper begin at the beginning and proceed to later stages?
2. Are the paragraphs arranged in logical order, one paragraph naturally following another?
3. Is the conclusion of the paper adequately anticipated and supported by preceding material?

Development
1. Is each paragraph adequate in material, unified in substance, and correctly proportioned in relation to other paragraphs in the paper?
2. Does the sum of the paragraphs reveal enough material to

convince readers of the point you are making? Conversely, have you included unnecessary or irrelevant material?

3. Are there adequate and clear transitions between paragraphs and between ideas?

4. Does the paper contain any logical loopholes, or flaws in reasoning, that will weaken your argument?

Sentence Structure

1. Does the paper contain any fused sentences? any comma faults? any unjustified sentence fragments?

2. Are there any dangling modifiers? any misplaced modifiers? any awkward split constructions?

3. Does the paper contain any sentences that reveal faulty parallelism, faulty coordination or subordination, and other illogical constructions?

4. Does the paper have any inconsistencies in tense, tone, or mood?

Diction, Grammar, and Usage

1. Is each word in the paper as suitable and effective as possible? Does the paper contain stale expressions, unnecessary words, or inappropriate examples of jargon and slang?

2. Does the paper contain any glaring errors in usage— incorrect reference of pronouns, faulty agreement, incorrect verb forms, mistakes in the case of pronouns?

Mechanics

1. Does the paper contain any misspelled words?

2. Is all the punctuation logical, necessary, and a clear aid to communication?

3. Is the paper neat in appearance and has it been prepared in accordance with prescribed form? (See Section 75.)

4. Has the paper been carefully proofread to eliminate careless errors of any kind? (See Section 74.)

rev

73b

EXERCISE 46

Make an honest analysis of the time spent on three of your compositions written outside class. Estimate the amount of time spent in preplanning, in writing, and in revising and proofreading.

EXERCISE 47

Rewrite a paper that you have turned in and gotten back. Submit both papers either to your instructor or to another student for comments on the two versions.

EXERCISE 48

The following is a short paper written outside of class. Read it carefully, marking all the errors and shortcomings you see. Give the paper a grade. Then write a comment that should help the writer in future papers.

THREE SERIOUS ERRORS IN ENGLISH

There were three reasons why I didn't get through. English 101 the first time. One of them being the sentence fragment. Time and time again I made this error. I did just about everything I could to prevent this error, but it seem to be a hopeless case. I could recognize the mistake when it was pointed out to me, but in proff reading I couldn't find them.

The sentence fragment gave me quite alot of trouble and kept my grades low; but another error, which put my grades down even lower, was spelling. In most cases it was'nt not knowing how to spell a particular word, it was carelessness more then anything else. I would misspell "there" and "their" all of the time. I knew the differences between the two; I was just careless in writeing them.

The last and biggest of my problems was the run-on-sentence. This I think was my biggest and worst mistake; if none of the other errors were on my themes you could be sure that the run-on-sentence was there to take care of the grade.

74. Proofreading

When we read, we usually see merely the outlines, or shells, of words. Only poor readers need to see individual letters as such; most of us comprehend words and even groups of words at a glance. But have you ever noticed how much easier it is to detect errors in someone else's writing than in your own? This may be because in reading someone else's writing you are looking for mistakes. Or it may be that you look more carefully at someone else's writing than at your own because you are unfamiliar with it and have to focus more sharply in order to comprehend. You already "know" what you yourself are saying.

Whatever the reason for closer scrutiny of other people's writing, in proofreading our own we must narrow the range of our vision and thereby pick up mistakes hitherto unnoticed. In short, we detect careless errors not by reading but by *proofreading,* which may be defined as reading carefully and intently for the sole purpose of detecting errors in spelling, punctuation, sentence structure, and other matters. Proofreading is a formation from "reading proof," *proof* being a term from printing that is applied to the first impression of composed type. Applied to your papers, proofreading means careful scanning of a finished product to determine what needs to be corrected.

Much of the effectiveness of proofreading depends on the spread of your vision. The following triangle will show how wide your vision (sight spread) is. Look at the top of the triangle and then down. How far down can you go and still identify each letter in each line at a single glance? Your central vision is as wide as the line above the one where you cannot identify each letter without moving your eyes at all.

```
                a
              a   r
            a   r   d
          a   r   d   c
        a   r   d   c   f
      a   r   d   c   f   g
    a   r   d   c   f   g   x
  a   r   d   c   f   g   x   y
  a   r   d   c   f   g   x   y   z
a   r   d   c   f   g   x   y   z   p
a   r   d   c   f   g   x   y   z   p   w
```

People differ in their range of vision, as they do in nearly everything else. But many people have difficulty identifying more than six letters at a single glance. Some have a span of vision embracing only three or four letters. Whatever your span, you should not try to exceed it when you are carefully checking for errors. If you do, you are reading—perhaps with excellent understanding—but you are not proofreading.

pfr

74

EXERCISE 49

Following the suggestions in this section, carefully proofread a paper that you are ready to hand in. How many mistakes did you find that needed correcting? Make a list of them and write a short paper about your findings.

EXERCISE 50

Write a paragraph of about 100 words with this topic sentence: "Careless errors in writing hinder communication as much as any kind of static hinders conversation."

EXERCISE 51

With a fellow student, exchange essays that each of you is ready to submit to an instructor. Carefully proofread the other student's paper. What are your findings?

75. Manuscript form

Interesting and well-planned as your paper may be, it is unlikely to win approval if it is untidy and illegible. Try to give your ideas the outward appearance that will guarantee ready communication.

75a. Conform to standards in preparing manuscript.

If you have received directions for the preparation of manuscripts, follow those. Otherwise, use the following as a guide for your final draft:

1. *Paper.* Use good-quality, preferably white bond, standard-sized stationery, 8½ by 11 inches. Use ruled paper for handwritten work.

2. *Title.* Center the title on the first line of ruled paper or about two inches from the top of unruled paper. Capitalize the first word and all other important words in the title. (See Section 31.) Do not use a period after the title, but use a question mark if necessary. Do not underline the title or enclose it in quotation marks unless it is itself a quotation.

3. *Beginning.* On ruled paper, leave one line blank between the title and the beginning of the essay; then write on each line or every other line, as directed by your instructor. On unruled paper, begin the paper about one inch below the title and leave about one-half inch between lines.

4. *Margins.* Leave a margin of at least one inch on the left side of each page. Standard theme paper may have a margin of one inch ruled off; leave a similar blank space on paper not having this vertical line. Leave a similar line on the right. Make the margins even and fairly uniform down the page. At the bottom, leave a margin of about one inch.

5. *Indentations.* Indent the first line of every paragraph about one inch. Use indentations of equal length for all paragraphs in the same paper. Make no exception if you use numbered paragraphs. On the second and following pages, indent the first line only if it is the beginning of a paragraph.

If, by chance, you have forgotten to indent a paragraph, show the paragraph division by placing the sign ¶ before the word beginning the paragraph. Cancel an unnecessary paragraph division by writing "no ¶" in the margin.

6. *Insertions and closures.* Use a caret (∧) when inserting an omitted word or expression. Use the sign ⌒ to join letters that have accidentally been separated.

7. *Cancellations.* Draw a line through material that you wish to cancel. Do not use parentheses on brackets to cancel words.

8. *Numbering of pages.* Number your pages with Arabic numerals in the upper right-hand corner of each page.

9. *Endorsement.* Write the following items in the order desired by your department or your instructor: With pages in proper order, fold the paper lengthwise through the middle (unless you are asked to leave it flat). On the right-hand side of the back of the last page write your name, the course title, the instructor's name (be sure to spell it right), the date, and the number of the paper. If the paper is unfolded, this information should be included on a separate title page.

**ms
form**

75b

75b. Make your handwriting legible.

Illegible writing taxes the patience of readers and causes them to give so much attention to the words themselves that their thoughts are turned away from the important ideas that should be considered. Make your handwriting easily readable by observing the following suggestions:

1. Do not crowd your writing. Make sure words are separated from each other and that each letter is legibly separated from its neighbors. Leave sufficient space between lines.

2. Join the consecutive letters of a word.

3. Form your letters carefully and consistently. Dot every *i* and *j*. Cross every *t*. Make the letters *m, n, u,* and *v* distinct and distinguish between small and capital letters.

4. Write with a good pen, using black or blue-black ink.

75c. Preferably, type your essay and other written work.

Not only is typescript more legible than handwriting; you can detect errors more easily in typescript than in handwriting. Observe the following conventions in typing:

1. *Paper.* Use standard-weight paper for the reader's copy; use onionskin only for the carbon copy that you keep (and be sure you do make and keep a copy). Avoid "erasable" coated papers; a slight touch is enough to smudge the typing on such papers, and errors can be corrected as easily on standard-weight paper by using correction paper or correction fluid.

2. *Title.* Center the title about two inches (12 lines) from the top of the sheet.

3. *Margins.* Leave margins of an inch or more at both left and right (one inch equals 10 pica spaces, 12 elite spaces). Leave a 1½-inch margin at the bottom. (It is easier if you measure the bottom margin before inserting the sheet in your typewriter. Make a small pencil mark where the last line of type should be and erase the mark after the page has been typed.)

4. *Spacing.* Double-space all lines except for lengthy quoted material. (See Section 27b.) Single-space in business letters, which have double-spacing only between paragraphs.

5. *Indentations.* Indent paragraph beginnings either 5 or 10 spaces.

6. *Special characters.* To form a dash, use two hyphens (-) with no space preceding or following them. If your typewriter has no key for the exclamation point, form one by striking a

ms form

75c

period, backspacing, and striking an apostrophe. For numbers, use a small "1" for the Arabic "one" (if you have no special key for the Arabic "one") and a capital "I" for the Roman "one." Write in brackets ([ ]) in ink.

7. *Spacing within lines.* After a period, question mark, or exclamation point, space twice; after internal punctuation marks, including the period after abbreviations and initials, space once.

8. *Endorsement.* The endorsement on a typewritten paper is usually placed in an upper corner of the first page.

If you have carried out your revision thoroughly, flaws in the final draft are only slips of the pen or errors in typing. Because such slips do occur, proofread the final draft with care. Do this with pen or pencil in hand, pointing to every word and punctuation mark. Errors in typed copy may be neatly corrected in ink; a typewritten page is not sacred.

**ms
form**

75c

VIII.
Special Compositions

The following sections deal with the précis, the paraphrase, the letter, the report, and the library paper. The précis and the paraphrase may not turn up as writing assignments in your English course, but they are valuable study aids in every course you take. You are likely to use the letter and the report more often in your postcollege years than now; learning how to write them is an investment for now and the future. Preparing a library paper and understanding what you are doing is one of the most valuable intellectual experiences college can offer.

76. The précis

Many questions asked on examinations require answers that summarize. Each day we are called on to give, in written or oral form, condensed versions of events, ideas, or impressions. Radio and TV news commentators furnish what are essentially summaries of the latest news developments. Magazines like *Time* and *Newsweek* contain short articles that are really condensations of news accounts. Business and industrial executives frequently ask employees to submit brief reports concerning developments in their departments or trends in business or research, or to write brief introductory summaries of longer reports.

A summary, as a condensed version of a longer passage or a more extended account, has several names: *abstract, abridgment, condensation, digest, epitome, précis, résumé, synopsis,* and more. All productions of this kind are here referred to as précis, although the term *summary* would serve as well.

A *précis*—the word serves for both singular and plural and is pronounced "pray-see"—is a brief summary or abstract of the essential thought of a longer composition. It provides a miniature of the original selection, reproducing the same proportions on a smaller scale, the same ideas, the same mood and tone as far as is possible. Makers of précis cannot interpret or comment; their sole function is to give a reduction of the author's exact and essential meaning, including all important details. Whether or not you agree or disagree with the author of what you are summarizing makes no difference in writing a précis. It's easy to avoid simple agreement or disagreement, but it is more difficult—and just as important—to make sure that the words you use do not reflect your own opinions.

76a. Read the selection carefully.

When assigned a précis to write, you will need to read carefully, analytically, and reflectively in order to group the central ideas. In doing such reading, follow two steps:

1. Give the material a thorough reading once in order to get a clear understanding of the whole.
2. Reread paragraph by paragraph in order to grasp each paragraph topic and notice how it has been developed.

Look up the meanings of words and phrases about which you are in doubt. Look for important or key expressions that must be used in your précis if it is to preserve the essential meaning and flavor of the original selection. See how the material has been organized, what stylistic devices the writer has used, what kinds of illustrations support the main thought.

76b. Use your own words.

As you read, restate the main idea of each paragraph clearly and concisely. Quoting sentences, perhaps topic sentences, from each paragraph results in a sentence outline, not a précis. You must use your own words for the most part, although some quoting is permissible; ordinarily, however, the phrasing of the original will not be suitable. Once you have mastered the thought of the material, your problem is one of original composition; your own analysis and statement of the major thought are what count.

76c. Limit the number of words used.

The length of a complete précis cannot be determined arbitrarily, but aim at a condensation that is one-third to one-fourth as long as the original. Omit nothing of real importance but remember that the central purpose of a précis is condensation.

76d. Follow the plan of the original.

Follow the order of the original so that the condensation will be accurate. Thoughts and facts should not be rearranged; if they are, the essence of the original may be distorted. Give attention to proportion. Try to preserve the mood and tone of the original.

76e. Use effective English.

The completed précis should be a model of exact and emphatic word choice and clear, effective sentence construction, because it must be intelligible to a reader who has not seen the original. Bring together your various summarizing statements with suitable transitions. Your passage from one sentence to another should be smooth and unobtrusive, emphasizing the unity and coherence of the summary. As you proceed, you may need to contract certain parts. Although the précis is not likely to be so well written as the original, it should read smoothly and possess the virtues of an effective composition in its own right.

The following is a précis made by a student. Judge it in terms of the suggestions just made.

ORIGINAL

But as for the bulk of mankind, they are clearly devoid of any degree of taste. It is a quality in which they advance very little beyond a state of infancy. The first thing a child is fond of in a book is a picture, the second is a story, and the third a jest. Here then is the true Pons Asinorum, which very few readers ever get over. [69 words]

—HENRY FIELDING

PRECIS

Most people lack taste; they remain childlike. Readers, like children, rarely ever get over the "bridge of asses" constituted by pictures, stories, and jokes. [24 words]

EXERCISE 1

Write a précis of these two paragraphs from Robinson's essay "On Various Kinds of Thinking."

A third kind of thinking is stimulated when anyone questions our beliefs and opinions. We sometimes find ourselves changing our minds without any resistance or heavy emotion, but if we are told that we are wrong we resent the imputation and harden our hearts. We are incredibly heedless in the formation of our beliefs, but find ourselves filled with an illicit passion for them when anyone proposes to rob us of their companionship. It is obviously not the ideas themselves that are dear to us, but our self-esteem, which is threatened. We are by nature stubbornly pledged to defend our own from attack, whether it be our person, our family, our property, or our opinion. A United States Senator once remarked to a friend of mine that God Almighty could not make him change his mind on our Latin-American policy. We may surrender, but rarely confess ourselves vanquished. In the intellectual world at least, peace is without victory.

Few of us take the pains to study the origin of our cherished convictions; indeed, we have a natural repugnance to so doing. We like to continue to believe what we have been accustomed to accept as true, and the resentment aroused when doubt is cast upon any of our assumptions leads us to seek every manner of excuse for clinging to them. The result is that most of our so-called reasoning consists in finding arguments for going on believing as we already do. [242 words]

EXERCISE 2

Write a précis of this paragraph from Gloria Steinem's "What It Would Be Like if Women Win."

Men now suffer from more diseases due to stress, heart attacks, ulcers, a higher suicide rate, greater difficulty living alone, less adaptability to change and, in general, a shorter life span than women. There is some scientific evidence that what produces physical problems is not work itself, but the inability to choose which work, and how much. With women bearing half the financial responsibility, and with the idea of "masculine" jobs gone, men might well feel freer and live longer. [80 words]

77. The paraphrase

The *paraphrase* is a kind of report on reading that is frequently required in college work. Whereas a précis is a digest of the essential meaning of an original passage, a paraphrase is a full-length statement of that meaning. A paraphrase presents a free rendering of the sense of a passage, fully and proportionately, but in words different from the original.

The paraphrase is used to make clear any material that is vague, obscure, or difficult, a process that usually consists of both simplification and modernization. You may have read a difficult poem or discussion that you could not make sense of until you put it in your own words. After you did so, its meaning was clear, and you felt that you had actually translated the passage into your own thoughts. Much of the learning in classrooms begins with paraphrasing ideas expressed in assignments from textbooks and other materials. In other words, almost every day you need to reshape source material.

Three common uses of paraphrase are the following: (1) paraphrasing technical, semitechnical, or otherwise difficult materials into understandable nontechnical English; (2) paraphrasing poems into prose as a test of your understanding; (3) paraphrasing poetry or prose of earlier periods into present-day prose.

If the material to be paraphrased is poetry, remember these points: (1) A line of poetry is a *poetic* unit, not a *sense* unit; it need not be and very likely is not a sentence. As a first step, write out the poem as if it were prose; then reread it with special attention to punctuation marks and the purposes they serve. (2) Poetry, for poetic reasons, often uses inverted, suspended, or transposed word order; rearrange these words in normal English word order—subject and modifiers, predicate and modifiers, object and modifiers.

In making a paraphrase, follow these suggestions:

77a. Study the original passage.

Study here means that you should read the original as often as necessary to approach an understanding of its full and exact meaning. It is impossible to paraphrase a passage until you are familiar with its purpose, organization, development, and essential content. Some phrases and sentences you will probably have to reread several times, carefully and reflectively, before their meaning becomes clear. If the passage contains obscure words and allusions, consult a dictionary or other reference work to determine their meanings.

77b. Use your own words.

Find understandable equivalents for words and phrases that are obscure, but do not strain for synonyms. Use words from the original if their meaning is unmistakably clear, but do not hesitate

para

77b

to use your own words and phrases where simplification, clarity, or modernization require them.

77c. Leave out nothing of importance.

A paraphrase is a restatement and, as such, should contain the thought of the original in its entirety. Omitting significant detail is a violation of the original and results in distortion.

77d. Add nothing that is not in the original.

Interpretation and explanation should be confined to making clear what the original author had in mind. Whether you like or dislike what the writer has said, whether you agree or disagree with the original, whether you think its logic is sound or faulty— these considerations do not enter into the making of a paraphrase. Your making of a paraphrase, of course, does not mean that you cease to think; it means that your thinking produces a full-length statement of an author's meaning.

The following is a paraphrase made by a student. Criticize it in terms of the suggestions just given.

On First Looking Into Chapman's Homer
Much have I travell'd in the realms of gold,
And many goodly states and kingdoms seen;
Round many western islands have I been
Which bards in fealty to Apollo hold.
Oft of one wide expanse had I been told
That deep-brow'd Homer ruled as his demesne:
Yet did I never breathe its pure serene
Till I heard Chapman speak out loud and bold:
Then felt I like some watcher of the skies
When a new planet swims into his ken;
Or like stout Cortez, when with eagle eyes
He stared at the Pacific—and all his men
Look'd at each other with a wild surmise—
Silent, upon a peak in Darien.

—JOHN KEATS

PARAPHRASE
I have read widely in the great classics of literature and have noted many examples of great poetry. I had often been told of the work of Homer and the poetry which he had created, but I never

really understood or appreciated its great beauty and power until I read Chapman's translation. Then I felt as awed as some astronomer who unexpectedly discovers a new planet, or as surprised and speechless as Cortez [Balboa] and his followers were when they saw the Pacific Ocean for the first time, from Panama.

EXERCISE 3

Paraphrase this sonnet by William Shakespeare:

Let me not to the marriage of true minds
Admit impediments. Love is not love
Which alters when it alteration finds,
Or bends with the remover to remove:
O, no! it is an ever-fixèd mark
That looks on tempests and is never shaken;
It is the star to every wandering bark,
Whose worth's unknown, although his height be taken.
Love's not Time's fool, though rosy lips and cheeks
Within his bending sickle's compass come;
Love alters not with his brief hours and weeks,
But bears it out even to the edge of doom.
* If this be error and upon me proved,*
* I never writ, nor no man ever loved.*

EXERCISE 4

Write a paraphrase of this paragraph from Lisa Hobbs' *Love and Liberation:*

What has happened is simply that our society has become one giant rational construct. It is an intellectual abstraction and no longer relates to the warm, groping, shabby, and sometimes hilarious realities of our human nature. These concepts under which we live, which force us forever to compete, to play sexually stereotyped roles, to marry as we do, raise children as we do, make war as we do, make love as we do, work as we do, and relate as we do—these concepts have polluted our souls.

78. The letter

let

78

During your college years you probably will write many more letters than formal papers, and after graduation you may find it necessary to write even more letters than you did in college. From the standpoints of utility and frequency, no other form of writing is as important, for the ability to write a good letter can accomplish much more than is commonly realized. Important business firms waste little time on poorly written applications, and often business and social contacts are hindered by ignorance of appropriate forms and conventions.

The two main kinds of letters are *informal* (or friendly) and *business* letters. This section concentrates on business letters, but it might not be amiss to suggest that in writing friendly letters you keep these suggestions in mind:

1. Think about your reader, not only about yourself.
2. Write legibly.
3. Take your time.
4. Provide details.
5. Adapt what you write to your intended reader.

A third kind of letter, the *formal* letter, includes invitations and replies, the stylized patterns for which are to be found in reference books on etiquette.

A writer of business letters is concerned primarily with *presentation* and *content,* or, respectively, arrangement and expression of material and the subject matter included. The following sections introduce general principles for use in business correspondence both now and later.

78a. Effective methods of presentation

A good business letter creates a pleasing impression the moment it is taken from its envelope. Quality of paper, neatness of typing or writing, and arrangement of letter parts are almost as important to the total effect as content is. Correctness and attractiveness in *form* reflect a courteous attitude toward the reader.

Stationery

Use good-quality, white unruled paper of standard size, 8½ by 11 inches, even for longhand letters. Do not use colored or unusual-sized sheets.

Typing

Type your letters, if possible, with a fresh black ribbon to ensure legibility; do not allow strikeovers or visible erasures to appear in the final version. If you lack a typewriter, write legible longhand with black or blue-black ink.

Form

Good business letters are arranged in a form that has now become standardized. It consists of six parts:

1. The heading
2. The inside address
3. The greeting, or salutation

4. The body
5. The complimentary close
6. The signature

Each part has certain set forms that must not be ignored or altered if your letter is to be conventional, attractive, and easy to read. Study the letters in this section for the position of parts, illustrations of common usages, and balanced arrangement of conventional forms.

1. The Heading

The heading contains the sender's full address—street, city, state, ZIP code—and the date of writing. It is placed in the upper-right- or left-hand part of the sheet, an inch or more below the top edge. (See the section on "*Margins*.") If it is set in the upper right-hand part, its longest line should end flush with the right margin. It is single-spaced. Avoid abbreviations, and don't use *st, nd, rd,* or *d* after the day. On stationery with a letterhead, only the date is added, ending flush with the right margin or centered directly beneath the letterhead. Use no punctuation at the ends of lines except periods after conventional abbreviations; this system, now widely used, is called "open punctuation."

2. The Inside Address

The name and address of the person or company you are writing to should appear from two to four spaces below the heading and flush with the left margin. It is single-spaced. Again, avoid all but conventional abbreviations, and, in harmony with the heading, use no punctuation at the ends of lines except abbreviation periods.

Some title should precede the name of the person addressed: *Mr., Ms., Mrs., Miss.* A business title rarely precedes the name,

let

78a

529

but a person of professional standing may be addressed as *Dr., The Reverend, President, Dean, Senator, Professor, General,* etc.

Note: For the proper titles of a divorced woman; armed services, diplomatic, government, legal, academic, religious (Protestant, Catholic, Jewish) personnel; and nobility in England, France, Germany, Italy, and Spain, complete information is given in some books of etiquette and in some dictionaries.

If only the last name of the person written to is known, or only the person's position in a firm, the letter is addressed to the firm, with *Attention: Mr. ———; Attention: Ms. ———;* or *Attention: Director of Personnel* (or whatever) added. The "attention" line usually appears two spaces below the inside address and two above the greeting; it has no effect on the greeting itself, which is always determined from the first line of the inside address.

3. The Greeting, or Salutation

The greeting (salutation) is placed two spaces below the inside address and flush with the left-hand margin. It is preferably punctuated with a colon, not a comma, semicolon, dash, or colon and dash. The following forms of salutation are common. Notice that *dear* is capitalized only when it is the first word.

Dear Dr. Bard:	Dear Mrs. (Ms., Miss) Lord:
My dear Dr. Bard:	My dear Mrs. (Ms., Miss) Lord:
Dear Sir:	Dear Madam:

The salutation, "Gentlemen," is usually used only when the letter is addressed to a firm or institution rather than an individual.

For people with special titles mentioned in the earlier section on "The Inside Address," consult a reference book for the appropriate greeting to fit the title.

4. The Body

The body of the letter contains the message and begins two spaces below the greeting. Most business letters are single-spaced, although a short message may be double-spaced for attractive arrangement on a large page. Single-spaced letters require two spaces between each paragraph. Paragraphs may be in block form (if the heading and inside address correspond in form) or indented. They may be indented, for clearness and effectiveness, even when the block system is used in other parts. (See the section on "Full Block and Modified Block Forms.")

If double spacing is used in the body of the letter, paragraphs are more clearly indicated by indentation. On the typewriter, in-

let

78a

dentation may be five or ten spaces; some letter writers indent one space beyond the length of the greeting line.

Paragraphs in business letters are shorter than in most other kinds of prose; they usually vary in length from two to six lines. Longer paragraphs are rare; one-line paragraphs are often used.

Messages that are too long for one page are continued on a second page, never on the back of a sheet. However, the second page should contain at least two lines, preferably more, in addition to the complimentary close and the signature. A paragraph may be continued from one page to the other, but at least two lines of the paragraph should appear on the page on which it begins or ends. Each additional page should carry a top-line identification, such as the addressee's initials or name, the page number, and the date: "H. M. Brown—September 12, 1980—Page 2."

5. The Complimentary Close

The close is usually placed at the middle or slightly to the right of the middle of the page, two spaces below the last line of the body of the letter. Only the first word is capitalized. Punctuation is usually a comma. Common forms of the complimentary close are the following:

Cordially,	Very sincerely yours,
Yours cordially,	Yours very sincerely,
Cordially yours,	Yours very truly,
Yours sincerely,	Very truly yours,
Sincerely yours,	Yours truly,

Respectfully yours is often conventionally used in letters to public officials, to clergy and others in religious orders, and to those ranking above the writer in academic circles, such as a college dean or president.

The close is independent of the last paragraph of the letter and should not be linked to it by a participial phrase such as "Thanking you in advance," "I remain," or "Hoping for an early reply." Clever or original forms such as "Enthusiastically yours," "Apologetically yours," "Yours for lower taxes," and the like are to be avoided except in personal letters.

6. The Signature

The signature is placed directly below the complimentary close. If the signature (name) is typewritten, at least four spaces are allowed for the insertion of a handwritten signature. Unless a letter is mimeographed or is plainly a circular letter, it should always have a legible handwritten signature in ink.

An unmarried woman may use simply *Ms.* or may place the title *Miss* in parentheses before her name; if either is included in the typewritten signature, it is not needed in the written signature:

Ms. Elizabeth West   (Miss) Elizabeth West

A married woman may use simply *Ms.* with the name she is known by, or may sign her own full name, followed by her married name in parentheses:

Ms. Anne Shelton   (or)   Anne Morris Shelton
                                    (Mrs. Paul R. Shelton)

If she wishes, a woman may choose to follow the common practice of men in placing no title before a written or typed name, that is, omitting titles such as *Mr., Dr.,* or *Rev.* But the writer's business title is often given: *General Manager, Superintendent, Vice President,* and so forth. Letter convention opposes putting an address under the signature; its proper place is in the heading.

Margins

Balanced layout of the letter on the page is determined by the length of the message. The entire letter, including heading, inside address, complimentary close, and signature, should have the appearance of a rectangle, with the top and bottom margins slightly wider than those at the sides. Side margins are at least an inch wide, and care should be taken to maintain as even a right margin as possible. Short business letters should be approximately centered, with wide margins.

For firms that use window envelopes, which require the inside address to be in the same position on every letter, long or short, the *standard line form* has been developed. The inside address begins a certain number of lines from the top edge. The first line of the body begins two spaces below the salutation; margins are smaller and uniform, about an inch, on each letter; and the typed lines cross the page, whether the letter is long or short.

Full block and modified block forms

Arrangement of the lines of the heading and of the inside address may follow the *full block* or the *modified block* system. In both, the second and third lines of the heading and of the inside address, respectively, begin directly underneath the beginning of the first line. In the full block form, all the parts of the letter, including the heading, complimentary close, and signature, begin at the left-hand margin. In the modified block form, the heading, complimentary close, and signature are on the right side of the letter.

The envelope

The envelope carries the sender's name and return address in the upper left-hand corner and the addressee's name slightly below the center and to the right. The full address should be used, in harmony with the inside address on the letter, although double spacing of a three-line address on an envelope is helpful to the Post Office Department, which prefers indented lines as well as the placing of the state on a separate line, followed by the zip code on the same line.

Conventional folding of the letter depends on the size of the envelope. When using the large No. 10 (9½″ by 4⅛″) envelope, fold the lower third of the sheet over the message, fold the upper part down to within a half-inch of the creased edge, and put the upper folded edge in the envelope first.

When using the smaller No. 6¾ (6½″ by 3⅝″), envelope, fold the lower part of the letter page over the message to within approximately one-half inch of the top of the page. Next, fold from the right slightly more than one-third, then from the left, leaving the left flap edge slightly short of the right folded edge. Insert the left folded edge into the envelope first.

The reason for these folds is obvious. If the reader opens your letter in the conventional way, the letter comes out of the envelope half-unfolding itself, top edge and written face up, ready to read.

Of course, for a window-envelope the letter is folded so that the inside address fits the "window" and thus becomes the outside address as well.

78b. Arrange the content effectively.

In addition to following the general principles of effective writing, business letters should be *clear, concise, complete,* and *courteous.* Since the object of a business letter is to convey information, and since you hope to secure the reader's attention, you should carefully plan every letter and its phrasing.

1. Opening sentence

Open the letter with a statement of its subject or its purpose, a courteous request, a direct question, an important statement, or several of these in combination. Avoid clichés like those listed under "Language" below. Include briefly in the opening sentences or paragraph any pertinent background information that will clarify your message. Make the purpose of your letter evident, and arrange your thoughts in logical, easy-to-follow units. Separate ideas require separate paragraphs and should be developed according to the principles discussed in Sections 54 and 55.

2. Closing sentence

Your letter should close strongly. As indicated under "The Complimentary Close," avoid weak participial or prepositional phrases. Make your last group of words a complete sentence: an invitation, a direct question, a courteous request, a restatement of the subject of the letter, or some other significant comment.

3. Language

Remember your reader: Avoid using overly formal English, but at the same time avoid using trite, outworn, "business" expressions like the following:

according to my records	in receipt of
am pleased to advise	meets your approval
as per	past favors
as soon as possible	permit us
an early date	recent date
at this writing	regret to advise
at your earliest convenience	take the liberty of
attached hereto	thank you in advance
beg to acknowledge (state, advise, etc.)	under separate cover
	valued wishes
contents noted	we trust
enclosed herewith	wish to advise (state, inform)
enclosed please find	would advise (state, inform)
has come to hand	you may rest assured

Use a soundly idiomatic style. Colloquialisms are permissible but avoid slang or a telegraphic style. Effective letters use the same courteous and friendly language as in business conversation over the telephone.

4. Types of business letters

The numerous types of business letters are classified according to their content or message. The most common kinds are the following:

1. Order letters and acknowledgments of orders
2. Letters asking or granting adjustments
3. Sales letters
4. Inquiries and replies; also other letters of information
5. Credit letters (designed to encourage buying now and paying later)
6. Collection letters (designed to encourage paying now)
7. Letters of application
8. Letters of recommendation or introduction

For detailed discussion of the various types of letters used in the transaction of business, you are referred to books listed in the card catalog of your library under "Business Letters" or "Letter Writing—Business."

Your most immediate and pressing need for information about conventional business letters may concern the *letter of application.* What follows is designed to help you secure the summer or after-hours or after-college job that you want and need.

An effective letter of application stresses throughout the writer's ability and desire to be of benefit to the prospective employer. Always emphasize what you, the applicant with your qualifications, can do for your employer, not what the latter can do for you. Your letter should be courteous, straightforward, and honest, offering services without pleading or demanding.

Open your letter by applying for a specific position and indicating how you learned of the opening: from a friend, an agency, a "Help Wanted" advertisement, or whomever. If your application is unsolicited, give your special reason for applying. Present your qualifications—education, experience, interest, and aptitude—and

let

78b

535

612 East Maple Road
Lafayette, Indiana 47905
February 10, 1980

Cincinnati Film Supply Company
412 West Main Street
Cincinnati, Ohio 45202

Gentlemen:

From your February catalog, please send me by parcel post the following 2″ × 2″ color slides:

Cat. No.	No. of Sets	Name	Unit Price	Total
CK 159	1	California Highways	$2.20	2.20
CK 312	2	California Beaches	3.30	6.60
PK 168	1	Yosemite National Park	2.75	2.75
PK 169	1	Yellowstone National Park	2.75	2.75
TK 98	3	1978 Tournament of Roses	3.30	9.90
				24.20
		Estimated parcel post charge		.50
		Total		24.70

My check for $24.70 is enclosed.

Very truly yours,

Edward J. Ryan, Jr.

Edward J. Ryan, Jr.

Encl.

emphasize those items that would be particularly useful to the employer. Devote a brief paragraph to personal information: age, health, and other pertinent details. Include two or three references, listing them separately, either in the body of the letter or immediately after the close, with full names, titles, and addresses. Close your letter by requesting an interview at the employer's convenience. If you are in the same city, indicate where you may be reached by telephone.

Note: Always receive permission from the persons whom you wish to suggest as references, and remember that it is courteous to write letters thanking them for their help.

The most effective letter of application is twofold: the letter itself and an *information record, vita,* or *résumé,* carefully prepared first. The letter itself is fairly brief: direct application with, usually, the source of information; a paragraph or two stressing pertinent points in the information record or additional information, without repeating material in the record; and a closing paragraph requesting an interview, with pertinent details such as time, place, and the like. The information record gives in classified form all the applicant's assets with a bearing on the position.

---

612 East Maple Road
Lafayette, Indiana 47905
February 23, 1980

Cincinnati Film Supply Company
412 West Main Street
Cincinnati, Ohio 45202

Attention: Adjustment Manager

Gentlemen:

My February 10 order, which arrived today, contained three sets of the 1948 Tournament of Roses instead of the three sets of the 1978 Tournament of Roses.

I am therefore returning by parcel post these three sets, to be replaced by the 1978 sets ordered.

Very truly yours,

Edward J. Ryan, Jr.
Edward J. Ryan, Jr.

---

let

78b

The content of the two-part letter of application is illustrated in the following:

1. The letter itself, sent by Julia M. Taylor, a junior at the University of Central Illinois at Concord, Illinois, to Mr. Kirby James, Allegheny Central Industries, Pittsburgh, Pennsylvania 15219, and dated January 18, 1980:

Mr. Laurence Frazier, your area representative, has told me that you are now accepting applications for management trainees. Please consider me an applicant for one of the positions.

Enclosed is an Information Record, giving my qualifications for the position. The university courses I have listed are my favorites, and in those that I have completed I have maintained a B average.

My high school and college experiences, my special assets, and even many of my hobbies all point, so my University counselor tells me, to a future in which I should make management, and especially personnel, my life's work.

I should like to have the chance to demonstrate the benefits I can bring to your company through your training program.

May I have an interview? I will be home for the Spring holiday at Easter, [Month and Date]. During those vacation days, I can come to your office at your convenience.

2. The information record:

INFORMATION RECORD
concerning
JULIA M. TAYLOR

PERSONAL INFORMATION

Age: 21	Home Address: 577 East Garden
Height: 5 feet, 6 inches	Road, Pittsburgh, Pennsylvania 15204
	Telephone: (412) 564-1564
Weight: 135 pounds	College Address: 912 Stanford
Health: Excellent	Street, Concord, Illinois
	62526 Telephone: (309) 865-1439

EDUCATION

High School: Audubon High School, McKeesport, Pennsylvania
　　　　　　　　Graduated, June 1976

College: University of Central Illinois,
Concord, Illinois
Degree: Bachelor of Arts, expected June
1980
Major: English (American Literature)
Minor: Economics
Scholarship standing: upper fourth of
class
Courses bearing on application, already
completed:
  English 330--Advanced Composition
  English 380--Modern English Grammar
    and Usage
  Speech 212--Informal Speaking
  Speech 321--Group Discussion
  Psychology 120--Introduction to
   Psychology
  Psychology 334--Group Dynamics
  Economics 205--The American Business
    System
  Economics 310--Economic Theory
Courses planned for second semester:
  Psychology 345--Psychology of
    Leadership
  Education 375--Testing and
    Measurements

EXPERIENCE

Four years experience in Student Government, arranging
committees to deal with various aspects of the
homecoming celebrations

Assisting (this college year, three afternoons a week)
in the office of the Dean of Students in the
administering of aptitude tests for the Placement
Service

SPECIAL ASSETS

Experience (from the foregoing) in arranging and
supervising groups

Four years experience (in English classes and Student
Government work) in the drafting of written
communications

Familiarity in the Dean of Students' office with
generally used instruments for measuring interest
and aptitude

Genuine interest in working with people

REFERENCES (by permission, for education, experience,
and character)

Professor Harold J. Creek, Department of English,

let

78b

539

University of Central Illinois, Concord, Illinois
62526
Dr. Leila Semmeredge, Dean of Students, University of
Central Illinois, Concord, Illinois 62526
Professor Thomas R. Bloom, Department of Economics,
University of Central Illinois, Concord, Illinois
62526
Rev. F. X. McNulty, Pastor, St. Sylvester's Church,
Pittsburgh, Pennsylvania 15204

EXERCISE 5

Collect and bring to class at least eight examples of business letters.
(Perhaps a relative or business acquaintance may lend you some letters.)
Study the letterheads used. Note especially both the usual and unusual
features of the six parts of the letters (heading, inside address, greeting,
body, complimentary close, signature). Notice the quality of paper used,
the spacing and length of the paragraphs, and the tone of the letters.

EXERCISE 6

Write a letter of inquiry to your state historical society concerning some
old industries in your town.

EXERCISE 7

Write a request for a refund on an unused bus ticket.

EXERCISE 8

From a magazine advertisement, write a letter ordering the item or
items advertised.

EXERCISE 9

Answer the following want ad: "WANTED: Counselors and aides for
boys' and girls' camps, June through August. Children are from 8 to 13.
Give full details concerning qualifications. Apex Summer Camps, Lake
Ormandy, Ohio."

Answer the following want ad: "WANTED: Student to wait tables and serve as cashier in local tearoom. Hours 3 to 6. Time for study during work. Give age, references, and previous experience, if any. Dept. S-7, *Courier,* New Bedford, Mass."

79. The report

A *report* is an account or statement describing in detail an event, situation, or circumstance, usually as a result of observation or inquiry. As a verb, *report* means literally to "carry back" and more generally means to "relate what has been learned by seeing and investigating."

If you witness a person entering a thicket in which you have noticed a reptile and you cry, "Look out for the snake," you have produced an efficient report. This is, you have clearly, briefly, and effectively conveyed important and useful information on a single topic about which you have become knowledgeable.

Report writing, however, is usually less simple and spontaneous than this warning about a snake. It may involve two or three pages of expository writing or, possibly, many pages bound in a folder containing pictures, diagrams, and charts. Regardless of length or form, reports and letters are likely to be the two forms of writing that you will use and depend upon most in later life.

A report can appear in the form of a research paper (see Section 80) or a letter (see Section 78) or even a précis (see Section 76), but most often it is a summary of activity based on an experiment or an investigation. For example, the activities of an organized group may require reports. Whether you are an officer in a civic group, the chairperson of a union committee, an accountant, or a research scientist, you will do a better job if you can submit a well-prepared, well-written report.

Report writing is becoming increasingly popular as an assignment in first-year English. Realizing that sometimes the preparation of a full-length library paper is taxing and is more time-consuming than some students can manage, more instructors than ever before are assigning reports. Such papers demand careful investigation, close observation, and often some library use. But reports are not usually expected to be as lengthy as library papers and normally do not require as full documentation (footnotes and bibliography).

79a. Planning a report

A good report contains enough accurate and pertinent information to accomplish the job it is designed to accomplish—and not one bit more. In order to ensure adequate but not excess coverage, outline the report (see Section 64) before you begin or frame an outline as you proceed. No satisfactory report was ever written without some sort of plan prepared in advance or developed as the writing progressed.

Such a scheme for an informal report might cover these questions:

1. Who asked you to study the problem? When? Why?
2. Precisely what is the subject to be reported on?
3. How was the investigation made? [Authorities consulted, people interviewed, places visited, tests made, reading done]
4. What are the specific results or recommendations?

In a formal or lengthy report, a summary of the methods used to obtain information and of the results or recommendations comes first. This summary is followed by the main body of the report, which discusses these summary points in detail. A list of topics on "Club Conditions in This College" might resemble the following:

1. Summary
2. Members of the investigating committee
3. Methods of conducting the survey
4. Number and kinds of clubs investigated
5. Means of selecting club members
6. Activities of the clubs involved in this study
7. Club contributions to the college
8. Clubs and elections
9. Clubs and the community
10. Effects of clubs on the student body

79b. Summarizing a report

The plan of an effective report is usually dictated by the opening summary, as in the following illustration:

> The purpose of this report is to determine (1) whether the program designed to give new employees an understanding of the products and social significance of the company has actually justified its cost in time and money; and (2) whether changes are needed to improve the program if it is retained.
>
> The investigation has been based on four sources of information: (1) interviews with employees who have completed the program; (2) interviews with supervisory personnel; (3) statistical comparisons of work efficiency between those who have and have not taken the program; (4) published reports on related programs at four other industrial centers.
>
> The report establishes the value of the program and recommends its continuation. Suggestions for improvement: (1) Top-level executives should contribute more actively to the program through individual interviews with employees and by lectures to groups. (2) Greater use of visual-aid material is needed to explain certain complex company operations. (3) The orientation course should be extended by two weeks.

Brief and informal reports do not require written summaries, but every report should be so organized and presented that it can be summarized in some way.

1. Selectivity

No report reveals everything that is known about any subject. Good report writers indicate careful planning and ability as much by what they omit as by what they include. Even so, competent reporters never regret collecting more material than they can use. Only if they collect more than they need can they write "from strength" by having in reserve more than is required.

2. Objectivity

Investigators who know in advance what answers they wish to get and use data to support their predetermined points of view are neither fair nor competent reporters. A report should be approached without personal prejudice. Results and recommenda-

rpt

79b

tions should be based on materials that have been collected and organized with an open mind. An effective report contains no exaggeration and few superlatives. The reliable report writer presents what he or she feels certain are facts, presents those facts as clearly and objectively as possible, and makes recommendations without resorting to emotional appeals.

3. Directness

Each paragraph in a report may begin with a topic sentence. (See Section 51.) A reader who, after absorbing the opening summary, wishes to examine in detail a particular part of the report should be able to locate that part by glancing at topic sentences only. Good report writers come to each main point at once and add no unnecessary details.

4. Visual representation

Some reports present opportunities for graphic representation. You do not need to develop professional skill in visual devices, but you should be aware that charts, maps, graphs, photographs, drawings, and diagrams may be helpful. If your report would be aided by the use of illustrative material, discuss the matter with your instructor or consult a reliable reference book on the graphic representation of data.

79c. Topics for reports

Most likely, your instructor will assign a specific topic, or at least a general subject area, for a report. If you are not given such an assignment, refer to Sections 61–63 for possible ideas. Also, look about you. Here are some general subjects that students have reported on with considerable success:

1. A factory producing batteries was polluting a local stream by discharging wastes. A careful investigation revealed the extent of the pollution and resulted in environmental action.
2. An election for student offices was bitter and prolonged. A

report on the actual campaign resulted in recommendations for a new system of elections.

3. The coach of an athletic team was charged with using injured players and with being insensitive to the educational needs and responsibilities of student athletes. A report cleared the coach of the first charge and offered recommendations for tutoring delinquent students.

4. A student became interested in how movie theater managers selected films for showing in his hometown. The result: an informative report on block booking, local interests, and the economics of theater management.

5. The owner of a local department store complained about the amount of stealing done by employees and customers. An excellent report revealed the methods used to prevent pilferage and made recommendations for improving them that were put into effect.

Topics for reports should not be difficult to find. Here are five suggestions that may appeal to you, either as they are stated or modified to suit your circumstances and interests:

1. A survey of the recreational facilities in your town (or college community): playgrounds, athletic fields, public swimming pools, skating rinks, dance halls, theaters, etc.

2. A report on the steps you took, the procedures you followed, and the difficulties you encountered in preparing a library paper. (See Section 80.)

3. A report on some specific situation or development in the administration of your town, such as a sewer project, or a local bond issue, or school busing, or garbage recycling.

4. A survey of the food service at your institution (cafeteria, dining hall, snack bar, etc.).

5. A survey of the attitudes and opinions of fellow students and teachers concerning some significant topic such as legal abortion, the pricing policy of the OPEC nations, the Israeli–Arab situation, the legalization of marijuana, the question of secret fraternities and clubs, or the strengths and weaknesses of the examination system.

rpt

79c

80. The library paper

A *library paper*—sometimes called a *term* or *research paper*—is supposed to be a well-documented, formal, carefully prepared composition somewhere between 1,500 and 6,000 words. It involves making a search for information about a particular topic and presenting and interpreting your findings. An effective library paper is an orderly, systematic study undertaken for a specific purpose. It is never a mere reading report or a hodgepodge of summaries and quotations.

THE LIBRARY

The primary source for any research paper that you are likely to undertake is a library. The vast resources of a library cannot be yours, however, until you learn how to *use* it with ease and without wasting time, motion, or effort. Libraries differ in size, holdings, and physical arrangement, yet the basic principles that determine library organization are so standardized as to enable you to use *any* library, provided you understand the following:

1. The physical arrangement of a library
2. The catalog system and its use
3. The uses of periodical indexes
4. Reference books and their resources

80a. Arrangement of library

Before losing time by discovering the resources of the library through trial and error, devote a free hour (or several of them) to a tour of its physical facilities. Your use of the library will be far more efficient if you know the locations of the main items available there.

Examine the main reading room, reserved-book room, study alcoves, reference section, and periodical room. Your particular library may not include such divisions, but it will have a similar organization on either a smaller or a larger scale. Find out where

lib

80a

the loan desk and catalog are located and where current magazines and newspapers are filed. Books of fiction (novels and stories) are arranged in most libraries in sections by themselves, shelved alphabetically by author. Stroll through the room or section where reference books are located and discover the kinds and locations of books there. In short, thoroughly knowing your way around a library will save time, trouble, annoyance, and disappointment for you, your teacher, and the library staff.

Your library may have available a handbook that explains the organization of the library and sets forth regulations for its use. If so, examine this publication carefully. In addition, both your instructor and the librarian will answer reasonable questions about the physical arrangements of the library and the most efficient means of using its resources.

80b. The library catalog

The most important part of a library is the main collection of books. To obtain any book, you need to consult the catalog, which is the index of the whole library. It usually consists of 3-by-5–inch cards filed alphabetically in long trays or drawers in a series of filing cabinets; on the front of each drawer is a label (for example, "A–ABN") giving the alphabetical limits of the cards in that drawer. Information is filed in the catalog in three ways, by (1) author, (2) title, and (3) subject. Each book in the library is therefore represented by several cards, which are printed and supplied by the Library of Congress and thus are uniform in all libraries. These cards are usually identical, except that certain lines may be typed across the top, giving the title, joint author, or subject headings (i.e., entries for the subject with which the book deals).

Whatever the cataloging system is (cards, bound-book listings, microfilm), the same information appears—author, subject, title— and will show the numbers that will help you locate the book you are seeking.

In addition to unlocking the resources of a library, the catalog provides the call number by means of which each book is located on the shelves. Many libraries are arranged so that all books are placed on open shelves that are easily accessible to readers. If this is the system used in your library, then the call number will help

lib

80b

you quickly locate the volume you are seeking. In other libraries, the main collection of books is shelved in closed stacks. In order to get a book, you must fill out a call slip furnished by the library and present it at the circulation or loan desk. A copy of the book you wish will be located by a library worker, through the use of its call number, and made available to you.

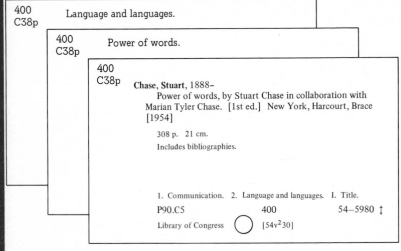

Subject, title, and author cards.

All libraries file by entry, that is, according to what appears first on the card, whether author, subject, or title. Articles (*a, an, the*) that comprise the first word of a title are ignored. Most libraries file letter by letter, including spaces, to the end of the word. This means that the title card "*The American Way*" would be filed in front of the subject card "AMERICANISMS," just as all cards beginning with "New York" would be filed in front of the cards with "Newark" as the entry word. Libraries that use a system of strictly alphabetical order would, of course, file *-isms* before *way* and *-ark* before *York*. It may be noted that encyclopedias, as well as library catalogs, differ in this fundamental rule.

Cards for books *about* an author (which are considered subject entries and are typed in red or in black capitals) are filed after cards for books *by* that author.

Author cards that have the same surname as the entry word are filed according to the given name (e.g., "Baker, Arthur" before

"Baker, Charles"). Always note carefully the first name, or at least the initials, of an author and the *exact* title of the book you wish.

Abbreviations and numerals are filed just as they would be if the words they represent were spelled out.

When an entry name is the same, all authors by that name precede all subjects, and all subjects come before all titles. Hence, "Washington, George" (books by); "WASHINGTON, GEORGE" (books about); and "*Washington Merry-go-round*" (title) are filed in that order.

80c. Periodical indexes

Most libraries display current, and sometimes recent, issues of magazines on racks or in a special periodical room. Older issues of many magazines and of some newspapers are bound in book form or are recorded on microfilm. You will find what you need from back issues by consulting periodical indexes. These are helpful guides to articles and other material that might lie buried except for the ready aid provided by indexes.

When you consult a periodical index, turn first to the front. Here you will find full, helpful instructions for use of the volume and also a list of the periodicals indexed.

For example, here are two entries from *Readers' Guide to Periodical Literature* and their meanings.

> **SOLOMON, Neil**
> Dr Solomon's new miracle diet for your hair,
> skin, sex life. Harp Baz 111:36+ Ap '78

This entry means that Neil Solomon published an article entitled "Dr. Solomon's New Miracle Diet for Your Hair, Skin, and Sex Life," in the *Harper's Bazaar* for April 1978. The volume number is 111. The article begins on page 36 and continues on later pages. This entry:

> **SOLAR heating**
> Something new under the sun. il Redbook 150:
> 206-8+ Ap '78

means that an illustrated article on the subject of solar heating, entitled "Something New Under the Sun," will be found in *Redbook Magazine* for April 1978. The volume number is 150. The article runs on pages 206 through 208 and is continued on later pages.

Indexes are of two kinds. *General indexes* list the contents of magazines and a few newspapers of wide circulation and interest. Unless you are working on some highly specialized and rather unusual subject, a general index, such as *Readers' Guide to Periodical Literature, Facts on File, The New York Times Index,* or *Social Sciences and Humanities Index,* will meet your needs. *Special indexes,* which occasionally are more helpful than general ones, restrict themselves to one particular area. *Agricultural Index, Applied Science and Technology Index, Art Index, Chemical Abstracts, Engineering Index,* and *Psychological Abstracts* are examples of special indexes.

Here are some brief comments on the ten periodical indexes that are likely to be of most use to you:

1. *Annual Magazines Subject-Index,* 1908–1949.
   A subject index (until it was discontinued) to a selected list of American and British periodicals and professional or cultural-society publications dealing mainly with history, travel, and art.
2. *Bibliographic Index: A Cumulative Bibliography of Bibliographies,* 1937—.
   A subject index to separately published bibliographies and to bibliographies that are included each year in several hundred books and approximately 1500 periodicals.
3. *Public Affairs Information Service Bulletin,* 1915—.
   A cumulative subject index to current books, pamphlets, periodicals, government documents, and other library material in the fields of economics and public affairs.
4. *Facts on File,* 1940—.
   A weekly world news digest with a cumulative index, including world, national, and foreign affairs, Latin America, finance and economics, art and science, education and religion, sports, obituaries, and other miscellany.
5. *Index to Legal Periodicals,* 1908—.
   A cumulative subject and author index to articles in law journals.
6. *Social Sciences and Humanities Index,* formerly *The International Index to Periodicals,* 1907—.
   A cumulative author and subject index to articles in domestic and foreign periodicals dealing with literature, history, social science, religion, drama, and pure science. It is a supplement to *Readers' Guide.*
7. *The New York Times Index,* 1913—.
   A cumulative guide to events of national importance by reference to day, page, and column of *The New York Times.* Material is entered by subject, person, and organization. The only index to an American newspaper, it is an indirect guide to events in other newspapers.
8. *Nineteenth Century Readers' Guide to Periodical Literature,* 1890–1899, with supplementary indexing, 1900–1922, 2 vols.
9. *Poole's Index to Periodical Literature,* 1802–1906.
   An index of articles, by subject only, in American and British periodicals, 7 vols.

10. *Readers' Guide to Periodical Literature,* 1900—.
A cumulative index, most useful to the general reader, to over 100 popular and semipopular magazines. Entries are according to author, subject, and fiction title.

80d. Reference books

Unless you already know what books and magazine articles are suited to your needs, you should start with condensed, authoritative articles in reference books. Any book may be used for reference purposes, but reference books are usually comprehensive in scope, condensed in treatment, and arranged according to some special plan to facilitate the ready and accurate finding of information. Such works are usually located on shelves open to the student in the main reading room or in a nearby reference room.

Your teacher or a reference librarian can tell you which of the scores of reference books available are likely to be most helpful with a particular subject. In addition, if your library has a copy of any of the following titles, examine it for useful, timesaving hints on using reference books:

General Reference Guides
Barton, Mary Neill. *Reference Books: A Brief Guide for Students and Other Users of the Library,* 8th ed. Baltimore: Enoch Pratt Free Library, 1977.
Murphey, Robert W. *How and Where to Look It Up.* New York: McGraw-Hill, 1958.
Prakken, Sarah L. *Reader's Adviser: Layman's Guide to Literature,* 12th ed. New York: R. R. Bowker, 1974.
Sheehy, Eugene P. *Guide to Reference Books,* 9th ed. Chicago: American Library Association, 1976.
Wynar, Bohdan S., ed. *Reference Books in Paperback: An Annotated Guide,* 2d ed. Littleton, Colorado: Libraries Unlimited, 1976.

Reference works are so numerous and so varied in content and quality that no fully adequate discussion can be provided here. But you should become acquainted with at least such important works as these:

General Encyclopedias
Collier's Encyclopedia. 24 vols. (Kept up to date with an annual volume, *Collier's Year Book Covering National and International Events.*)
Columbia Encyclopedia, 3d ed.
Columbia-Viking Desk Encyclopedia, 2d ed.
Encyclopaedia Britannica. 30 vols. (Kept up to date with an annual volume, *Britannica Book of the Year: A Record of the March of Events.*)

lib

80d

Encyclopedia Americana. 30 vols. (Kept up to date with an annual volume, *The Americana Annual: An Encyclopedia of Current Events.*)

Lincoln Library of Essential Information.

New International Encyclopaedia. 25 vols. (Kept up to date with an annual volume, *New International Year Book: A Compendium of the World's Progress*).

Seligman, Edwin R. A., and Alvin Johnson, eds. *Encyclopaedia of the Social Sciences* (commonly known as ESS). 15 vols. (Less comprehensive than the other volumes listed, it deals with many subjects directly and indirectly related to the social sciences.)

World Book Encyclopedia. 22 vols. (Kept up to date with an annual volume, *World Book Year Book: An Annual Supplement.*)

General Dictionaries

Funk and Wagnalls New Standard Dictionary of the English Language.

Murray, Sir James A. H., and others, eds. *A New English Dictionary on Historical Principles,* reissued as *The Oxford English Dictionary.* 13 vols. (Commonly referred to as the NED or OED.)

The Random House Dictionary of the English Language.

Webster's New International Dictionary of the English Language.

Yearbooks

In addition to the annual yearbooks of the various encyclopedias (see above).

Annual Register: A Review of Public Events at Home and Abroad (British).

Europa Yearbook. 2 vols. (Vol. I, Europe; Vol. II, Africa, The Americas, Asia, Australasia.)

Information Please Almanac. (Miscellaneous information in compact form.)

International Yearbook and Statesmen's Who's Who. (Data on countries and political leaders.)

Statesman's Year-book: Statistical and Historical Annual of the States of the World. (Over 100 annual volumes have been published.)

United Nations Yearbook.

World Almanac and Book of Facts. (Miscellaneous information.)

Special Reference Books

Special reference works are available dealing with subjects like biography, drama and theater, history, language, literature, science, business and economics, education, music and dance, painting, architecture, philosophy, psychology, religion, and so forth.

Space prohibits giving a full listing of the scores of special-subject reference works available, but here is a sampling of works that are likely to be helpful:

A. BIOGRAPHY

Barnhart, C. L., ed., *New Century Cyclopdia of Names.* 3 vols.

Biography Index, 1947—. (A cumulative index to biographical material in books and magazines.)

Current Biography: Who's News and Why, 1940—. (Eleven monthly issues, cumulated in one alphabet annually, of "personalities prominent on the international scene, in the arts, sciences, industry, politics, education, and entertainment.")

Dargan, Marion. *Guide to American Biography,* 1607–1933. (Suggests original and secondary sources.)

Ethridge, James M., ed. *Contemporary Authors: A Bio-Bibliographical Guide to Current Authors and Their Works.*

Johnson, Allen, and Dumas Malone, eds. *Dictionary of American Biography.* 21 vols. (Commonly known as DAB; it includes outstanding Americans who are no longer living).

Kunitz, Stanley J., and Howard Haycraft, eds. *American Authors, 1600–1900.* (Includes 1300 biographies and 400 portraits.)

Kunitz, Stanley J., and Howard Haycraft, eds. *British Authors of the Nineteenth Century.* (Includes 1000 biographies and 350 portraits.)

Kunitz, Stanley J., and Howard Haycraft, eds. *Twentieth Century Authors* and *First Supplement.* (Includes over 1850 biographies and 1700 portraits.)

Magill, Frank N. *Cyclopedia of World Authors.* (Biographies of 753 world-famous authors.)

National Cyclopedia of American Biography. 47 vols. (In progress.)

New York Times, Biographical Edition. (Loose-leaf monthly.)

Notable American Women, 1607–1950. 3 vols.

Stephen, Leslie, and Sidney Lee, eds. *Dictionary of National Biography.* 63 vols. originally; reissued in 22 vols., several supplements. (Commonly known as DNB; it includes outstanding Englishmen who are no longer living.)

Webster's Biographical Dictionary.

Who's Who. (Principally British; includes only living people; for those who have died recently, see earlier volumes or volumes entitled *Who Was Who.*)

Who's Who in America. (Includes only notable living people; for those who have died recently, see earlier volumes or volumes entitled *Who Was Who in America.*)

Specialized books giving biographies of contemporary people in various fields and in foreign countries include *American Men of Science; Directory of American Scholars; Leaders in Education; Who's Who in American Art; Who's Who in Engineering; Who's Who in the Theatre; Who's Who of American Women;* and *Who's Who in the East (Midwest, West, South and South West, Canada, France, Latin America, the United Nations).*

B. DRAMA AND THEATER

Baker, Blanch M., comp. *Theatre and Allied Arts.*

Firkins, Ina Ten Eyck. *Index to Plays,* 1800–1926, with Supplement to 1934. (These two volumes index 11,156 plays by 3,538 authors.)

Hartnoll, Phyllis, ed. *The Oxford Companion to the Theatre.*

Ottemiller, John H. *Index to Plays in Collections,* 1900–1962, 4th ed. (An index to 6993 copies of 2536 different plays by 1300 different authors in 814 collections—from ancient times to the present.)
Sobel, Bernard. *The New Theatre Handbook and Digest of Plays.*
West, Dorothy H., and Dorothy M. Peake. *Play Index,* 1949–1952.

C. HISTORY
Adams, James Truslow, ed. *Dictionary of American History.* 7 vols.
Bury, J. B., and others, eds. *Cambridge Ancient History.*
Damon, Charles R., comp. *American Dictionary of Dates,* 458–1920. 3 vols.
Douglas, George W. *The American Book of Days.*
Guide to the Study of the United States of America.
Gwatkin, H. M., J. P. Whitney, and others, etc. *Cambridge Medieval History.*
Handlin, Oscar, and others. *Harvard Guide to American History.*
Harper's Encyclopaedia of United States History from 458 A.D. to 1912. 10 vols.
Hockett, Homer C. *The Critical Method in Historical Research and Writing.*
Langer, William L. *An Encyclopedia of World History.*
Keller, Helen Rex. *Dictionary of Dates.* 2 vols.
Magill, Frank N. *Great Events from History.* 9 vols.
Morris, Richard B., ed. *Encyclopedia of American History,* rev. ed.
Social Sciences and Humanities Index, 1965—. (Cumulative author and subject index to over 200 magazines; supplements *Readers' Guide* and succeeds *International Index to Periodicals.*)
Ward, A. W., and others, eds. *Cambridge Modern History.*
Webster's Geographical Dictionary.
Writings on American History, 1906–1940, 1948—. (An annual index, arranged by author, title, and subject, to materials in books and periodicals dealing with U.S. history.)

D. LANGUAGE
Baugh, Albert C., *A History of the English Language.*
Berrey, Lester V., and Melvin Van den Bark. *American Thesaurus of Slang: A Complete Reference Book of Colloquial Speech.*
Crabb's English Synonyms.
Craigie, Sir William A., and James R. Hulbert, eds. *A Dictionary of American English on Historical Principles.* 4 vols.
Evans, Bergen, and Cornelia Evans. *A Dictionary of Contemporary American Usage.*
Fowler, Henry W. *A Dictionary of Modern English Usage.*
Kennedy, Arthur G. *A Bibliography of Writings on the English Language from the Beginning of Printing to the End of 1922.*
Mathews, Mitford M., ed. *A Dictionary of Americanisms on Historical Principles.* 2 vols.
Nicholson, Margaret. *Dictionary of American-English Usage.*
Partridge, Eric. *A Dictionary of Slang and Unconventional English,* 4th ed.
———. *Slang Today and Yesterday.*
Roget's *International Thesaurus of English Words and Phrases.* (Revised constantly; title may vary slightly.)

lib
80d

Webster's Dictionary of Synonyms.
Wentworth, Harold. *American Dialect Dictionary.*
Wentworth, Harold, and Stuart B. Flexner. *Dictionary of American Slang.*

E. LITERATURE
A.L.A. Index . . . to General Literature, with Supplement. (A guide down to 1910; a subject index, still useful for older books.)
Barnhart, C. L., ed. *The New Century Handbook of English Literature.*
Bartlett, John. *Familiar Quotations.* (First published in 1855; constantly revised by succeeding editors.)
Bateson, F. W., ed. *Cambridge Bibliography of English Literature.* 4 vols.; vol. 5, *Supplement,* ed. by George Watson, also the editor of a condensed one-volume version, *The Concise Bibliography of English Literature,* 600–1950.)
Blanck, Jacob, comp. *Bibliography of American Literature.* (Begun and continuing; 8 or 9 vols. to date.)
Book Review Digest, 1905—. (An index to reviews of some 4000 general books appearing in some 74 American and British periodicals; it is published 11 times a year, but it is cumulated semiannually and annually.)
Burke, William J., and W. D. Howe, eds. *American Authors and Books,* 1640–1940.
Cary, M., and others, eds. *Oxford Classical Dictionary.*
Cumulative Book Index: A World List of Books in the English Language, 1929— (Author, title, and subject entries are in one alphabet; published monthly, except August, and cumulated frequently during the year, annually, and in four- or five-year cumulations; information given includes publisher, price, and date of publication; for books in print before the *Cumulative Book Index* started, see *United States Catalog,* 1st, 2nd, 3rd, and 4th eds.)
Essay and General Literature Index, 1900—. (An index to essays and articles in volumes of collections of essays and miscellaneous works; supplements the *A.L.A. Index;* published semiannually.)
Funk and Wagnalls Standard Dictionary of Folklore, Mythology and Legend. 2 vols.
Hart, James D. *Oxford Companion to American Literature.*
Harvey, Paul. *Oxford Companion to Classical Literature.*
———, *Oxford Companion to English Literature.*
Jones, Howard Mumford, and Richard M. Ludwig. *Guide to American Literature and Its Backgrounds Since 1890.*
Kennedy, Arthur G., and Donald B. Sands. *A Concise Bibliography for Students of English.*
Leary, Lewis, G. *Articles on American Literature,* 1900–1950.
Magill, Frank N., ed. *Quotations in Context.* (Contains 2020 quotations from world literature revealing who said what under what circumstances).
———, *Cyclopedia of Literary Characters.* (Contains 16,000 characters from world literature, listed and identified.)
Mencken, H. L., ed. *A New Dictionary of Quotations on Historical Principles from Ancient and Modern Sources.*

lib

80d

Millett, Fred B. *Contemporary American Authors.*

Modern Humanities Research Association. *Annual Bibliography of the English Language and Literature,* 1920—.

Oxford Dictionary of Quotations.

Publications of the Modern Language Association of America. (Each year an early issue of this quarterly contains an extensive bibliography of the previous year's writings on language and literature: American, English, modern European.)

Sanders, Chauncey. *An Introduction to Research in English Literary History.*

Sandys, John E. *Companion to Latin Studies.*

Smith, Horatio, ed. *Columbia Dictionary of Modern European Literature.* (Contains 1167 articles by 239 specialists, dealing with later nineteenth- and twentieth-century authors; 31 literatures are represented.)

Social Sciences and Humanities Index, 1965—. (Cumulative author and subject index to over 200 magazines; supplements *Readers' Guide* and succeeds *International Index to Periodicals.*)

Spiller, Robert E., and others, eds. *Literary History of the United States.* 3 vols. *Bibliography Supplement,* ed. Richard M. Ludwig.

Steinberg, S. H., ed. *Cassell's Encyclopaedia of Literature.* 2 vols.

Stevenson, Burton E. *The Home Book of Quotations, Classical and Modern.*

Thrall, William F., and Addison Hibbard. *A Handbook to Literature.*

Trent, William P., and others, eds. *Cambridge History of American Literature.* 4 vols.

Ward, A. W., and A. R. Waller, eds. *Cambridge History of English Literature.* 15 vols.

Whibley, Leonard. *Companion to Greek Studies.*

F. SCIENCE

Agricultural Index, 1916–1964. (A cumulative subject index to a selected but extensive list of agricultural magazines, books, and bulletins; succeeded by *Biological and Agricultural Index.*)

Applied Science and Technology Index, 1958—. (A cumulative subject index to about 200 periodicals dealing with applied science and technology subjects; formerly *Industrial Arts Index.*)

Biological and Agricultural Index, 1964—. (A cumulative subject index to periodicals in the fields of biology, agriculture, and related sciences; continues *Agricultural Index.*)

Crane, Evan J., and others, eds. *A Guide to the Literature of Chemistry.*

Engineering Index, 1884—. (With changes over the years, this index has been since 1928 a selective subject–author index to periodicals in all engineering fields; it is published annually, but technical libraries receive weekly cards containing the information that is eventually published in the annual volumes.)

Gentle, Ernest J., and others. *Aviation and Space Dictionary.*

Industrial Arts Index, 1913–1958. (A cumulative subject index to a selected but extensive list of business, finance, applied science, and technology periodicals, books, and pamphlets; continued by *Applied Science and Technology Index.*)

Jones, Franklin, and Paul B. Schubert, eds. *Engineering Encyclopedia.* (Treats 4500 important engineering subjects.)

McGraw-Hill Encyclopedia of Science and Technology. 15 vols. (An international reference work, kept up to date by the *McGraw-Hill Yearbook of Science and Technology.*)

Newman, James R., ed. *Harper Encyclopedia of Science.* 4 vols.

O'Rourke, Charles E., ed. *General Engineering Handbook.*

Parke, Nathan G. *Guide to the Literature of Mathematics and Physics.*

Sarton, George. *Introduction to the History of Science.*

Technical Book Review Index, 1935—. (A cumulative guide to reviews of scientific and technical books in scientific, technical, and trade journals.)

Van Nostrand's Scientific Encyclopedia.

Whitford, R. H. *Physics Literature: A Reference Manual.*

THE RESEARCH PAPER

With this information about the primary role of the library in investigative papers, we can consider the research project itself. The pages that follow deal with a paper begun from scratch and depending on library investigation. The suggestions offered should be adequate for even a moderately long paper. Its preparation and writing depend on four major steps: (1) choosing and analyzing the subject; (2) making a thorough investigation of the subject; (3) preparing an outline; and (4) writing and revising.

80e. Choose and analyze your subject carefully.

1. Choose a subject in which you are already interested or in which you can become interested. Do not select a difficult or technical subject that will not interest your readers.

2. Do not select too large or too small a subject. Your experience in writing shorter papers should be helpful here; if you have a clear idea of the size of topic needed for 1,000 words, that judgment will tell you that a topic of the same size will not be adequate for 5,000 words. You do not want to have to pad, to repeat yourself, to make the paper dull. The size of your outline (see Section 64) will also help you gauge how suitable your topic is—whether it needs to be trimmed or lengthened.

3. Choose a topic on which enough has been written to supply you with adequate information. Keep in mind, too, the resources of the library where you will do your work; for example, avoid a subject that depends heavily on back copies

res
pap

80e

of magazines that your library does not have either bound or on microfilm or tape. Also, base your paper on material from several kinds of sources: reference books, periodicals, books, even newspapers and personal interviews.

4. Select a central purpose, a controlling idea, and state it in a thesis, or theme, sentence. Any assembling of material presupposes that it supports some proposition, some general statement or idea, and all the information you finally use should lead toward your conclusions, the most important part of any research paper. You may change your attitude toward, and treatment of, your subject when you have assembled and contemplated your materials, for you should never start out with a rigid, preconceived idea to be established in spite of all facts and evidence. That is why you are advised to begin with a general statement or idea rather than a specific one. But the idea must be there to start with so that you can select your reading material and make sure you develop a single subject fairly.

5. Select, but modify if necessary, the basic type of writing for your research paper. Your report may be *descriptive exposition:* It may describe and explain the processes involved in the manufacture of some product, or the salient facts about a region or situation or movement. It may be *narrative:* a report of exactly what took place on a certain occasion. It may be *argumentative:* setting forth facts in favor of, or opposed to, some plan, movement, or proposal. Or it may be *analytical:* that is, it may analyze the component parts and significance of a somewhat abstract subject, or may take a comparison–contrast approach and treat the likenesses and differences between two systems. But whatever type of writing you choose, your research paper must have a clear, unmistakable purpose.

Since your choice of topic depends on your interests and those of your prospective reader or readers, literally hundreds of topics are available, many of which are suggested by these broad fields:

applied science	architecture, etc.)
biography	history
economics	land, sea, air
education	language
fine arts (music, painting, sculpture, ceramics,	literature

manufacturing	pure science
politics	religion
psychology	space exploration

Of course, these fields are starting places, not topics. Once you have selected a field, narrow it to something like this:

An outstanding or memorable episode or day or month or year in a well-known person's life

An account of the education of a famous person

Someone in public office: president, vice-president, senator, governor, etc.

The friendship of two well-known people, or some phase of that friendship

The love affair of a famous couple

The reception, influence, or effect of some book, invention, or process, or its reputation about 10, 25, 50, 100 years later

The reputation of an author after 25, 50, or 100 years

The major or minor achievements of a biologist, chemist, discoverer, explorer, soldier, inventor, manufacturer, speaker, traveler, writer, etc.

Space research and exploration: planets, satellites, rockets, space colonies, space medicine, and so forth

The next 5 (10) years in space exploration, or the last 5 (10) years in space exploration

Famous historical events, trials, sporting events, etc.

Famous or well-known battles or phases of battles (land, sea, air)

Famous or memorable shipwrecks, storms, fires, floods, tornadoes

A famous structure, completed or proposed: harbor, canal, bridge, building, ship, tower, cathedral, pyramid, dam, tunnel, railroad, highway, airport, and so forth

Famous places: summer resorts, winter resorts, health resorts, world capitals, cities, rivers, canyons, parks, etc.

Foods: nutritive value of foods, home freezing of fruits and vegetables, recent methods of food preservation, so-called junk foods

Language: Briticisms and Americanisms; Latin and Greek prefixes, suffixes, roots in English; neologisms; localisms; dialect; logic and language; profanity; place names; spelling reform; making a dictionary

**res
pap**

80e

Then limit the area selected still further, looking for a specific instance of the topic. Consider the following examples:

The Presidential Campaign of the Bicentennial Year
Gerald Ford's First Month as President
The Friendship of C. S. Lewis and J. R. R. Tolkien
Robert Browning's Courtship of Elizabeth Barrett
Noah Webster's First Dictionary
Michael Sveda's Discovery of Cyclamates
The Space Shuttle *Enterprise*
Across the Atlantic by Balloon
The Trans-Alaska Pipeline
Gambling Casinos in New Jersey
Commercial Fishing: Five Billion Pounds of Fish
Idealism in Speech: Artificial Languages for the World
Reverse Discrimination in My Neighborhood
The Curious Application of "R" and "X" Ratings to Two Films

80f. Make a thorough investigation of the subject.

Your time and resources may be limited, but you should make as thorough a search as possible for relevant information in reference books, periodicals, the general collection of books in the library, and newspapers. Encyclopedias are not enough: A term paper has no real value unless it does more than merely dip into a subject. Use reference works, periodical indexes, the card catalog, and the general collection of books. From these resources, prepare a preliminary bibliography on 3-by-5–inch cards, that is, a list of books and magazine or newspaper articles that are *likely* to contribute material, with one title to a card. You save time if you give complete information on this preliminary bibliography card, since it will also serve as information for your final bibliography. Note that the material is arranged in the order in which it would appear in a final bibliography. Note also that the card contains the library call number—a timesaver if you have to return to the book for further checking. Put this library call number on each preliminary bibliography card as soon as you begin your library search for specific materials.

Bittner, William

Poe: A Biography

Boston: Little, Brown and Co.,
1962

928.1
P752 bi

80g. Take careful notes from your reading.

Taking careful notes from your reading is essential in preparing a library paper. But note-taking has other uses as well. As a college student, you will spend much time taking notes in your room, in the library, and in the classroom. Both now and later you will be faced with the problem of taking notes on books and articles that you may write about or use in reviewing for examinations. You will need, too, to take usable notes on lectures and other talks. Much of your academic success depends on your ability to take notes that are really helpful.

Note-taking should be a process of systematic thinking. Too frequently it is a hurried setting down of carelessly selected ideas on scraps of paper, or miscellaneous jottings in a notebook. If you wish to get maximum benefit from your reading, with intelligent labor saving, you should organize both the materials and the methods of note-taking in order to preserve notes for possible use at any future time, for example, until a long paper is written or an examination is over.

Materials

1. Many researchers believe that the most efficient note-taking is done on cards or slips of paper (3 by 5 or 4 by 6 inches or larger), *one note to a card*. A heading is put on each card and the cards are filed for later reference. The advantage of this

system is that all notes on the same subject, even if they are taken at widely separated times, can be kept together. The use of the card system—both bibliographical cards and content cards—is especially valuable in taking notes for a library paper.

2. Some students prefer to take notes on full-size or half-size sheets of paper or loose-leaf notebook paper. (Bound notebooks are usually unsatisfactory.) If you use such materials, keep all notes on a particular book or article together and organize your notes on the various phases of the subject as you proceed.

Methods

More important than the materials are the methods employed. To save time and trouble later and avoid a hodgepodge of quotations and undigested raw material, follow this suggested technique:

1. Before taking notes on a book, study its preface and table of contents to learn the scope and purpose of the book. If you are going to read only one chapter from a book, or a magazine article, skim through it first, then begin to read carefully and take notes. The book probably has an index (almost all nonfiction books do); save time by examining it for your particular subject or for related materials.

2. Record accurately and fully the following details about the source of information: author, book, title, article, chapter title, magazine title, date, volume, page numbers, and the like. After copying the information, check it immediately against the original.

3. Record accurately and fully the information itself. If you are quoting directly in order to use the material later either for direct quotation or in summarizing, make a word-by-word check at once. Be careful to copy *exactly* all direct quotations, preserving original spelling and punctuation; mark clearly any variations from standard style in your *first* notes, and do not forget to use quotation marks.

Your notes must be clear and full. Otherwise, you will have to make trip after trip to the library to supply missing information. Get all the information *the first time*. Make your notes *clear,* so that you can read and understand them later; *full,* so that you can supply adequate information about sources in both

footnotes and bibliography; *exact,* so that you can quote or paraphrase accurately; and *organized,* so that you can make ready
use of what you have assembled.

4. Condense your notes, which should be as full as needed but
   not so full that main ideas are obscured in a mass of detail.
   Make frequent use of topic sentences (see Section 51) and
   summaries (see Section 76).

5. Rearrange and regroup your notes as your work proceeds.
   Keep all notes on a single subject together, not mixed with
   others even if they are on the same general subject. This
   grouping is especially important whenever numerous books
   or articles are consulted.

6. Be careful to distinguish fact from opinion in your reading
   and in the notes themselves. In weighing opinions, consider
   the facts on which the opinions are based, the expert knowledge and possible bias of the author, and the date of publication of the material.

The sample note card shown here illustrates the suggested technique. The upper right corner gives the general subject, the upper
left the specific subject; then come a direct quotation, summary,
or paraphrase, and full bibliographical details. If a number of note
cards come from the same source, work out an abbreviated system
whereby your bibliographical references will be explained by your
preliminary or final bibliography card.

Poe as Poet   (Reaction to Science)

Poe realized that a Romantic poet
"can no longer sing because his
mythologies have been destroyed
by Science—"   p. 34

George Monteiro, "Edgar Poe and
the New Knowledge," *Southern Literary
Journal,* 4, 2 (1972).

res
pap

80g

Not all cards will be notes of material that is directly quoted. Many of them will summarize in your own words (see Section 76) the ideas of the source. Some will be paraphrases (see Section 77) giving a full-length statement of the source material in your own words. All cards should be complete enough to prevent your having to return to the source to discover how much of the material is direct quotation, how much is paraphrase, or what the bibliographical facts are.

80h. Prepare an outline for your research paper.

When you have read and taken notes on the available material, you can make a tentative outline of your research paper. Have in mind some general plan, one that you can adapt as you assemble material, and become familiar with it. Then, when you have worked long enough to reach definite conclusions and see the framework of the whole structure, you can rearrange your notes in final form under appropriate headings and prepare a topic or sentence outline from them. (See Section 64.)

In making an outline for your paper, bear in mind that the object of your investigation is to find out facts, arrange and interpret them, and present conclusions based on them. You are not necessarily a propagandist—rather, you are a discoverer of fact—but you must assimilate and absorb what seems to you the truth so that you can present it to a reader who will see the definite purpose you had in mind.

A tentative but general outline, adaptable for many but not all subjects, might include the following:

    I. Purpose of investigation
   II. Importance or significance of the subject
  III. Background or history of the subject
  IV. Discussion of the subject itself
   V. Conclusions

80i. Revise your research paper carefully.

After outlining your paper, write it. When you are satisfied with your draft, put it aside for a while. After this "cooling" period, you will be able to come back to it with more impartiality than was possible just after you had finished it. Shortcomings in content and purpose will be more apparent, and you can give your paper its final form. One reading should be for the sole purpose of making certain that footnotes are accurately and uniformly listed and the bibliography is correctly and consistently arranged. Then make your final draft and proofread it carefully.

80j. Use notes to document your research paper adequately and properly.

In addition to being correct, clear, effective, and appropriate, every investigative paper must be carefully documented. The following suggestions enable you to provide your library paper with adequate and accurately composed *footnotes* (if your notes are at the bottom of the page) or *notes* (if they are collected in a section at the end of the paper), and a bibliography.

What to footnote

The purpose of a footnote (or a note) is to acknowledge the authority for some fact stated or some material quoted, or to develop some point that is referred to more or less incidentally in the body of the paper.

Generally known facts do not require substantiation in footnotes, nor do well-known quotations, usually. With other materials you must avoid charges of plagiarism, and unless the ideas and phrasing in your paper are completely your own, you should refer the reader to some source for your statement. To be entirely honest, you will acknowledge every source of indebtedness, even when no direct quotation is used.

Occasionally you may wish to develop, interpret, or refute some idea but do not wish an extended comment to interfere with the flow and unity of your paper. Use a footnote, but since footnotes for such purposes run the risk of becoming distracting to the reader, do not overuse them.

How many footnotes should appear in a research paper? Only as many as are necessary. One investigation may call for twice as many as another. Some pages may need a half-dozen or more; others may need none or only one or two. Use footnotes or notes to acknowledge credit where it is due and to supply discussion only when necessary for understanding.

80k. Adopt a standard form of notation and be consistent in its use.

Methods of documentation are numerous, but whatever system you employ should be consistent throughout your paper and immediately clear to the reader. The Modern Language Association of America's *MLA Handbook* recommends the following forms for citation of books and periodicals:

Books

A. BOOKS BY ONE AUTHOR:

[1]Susanne K. Langer, Feeling and Form: A Theory of Art (New York: Scribner's, 1953), p. 96.

If the author's full name has been given in the text of your paper, the note reads as follows:

[1]Feeling and Form: A Theory of Art (New York: Scribner's, 1953), p. 96.

If both the author's full name and the title of the book have been given in the text, the footnote reads as follows:

[3](New York: Scribner's, 1953), p. 96.

B. BOOKS BY TWO OR MORE AUTHORS:

[4]Edwin Shiedman and Norman Faberow, Clues to Suicide (New York: McGraw-Hill, 1957), p. 14.

C. BOOKS PREPARED BY AN EDITOR OR EDITORS:

[5]Jerry Griffith and L. E. Miner, ed., The Second and Third Lincolnland Conferences of Dialectology (University, Ala.: Univ. of Alabama Press, 1972), p. xi.

When the information cited comes not from the primary source but from another writer's use of it, use the following form:

[6]Cotton Mather, Memorable Provinces, 1689. Quoted from David Levin, What Happened in Salem? (New York: Harcourt Brace Jovanovich, 1960), pp. 96–97.

D. TRANSLATIONS:

[7]Alexander I. Solzhenitsyn, The First Circle, trans. Thomas P. Whitney (New York: Harper & Row, 1968), p. 269.

E. BOOKS CONSISTING OF TWO OR MORE VOLUMES:

[8]James Boswell, The Life of Samuel Johnson, ed. Edward G. Fletcher (New York: Heritage, 1963), II, 145.

Articles (Essays, Stories)

A. FROM A MAGAZINE:

[9]William Graves, "The Imperiled Giants," National Geographic, Dec. 1976, p. 739.

B. FROM A SCHOLARLY JOURNAL:

[10]Julian Smith, "Hemingway and the Thing Left Out," Journal of Modern Literature, 1 (1970–71), 180.

C. FROM A COLLECTION:

[11]Richard M. Dorson, "The Eclipse of Solar Mythology," in The Study of Folklore, ed. Alan Dundes (Englewood Cliffs, N.J.: Prentice–Hall, 1965), p. 78.

D. FROM A NEWSPAPER:

[12]James J. Kilpatrick, "Trying to Reap Some Good out of the Deaths of 144," Raleigh News and Observer, October 10, 1978, sec. I, p. 5.

E. FROM AN ENCYCLOPEDIA:

[13]J. B. Rhine, "Psychical Research of Parapsychology," Encyclopedia Americana, 1969 ed.

801. Use the following standard footnote abbreviations.

In notes in research papers, abbreviations are permissible and economical of space. If the need for abbreviation arises, use these forms:

anon. "anonymous"
ante "before"
art., arts. "article(s)"

c., ca. "about," "approximate date"

cf. (confer) "compare." Do not use to mean "see."

ch., chs. "chapter(s)"

comp. "compiler," "compiled"

ed., eds. "editor(s)", "edition(s)"; *ed.* also means "edited by"

e.g. (exempli gratia) "for example"

f., ff. "following line(s)," "following pages." Ordinarily, use exact reference instead; that is, use "pp. 59–63" rather than "pp. 59 ff."

fig., figs. "figure(s)"

ibid. (ibidem) "in the same place." If a note refers to the same source as the one referred to in the note immediately preceding it, the abbreviation *ibid.* may be used. If the volume, page, title, and author are the same, use *ibid.* alone. If the volume and page differ, use, for example, *ibid.,* III, 206. *Ibid.* usually comes at the beginning of a note and is capitalized for that reason only.

i.e. (id est) "that is"

l., ll. "line(s)"

loc. cit. (loco citato) "in the place cited." Use of this abbreviation is not recommended, but if the reference is to the *exact* passage covered by an earlier reference not *immediately* preceding, *loc. cit.* may be used. Never follow *loc. cit* with a page number.

MS, MSS "manuscript(s)"

n., nn. "note(s)"

N.B. (nota bene) "take notice, mark well"

op. cit. (opere citato) "in the work cited." After the first full reference to a given work, provided that no other work by the same author is mentioned in the paper, succeeding references may be indicated by the author's surname, followed by *op. cit.* and the volume and page numbers. Use of *op. cit.* is not recommended.

p., pp. "page(s)"

par., pars. "paragraph(s)"

passim To be used when no specific page reference can be given; it means "everywhere," "throughout," "here and there."

pseud. "pseudonym"

pt., pts. "part(s)"

q.v. (quod vide); Latin for "which see"

sec., secs. "section(s)"

sic "thus," "so." Used between brackets in a quotation to show that the preceding material has been followed exactly even if there is an obvious factual error or an error in spelling, grammar, punctuation, or word use.

v., vv. "verse(s)"

vol., vols. "volume(s)"

Note: *Loc. cit.* and *op. cit.* are seldom seen in research writing that follows the form recommended by the *MLA;* instead, the author's name, with a short title, is used for footnote references after the first. For example:

First Entry:

[1]Eugene T. Gendlin, <u>Experiencing and the Creation of Meaning</u> (Toronto: Free Press, 1962), p. 35.

Subsequent Entry for the Same Book:

[5]Gendlin, <u>Experiencing</u>, p. 88.

First Entry:

[1]Victor B. Scheffer, "Exploring the Lives of Whales," <u>National Geographic</u>, Dec. 1976, p. 754.

Subsequent Entry for the Same Article:

[5]Scheffer, "Lives of Whales," p. 761.

80m. Place the footnote or endnote numeral and the note itself properly.

Unless otherwise instructed, you should apply the following guidelines:

1. In the text, refer to a note by means of an Arabic numeral placed above and to the right of the word to be commented on or documented. If the reference is to a statement or quotation, place the numeral at the end of the quoted passage, after the punctuation.

2. If your instructor so directs, gather the notes in a section headed "Notes" at the end of the paper. Otherwise, place them as footnotes at the bottom of each page.

3. Before a note, repeat the number used in the text. Place this number above the line also. Do not use asterisks or other symbols in place of Arabic numerals.

res
pap

80m

4. Number the footnotes or endnotes consecutively throughout the paper or, in a very long paper, consecutively throughout each chapter.

5. If you use footnotes, separate the first footnote on a page from the text above it by leaving three blank lines between the text and the note.

6. If you type, double-space throughout the notes as well as within the text.

80n. Use the name–and–year (author and date) documentation system when appropriate.

This system, widely used in the social and physical sciences, does not separate identifying notes from the text. With this system, the name of the author and the year of publication are placed in parentheses immediately following the information you are documenting. The following examples show how to cite the source or identify a direct quotation using this method:

> Although the ability to extrapolate present trends is vital to the science fiction writer, and despite the fact that this ability would be extremely helpful in government, few people in Washington would confess to reading the stuff (Allen 1975).

> The lack of scholarly attention to recent works of fiction is nothing new. In the 1940's "the survey of English literature ended abruptly with the works of Thomas Hardy" (Warrick 1978, p. xi.).

As the second example shows, a page number may be inserted when that information is useful.

With the name-and-year system, the form of the bibliography is important, since the citations in the text refer the reader to the bibliography alone, not to a page of notes. Arrange it in alphabetical order according to the author's last name or some identifying word if the article is anonymous. Then comes the year of publication, followed by a period. Here are some sample entries:

Books

Allen, Dick, and Lori Allen, 1975. Looking Ahead: The Vision of Science Fiction. New York: Harcourt Brace Jovanovich.

Articles

Bennett, William H. 1970. "The Stress Patterns of Gothic," <u>PMLA</u>, 85: 463–72.

Notice that the volume number, 85, is separated from the inclusive page numbers by a colon.

If you cite two or more books by the same author, arrange them in chronological order by publication date:

Hudson, R. A., 1973. "Tense and Time Reference in Reduced Relative Clauses," <u>Linguistic Inquiry</u>, 4:251–56.
——. 1974. "Systemic Generative Grammar," <u>Linguistics</u>, 139: 5–42.
——. 1975. "The Meaning of Questions," <u>Language</u>, 51:1–31.

Works by the same author published in the same year are assigned an identifying letter: They are arranged in alphabetical order by title, and the first is listed as "a," the second as "b," and so on:

Ross, J. R. 1969a. "Auxiliaries as Main Verbs," <u>Studies in Philosophical Linguistics</u>. Evanston, Ill.: Great Expectations.
——. 1969b. "Guess Who?" <u>Chicago Linguistic Society</u>, 5: 252–86.

80o. Use a bibliography to document your research paper adequately.

A *bibliography* is a list of reference materials related to a given subject that is placed at the end of a manuscript. It is usually a list containing the names of all the works actually quoted from or otherwise used in the paper and its preparation. Thus, a bibliography may contain more references than the sum of all the footnote or endnote references. Every formally prepared research paper should contain a bibliography.

Usage in the arrangement of bibliographical items varies, but unless your instructor directs you otherwise, adhere to the following examples prepared from the recommendations of the *MLA Handbook*. Note carefully these features: alphabetical arrangement of items; order of material within each item; capitalization; punctuation; use of italics or underlining, Arabic numerals, and abbreviations.

If the items in your bibliography are numerous, you may want

res pap

80o

to classify them in groups: books, magazine articles, public documents, reports, newspaper accounts, and the like. But it is unlikely that you would have sufficient references to justify separate groups; unless you are directed to group your items, arrange them in a single alphabetical list.

A sentence or phrase beneath each item describing its contents and scope is sometimes helpful and desirable. Such statements make the bibliography an *annotated* bibliography. The individual comments are called *annotations*.

Place the bibliography at the end of the research paper; number its pages consecutively with the paper; and begin it on a separate page, not on the last page of the text. Give it a title that fits it precisely, such as "List of Works Consulted," "List of Works Cited," or "A Selected Bibliography." It should include all the first references in your footnotes or endnotes. If the paper is typewritten, double-space throughout the bibliography and indent any part of an item that runs over to the next line or lines.

The following, an example of a short bibliography, follows the preferred method of including all materials in one alphabetical arrangement:

Dameron, J. Lasley, and Irby B. Cauthen, Jr. Edgar
    Allan Poe: A Bibliography of Criticism: 1827–1967.
    Charlottesville, Va.: Univ. Press of Virginia,
    1974.
"Edgar Allan Poe," Encyclopaedia Britannica. 1967 ed.
Gerber, Gerald E. "Additional Sources for 'The Masque
    of the Red Death.' " American Literature, 37 (March
    1965), 52–54.
Jacobs, William Jay. Edgar Allan Poe: Genius in
    Torment. New York: McGraw–Hill, 1975.
Mabbott, Thomas O., ed. Collected Works of Edgar
    Allan Poe. Vol. I: Poems. Cambridge, Mass.:
    Belknap, 1969.
Moldenhauer, Joseph J., Compl. A Descriptive Catalog
    of Edgar Allan Poe Manuscripts in the Humanities
    Research Center Library, the University of Texas at
    Austin. Supplement to Texas Quarterly, 11, no. 2
    (1973).
Monahan, Dean W. "Edgar Allan Poe and the Theme of
    the Fall." Dissertation. Penn State 1969.
Monteiro, George. "Edgar Poe and the New Knowledge."
    Southern Literary Journal, 4, no. 2 (1972), 34–40.
Pollin, Burton R. "The Temperance Movement and Its
    Friends Look at Poe." Costerus, 2 (1972), 119–44.
Ricardou, Jean. "Gold in the Bug." Trans. Frank
    Towne. Poe Studies, 9 (1976), 33–39.
Spiller, Robert E., et al., eds. Literary History of

the United States. 3rd ed. 2 vols. New York: Macmillan, 1963.

Stein, Allen F. "Another Source for 'The Raven.' " American Notes and Queries, 9 (1971), 85–87.

Stovall, Floyd. "The Conscious Art of Edgar Allan Poe." College English, 24 (March 1963), 417–421.

Wright, Nathalia. "Roderick Usher: Poe's Turn-of-the-Century Artist." In Artful Thunder: Versions of the Romantic Tradition in American Literature. Ed. Robert J. DeMott and Sanford E. Marovitz. Kent, Ohio: Kent State Univ. Press, 1975.

A SPECIMEN LIBRARY PAPER

A specimen library paper follows. It should clarify the numerous points made in this discussion. Study it with care. It was planned, written, and revised by a student, Michael Williford, and is used with the permission of the author.

You may be requested to provide a title page for any library paper you submit. Such a page is simple to prepare and hence is not illustrated here. You may also wish (or be required) to provide a copy of your final outline (see Section 64) when you turn in your completed paper.

Hemingway's Margaret Macomber

In Ernest Hemingway's "The Short Happy Life of Francis Macomber," the most tragic figure is Margaret Macomber. Critics have labelled her a classic example of the domineering American bitch,[1] yet Margaret is the most elusive and subtly drawn character in the story. Once she is freed from the view that Wilson is Hemingway's spokesman, one can see that she is not a stereotyped domineering woman, but the only character who gains any insight concerning herself and the tragic action that kills her husband.[2]

If the domination of her husband was Margaret's chief desire, it is surprising that she should be so upset by her husband's display of weakness in stalking

---

[1]Anne Greco, "Margot Macomber: 'Bitch Goddess,' Exonerated," Fitzgerald/Hemingway Annual 1972, ed. Matthew J. Bruccoli and C. E. Frazer Clark, Jr. (Dayton: National Cash Register, 1973), p. 276.

[2]Virgil Hutton, "The Short Happy Life of Macomber," University Review, 30 (1964), 260.

lib
pap

573

the wounded lion, since Macomber's cowardice is a flaw that would only strengthen her control. Furthermore, Margaret's having "done the best she could for many years back"[3]--perhaps trying to make her marriage work--again contradicts the stereotyped image. The problem is that Margaret's bitchery has been accepted as her characteristic behavior; however, all that the story shows is what she does as a special reaction to a specific event.[4] In fact, Margaret is putting on an act to repay her husband for failing her through his cowardice; that her behavior is a sudden change is suggested by Wilson's surprise at her switch from a fine, understanding woman to an "enamelled" sadist, and his momentary guess that she might be trying to put up "a good show."[5] Virgil Hutton argues that although Wilson suspects that Margaret might be behaving differently, the guide "cannot integrate the seemingly contradictory parts of Margaret, and finally accepts the ostentatious display of bitchery as her whole character."[6]

Margaret's extreme reaction to her husband's failure, committing adultery with Wilson, shows how deeply she feels that her years of effort have been betrayed. Her revenge is unjustified, but Margaret, a product of upper-class American society, is like her husband a victim of Wilson's stereotyped notions of fear and bravery. The story describes Margaret's freeing herself from those notions; this is certainly a fundamental change in her attitude, but a change leading to understanding, not to murder.[7]

Before the lion hunt, Macomber remains alone with his fear because his wife sees no reason for anyone to be afraid. Margaret sees the hunt as an adventurous game. She feels "marvellous" and "very excited"; she thinks the lion's roar is "very impressive," and reassures her husband that she knows he will kill the lion "marvellously" (pp. 228-29).

But immediately after the automobile chase of the buffalo, the day after the lion hunt, the turmoil within Margaret cracks her show of gaiety.[8] She is

[3]Ernest Hemingway, "The Short Happy Life of Francis Macomber," in Sylvan Barnet, ed., An Introduction to Literature, 6th ed. (Boston: Little, Brown, 1977), p. 244. All quotations from the story are from this edition and will be included in the text.

[4]Hutton, p. 261.

[5]Ibid.

[6]Ibid., p. 262.

[7]R. F. Fleissner, "The Macomber Case: A Sherlockian Analysis," Baker Street Journal, 20:3 (1969), 155.

[8]Greco, p. 278.

"very white faced," and says, "It was frightful. I've
never been more frightened in my life" (p. 241).
Significantly, she uses the word--frightful--that
Macomber used to describe the lion's roar. But the
reversal in their positions occurs only after they
examine the dead buffalo.[9] "With delight" Macomber
views the buffalo, but Margaret says, "He's hateful
looking" (p. 242). Now, in addition to her white face,
she looks ill. But Macomber rattles on, in terms that
recall Margaret's earlier fatuities:
　"Wasn't it marvellous, Margot?"
　"I hated it."
　"Why?"
　"I hated it," she said bitterly. "I loathed it."
(p. 243) Her thoughts are now the opposite of what
they were before; in classical terms, the peripeteia
has occurred because of Margaret's discovery.[10] By
experiencing fear and by looking at the dead buffalo
she realizes the potential deadliness of the hunt.[11]
After seeing the change in her husband, Margaret
becomes "very afraid," but afraid that he may be
killed. But Wilson, who knows nothing of her change,
thinks that her fear is that Macomber may leave her.[12]
　The climax of the story occurs when the wounded
buffalo charges, but Macomber does not run; instead,
he stands his ground. No longer seeing Wilson or
depending on him, Macomber faces the danger on his
own, "aiming carefully" as he shoots once more "with
the buffalo's huge bulk almost on him" (p. 245). The
animal is so close that "he could see the little
wicked eyes," and he sees too that since "the head
started to lower" (p. 245), his last bullet must have
taken effect. Then, in that triumphant moment, the
bullet his wife has fired kills him instantly.
　Wilson's assumption at this point--that Margaret has
murdered her husband--must be weighed carefully in
relation to what the text says: "Mrs. Macomber . . .
had shot at the buffalo . . . as it seemed about to
gore Macomber . . ." (p. 246). The danger was indeed
acute: the animal falls "not two yards" from him. In
that proximity and under that excitement Mrs.
Macomber, who has not been shown to be an experienced
shot or even a participant in the previous hunting,
might have killed her husband accidentally.[13] And of

[9]Ibid.
[10]Warren Beck, "The Shorter Happy Life of Mrs.
Macomber," Modern Fiction Studies, 1:4 (1955), 33.
[11]Ibid., p. 34.
[12]Ibid.
[13]Arnold E. Davidson, "The Ambivalent End of Francis
Macomber's Short, Happy Life," Hemingway Notes, 2:7
(1972), 16.

**lib
pap**

chief significance is that the buffalo "seemed about to gore Macomber." This is what she sees: not that Francis, having learned to be brave, will leave her, but that in his bravery he is about to be killed. If she had wanted him dead, she could have left it to the buffalo.[14] Furthermore, not only does the story supply evidence about Margaret Macomber which contradicts Wilson's views, but we have also the word of Ernest Hemingway, the author (or at least, the third-person omniscient narrator), who writes that she "shot at the buffalo."

After full consideration, it seems that Margaret Macomber is not the destructive "bitch goddess," who shatters her husband's manhood and then intentionally cuts short his newly found life.[15] On the contrary, it would seem that her oral attacks on him, especially after he runs away from the wounded lion, are an attempt to force her husband to realize his disgrace so that he might work out some means of atonement.[16] Ironically, by committing adultery, Margaret causes Francis to change his fear into hate, and the change of emotion enables him to perform an act of great courage. Finally, despite Wilson's assertion that Margaret intentionally murdered her husband, it would seem that she was consciously trying to save him from a very real danger.[17]

Finally, there is the ending to consider. Although Margaret is crying hysterically, Wilson, as we noted, believes she has murdered Francis, and taunts her: "That was a pretty thing to do" (p. 246). To believe that Wilson is right, we have to believe that he has suddenly gathered a lot of information that has been missed by readers of the story: he has somehow learned that Mrs. Macomber is a good enough shot to hit a man's head with an unfamiliar rifle from some distance away. He has learned too, according to his second comment, that Macomber was going to leave Margaret, although he hadn't thought that just a few pages before. If Wilson was a sensitive observer, these thoughts might carry more weight, but he is a man who can think "Hell of a good bull" (p. 246), and judge the spread of its horns to be fifty inches just minutes after a man he had come to respect and like has been killed. No, Wilson thinks in stereotypes: he can say of American women, "they're all cruel" (p. 226), and speak of them as "the hardest in the world; the hardest, the cruelest, the most predatory and the most attractive . . ." (p. 225). Given that view, he would naturally assume that Margaret had murdered her husband.

[14]Ibid.
[15]Greco, p. 279.
[16]Ibid.
[17]Fleissner, p. 156.

Margaret has little chance against prejudice like
this. At this time, she can do no more than weep and
say "Stop it." But if she has seen Macomber fit her
own stereotype of a brave man, and then die just as
she has learned the foolishness of that stereotype,
then she is just as much a victim as Macomber, and
although her life will be longer, it will not be
happier.

Bibliography

Beck, Warren, "The Shorter Happy Life of Mrs.
Macomber." Modern Fiction Studies, 1:4 (1955), 28–
37.
Davidson, Arnold E. "The Ambivalent End of Francis
Macomber's Short, Happy Life." Hemingway Notes, 2:7
(1972), 14–16.
Fleissner, R. F. "The Macomber Case: A Sherlockian
Analysis." Baker Street Journal, 20:3 (1969), 154–
56.
Greco, Anne. "Margot Macomber: 'Bitch Goddess,'
Exonerated." Fitzgerald/Hemingway Annual 1972. Ed.
Matthew J. Bruccoli and C. E. Frazer Clark, Jr.
Dayton: National Cash Register Company, 1973.
Hemingway, Ernest. "The Short Happy Life of Francis
Macomber." In An Introduction to Literature, 6th
ed. Ed. Sylvan Barnet, Morton Berman, and William
Burto. Boston: Little, Brown, 1977.
Hutton, Virgil. "The Short Happy Life of Macomber."
University Review, 30 (1964), 253–63.

EXERCISE 11

Make a floor plan of the library you use, showing the location of the
main reading room, the more general kinds of reference books, and the
trays containing the card catalog.

EXERCISE 12

In your library, what is the (a) most recent book by William Faulkner,
(b) most recent book about Faulkner, (c) most recent magazine story or
article by Faulkner, (d) most recent article about Faulkner, (e) most recent
review of a book by Faulkner?

**lib
pap**

EXERCISE 13

How many books does your library have about Eleanor Roosevelt,
Charles Dickens, Theodore Roosevelt, Winston Churchill? Copy the title,
author, and call number of one book about each person named.

EXERCISE 14

Who are the authors of the following works?

1. *An American Tragedy*
2. *Leaves of Grass*
3. *Crossing the Water*
4. *Henry Esmond*
5. *Color*
6. *A Curtain of Green and Other Stories*
7. *Native Son*
8. *Madame Bovary*
9. *War and Peace*
10. *But Will It Sell?*

EXERCISE 15

Who are the following? What did they do? When did they live? When did they die? (1) Thomas à Becket; (2) Thomas à Kempis; (3) Thomas Aquinas; (4) Thomas Browne; (5) Thomas Hardy; (6) Thomas Henry Huxley; (7) Thomas Woodrow Wilson; (8) Thomas Carlyle; (9) Thomas A. Edison; (10) Thomas Jefferson.

EXERCISE 16

List the sources that you think would be the best places to find the following:

1. A brief biography of one of your two U.S. senators.
2. A quotation from Shakespeare of which you remember only one key word.
3. The total number of baseball records broken in the 1966 World Series.
4. A synopsis and analysis of Arthur Miller's play, *Death of a Salesman*.
5. A recent biographical sketch of the concert pianist Rudolf Serkin.
6. A list of essays and articles about Ezra Pound that have appeared in books and magazines.
7. The origin of the English word *barrister*.
8. Whether the "Garrick Club" was an organization, a golf club, or a weapon.
9. A good general discussion of American jazz.
10. A recent magazine article on inheritance taxes.

EXERCISE 17

After you have become familiar with your library, choose *one* of the following sentences. Use it as the first (topic) sentence for a paragraph of about 100–150 words.

1. Several things impressed me about our library.
2. The _____ room in the library is an interesting place.
3. Here are directions for borrowing books from the library.
4. The library has a _____ room.
5. A library is a busy place.
6. You can even have dates in the library.

Index

Ind

Ind

Ind

Ind

Ind